food for fifty

FOOD FOR *Fifty*

FOURTH EDITION

compiled by

Sina Faye Fowler, M.S.

Restaurant Dietitian,
Quality Control Section,
Western Electric Company
Chicago, Illinois

Bessie Brooks West, M.A.

Professor Emeritus of
  Institutional Management,

formerly *Head of Department,*
Kansas State University

Grace Severance Shugart, M.S.

Head of Institutional Management
  Department,
Kansas State University

John Wiley & Sons, Inc., New York • London

FOURTH EDITION

Second Printing, March, 1963

LIBRARY OF CONGRESS CATALOG CARD NUMBER: 61-14809

PRINTED IN THE UNITED STATES OF AMERICA

preface

The first edition of *Food for Fifty* was published in 1937. The wide and generous acceptance given to this and two later editions has encouraged the authors to undertake the preparation of a fourth edition.

Food for Fifty was originally planned to supplement the textbook *Food Service in Institutions*, published by John Wiley and Sons for college instruction in the area of institutional food services and their management. It also has been used extensively by home economics teachers called upon to assume the responsibilities of planning, preparing, and serving special community meals and school lunches; by dietitians in hospitals, residence halls, and related food services; by those in charge of fraternity and sorority dining rooms; and by managers of commercial food services.

In this revision, one major purpose of the book, as presented in the original foreword, remains unchanged, namely "to provide a limited number of carefully tested and standardized institutional formulae for class use in institutional food management classes and in institutional food services."

A second purpose is the presentation of general information relevant to the effective production of high-quality food and to the development of high standards in institutional food service. Included in the subject matter covered are tables of weights and their approximate equivalents in measure; amounts of food as purchased to serve fifty and amounts of food as prepared to serve this number; equivalent substitutions such as shortening, thickening, and leavening agents; cooking times; and other pertinent information.

The decade that has passed since the last revision has brought marked changes in the food supplies available on the market and in the processing to which many foods have been subjected. Recommended cooking procedures have been widely modified as a result of research findings. These changes necessitated a complete revision of all sections of this manuscript.

It is our pleasure to express thanks to Margaret M. Justin, Dean Emeritus, School of Home Economics, Kansas State University, and to our colleagues on the staff of the Department of Institutional Management, as well as to former students and other coworkers in the institutional field who have given liberally from their experience to aid in the completion of this task. To these, our efforts are dedicated. Grateful acknowledgment of permission granted for the use of illustrations in the fourth edition are made throughout the text.

SINA FAYE FOWLER
BESSIE BROOKS WEST
GRACE SEVERANCE SHUGART

Manhattan, Kansas
April, 1961

contents

DEEP-FAT FRYING   32

SPICES AND SEASONINGS   34

COOKERY TERMS   35

part two • recipes

GENERAL INFORMATION   41

INCREASING AND DECREASING RECIPES   42

APPETIZERS   44

BEVERAGES   49

BREADS   57

DESSERTS   86

MEAT   155

POULTRY   179

part three · menu planning

part four • special meals

part one • general information

general information

● AMOUNTS OF FOOD TO SERVE 50

Approximate Amounts of Foods as Purchased to Serve 50

Food	Serving Unit	Order
I. Bakery Products		
Hard rolls	1–1½	4½–6½ doz.
Pan rolls	1½–2	6–8½ doz.
Pullman loaf, 30 oz.	1–2 slices	2–3 loaves
II. Beverages		
Cider	½ c.	6½ qt.
Cocoa	1 c.	8 oz.
Cocoa, instant	1 c.	2½ lb.
Coffee	1 c.	1–1¼ lb.
Coffee, instant	1 c.	1 6-oz. jar
Grape juice	½ c.	6½ qt.
Lemons, for lemonade	1 glass	3 doz.
Oranges, for juice	⅓ c.	6 doz. medium
Orange juice, frozen	½ c.	4 12-oz. cans
Tea (amount will vary with quality and blend)		
Hot	1 c.	2 oz.
Iced	1 glass	6 oz.
Tomato juice	{ ½ c.	4 46-oz. cans
	{ ⅓ c.	5 qt.
III. Cereals and Cereal Products		
Cereal, to cook		
Corn meal	6 oz.	3 lb.
Cream of Wheat	5 oz.	2 lb.
Farina	5 oz.	2 lb.
Grits, hominy	5 oz.	3 lb.
Grits, wheat	5 oz.	2 lb.
Macaroni	5 oz.	4–5 lb.
Noodles	5 oz.	4 lb.
Pettijohns	5 oz.	3 lb.
Rice	5 oz.	3–4 lb.
Rolled oats	5 oz.	3 lb.

Approximate Amounts of Foods as Purchased to Serve 50 (Continued)

Food	Serving Unit	Order
Spaghetti	5 oz.	4–5 lb.
Cereal, prepared		
All Bran, 16-oz pkg.	½ c. (scant)	3 pkg.
Bran flakes, 10-oz. pkg.	¾ c.	5 pkg.
Crackers, graham	2 crackers	2 lb.
Crackers, 2 x 2 in.	2 crackers	1 lb.
Cornflakes, 8-oz. pkg.	⅘ c.	5 pkg.
Grapenuts, 12-oz. pkg.	¼ c. (scant)	4 pkg.
Krumbles, 8-oz. pkg.	1 c. (scant)	6 pkg.
Puffed Wheat, 3½-oz. pkg.	1 c.	6 pkg.
Puffed Rice, 4-oz. pkg.	1 c.	6 pkg.
Rice Krispies, 6-oz. pkg.	⅔ c.	6 pkg.
Whole wheat flakes, 10-oz. pkg.	⅔ c.	5 pkg.
Shredded Wheat, 12-oz. pkg.	2 biscuits	7 pkg.
Wheat Krispies, 10½-oz. pkg.	⅔ c.	4 pkg.
IV. Dairy Products and Eggs		
Butter for table (allow more if serving hot bread)	1–1½ pats	1–1½ lb.
Butter for sandwiches	2 t.	1 lb.
Butter for vegetables		½ lb.
Cream, coffee	1 T.	1 qt.
Cream, whipping for garnish	1 T.	1 pt.
Cheese, cottage	⅓ c.	10 lb.
Cheese, Longhorn	1½ oz.	4¾ lb.
Cheese, for sandwiches	1¼ oz.	4 lb.
Eggs	1–2	4⅙–8⅓ doz.
Ice cream, bulk	No. 12 dipper	2 gal.
Ice cream, brick		7–8 bricks
Ice or sherbet, with meal	No. 16 dipper	1½ gal.
Milk	6 oz. glass	2½ gal.
V. Fruits		
Canned fruits		2 No. 10 cans
Dried fruits		
Apricots	3 oz.	4½ lb.
Dates	5–6 each	4½ lb.
Figs, uncooked	2 each	2¼ lb.
Peaches	3 oz.	4½ lb.
Prunes	3 oz.	5½ lb.
Raisins	2⅓ oz.	4 lb.
Fresh fruits		
Apples for sauce	3 oz.	15 lb.
Apples, for 8-in. pie	6–7 cuts per pie	15 lb.
Bananas, to serve whole, small size	1 each	16 lb.

Approximate Amounts of Foods as Purchased to Serve 50 (Continued)

FOOD	SERVING UNIT	ORDER
Bananas, for 8-in. pie	6–7 cuts per pie	5 lb.
Blackberries, for 8-in. pie	6–7 cuts per pie	6–8 qt.
Cherries, red, for 8-in. pie	6–7 cuts per pie	8–10 qt.
Cranberries, for sauce	¼ c.	3 lb.
Pineapple (each 2 lb.)	½ c. diced	5 pineapples
Strawberries, for shortcake	½ c.	6–8 qt.
Frozen fruits		
Apricots, dessert	3 oz.	10 lb. (4 40-oz. pkg.)
Apples, pie	3 oz.	10 lb. (4 40-oz. pkg.)
Cherries, pie	3 oz.	10 lb. (4 40-oz. pkg.)
Peaches, sliced	3 oz.	10 lb. (4 40-oz. pkg.)
Rhubarb, cut	2¼ oz.	7½ lb. (3 pkg.)
Fruit topping (for ice cream)	1½ oz.	5 lb. (2 pkg.)
Juices		
Canned	4 oz. (½ c.)	4 46-oz. cans
Frozen	4 oz. (½ c.)	4 12-oz. cans
VI. Meats	COOKED WT.	
Beef		
Chuck roast, boneless	2½ oz.	20 lb.
Country fried steak (round), ½ in. thick	3 oz.	15 lb.
Creamed beef, ground meat	3 oz.	10 lb.
Ground meat, patties	3½ oz.	14 lb.
Heart	3 oz.	20 lb.
Liver	3 oz.	10 lb.
Loin, boneless	3 oz.	20 lb.
Pot roast, chuck	3 oz.	20–22 lb.
Rib roast, standing	2 oz.	25–28 lb.
Rib roast, boned, rolled	3–4 oz.	20 lb.
Round, boneless	2 oz.	20–22 lb.
Steaks to broil, sirloin	4–4½ oz.	18–20 lb.
Steaks to broil, T-bone	8 oz.	25 lb.
Stew with vegetables	5½ oz.	15 lb.
Swiss steak (round), ¾ in. thick	3½ oz.	16 lb.
Tongue	3 oz.	18–20 lb.
Veal		
Breaded veal round	3 oz.	12½ lb.
Birds, round, thin	3½ oz.	12½ lb.
Chops 3/1°	1 each	17 lb.
Cutlets 4/1 †	3 oz.	12½ lb.

° Three to 1 lb.
† Four to 1 lb.

Approximate Amounts of Foods as Purchased to Serve 50 (Continued)

Food	Serving Unit	Order
Loaf, 8 lb. veal, 4 lb. pork	3 oz.	12 lb.
Fish		
Fish, fillets	4 oz.	12½–15 lb.
Fish, whole (dressed)	2½ oz.	40 lb.
Oysters (size 116–210)		1½–2 gal.
Scallops	3 oz.	10 lb.
Shrimp	2½ oz.	10–12 lb.
Lamb		
Chops, rib 4/1†	2 each	25 lb.
Roast leg, 6 lb. each	2½ oz.	4 legs
Pork		
Cold cuts		
Braunschweiger	2½ oz.	8½ lb.
Salami	2 oz.	6½ lb.
Frankfurters 12/1	2 each	8–10 lb.
Ham, cured, boneless		
Baked	2 oz.	18 lb.
Baked, sliced	2 oz.	16–20 lb.
Loaf—8 lb. cured,		
4 lb. fresh	3 oz.	12 lb.
Grilled	3 oz.	15–18 lb.
Boiled, sliced	2 oz.	8 lb.
Creamed	2½ oz.	6 lb.
Pork cutlets 4/1	1 each	12½ lb.
Roast, loin, boneless	3 oz.	16–20 lb.
Pork chops, 3/1 or 4/1	1 each	12½–16 lb.
Roast, ham, boneless	3 oz.	15–18 lb.
Sausage 4/1	1 cake each	12½ lb.
Sausage, link 16/1	2 each	6¼ lb.
Stew	2½ oz.	12–15 lb.
VII. Poultry		
Chicken, ready to cook		
A la King	6 oz.	18–20 lb., 4 hens 4½–5 lb. each
Baked	4 oz.	30 lb., 8 hens 5–6 lb. each
Creamed	5 oz.	18–20 lb., 4 hens 4½–5 lb. each
Fried	¼ or ½ chicken	13–25 fryers 2½–3½ lb. each
Scalloped	6 oz.	20 lb., 4 hens 4½–5 lb. each
Stewed	5 oz.	35–40 lb., 8 hens 4½–5 lb. each
Turkey, roast	2½ oz.	35–40 lb.
Turkey roll	3 oz.	12–15 lb.

† Four to 1 lb.

Approximate Amounts of Foods as Purchased to Serve 50 (Continued)

FOOD	SERVING UNIT	ORDER
VIII. Vegetables		
Canned vegetables	4 oz.	2 No. 10 cans
Dried vegetables		
Beans, kidney	4 oz.	5 lb.
Beans, Lima	4 oz.	5 lb.
Beans, navy, baked	5 oz.	5 lb.
Peas, split	4 oz.	5 lb.
Fresh vegetables, as purchased		
Asparagus	3 oz.	18–20 lb.
Beans, green	3 oz.	10–12 lb.
Beans, Lima	3 oz.	22–25 lb.
Beets, topped	3 oz.	12–14 lb.
Broccoli	3 oz.	16–20 lb.
Brussels sprouts	2½–3 oz.	10–12 lb.
Cabbage, to cook	2½–3 oz.	12 lb.
Cabbage, raw	1–2 oz.	8 lb.
Carrots, topped	3 oz.	12½ lb.
Carrots, for relishes	2–3 strips	2–2½ lb.
Cauliflower	3 oz.	28–32 lb.
Celery, for relishes	1–2-in. piece	2 lb.
Cucumber, 9 in.	2 slices	4
Eggplant, 1¼ lb. each	2–2½ oz.	8
Lettuce, head	1½–2 oz.	8–10 heads
Lettuce, head, garnish		4–5 heads
Lettuce, leaf, garnish		2–3 lb.
Onions, whole	1 medium	12½ lb.
Parsnips	3–3½ oz.	12½–15 lb.
Peas in shell	2½ oz.	25 lb.
Potatoes, Irish, baked	6 oz.	20 lb.
Potatoes, to mash	4 oz.	12 lb.
Potatoes, to brown	3½–4 oz.	15–18 lb.
Potatoes, to scallop	5 oz.	15 lb.
Potatoes, sweet	4½–5 oz.	18–20 lb.
Radishes	2 each	10 bunches
Spinach, to cook	3 oz.	12–15 lb.
Spinach, for salad	1 oz.	5–6 lb.
Squash, to mash	3 oz.	12–15 lb.
Squash, to bake	3 oz.	12–15 lb.
Tomatoes, small	1 each	12–15 lb.
Tomatoes, sliced	3 oz.	10–12½ lb.
Turnips, diced	3 oz.	12–15 lb.
Turnips, to mash	3 oz.	15 lb.
Frozen vegetables		
Asparagus tips	3 oz.	10 lb. (4 40-oz. pkg.)
Beans, cut green	2½ oz.	7½ lb. (3 40-oz. pkg.)

Approximate Amounts of Foods as Purchased to Serve 50 (Continued)

Food	Serving Unit	Order
Beans, baby Lima	3 oz.	10 lb. (4 40-oz. pkg.)
Beans, Fordhook	3 oz.	10 lb. (4 40-oz. pkg.)
Broccoli	3 oz.	10 lb. (4 40-oz. pkg.)
Brussels sprouts	3 oz.	10 lb. (4 40-oz. pkg.)
Cauliflower	3 oz.	10 lb. (4 40-oz. pkg.)
Corn, whole kernel	2½ oz.	7½ lb. (3 40-oz. pkg.)
Peas	2½ oz.	7½ lb. (3 40-oz. pkg.)
Spinach	3 oz.	10 lb. (4 40-oz. pkg.)

IX. Miscellaneous
  Nuts

Food	Serving Unit	Order
Pecan meats for tea	2 t.	¾–1 lb.
Jumbo peanuts for tea	2 t.	¾–1 lb.
Mixed nuts for nut cups		1½ lb.

  Relishes

Food	Serving Unit	Order
Carrots, strips, 3 in.	2–3 pieces	2–2½ lb.
Celery curls, 2½-in. pieces	1 piece	2 medium stalks (2¼ lb. A.P.)
Olives, green, medium	3–4	2 qt. 88–94 to qt.
Pickles, 3 in.	½ pickle	1½ lb.

  Sweets

Food	Serving Unit	Order
Candies, small		1 lb.
Honey	2 T.	5 lb.
Jam	2 T.	3 lb.
Jelly	2 T.	3 lb.
Sirup	¼ c.	3¼ qt.
Sugar, loaf	1–2 cubes	1½ lb.
Sugar, granulated	1½ t.	¾ lb.

Approximate Amounts of Prepared Foods to Serve 50

Food	Serving Unit	Quantity
I. Beverages		
Cocoa, coffee	6 oz. (1 teacup)	2½ gal.
Lemonade	8 oz. (1 glass)	3 gal.
Tea, hot	6 oz. (1 teacup)	2½ gal.
Tea, iced	8 oz. (1 glass)	3 gal.
Punch	{ 3 oz. (1 punch cup)	1¼ gal.
	{ 6 oz.	2½ gal.

Approximate Amounts of Prepared Foods to Serve 50 (Continued)

Food	Serving Unit	Quantity
II. Breads		
Bread, thin for sandwiches	2 oz. (2 slices)	7 lb. bread
Bread, quick loaf (brown, nut, orange)	2 to 3 slices	5 loaves 4 x 9 in.
Rolls, breakfast	3 oz. (1 roll)	4⅓–4½ doz.
Rolls, raised yeast (men's group)	3 oz. (2 rolls) av.	9 doz.
Rolls, raised yeast (women's group)	1½ oz. (1½ rolls) av.	6 doz.
Rolls, raised yeast (mixed group)	1½ oz. (1¾ rolls) av.	8 doz.
Coffee cake, quick	2 oz. (1 piece 2 x 2½ in.)	1 pan 12 x 20 in.
Coffee cake, yeast	3 oz. (1 piece 2 x 2½ in.)	1 pan 12 x 20 in.
Corn bread	2 pieces (3 x 3 in.)	2 pan 12 x 20 in.
Muffins	2 oz. (2 muffins)	9 doz.
Biscuits (men's group)	3 oz. (3 biscuits)	12½ doz.
Biscuits (women's group)	2 oz. (2 biscuits)	9 doz.
Griddle cakes	3½ oz. (2 cakes)	6½ qt. batter
Waffles	3 oz. (1 waffle)	6½ qt. batter
Doughnuts, cake type	1½ oz. (2 doughnuts)	9 doz.
Doughnuts, yeast type	1½ oz. (2 doughnuts)	9 doz.
Toast, French	4 oz. (2 slices)	7 lb. bread
Toast, buttered or cinnamon	2 oz. (2 slices)	7 lb. bread
III. Cereal Products, cooked		
Farina, Cream of Wheat	5 oz. (⅔–¾ c.)	8½–9½ qt.
Grits, hominy	5 oz. (⅔ c.)	2 gal.
Macaroni	5 oz. (⅔ c.)	2 gal.
Spaghetti	5 oz. (⅔ c.)	2 gal.
Noodles	5 oz. (⅔ c.)	2 gal.
Rice, for cereal	5 oz. (⅔ c.)	2 gal.
Rice, as vegetable	4 oz. (¼–½ c.)	3½–6¼ qt.
Rolled oats, Pettijohns	5 oz. (⅔ c.)	2 gal.
Corn meal	6 oz. (⅔ c.)	2 gal.
Bread stuffing	1–1½ oz.	7¼ qt.
IV. Desserts		
Cake		
Layer, 2 (10-in.)	2½ oz.	3 cakes
Pound or Loaf	3 oz.	4 loaves
Sheet cake	2½ oz.	1 sheet 12 x 20 in.

Approximate Amounts of Prepared Foods to Serve 50 (Continued)

Food	Serving Unit	Quantity
Fruit cake	2½ oz.	8 lb. (2 cakes)
Cup cakes	1½ oz.	4½ doz.
Angel food cake,		
plain	1 oz.	3 10-in. cakes
Cake frosting		
Layer cake, 2 (10-in.)	3 cakes	2¼–2½ qt.
Sheet cake	1 cake	1–1½ qt.
Angel Food	3 cakes	2–2½ qt.
Fruit cup, fresh	3 oz. (½ c.)	6 qt.
Ice cream sundae, bulk	⅓ c. No. 12 dipper	8 qt.
Ice cream, plain, bulk	⅓ c. No. 12 dipper	8 qt.
Ice cream (for à la		
mode) bulk	¼ c. No. 16 dipper	6 qt.
Pies (8-in.)	6 cuts per pie	8 pies
Filling		
Fruit	2½–3 c. per pie	5–6 qt.
Cream	3 c. per pie	6 qt.
Custard or pumpkin	3 c. per pie	6 qt.
Pastry		
For 2-crust pie	12 oz. per pie	6 lb.
For 1-crust pie	6½ oz. per pie	3¼ lb.
Meringue	3 oz. per pie	1½ lb.
Puddings		
Cornstarch or		
Tapioca	½ c. No. 10 dipper	6¼ qt.
Gelatin dessert	½ c.	6¼ qt.
Whips, fruit	½ c.	6¼ qt.
Steamed pudding	2½ oz. No. 16 dipper	4½ doz.
Baked pudding	3 oz.	1 pan 12 x 20 in.
V. Meats, cooked		
Chicken, cubed	1½ oz.	4 qt.
Chicken or ham,		
creamed	½–⅔ c.	6½–8½ qt.
Ham, boiled, sliced	3 oz.	9½ lb.
Meat loaf	4 oz.	5 loaves
Beef stew	⅔ c.	9 qt.
Roast beef, boneless	2½ oz.	8½ lb.
VI. Luncheon Dishes		
Macaroni and cheese	½ c.	1 pan 12 x 20 x 4 in.
Eggs à la king	½ c.	6½ qt.
Cheese soufflé	½ c.	3 pans 12 x 10 x 2 in.
Chili	1 c.	12½ qt.
VII. Sauces and Dressings		
Gravy	3–4 T.	3–4 qt.
Sauce, meat accom-		
paniment	2 T.	2 qt.

Approximate Amounts of Prepared Foods to Serve 50 (Continued)

Food	Serving Unit	Quantity
Pudding sauce	2–3 T.	2–3 qt.
Vegetable sauce	2–3 T.	2–3 qt.
Salad dressing, thin	1 T.	1 qt.
VIII. Salads		
Bulky vegetable	⅔ c.	2 gal.
Fish or meat	⅔ c.	2 gal.
Fruit	⅓ c.	4¼ qt.
Gelatin, liquid	½ c.	6 qt.
Potato	½ c.	6¼ qt.
IX. Soups		
Soup, first course	⅔ c.	2 gal.
Soup, main course	1 c.	3 gal.
X. Vegetables		
Buttered	½ c.	6 qt.
Creamed, diced	½ c.	6 qt.
Kidney and other dry		
beans	½–¾ c.	6¼–9½ qt.
Potatoes, mashed	½ c.	6¼ qt.
Potatoes, creamed	½ c.	6¼ qt.
Potatoes, chips	¾–1 oz.	2½–3 lb.
Potatoes, French fried		12–15 lb.

● TABLES OF WEIGHTS AND MEASURES

Weights, Measures, and Their Abbreviations

Abbreviations		Equivalent
f.g.	few grains	
ml.	milliliter	
t.	teaspoon	5 ml. = 1 t.
T.	tablespoon	3 t. = 1 T.
c.	cup	16 T. = 1 c.
pt.	pint	2 c. = 1 pt.
qt.	quart	2 pt. = 1 qt.
l.	liter	1 l. = 1000 ml. or 1.06 qt.
gal.	gallon	4 qt. = 1 gal.
pk.	peck	8 qt. = 1 pk.
bu.	bushel	4 pk. = 1 bu.
g.	gram	
oz.	ounce	28.35 g. = 1 oz. (2 T. fluid)
lb.	pound	16 oz. = 1 lb. or 453.6 g.
kg.	kilogram	2.2 lb. = 1 kg.

Food Weights and Approximate Equivalents in Measure

Food	Weight	Approximate Measure
Allspice	1 oz.	4½ T.
Almonds, blanched	1 lb.	3 c.
Apples, A.P.°	1 lb.	3–4 medium
Apples, A.P.	1½ lb.	1 qt. sliced
Apples, diced, ½-inch cubes, peeled	1 lb.	4½ c.
Applesauce	1 lb.	2 c.
Apples, canned, pie pack	1½ lb.	1 qt.
Apricots, dried, A.P.	1 lb.	3 c.
Apricots, dried, cooked, no juice	1 lb.	4½–5 c.
Apricots, fresh	1 lb.	8 apricots
Apricots, canned, halves, without juice	1 lb.	2 c. or 21 halves
Apricots, pie pack	1 lb.	1¾ c.
Asparagus, fresh	1 lb.	16–20 stalks
Asparagus, canned tips, drained	1 lb.	17–19 stalks
Asparagus, canned, cuts, drained	1 lb.	2½ c.
Avocado	1 lb.	2 medium
Bacon, raw	1 lb.	15–25 slices
Bacon, cooked	1 lb.	85–95 slices
Baking powder	1 oz.	2 T.
Baking powder	1 lb.	2 c.
Bananas, A.P.	1 lb.	3 medium
Bananas, diced	1 lb.	2–2½ c.
Barley, pearl	1 lb.	2 c.
Beans, baked	1 lb.	2 c.
Beans, dried, Lima, A.P.	1 lb.	2½ c.
Beans, dried, Lima, 1 lb. A.P., after cooking	2 lb. 9 oz.	6 c.
Beans, Lima, fresh or canned	1 lb.	2 c.
Beans, kidney, A.P.	1 lb.	2⅔ c.
Beans, kidney, 1 lb., A.P., after cooking	2 lb. 6 oz.	6–7 c.
Beans, navy, A.P.	1 lb.	2½ c.
Beans, navy, 1 lb. A.P., after cooking	2 lb. 3 oz.	5½–6 c.
Beans, snap, cut, cooked, without juice	1 lb.	3½ c.
Bean sprouts	1 lb.	1 qt.
Beef, dried, solid pack	1 lb.	1 qt.
Beef, ground, raw	1 lb.	2 c.
Beef, cooked, diced	1 lb.	3 c.

° A.P. denotes "as purchased."

Food Weights and Approximate Equivalents in Measure (Continued)

Food	Weight	Approximate Measure
Beets, medium	1 lb.	3–4 beets
Beets, cooked, diced	1 lb.	2½–2¾ c.
Beets, cooked, sliced	1 lb.	2½ c.
Blackberries, fresh	1 lb.	2–2½ c.
Blackberries, pie pack	1 lb.	2½ c.
Bran, dry	1 lb.	2 qt.
Bran, all bran	8 oz.	1 qt.
Bran, flakes	1 lb.	3 qt.
Bread, loaf	1 lb.	18 slices, ½ in. each
Bread, sandwich	2 lb.	36–40 slices, thin
Bread, soft, broken	1 lb.	2½ qt.
Bread, dry, broken	1 lb.	8–9 c.
Bread, fresh	2 lb.	1 lb. dry crumbs
Bread crumbs, dry, ground	1 lb.	4 c.
Bread crumbs, soft	1 lb.	2 qt.
Brussels sprouts, A.P.	1 lb.	1 qt.
Butter	1 lb.	2 c.
Cabbage, shredded, E.P.† (raw)	1 lb.	1 qt. lightly packed
Cabbage, A.P., shredded, cooked	1 lb.	1½ c.
Cake crumbs, soft	1 lb.	6 c.
Cantaloupe	18 oz.	1 melon, 4½ in. diameter
Carrots, diced	1 lb.	3–3¼ c.
Carrots, ground, raw, E.P.	1 lb.	3 c.
Carrots, diced, cooked	1 lb.	3 c.
Carrots	1 lb.	4 to 5 medium
Cauliflower, head	12 oz.	1 small
Celery cabbage, shredded	1 lb.	6 c.
Celery, diced, E.P.	1 lb.	1 qt.
Celery, diced (depending on size)	1–2 bunches	1 qt.
Celery seed	1 oz.	4 T.
Cheese, cottage	1 lb.	2 c.
Cheese, grated or ground	1 lb.	1 qt.
Cheese, Philadelphia cream	3 oz.	⅓ c.
Cherries, red, pie pack, without juice	1 lb.	3 c. (scant)
Cherries, glacé	1 lb.	96 cherries or 2½ c.
Cherries, Royal Anne, drained	1 lb.	2¼ c.
Chicken, ready-to-cook	4–4½ lb.	1 qt. cooked, diced
Chicken, cooked, cubed	1 lb.	3 c.

† E.P. denotes "edible portion."

Food Weights and Approximate Equivalents in Measure (Continued)

Food	Weight	Approximate Measure
Chili powder	1 oz.	4 T.
Chili sauce	14 oz.	1¼ c.
Chocolate	1 lb.	16 squares
Chocolate, grated	1 lb.	3½ c.
Chocolate, melted	1 lb.	2 c. (scant)
Cinnamon, ground	1 oz.	4 T.
Cinnamon, ground	1 lb.	4 c.
Cinnamon, stick	¾ oz.	4 sticks, 5 in. long
Citron, dried, chopped	1 lb.	2½ c.
Cloves, ground	1 oz.	5 T.
Cloves, whole	3 oz.	1 c.
Cocoa	1 lb.	4 c.
Coconut, prepared, shredded	1 lb.	6–7 c.
Coconut, moist, canned	1 lb.	5⅓ c.
Coffee, ground coarse	1 lb.	5–5½ c.
Coffee, instant	1 oz.	½ c.
Coffee, pulverized	1 lb.	5 c.
Corn, canned	1 lb.	1¾–2 c.
Cornflakes	1 lb.	4 qt.
Corn meal, coarse	1 lb.	3 c.
Corn meal, after cooking	1 lb.	3 qt.
Corn sirup	1 lb.	1⅓ c.
Cornstarch	1 oz.	3½ T.
Cornstarch	1 lb.	3½ c.
Crabmeat, flaked	½ lb.	3 c.
Crackers, graham	1 lb.	58–66 crackers
Crackers, 2⅝ in. sq.	12 oz.	50 crackers
Crackers, 2 x 2 in.	1 lb.	108 crackers
Cracker crumbs, medium fine	1 lb.	5–6 c.
Cranberries, raw	1 lb.	1 qt.
Cranberries, cooked	1 lb.	1 qt.
Cranberries, sauce, jellied	1 lb.	2 c.
Cranberries, dehydrated, sliced	1 lb.	8½ c.
Cream of tartar	1 oz.	3 T.
Cream of Wheat, A.P.	1 lb.	2⅔ c.
Cucumbers, diced, E.P.	1 lb.	3 c.
Currants, dried	1 lb.	3 c.

Food Weights and Approximate Equivalents in Measure (Continued)

Food	Weight	Approximate Measure
Curry powder	1 oz.	4 T.
Dates, pitted	1 lb.	2½ c.
Eggplant	1 lb.	8 slices 4 x ½ in.
Eggs, whole, A.P.	1 lb.	8–9 eggs
Eggs, whole°	1 lb.	2 c. (9–11 eggs)
Eggs, whites	1 lb.	2 c. (17–20 eggs)
Eggs, yolks	1 lb.	2 c. (19–22 eggs)
Eggs, hard cooked, chopped	1½ lb.	1 qt.
Eggs, dried	1 lb.	4 c.
Eggs, frozen, whole	1 lb.	2 c. (10 eggs)
Eggs, whites, dried	1 lb.	5 c.
Eggs, yolks, dried	1 lb.	5⅔ c.
Farina, cooked	6 oz.	¾ c.
Farina, A.P.	1 lb.	3 c.
Farina, 1 lb. A.P., after cooking	8 lb.	3¾ qt.
Figs, dry, cut fine	1 lb.	2½ c.
Flour, all-purpose	1 lb.	4 c.
Flour, white, bread, unsifted	1 lb.	3½ c. (scant)
Flour, white, bread, sifted	1 lb.	4 c.
Flour, cake, sifted †	1 lb.	4¾ c.
Flour, whole wheat	1 lb.	3¾ c.
Flour, rye	1 lb.	5¾ c.
Flour, soya, low fat	1 lb.	5 c.
Gelatin, granulated	1 oz.	4 T.
Gelatin, granulated	1 lb.	3 c.
Gelatin, prepared, flavored	1 lb.	2⅓ c.
Ginger, ground	1 oz.	5 T.
Ginger, ground	1 lb.	5 c.
Ginger, candied	1 oz.	1 piece 2 x 2 x ⅜ in.
Grapefruit, size 64	1 lb.	1 grapefruit
Grapenuts	1 lb.	4 c.
Grapes, cut, seeded, E.P.	1 lb.	2¾ c.
Grapes, on stem	1 lb.	1 qt.
Ham, cooked, diced	1 lb.	3 c. (+)
Ham, cooked, ground	1 lb.	2 c.
Ham, 1 lb. A.P., after cooking	8 oz.	1 c. cooked

° One case (30 doz.) eggs weighs approximately 41 to 43 lb. and yields approximately 35 lb. liquid whole eggs.

† Or pastry flour.

Food Weights and Approximate Equivalents in Measure (Continued)

FOOD	WEIGHT	APPROXIMATE MEASURE
Hominy, coarse	1 lb.	2½ c.
Hominy grits, raw	1 lb.	3 c.
Hominy grits, 1 lb. A.P., after cooking	6½ lb.	3¼ qt.
Honey	1 lb.	1⅓ c.
Horseradish	1 oz.	2 T.
Jam	1 lb.	1⅓ c.
Jelly	1 lb.	1½ c.
Krumbles	1 lb.	16 c.
Lard	1 lb.	2 c.
Lemons, size 165	1 lb.	4–5 lemons
Lemon juice	1 lb.	2 c. (8–10 lemons)
Lettuce, average head	9 oz.	1
Lettuce, shredded	1 lb.	6–8 c.
Lettuce, leaf	1 lb.	25–30 salad garnishes
Macaroni, 1-inch pieces, A.P.	1 lb.	4 c.
Macaroni, 1 lb., after cooking	4 lb.	2¼ qt.
Macaroni, cooked	1 lb.	2½ c.
Margarine	1 lb.	2 c.
Marshmallows (1¼ in.)	1 lb.	80
Mayonnaise	1 lb.	2 c. (scant)
Meat, chopped, cooked	1 lb.	2 c.
Milk, fluid, whole	1 lb. 1 oz.	2 c.
Milk, sweetened condensed	1 lb.	1½ c.
Milk, evaporated	1 lb.	1¾ c.
Milk, evaporated, tall can	14½ oz.	1⅔ c.
Milk, nonfat, dry	1 lb.	4 c.
Milk, nonfat, dry	1 oz.	4 T.
Mincemeat	1 lb.	2 c.
Molasses	1 lb.	1⅓ c.
Mushrooms, 1 lb. sliced, fresh, fried		1½ c.
Mushrooms, canned	1 lb.	2 c.
Mustard, ground, dry	1 lb.	4½ c.
Mustard, prepared	1 oz.	4 T.
Mustard seed	1 oz.	2½ T.
Noodles, dry, A.P.	1 lb.	6 c.
Noodles, 1 lb. A.P., after cooking	3 lb.	2¼ qt.

Food Weights and Approximate Equivalents in Measure (Continued)

Food	Weight	Approximate Measure
Nutmeats	1 lb.	3½ c.
Nutmeg, ground	1 oz.	3½ T.
Oats, rolled, A.P. (quick)	1 lb.	6 c.
Oats, rolled, 1 lb. A.P. (quick), after cooking	2½ lb.	4 qt.
Oil, vegetable	1 lb.	2–2⅛ c.
Olives, green, small size 180–200, 1 qt.		109–116 olives
Olives, ripe, small size 120–150, 1 qt.		152 olives
Olives, A.P.	4½ lb.	3 c. chopped
Onions, A.P.	1 lb.	4–5 medium
Onions, chopped	1 lb.	2–3 c.
Onions, dehydrated, chopped	1 lb.	7½ c.
Onions, dehydrated, chopped, 1 lb. A.P., after cooking	4½–5 lb.	7½–11 c.°
Onions, dehydrated, sliced	1 lb.	12 c.
Onions, dehydrated, sliced, 1 lb. A.P., after cooking	4 lb. 6 oz.–5 lb.	12–18 c.°
Onions, dehydrated, 2 No. 10 cans	3½ lb.	50 lb. raw (equivalent)
Oranges, size 72	1 lb.	2
Oranges, diced with juice (size 150)	3 lb.	1 qt.
Orange juice	6 oz.	¾ qt. reconstituted
Oysters, 1 qt.	2 lb.	40 large, 60 small
Paprika	1 oz.	4 T.
Parsnips, A.P.	1 lb.	4
Peanuts, E.P.	1 lb.	3¼ c.
Peanut butter	1 lb.	1¾ c.
Peaches, medium, A.P.	1 lb.	4
Peaches, canned, sliced, drained	1 lb.	2 c.
Peas, A.P. in pod	1 lb.	1 c. shelled
Peas, canned, drained	1¼ lb.	2–2½ c.
Peas, dried, split	1 lb.	2⅓ c.
Peas, 1 lb. dried, after cooking	2½ lb.	5½ c.
Pears, fresh, A.P.	1 lb.	3–4
Pears, canned, drained, diced	1 lb.	2½ c.
Pears, halves, large, drained	1 lb. 14 oz.	1 qt. (9 halves)

° 2-hr. rehydration gives 10% more volume than 30 min.; overnight rehydration, 10% more volume than 2 hr.

Food Weights and Approximate Equivalents in Measure (Continued)

FOOD	WEIGHT	APPROXIMATE MEASURE
Pecans	1 lb. E.P.	3¾ c.
Peppers, green	1 lb.	7–9 medium
Peppers, green, chopped	1 lb.	3 c.
Pepper, ground	1 oz.	4 T.
Pepper, ground	1 lb.	4 c.
Pickles, chopped	1 lb.	3 c.
Pickles, halves, 3 in.	1 lb.	3 c. or 36 halves
Pimiento, chopped	1 lb.	2½ c.
Pineapple, canned tidbits	1 lb.	2 c.
Pineapple, fresh	2 lb.	1 pineapple, 2–3 c.
Pineapple, canned, slices, drained	1 lb.	8–12 slices
Poppy seed	5 oz.	1 c.
Potatoes, white, medium, A.P.	1 lb.	3
Potatoes, 2 lb. A.P., after cooking (diced and creamed or mashed)		1 qt.
Potatoes, sweet	1 lb.	3 medium
Potato chips	1 lb.	4–5 qt.
Potato chips	¾–1 oz.	1 serving
Prunes, dried, A.P., size 30 to 40	1 lb.	2½ c.
Prunes, dried, 1 lb. A.P., after cooking	2 lb.	3–4 c.
Prunes, cooked, pitted	1 lb.	3¼ c.
Pumpkin, cooked	1 lb.	2½ c.
Raisins, A.P.	1 lb.	3 c.
Raisins, 1 lb. A.P., after cooking	1 lb. 12 oz.	1 qt.
Raspberries, A.P.	1 lb.	3⅜ c.
Rhubarb, raw, 1-in. pieces	1 lb.	4 c.
Rhubarb, 1 lb. E.P., after cooking		2½ c.
Rice, A.P.	1 lb.	2 c.
Rice, 1 lb. A.P., after cooking	4–4½ lb.	2 qt.
Rice, puffed	1 oz.	1⅔ c.
Rutabagas, raw, cubed, E.P.	1 lb.	3⅓ c.
Sage, finely ground	1 lb.	8 c.
Sage, finely ground	1 oz.	½ c.
Salad dressing, cooked	1 lb.	2 c.
Salmon, canned	1 lb.	2 c.
Salt	1 oz.	1½ T.
Sardines, canned	1 lb.	48, 3 in. long

Food Weights and Approximate Equivalents in Measure (Continued)

Food	Weight	Approximate Measure
Sausage, link, small	1 lb.	16–17
Sauerkraut	1 lb.	3 c. packed
Sesame seed	1 oz.	3 T.
Shortening, hydrogenated fats	1 lb.	2¼ c.
Shrimp, small, cleaned	1 lb.	3¼ c.
Soda	1 oz.	2⅓ T.
Soybeans	1 lb.	2¼ c.
Spaghetti, 2-in. pieces	1 lb.	5 c.
Spaghetti, 1 lb. A.P., cooked	4 lb.	2½ qt.
Spinach, raw	1 lb.	5 qt. (lightly packed)
Spinach, 1 lb. raw, E.P., after cooking	13 oz.	2¾ c.
Spinach, canned	1 lb.	2 c.
Squash, summer, A.P.	2 lb.	1 squash, 5-in. diameter
Squash, Hubbard, cooked	1 lb.	2 c.
Strawberries, A.P.	1 lb.	2¼ c.
Suet, ground	1 lb.	3¾ c.
Sugar, brown, light pack	1 lb.	3 c.
Sugar, brown, solid pack	1 lb.	2 c.
Sugar, cubes	1 lb.	96 cubes
Sugar, granulated	1 lb.	2 c.
Sugar, powdered, XXXX sifted	1 lb.	3 c.
Sweetbreads, 5 lb. A.P.		1¾ qt. cooked
Tapioca, quick cooking	1 lb.	3 c.
Tapioca, pearl	1 lb.	2¾ c.
Tapioca, 1 lb. after cooking		7½ c.
Tea	1 lb.	6 c.
Tomatoes, canned	1 lb.	2 c.
Tomatoes, fresh	1 lb.	3–4 medium
Tomatoes, fresh, diced	1 lb.	2¼ c.
Tomatoes, dehydrated, flaked	1 lb.	2¾ c.
Tomatoes, dehydrated, flaked, 1 lb. A.P., after reconstituting (1 gal. water)	1 lb.	11 c.
Turkey A.P. dressed weight	14 lb.	11–12 c. diced, cooked meat
Turnips, A.P.	1 lb.	2–3

Food Weights and Approximate Equivalents in Measure (Continued)

FOOD	WEIGHT	APPROXIMATE MEASURE
Tuna	1 lb.	2 c.
Vanilla	½ oz.	1 T.
Vinegar	1 lb.	2 c.
Walnuts, English, 1 lb. E.P.	1 lb.	4 c.
Watercress	1 lb.	5 bunches
Watermelon	1 lb.	1-in. slice, 6-in. diameter
Wheat, puffed	1 lb.	32 c.
Wheat, shredded	1 lb.	15–16 biscuits

Approximate Weights of Fresh Fruits and Vegetables

COMMODITY	UNIT	APPROXIMATE NET WEIGHT POUNDS	COMMON COUNT OR NUMBER PER UNIT
Apples	Box	48	88–138
	Bushel	45–50	100 medium
Apricots	Lug	18 and 22	6–10
	Crate	24	
Artichokes, globe	Box	24	24, 30, 36
Asparagus	Crate	12 and 30	12 bunches
	Bunch	2½–3	per box
Avocado	Box		12–20 count per box
Bananas	Box	40	Medium 3 per lb.
Beans, snap	Hamper, bushel	28–30	
Beets, topped	Sack, bushel	50	
Beets, with tops	Crate	Varies	2–3 doz. bunches
Cabbage	Sack	50	15 medium
	Crate	50 and 75	
Celery cabbage	Bushel	45	12–14
	Lug	15	
Cantaloupe	Crate	70	23–45

Approximate Weights of Fresh Fruits and Vegetables (Continued)

COMMODITY	UNIT	APPROXIMATE NET WEIGHT POUNDS	COMMON COUNT OR NUMBER PER UNIT
Carrots, topped	Sack	50	
Carrots, cello, package	Crate	48	1-lb. package
Cauliflower, trimmed	Crate	30	9–12 heads
Cauliflower, cello	Crate	20	12–14 heads
Celery	Crate	45	24, 30, 36 stalks
Cherries, bing, unstemmed	Lug	12 and 15	
Corn, whole ears	Crate, sack	35–40	5 doz.
Cranberries	Box	24	24 1-lb. cello pkg. per case
Cucumbers	Bushel	48–50	10–12
	Basket	18	2 doz.
Eggplant	Bushel	30	24–30
Grapefruit	Carton (½ crate)	36	18–48 count per carton
	Crate (also carton)	70–80	36 count per crate
Grapes	Lug	28	
	Basket	10	
Lemons	Carton (½ crate)	40	95–235 per carton
Limes	Carton	10	80–84
	Box	40	475, 550
Lettuce, head	Carton	40–50	24–30
Lettuce, leaf	Basket	15	
Lettuce, bibb	Basket	15	30–36 heads
Melons, honeydew	Crate		6–12
Melons, watermelon		25–50	
Onions, dry	Sack	50	5/1 # medium
Onions, green	Crate	30	8 doz. bunches
Oranges (Calif.)	Carton (½ crate)	40	48–180 per carton
Oranges (Fla.)	Carton (½ crate)	40	82–100 count per carton

Approximate Weights of Fresh Fruits and Vegetables (Continued)

COMMODITY	UNIT	APPROXIMATE NET WEIGHT POUNDS	COMMON COUNT OR NUMBER PER UNIT
Parsley	Bushel	15–20	5 doz. bunches
Parsnips	Bushel	45	
	Carton	12	12 1-lb. packages
Peaches	Bushel	50	80–88
	Lug	18–24	55 medium
Pears	Box	50	80–180 count per box
Peas	Bushel	30–35	
Peppers, green	Bushel	25–28	110 medium
Pineapple	Crate	18–20	9–15
Plums	Crate	28	4 x 5
	4 baskets to box	26	5 x 5
Potatoes, Irish	Sack	100	
Potatoes, for baking	Carton	50	60–140
Potatoes, sweet	Hamper	50	
Rhubarb, hothouse	Lug	20	
Rutabaga	Sack	50	
Spinach	Bushel	18	
	Crate	25	
Spinach, cello	Case		12 10-oz. bags
Squash, summer	Basket	10	
	Hamper	25	
Squash, winter	Bushel	50	
	Crate	70–80	
Strawberries	Flat		12 pt. boxes
	Crate		16 qt. or 24 pt.
Tangerines	Crate	45 lb.	150, 176
Tomatoes, repack	Lug	28	5 x 6, 6 x 6
	½ bushel	25	
	Basket	5 and 10	
Turnips	Sack or bushel	50	

Approximate Waste in the Preparation of Fresh Fruits and Vegetables[1]

FRUITS	AVERAGE % WASTE	VEGETABLES	AVERAGE % WASTE
Apple	27	Asparagus	49
Avocado	40	Beans, green	16
Banana, peeled	42	Broccoli	38
Blueberries	16	Cabbage, green	21
Cranberries	3	Carrots	24
Cherries, pitted	21	Cauliflower	69
Cantaloupe, with rind	63	Celery	29
Cantaloupe, peeled	39	Chicory	29
(served without rind)		Cucumber	28
Grapefruit, sections	52	Eggplant	22
and juice		Lettuce, head	31
Grapes, seedless	5	Onions, mature	11
Honeydew, served		Peas, green	63
without rind	46	Peppers, green	22
Orange sections	43	Potatoes	16
Peaches (average)	20	Potatoes, sweet	20
Pears	33	Radishes	40
Pineapple	52	Spinach	64
Plums	7	Squash, Acorn	34
Strawberries	16	Squash, Hubbard	41
Watermelon	54	Squash, Zucchini	2
		Tomatoes	14
		Turnips	20

NOTE: To change the prepared raw food weight to as purchased weight:

1. Subtract the % waste from 100 to obtain % yield.
2. Divide the known prepared raw food weight by the % yield obtained in (1), then multiply by 100, to obtain the A.P. (as purchased) weight.

[1] Adapted from Elsie H. Dawson, Elsie F. Dochterman, and Ruth S. Vettel, "Food Yields in Institutional Food Service," *Journal of the American Dietetic Association* (1958), Vol. 34, pp. 267–272.

A Guide to Common Can Sizes[1]

SIZE CAN	AVERAGE WEIGHT	APPROXIMATE MEASURE	USES	AVERAGE No. 4-oz. SERVINGS
6 oz.	6 oz.	¾ c. (6 fl. oz.)	Frozen concentrated and single strength juices	6
8 oz.	8 oz.	1 c. (7¾ fl. oz.)	Fruits, vegetables, specialty items	2
No. 1 (Picnic)	10½ oz.	1¼ c. (9½ fl. oz.)	Condensed soups, some fruits, vegetables, meat and fish products	2–3
No. 300	15½ oz.	1¾ c. (13½ fl. oz.)	Specialty items, such as beans with pork, spaghetti, chili con carne, some fruits, including cranberry sauce	4
No. 303	1 lb.	2 c. (15 fl. oz.)	Vegetables; fruits, such as cherries, fruit cocktail, applesauce	4
No. 2	1 lb. 4 oz.	2½ c. (1 pt. 2 fl. oz.)	Vegetables, many fruits, and juices	4–5
No. 2½	1 lb. 13 oz.	3½ c. (1 pt. 10 fl. oz.)	Fruits, such as peaches, pears, plums, and fruit cocktail; vegetables, such as tomatoes, pumpkin, sauerkraut	7
46 oz.	46 oz.	5¾ c. (1 qt. 14 fl. oz.)	Fruit and vegetable juices	9–11
No. 10	6 lb. 9 oz. (Vary from 6 lb.–6 lb. 14 oz.)	3 qt.	Most fruits and vegetables Most commonly used institutional size	25

A table showing approximately the number of small cans required to replace 1 No. 10 can follows:

> 7 No. 300 cans equal approximately 1 No. 10 can.
> 6 No. 303 cans equal approximately 1 No. 10 can.
> 5 No. 2 cans equal approximately 1 No. 10 can.
> 4 No. 2½ cans equal approximately 1 No. 10 can.
> 2 46-oz. cans equal approximately 1 No. 10 can.

[1] Adapted from *Purchase and Use of Canned Foods*, American Can Co., New York.

Approximate Dipper Equivalents

Dipper No.°	Approximate Equivalent		Suggested Use
	Measure	Weight	
60	1 T.		Small cookies, garnishes
40	1½ T.	¾ oz.	Drop cookies
30	2 T. +	1–1½ oz.	Drop cookies
24	2⅔ T. +	1½–1¾ oz.	Cream puffs
20	3 T. +	1¾–2 oz.	Muffins, cup cakes, sauces
16	4 T. (¼ c.)	2–2¼ oz.	Muffins, desserts, croquettes
12	5 T. + (⅓ c.)	2½–3 oz.	Croquettes, vegetables, muffins, desserts, salads
10	6 T. +	3–4 oz.	Desserts, meat patties, vegetables, hot cereals
8	8 T. (½ c.)	4–5 oz.	Luncheon dishes, creamed meats
6	10 T. +	6 oz.	Luncheon salads

° Portions per quart.

Approximate Ladle Equivalents

Measure	Weight	Suggested Use
⅛ c.	1 oz.	Sauces
¼ c.	2 oz.	Gravies, some sauces
½ c.	4 oz.	Stews, creamed dishes
¾ c.	6 oz.	Stews, creamed dishes
1 c.	8 oz.	Soup

Fractional Parts of Common Measures

Fraction	Tablespoon	Cup	Pint	Quart	Gallon
1	3 t.	16 T.	2 c.	2 pt.	4 qt.
⅞	2½ t. +	14 T.	1¾ c.	3½ c.	3½ qt.
¾	2¼ t.	12 T.	1½ c.	3 c.	3 qt.
⅔	2 t.	10⅔ T.	1⅓ c.	2⅔ c.	2⅔ qt.
⅝	2 t. (scant)	10 T.	1¼ c.	2½ c.	2½ qt.
½	1½ t.	8 T.	1 c.	2 c.	2 qt.
⅜	1⅛ t.	6 T.	¾ c.	1½ c.	1½ qt.
⅓	1 t.	5⅓ T.	⅔ c.	1⅓ c.	1⅓ qt.
¼	¾ t.	4 T.	½ c.	1 c.	1 qt.
⅛	½ t. (scant)	2 T.	¼ c.	½ c.	½ qt.
¹⁄₁₆	¼ t. (scant)	1 T.	2 T.	4 T.	1 c.

● FOOD SUBSTITUTIONS AND PROPORTIONS

Approximate Equivalent Substitutions

INGREDIENT	APPROXIMATE EQUIVALENT
I. Thickening Agents	
3½ whole eggs	
7 egg yolks	
1⅓ oz. minute tapioca	} 1 oz. flour
¾ oz. bread crumbs	
⅔ oz. cornstarch	
II. Shortening Agents	
1 lb. margarine	
⅞ lb. hydrogenated shortening plus 1 t. salt	
⅞ lb. lard plus 1 t. salt	
⅞ lb. oil (1⅜ c.) plus 1 t. salt	} 1 lb. butter
⅞ lb. chicken fat plus 1 t. salt	
2½ c. 36–40% cream	
5 c. 18–20% cream	
III. Leavening Agents°	
¼ t. soda plus ½ t. cream of tartar	} 1 t. baking powder
2 egg whites	
2 pkg. dry yeast	1 oz. compressed yeast
IV. Chocolate and Cocoa	
1 oz. or square chocolate	3 T. cocoa plus ½ T. fat
V. Milk and Cream	
¼ c. (approximately) dry whole milk plus 1 c. water	
¾ c. (approximately) non-fat dry milk solids plus 1 c. water and 3 T. butter	} 1 c. whole milk
½ c. evaporated milk plus ½ c. water	
⅞ c. milk plus 3 T. butter	1 c. cream, thin (18–20%)
¾ c. milk plus ⅓ c. butter	1 c. cream, heavy (36–40%)
1 c. sweet milk plus 1 T. lemon juice or vinegar°	1 c. sour milk
VI. Flour	
1 c. plus 2 T. cake flour	
⅞ c. corn meal	
1 c. graham flour	
1 c. rye flour	} 1 c. all-purpose flour
1½ c. bran	
1½ c. bread crumbs	
1 c. rolled oats	

° To substitute sour milk or buttermilk for sweet milk, add ½ t. soda and decrease baking powder by 2 t. per cup of milk. To sour reconstituted dry milk, add 1 c. cultured buttermilk to 1 gal. reconstituted dry milk.

Relative Proportions of Ingredients

INGREDIENT	RELATIVE PROPORTION
I. Seasonings	
Salt	1 to 2 t. to 1 lb. flour.
	1¼ t. to 1 lb. meat.
	2 t. to 1 qt. water (cereal)
II. Leavening Agents	
Baking powder, quick-acting (tartrate or phosphate)	2 to 2⅔ T. to 1 lb. flour.
Baking powder, slow-acting (S.A.S. or combination)	1½ to 2 T. to 1 lb. flour.
Baking soda	2 t. to 1 qt. sour milk or molasses.
Yeast	½ to 1 compressed yeast cake to 1 lb. flour (varies with ingredients and time allowed).
III. Thickening Agents	
Eggs	4 to 6 whole eggs to 1 qt. milk.
	8 to 12 egg yolks to 1 qt. milk.
	8 to 12 egg whites to 1 qt. milk.
Flour (1 T. flour is equivalent to ½–¾ T. cornstarch.)	½ oz to 1 qt. liquid—very thin sauce (cream soups, starchy vegetables).
	1 oz. to 1 qt. liquid—thin sauce (cream soups, non-starchy vegetables).
	2 oz. to 1 qt. liquid—medium sauce (creamed dishes, gravy).
	3 to 4 oz. to 1 qt. liquid—thick sauce (soufflés).
	4 to 5 oz. to 1 qt. liquid—very thick sauce (croquettes).
	1 lb. to 1 qt. liquid—pour batter (popovers).
	2 lb. to 1 qt. liquid—drop batter (cake, muffins).
	3 lb. to 1 qt. liquid—soft dough (biscuit, rolls).
	4 lb. to 1 qt. liquid—stiff dough (pastry, cookies, noodles).
Gelatin	2 T. to 1 qt. liquid—plain jellies (gelatin and fruit juices).
	2 T. to 1 qt. liquid—whips (gelatin and fruit juices whipped).
	3 T. to 1 qt. liquid—fruit jellies (gelatin, fruit juices, and chopped fruit).
	3 T. to 1 qt. liquid—vegetable jellies (gelatin and liquid and chopped vegetables).
	3 T. to 1 qt. liquid—sponges (gelatin and fruit juices and beaten egg whites).
	4 T. to 1 qt. liquid—Bavarian cream (gelatin and fruit juice and fruit pulp and whipped cream).

Dry-milk Solids

The substitution of dry milk for fluid milk is becoming increasingly important in institutional food services because of the comparatively low cost of dry milk and its ease of handling and storage. The nutritive value of dry milk is comparable to that of fluid milk.

Dry milk is available as whole, nonfat, and buttermilk. Nonfat dry milk solids have better keeping qualities than dry whole milk, although both should be kept dry and cool.

Dry-milk solids, either whole or nonfat, may be used in dry form or reconstituted as fluid milk. When dry milk is used in recipes containing a large proportion of dry ingredients, such as bread, biscuits, muffins, and cakes, the only change in method would be to mix the dry milk with the other dry ingredients and use water in place of fluid milk. For best results, dry milk should be weighed rather than measured. The proportion of dry milk to water varies with the kind of dry milk used. The proportions are found on the package. Additional amounts of dry milk may be added to increase the nutritive value of many foods. The amount to use depends on the effect the added milk has upon the palatability and physical qualities of the product.

To reconstitute nonfat dry milk, sprinkle it on top of warm water. Beat well with a rotary beater, wire whip, or power mixer until milk crystals are dissolved. Never add the dry milk to a boiling mixture. The reconstituted milk may be used immediately for cooking purposes. Refrigerate over night if it is to be used as a beverage.

Dried Whole-egg Solids[1]

Dried eggs are freshly packed from carefully inspected high-quality fresh eggs in No. 10 cans, 3 pounds per can. This is approximately equivalent to 100 shell eggs. Since only water and the shells have been removed, the food value of these eggs is practically the same as that of shell eggs.

Dried eggs must be stored in the refrigerator at 32° to 50° F. After a case has been opened, all unused dried eggs must be stored in a tightly covered container in the refrigerator.

Dried eggs may be combined with dry ingredients or reconstituted with water and used like shell eggs. However, they must be included

---

[1] Adapted from U. S. Department of Agriculture, Agricultural Marketing Service, *School Lunch Recipes Using Dried Whole Egg Solids*, AMS–194. 1959.

only in those dishes which are to be thoroughly cooked, such as baked breads, long-cooked casserole dishes, and baked desserts. Do not use dried eggs in egg-milk drinks, uncooked salad dressing, cream puddings, soft custards, ice creams, omelets, or scrambled eggs when cooked on top of the stove.

For best results, dried egg should be weighed, not measured. Dried egg and water, in the following proportions, are used to replace the shell egg called for in a recipe:

DRIED WHOLE EGG		WATER	SHELL-EGG EQUIVALENT
½ oz. (2½ T. sifted)	+	2½ T.	1
3 oz. (1 c., sifted)	+	1 c.	6
6 oz. (2 c., sifted)	+	2 c.	12

● BAKING TEMPERATURES

Terms for Oven Temperatures

TERM	TEMPERATURE	
	Degrees F.	Degrees C.
Very slow	250–275	121–135
Slow	300–325	149–163
Moderate	350–375	177–191
Hot	400–425	205–219
Very hot (quick)	450–475	232–246
Extremely hot	500–525	260–274

Temperatures and Times Used in Baking[1]

TYPE OF PRODUCT	APPROXIMATE TIME REQUIRED FOR BAKING	OVEN TEMPERATURE	
	(Minutes)	Degrees F.	Degrees C.
Bread			
Biscuits	10–15	425–450	218–232
Corn bread	30–40	400–425	204–218
Cream puffs	40–60	375	191
Muffins	20–25	400–425	204–218
Popovers	60	375	191
Quick loaf bread	60–75	350–375	177–191
Yeast bread	30–40	400	204
Yeast rolls: plain	15–25	400–425	204–218
sweet	20–30	375	191
Cakes, with fat			
Cup	15–25	350–375	177–191
Layer	20–35	350–375	177–191
Loaf	45–60	350	177
Cakes, without fat			
Angel food and sponge	30–45	350–375	177–191
Cookies			
Drop	8–15	350–400	177–204
Rolled	8–10	375	191
Egg, meat, milk, cheese dishes			
Cheese soufflé (baked in pan of hot water)	30–60	350	177
Custard, plain, corn, other (baked in pan of hot water)	30–60	350	177
Macaroni and cheese	25–30	350	177
Meat loaf	60–90	300	149
Meat pie	25–30	400	204
Rice pudding (raw rice)	120–180	300	149
Scalloped potatoes	60	350	177
Pastry			
1-crust pie (custard type)	30–40	400–425	204–218
Meringue on cooked filling in preheated shell	12–15	350	177
	or		
	4–4½	425	218
Shell only	10–12	450	232
2-crust pies and uncooked filling in prebaked shell	45–55	400–425	204–218
2-crust pies with cooked filling	30–45	425–450	218–232

[1] Adapted from *Handbook of Food Preparation,* American Home Economics Association, Washington, D. C. (1959), p. 30.

● SIRUPS AND CANDIES

Temperatures and Tests for Sirups and Candies

Product	Temperature of Sirup at Sea Level (Indicating Concentration Desired)*		Stage of Concentration Desired	Behavior at Stage Desired
	Degrees F.	Degrees C.		
Sirup	230–234	110–112	Thread	The sirup spins a 2-in. thread when dropped from fork or spoon.
Fondant Fudge Penoche	234–240	112–115	Soft ball	When dropped into very cold water, sirup forms a soft ball which flattens on removal from water.
Caramels	244–248	118–120	Firm ball	When dropped into very cold water, sirup forms a firm ball which does not flatten on removal from water.
Divinity Marshmallows Nougat Popcorn balls Salt-water taffy	250–266	121–130	Hard ball	When dropped into very cold water, sirup forms a ball which is hard enough to hold its shape, yet plastic.
Butterscotch Taffies	270–290	132–143	Soft crack	When dropped into very cold water, sirup separates into threads which are hard but not brittle.
Brittle glacé	300–310	149–154	Hard crack	When dropped into very cold water, sirup separates into threads which are hard and brittle.
Barley sugar	320	160	Clear liquid	Sugar liquefies.
Caramel	338	170	Brown liquid	Liquid becomes brown.

* It may be necessary to modify these temperatures for decreased atmospheric pressure.

Sugar Sirups

Sugar Sirup (thin): 2 lb. sugar and 1 qt. water, boil together; for a thicker sirup increase sugar to 2½ lb. and add 1 T. corn sirup to prevent crystallization. May be kept on hand for use in beverages or where recipe specifies simple sirup.

Burnt Sugar Sirup or *Caramel Flavoring:* 1 lb. sugar and 1 pt. boiling water. Put sugar in a pan and melt slowly, stirring constantly. Cook until light brown (caramelized), being careful not to scorch. Add boiling water. Cook slowly until a sirup is formed.

● DEEP-FAT FRYING

Methods of Preparing Food for Deep-fat Frying

Light coating. Dip prepared food in milk. Drain. Dredge with seasoned flour. (Use 1 lb. flour, 2 T. salt, and other seasonings as desired.)

Egg and crumb. Dip prepared food in flour (may omit), then in a mixture of egg and milk or water. Drain and roll in fine crumbs to cover. (Use 3 eggs to 1 c. milk or water for most products. In some cases 1 egg to 1 c. milk may be satisfactory.) Allow 12 oz. crumbs for 50 servings of most items.

Batter. Dip prepared food in a batter made in the following proportions: 12 oz. flour, 1½ t. salt, 2 t. baking powder, 3 T. melted fat, 2 c. milk, and 6 well-beaten eggs. This quantity is sufficient for 50 servings of most items.

Care of Fat and Fryer

For best results, select a bland-flavored frying fat with a high smoking point. Use the amount of fat recommended for the fryer. This should be enough to cover the food entirely. Clarify the fat regularly (at least once a day when fryer is in constant use) by straining through cheesecloth to remove accumulated sediment. Thoroughly wash, rinse, and dry fryer before replacing strained fat, then add enough fresh fat to bring back the required weight or amount necessary for best use of the deep fat frying equipment.

Proper care will prolong the life of the fat; but when undesirable flavors develop, fat should be discarded.

Deep-fat Frying Temperatures

Type of Product	Preparation	Temperature	Frying Time°
		Degrees F.	Minutes
Bananas	Skin and scrape. Cut in pieces 2 in. long. Sprinkle with powdered sugar and lemon juice. Let stand 30 min. Dip in batter.	375	1–3
Cauliflower, pre-cooked	See p. 314	370	3–5
Cheese balls	See p. 217	350	2–3
Chicken, disjointed,			
1½–2 lb. fryers	Light coating or egg and crumb	325	10–12
2–2½ lb. fryers	Light coating or egg and crumb	325	12–15
Chicken, half			
1½–2 lb. fryers	Light coating or egg and crumb	325	12–15
Croquettes (all previously cooked foods)	See p. 204	360–375	2–5
Cutlets, ½ in. thick	Egg and crumb	325–350	5–8
Doughnuts	See p. 65	360–375	3–5
Eggplant	See p. 324	370	5–7
Fish fillets	Egg and crumb	375	4–6
Fritters	See p. 231	370–380	2–5
Onion rings	Batter	350	3–4
Oysters	Egg and crumb	375	2–4
Potatoes, ½ in.	See p. 321		
Complete fry		365	6–8
Blanching		360	3–5
Browning		375	2–3
Frozen, fat blanched		375	2–3
Sandwiches	See p. 280	350–360	3–4
Scallops	Egg and crumb	360–375	3–4
Shrimp	Batter or egg and crumb	360–375	3–5
Timbale cases	See p. 84	350–365	2–3
Fish sticks	Egg and crumb	375	3–4
French toast	See p. 83	360	3–4

° The exact frying time will vary with the equipment used, size and temperature of the food pieces, and the amount of food placed in the fryer at one time. If the kettle is overloaded, foods may become grease-soaked. If food is frozen, use lower temperatures listed and allow additional cooking time.

● SPICES AND SEASONINGS

Use of Spices and Seasonings in Cooking

SPICE	USE
Allspice, whole	Pickling, gravies, consommé, boiled fish and meat, egg-plant, tomatoes, baked beans.
Allspice, ground	Baked products, puddings, relishes, some fruit preserves, gravies.
Anise seed, whole or ground	Coffee cakes, sweet rolls, cookies, candies.
Basil, whole or ground	Tomato juice, beef stew, chicken, tomatoes, Lima beans, peas, French dressing.
Bay leaves (laurel)	Pickling, stews, soups, roast beef, beets, tomatoes, kidney beans, string beans, eggplant.
Caraway seed, whole or ground	Rye bread, sprinkled over pork, liver, or kidney before cooking.
Cardamom (cardamum)	Pickling, flavoring in coffee cakes, Danish pastry, curries, and soups.
Celery seed, whole or ground	Pickling, salads, fish, salad dressings, cream cheese spread, ham spread, beef stew, meat loaf, croquettes, cabbage, cauliflower, onions, cole slaw.
Cayenne pepper	Lima beans, meats, fish, sauces, Mexican dishes.
Chili powder	Chili con carne, tamales, shell fish and oyster cocktail, sauces, cooked eggs, kidney beans, Spanish rice, meat sauces, gravies.
Cinnamon, ground	Puddings, pastry, rolls.
Cinnamon stick and Cassiabuds	Pickling, preserving, stewed fruits.
Cloves, whole	Pickling, hams, fruits, string beans.
Cloves, ground	Baked products, desserts, cranberry juice, tomato soup, Mulligatawny soup, pot roast, boiled beef, beets, onions, sweet potatoes, tomato sauce, tomato aspic.
Coriander, whole or ground	Pickling, curries, baked products.
Cumin (Cumino), whole	Mexican cookery, sausages, stews, soups. (Ingredient of curry and chili powder.)
Curry powder	Mulligatawny soup, lamb, veal stew, chicken, rice dishes, fish.
Dill seed, whole or ground	Pickling, sauerkraut, cabbage, cauliflower, turnips.
Fennel seed	Italian and Swedish cookery.
Ginger, whole	Pickling, beverages.
Ginger, ground	Baked products, barbecue sauce, pear salad.
Horseradish	Sauces, relishes.
Mace, ground	Fish, fish sauces, pickling, preserving, baked products, pastries, tomato juice.

Use of Spices and Seasonings in Cooking (Continued)

SPICE	USE
Marjoram, leaf or ground	Soups, stews, sausage, lamb, tomatoes, Swiss chard, spinach, peas, cottage cheese, French dressing.
Mint leaves	Peas, lamb, iced tea, sauces.
Mustard seed, whole	Pickling, salad garnish.
Mustard seed, ground	Salad dressing, sauces, baked beans, sandwich fillings.
Nutmeg, ground	Sauces (dessert), chicken, sweet potatoes, spinach, cauliflower, baked products, puddings, eggnog.
Oregano leaves (Mexican sage)	Pork. (Ingredient of chili powder.)
Paprika	Fish, salad dressing, garnishes, corn, stews.
Peppercorn (white and black)	Pickling, soups, meats.
Pepper, ground (white and black)	Meat, sauces, gravies, vegetables.
Poppy seed	Cake, cookies, topping for breads.
Rosemary leaves	Italian sausages, Italian dishes.
Sage, leaf or ground	Stuffing, sausage, cheese, soup, sauces.
Saffron	Baked products, special dishes.
Savory leaves	Poultry, meat.
Sesame seed	Rolls, breads.
Thyme, leaf or ground	Stews, meat loaf, soups, stuffing.
Tarragon leaves	Vinegar, dressing, pickles, sauces, mustard.
Turmeric, ground	Ingredient of curry powder, coloring for condiments.

● COOKERY TERMS

Cooking Processes and Methods

Baking: Cooking by dry heat, usually in an oven but occasionally on heated metals. This term is used interchangeably with **roasting** when applied to meats in uncovered containers.

Basting: Moistening meat or other food while cooking to add flavor and to prevent drying of the surface. Melted fat, meat drippings, water, or water and fat may be used for basting.

Beating: A brisk regular motion that lifts a mixture over and over and thereby introduces air or makes the mixture smooth.

Blanching: Preheating in boiling water or steam (1) to remove inactive enzymes and shrink food for canning, freezing, and drying, (2) to aid in the removal of skins from nuts, fruits, and some vegetables.

Blending: Thoroughly mixing two or more ingredients.

Boiling: Cooking in water or a liquid, mostly water, in which the bubbles are breaking on the surface and steam is given off. The boiling temperature of water at sea level is 100° C. (212° F.) but will be approximately 1° C. less for every 1000-foot elevation. The boiling point will be increased by the solution of solids in the water.

Braising: Cooking slowly in a covered utensil in a small amount of liquid. Meat stock, water, milk, or cream may be used for the liquid.

Breading: Dipping a food into an egg-milk mixture and then into fine dry crumbs.

Broiling: Cooking by direct heat. This may be done by placing the food under or over a clear flame.

Candying: Cooking in heavy sirup until plump and transparent, then draining and drying.

Caramelizing: Heating sugar, or food containing a high percentage of sugar, until a brown color and a characteristic flavor develops.

Chopping: Cutting food into fairly fine pieces with a knife or other sharp tool.

Creaming: The working of one or more foods until soft and creamy. This term is ordinarily applied to the mixing of fat and sugar.

Crisping: Heating foods such as cereals or crackers to remove excessive moisture.

Cutting in: The combining of a solid fat with dry ingredients by a horizontal motion with knives. A fat is thus combined with dry ingredients with the least amount of blending.

Dicing: Cutting into cubes.

Dredging: Coating or sprinkling a food with flour or other fine substance.

Egging and crumbing: Dipping a food into diluted, slightly beaten egg, and dredging with crumbs. This treatment is used to prevent soaking of the food with fat or to form a surface easily browned.

Folding: Combining ingredients by using two motions, cutting vertically through the mixture, and turning over and over by sliding the implement across the bottom of the mixing bowl with each turn.

Fricasseeing: Cooking by browning in a small amount of fat, then stewing or steaming. This method is most often applied to fowl or veal cut into pieces.

Frizzling: Cooking in a small amount of fat to produce a food that is crisp and brown with curled edges.

Frying: Cooking in hot fat. The food may be cooked in a small amount of fat (also called sautéing or pan frying), or in a deep layer of fat (also called deep-fat frying).

Glacéing: Coating with a thin sugar sirup cooked to the crack stage. It may also refer to a less concentrated mixture, containing thickening, and used for coating certain types of rolls or pastries.

Grilling: Cooking by direct heat.

Grinding: Changing a food to small particles.

Kneading: Manipulation with a pressing motion accompanied by folding and stretching.

Larding: The insertion of small strips of fat (lardoons) into or on top of uncooked lean meat or fish, to give flavor or prevent dryness.

Marinating: Placing a food into a marinade (usually an oil-acid mixture, such as French dressing).

Melting: Liquefying by the application of heat.

Mincing: Cutting or chopping food into very small pieces—not so fine and regular as grinding, yet finer than those produced by chopping.

Mixing: Uniting two or more ingredients.

Pan-broiling: Cooking, uncovered, on hot metal, such as a fry pan. The fat is removed as it accumulates. Liquid is never added.

Pan-frying: Cooking in a small amount of fat. (See *Frying.*)

Parboiling: Partially cooking a food by boiling, the cooking being completed by another method.

Parching: Browning by the application of dry heat usually applied to grains of corn.

Paring: Cutting off the outside covering, usually with a knife.

Peeling: Stripping off the outside covering.

Planking: Cooking or serving a food, usually fish or steak, on a hot wooden board or plank made especially for this purpose.

Poaching: Cooking in a hot liquid, the original shape of the food being retained.

Pot-roasting: Cooking large cuts of meat by braising.

Roasting: Cooking uncovered by dry heat. The term is usually applied to meat.

Sautéing: Cooking in a small amount of fat. (See *Frying.*)

Scalding: Heating a liquid to a point just below boiling.

Scalloping: Baking food, usually cut into pieces and covered with a liquid or sauce and crumbs. The food and sauce may be mixed together or arranged in alternate layers in a baking dish, with or without crumbs. *Escalloped* is a synonymous term.

Scoring: Making shallow lengthwise and crosswise slits on the surface of meat.

Searing: Browning the surface of meat by the application of intense heat for a short time.

Simmering: Cooking in a liquid in which bubbles form slowly and break just below the surface. The temperatures range from 85° C. (185° F.) to a temperature just below the boiling point.

Steaming: Cooking in steam with or without pressure. Steam may be applied directly to the food, as in a steamer, or to the vessel, as in a double boiler.

Steeping: The process of extracting flavors, colors, or other qualities by adding boiling water and allowing the mixture to stand. The mixture is always just below the boiling point.

Stewing: Simmering in a small amount of liquid.

Stirring: Mixing food materials with a circular motion. Food materials are blended or made into a uniform consistency by this process.

Toasting: The application of direct heat until the surface of the food is browned.

Whipping: Rapid beating to increase volume by the incorporation of air.

part two • recipes

recipes

● GENERAL INFORMATION

Yield

The recipes presented provide servings for 50 people, unless otherwise stated. It is recognized that many factors affect the probable yield. For example, a recipe that may serve adequate portions to 50 women may yield only 35 portions of the size considered acceptable in a men's residence hall.

Weights and Measures

Quantities of most dry ingredients weighing more than 1 oz. are given by weight, and all liquids are indicated by measure. If measures are used in place of weights, equivalents are given on pp. 12–20. Careful weighing and measuring of ingredients are essential to obtain a satisfactory product. Weights given are for food as purchased (A.P.), unless otherwise stated. If the weight given is for edible portion, it is designated as E.P.

Ingredients Used in Standardizing Recipes

Flour. In flour mixtures, the exact ratio between the flour and liquid will vary with the kind of flour. Cake flour was used in cake recipes, and all-purpose flour in other recipes.

Baking powder. Sodium-aluminum-sulphate-type baking powder (double-acting) was used in all recipes.

Eggs. Fresh shell eggs weighing approximately 2 oz. each were used in the preparation of recipes.

Fats. High ratio and/or hydrogenated fats were used in cake and pastry recipes. Butter or margarine was used in cookies and most sauce recipes. Solid fats, such as butter, margarine, and hydrogenated fats, were used interchangeably in recipes that specify only "fat." Unsaturated fat, including corn and vegetable oil, was used in recipes that specify salad oil.

Pan Sizes

Much work has been done by private agencies and equipment manufacturers on the standardization of institutional pans, but as yet no single acceptable standard has been established. A pan 12 x 20 x 4 in. has been indicated for many recipes in this book, as it usually yields 50 servings of satisfactory size. For foods such as scalloped dishes, it may be desirable to use 2 12 x 20 x 2 in. pans for 50 servings. This size pan is also more suitable than the deeper pans for products such as sheet cake or coffee cake; bun pans 18 x 26 in. are often preferred for rolls, jelly roll and cookies. The cooking time given in each recipe is based on the size of pan indicated in the recipe and the amount of food in the pan. If a smaller or larger pan is used, the cooking time should be adjusted accordingly. The number of pans placed in the oven at one time may affect the length of baking time.

● INCREASING AND DECREASING RECIPES

When recipes are increased or decreased, or ingredients are changed from weights to measures, there often arises the need for rounding off the weight or measure of certain items. The decision in each case will depend upon the ingredient and type of recipe. The following policy, however, is generally acceptable:

Rounding Off Calculated Weights and Measures[1]

Calculated Weighed Amount	Adjustment
5 lb. or more	To closest ¼ lb.
2–4 lb. 15 oz.	To closest full oz.
11 oz.–1 lb. 15½ oz.	To closest ½ oz.
2½–10¾ oz.	To closest ¼ oz.
Under 2½ oz.	

NOTE: If the amount cannot be easily weighed, convert it to measure.

[1] Adapted from Pearl J. Aldrich and Grace A. Miller, *Whole and Nonfat Dry Milk in Quantity Food Preparation.* Michigan State University Circular 223, October, 1956.

Rounding Off Calculated Weights and Measures (Continued)

CALCULATED MEASURE	ADJUSTMENT
5 gal. or more	To closest full qt.
5¼ qt.–4¾ gal.	To closest full c.
5¼ c.–5 qt.	To closest ½ c.
2¾–5 c.	To closest ¼ c.

CALCULATED MEASURE	ADJUSTMENT
1¼–2½ c.	To closest T.
9 T.–1 c. 3 T.	To closest t.
5–8 T.	To closest ½ t.
Under 4½ T.	To closest ¼ t.

Conversion of Ounces to Pounds

WEIGHT IN OUNCES	FRACTION OF POUND	DECIMAL OF POUND
1	$\frac{1}{16}$	0.0625
2	$\frac{1}{8}$	0.1250
3	$\frac{3}{16}$	0.1875
4	$\frac{1}{4}$	0.2500
5	$\frac{5}{16}$	0.3125
6	$\frac{3}{8}$	0.3750
7	$\frac{7}{16}$	0.4375
8	$\frac{1}{2}$	0.5000
9	$\frac{9}{16}$	0.5625
10	$\frac{5}{8}$	0.6250
11	$\frac{11}{16}$	0.6875
12	$\frac{3}{4}$	0.7500
13	$\frac{13}{16}$	0.8125
14	$\frac{7}{8}$	0.8750
15	$\frac{15}{16}$	0.9375
16	1 lb.	1.0000

When increasing or decreasing recipes, the division or multiplication of pounds and ounces is simplified when decimals are substituted for ounces. For example, when multiplying 1 lb. 7 oz. by 4, convert from ounces to the decimal part of a pound. Thus 1.437 lb. times 4 is 5.748 lb., which converted to ounces by use of the table above, would be 5 lb. 12 oz.

appetizers

Appetizers include hors d'oeuvres, canapés, cocktails, and soups, and are served at the beginning of a meal to stimulate the appetite. They should be attractive in appearance, pleasing in flavor, and well seasoned.

● HORS D'OEUVRES AND CANAPÉS

Hors d'oeuvres are relishes served at the beginning of the meal. They may be canapés, olives, stuffed celery, deviled eggs, pickles, radishes, cheese, fish, sausages, or a combination. Hors d'oeuvres may be arranged on individual plates and served as the first course, or a tray containing a variety may be passed prior to seating the guests.

Canapés are made by spreading a well-seasoned mixture of eggs, cheese, fish, or meat on a canapé base and garnishing with a bit of some colorful or interesting food. A well-seasoned canapé mixture is often served in a bowl, accompanied by crisp crackers or chips. Guests "dip" into the mixture to make their own canapés.

Hors d'Oeuvres

Apple-Cheese. Core and cut crisp tart red apples into wedges. Dip in fruit juice to prevent discoloration. Spread with a bit of Roquefort cheese softened with cream, and spear each wedge with a toothpick. Arrange sections close together in a circle around a whole red apple.

Carrot Curls. See p. 237.

Cheese Puffs. Prepare Cream Puffs (p. 152) and drop on baking sheet by level teaspoonful. Combine 8 oz. cream cheese, 4½-oz. can deviled ham, 1 t. grated onion, 1 T. horseradish, ½ t. Worcestershire sauce, and ¼ t. pepper. Blend until smooth. Fill each tiny puff with cheese mixture (5 doz.).

Cheese Straws. See p. 85.

Cherry Tomatoes. Select uniform firm tomatoes; wash, chill, and serve whole.

Chicken or Fish Puffs. Fill tiny cream puffs with chicken or fish salad.

44

Cocktail Wieners. Broil small cocktail-size wieners. Spear with cocktail picks and serve immediately.

Ginger-Cheese Balls. Combine 1 8-oz. package cream cheese, 2½ oz. crumbled Roquefort cheese, 2 T. candied ginger, shredded, and 2–4 T. cream. Mix well. Chill thoroughly. Make into small balls. Roll in chopped pecans.

Ham-Cheese Wedges. Spread 6 thin Pullman slices of ham or luncheon meat with cream cheese mixture and stack. Chill, cut into small wedges. Spear with cocktail picks.

Hot Cheese Balls. Prepare small cheese balls, using recipe on p. 217. Serve hot on cocktail picks with chilled tomato juice.

Hot Cheese Canapés. Combine 4 oz. sharp grated Cheddar cheese, ⅛ t. salt, and f.g. cayenne. Spread on toasted canapé base. Sprinkle with sesame seed. Toast and serve hot.

Cheese Wafers. Blend 4 oz. grated sharp Cheddar cheese and 8 oz. butter or margarine. Add ½ t. Worcestershire sauce, 6 oz. flour, ½ t. salt, and f.g. cayenne pepper, and mix thoroughly. Form into 1-in. roll. Wrap in waxed paper and chill for several hours. Slice in ¼-in. slices and bake on ungreased baking sheet for 12–15 min at 375° F.

Melon Cubes. Cut fresh honeydew, cantaloupe, or other melon into cubes. Dip in lemon juice and spear with cocktail picks.

Parsleyed Olives. Use a smooth cheese spread to cover small pimiento-stuffed olives. Roll in minced parsley and spear with colored cocktail picks.

Party Cheese Ball. Combine 3 oz. cream cheese, 4 oz. Blue cheese, 6 oz. sharp Cheddar cheese, 1 T. onion juice, f.d. Worcestershire sauce. Add 1 T. finely cut candied ginger if desired. Mix until smooth. Shape into a ball. Cover with pecans and chill. Serve in center of plate surrounded with crisp assorted crackers. Cheese mixture may also be formed into a long roll, wrapped in waxed paper, and chilled several hours. Slice and serve on crackers.

Pineapple-Shrimp. Spear a small whole shrimp and a pineapple cube on a cocktail pick. Serve with a cheese dip.

Strawberries. Arrange whole, perfect strawberries, with stems, around a bowl of sour cream.

Stuffed Celery. Cut prepared celery into 3-in. lengths and stuff with cream cheese and Roquefort dip, or pimiento cheese.

Stuffed Burr Gherkins. Place a whole almond in a half burr gherkin to form an "acorn," or stuff gherkin with red cherry.

Stuffed Cucumber. Pare cucumber and scoop out center. Fill with ham or shrimp mixture. Chill. Cut into ½-in. slices.

Stuffed Olives. Use ripe or green olives. Prepare thin carrot sticks about 3 in. long and pull 2 or 3 through center of each large pitted olive. Place in ice water to crisp.

Canapés

Canapé bases may include bread slices, cut into various shapes with cookie or sandwich cutter, and toasted or sautéd on one side; thin slices of pan rolls, toasted or sautéd; crisp thin crackers, wafers, corn or potato chips, bread sticks, tiny plain or cheese biscuits, small pancakes, or puff pastry shells. A combination of these makes interesting canapé bases and offers a wide variety for the hors d'oeuvres tray. Suggested canapé spreads and dips follow:

Anchovy. Combine and blend 4 T. anchovy paste, 4 T. cream cheese, 2 T. minced chives, 1 t. lemon juice, and 1 T. soft butter. Spread on canapé bases. Garnish with watercress and/or riced yolk and egg white.

Avocado-Shrimp. Mash 2 soft avocados; season with 1 T. lemon juice, 1 T. minced onion, and f.g. salt. Spread on crackers or canapé bases and top each with small whole shrimp.

Crabmeat and Parmesan Cheese. Mix 1 c. crabmeat, 1 T. onion browned lightly in butter, ¼ c. Parmesan cheese, and mayonnaise to moisten. Spread on canapé bases. Garnish with thin strips of red pepper or pimiento.

Chicken or Ham. Combine 2 c. chicken or ham, finely chopped, with creamed butter seasoned with ½ t. curry powder or chutney. Spread on canapé bases. Garnish with watercress and/or paprika.

Cheese-Mushroom. Sauté a 4-oz. can mushrooms, drained, in 4 T. of butter or margarine. Add ¼ c. heavy cream, few drops of onion juice, salt, pepper, and ¾ c. Cheddar cheese. Mash to a paste. Spread toasted bread rounds with creamed butter and then cheese-mushroom mixture. Garnish with grated cheese and thinly sliced ripe olives.

Carrot. Combine ½ c. ground raw carrot with 1 grated hard-cooked egg, a few drops of onion juice, ½ t. lemon juice, and enough French dressing to moisten. Spread on canapé base. Garnish with thinly sliced stuffed olive or parsley.

Crab or Lobster. Moisten crab or lobster meat with mayonnaise. Add finely cut celery if desired. Pile on canapé base spread with sweet butter.

Crabmeat or Lobster with Egg. Mash 1 6-oz. can crabmeat or lobster. Add 2 chopped hard-cooked eggs, ½ t. prepared mustard, 2 T. mayonnaise, 1 T. lemon juice, ½ t. curry powder. Blend. Spread on canapé base.

Deviled Ham. Blend 3 oz. of canned deviled ham and 1 T. of mayonnaise. Spread on canapé bases that have been toasted on one side. Garnish with parsley.

Pâté de foie gras (or Liverwurst). Mash ½ lb. liverwurst; add 1 t. lemon juice, ½ t. Worcestershire sauce, and cream to moisten. Spread on canapé bases. Garnish with outside border of riced hard-cooked egg yolks mixed with mayonnaise to moisten and season, and an inside border of finely chopped hard-cooked egg whites. Sprinkle with chopped parsley.

Sardine. Mash and bone 3 oz. sardines. Add 2 T. lemon juice and French dressing to moisten. Spread canapé bases with creamed butter and then with sardine mixture. Garnish with riced egg yolk in center and a border of chopped hard-cooked egg whites.

Avocado Dip. Mash 2 ripe avocados and blend with 1 c. cultured sour cream, ¼ t. salt, 1 t. onion juice, 2 T. prepared horseradish. Serve with cooked chilled shrimp.

California Dip. Combine 1 pt. cultured sour cream with 1 1½-oz. package dry onion soup. Blend thoroughly. Serve with crackers, potato or corn chips.

Cheddar Cheese Dip. Blend 4 oz. sharp Cheddar cheese, grated, with 2 t. minced green onion, ½ c. mayonnaise, and ¼ t. salt. Just before serving add ¼ c. chopped crisp bacon. Garnish with ¼ c. chopped toasted almonds. Serve with crisp crackers.

Cheese Bowl. Mix 2 c. cottage cheese, 1 c. grated sharp Cheddar cheese, 2 T. horse-radish, 3 finely chopped young green onions, f.g. cayenne, and 2 T. mayonnaise. Serve in bowl with crisp salty crackers.

Clam Dip. Combine 1 7-oz. can minced clams, 1 c. cottage cheese, 1 8-oz. package cream cheese, 2½ oz. Blue cheese, 2 t. lemon juice, 1½ t. Worcestershire sauce, ½ t. salt, f.d. Tabasco sauce. Thin with clam juice or cream. Blend well. Serve with crisp crackers, potato or corn chips.

Cream Cheese Dip. Blend 3 oz. cream cheese, 2 oz. crumbled Blue cheese, 1 t. onion juice, ⅛ t. salt, ⅛ t. pepper, f.d. Tabasco sauce, 2 T. cream. ¼ c. chopped pecans may be added. Serve with potato chips or pretzels.

Guacamole Dip. Mash 2 ripe avocados; add 1 T. lemon or lime juice, ½ t. salt, 1 T. finely grated onion, 1 ripe tomato, peeled and mashed. Mix well. Serve with potato chips or Melba toast.

Roquefort Dip. Blend 6 oz. cream cheese with 1 oz. Roquefort cheese; then fold in 1 c. whipped cream. Serve in bowl, garnish with paprika.

Tuna-Pineapple Dip. Blend 1 6½-oz. can tuna, 9 oz. drained crushed pineapple, 8 oz. cream cheese, and 3 T. pineapple juice. Serve in bowl with potato chips.

● COCKTAILS

Cocktails are made of pieces of fruit, fruit or vegetable juices, carbonated or alcoholic beverages, or a combination of these. They may also be made of sea food, such as oysters, shrimp, crab, or lobster, and served with a highly seasoned sauce.

Fruit Cup or Cocktail Suggestions[1]

Avocado. Cut avocado into cubes. Serve in small glasses with sauce made of 1 part catsup, 2 parts orange juice, and a few drops of onion juice.

Avocado-Fruit. Cut avocado into sections. Combine with pineapple chunks and grapefruit sections. Chill.

Cantaloupe-Berry. Combine melon balls with berries. Place in sherbet glasses and chill.

Crab Meat. Line cocktail glasses with lettuce. Fill with alternate layers of crab meat, chopped celery, or diced avocado and cocktail sauce (p. 291).

Cranberry-Ginger Ale. Add sugar to cranberry purée. Chill. Add an equal amount of chilled ginger ale. Serve in cocktail glasses. Garnish with a sprig of mint or paper-thin slices of orange.

Cranberry-Grapefruit. Arrange grapefruit sections in cocktail glasses. Cover with chilled cranberry juice.

Frosted Fruit Cup. Pineapple cubes, grapefruit and orange sections or berries topped with lime ice.

Fruit Coconut. Combine diced orange sections, pineapple, and shredded coconut. Chill.

[1] Ginger ale may be used as liquid in recipes designated as "cups."

Grape-Melon. Mix seedless grapes, diced honeydew melon, cubed orange sections, lemon juice, and sugar. Chill. Serve in sherbet glasses.

Grapefruit, broiled. Cut grapefruit in halves and remove centers and seeds. Cut fruit from skin with a sharp knife. Add 1 t. butter and 1 oz. sugar to each center. Broil in a hot oven until fruit turns a golden brown.

Honeydew. Combine chilled pineapple tidbits and juice with honeydew melon balls, seedless grapes, and a little grenadine sirup. Place a grape or ivy leaf under cocktail dishes.

Melon Cup. Cut small round balls from heart of ripe watermelon, cantaloupe, or honeydew melon, or use a combination of the three. Chill thoroughly. Cover with chilled ginger ale.

Mint Cup. Cubes of fresh or canned pineapple and pear with mint or lime ice.

Minted Pineapple. Just before serving, mix 2 No. 10 cans of pineapple tidbits and 1 lb. mints (white, soft). Garnish with a maraschino cherry.

Orange Cup. Orange sections with orange ice or orange sections sprinkled with powdered sugar, covered with pineapple and lemon juice, and garnished with mint leaf.

Oyster. Drain small oysters. Chill and serve in cocktail cups with cocktail sauce (p. 291) and wedge of lemon.

Papaya. Add chopped papaya, salt, and sugar to fresh grapefruit juice. Chill. Serve in frappé glasses. Garnish with cherries.

Pineapple Cup. Cubes of fresh pineapple and whole fresh strawberries.

Raspberry Cup. Fresh raspberries topped with raspberry ice.

Red Raspberry or Strawberry. Prepare fresh berries. Add sugar. Chill. Place in cocktail dishes. Add lime juice and garnish with mint leaves.

Rhubarb-Strawberry. Cut rhubarb into pieces. Cook, sweeten. Chill. Combine with strawberries.

Sherbet. Place no. 16 dipper of lime, pineapple, lemon, orange, or raspberry sherbet in a chilled sherbet dish. Pour 2 T. orange juice or ginger ale over sherbet just before serving.

Shrimp. Line cocktail glasses with lettuce. Add cooked shrimp, either whole or cut into pieces, depending on size. Serve with cocktail sauce (p. 291).

Shrimp-Avocado-Grapefruit. Arrange avocado wedges, grapefruit sections, and shrimp in lettuce lined cocktail glasses. Serve with cocktail sauce (p. 291).

Strawberry. Arrange a few green leaves on each plate. Form a mound of powdered sugar in the center. Around the sugar arrange 5 or 6 large unhulled strawberries.

Strawberry Cup. Fresh strawberries topped with strawberry ice.

Vegetable. Separate raw cauliflower into small flowerets. Mix with chili sauce, lemon juice, Worcestershire sauce, Tabasco sauce, salt, and celery cut very fine. Garnish with parsley.

For fruit and vegetable juice cocktails, see "Beverages," pp. 53–56.

beverages

Beverages on which the reputation of a food service has been made or lost include coffee, tea, chocolate, and cocoa, or a variation of these. The processes involved in preparing these beverages include filtration, percolation, and infusion. Each process is intended to draw out the characteristic color, odor, and flavor of the product in conformity with the general preferences of the regional area being served. Whatever the method used in preparation, the resulting beverage should be served very hot or iced.

● COFFEE

The most common methods of brewing coffee in an institutional food service are filtration, in which water is poured slowly over the coffee as in the usual type of urn, and percolation, in which hot water gradually passes through small spaces onto the ground coffee bean. The choice of method will depend upon the available equipment, how much coffee is to be made, the blend and kind of coffee, and the chemical composition of the water in that area. Regardless of the method used, certain precautions should always be observed:

1. The coffee must be accurately measured or weighed, fresh, and of a satisfactory blend and grind.

2. The water must be freshly drawn, freshly boiled, and accurately measured.

3. Coffee should be held at a temperature of 185° to 190°F. and never allowed to boil. Only coffee that has been made no longer than 1 hour can meet the high standard demanded by a discriminating clientele.

4. Care of equipment is of utmost importance for a satisfactory brew. The urn or other equipment should be cleaned immediately after each use, following instructions that come with the equipment.

The number of servings per pound of coffee will vary with the quality of the coffee bean, equipment used, and the cup size. A high-quality coffee properly made should yield on the average 52 4½-oz. servings, using a 6-oz. cup; 47 5-oz. servings, using a 6½-oz. cup; or 39 6-oz. servings, using an 8-oz. cup.

Hot Coffee

Amount		Ingredient	Method
2½–3 gal.		Water, boiling	
		Add	
1 lb.		Coffee	Mixed and placed in a large
	1 c.	Water, cold	cloth bag
	1	Egg	
		Bring to the boiling point (will require about 15 min.)	
			Yield: 2½ to 3 gal.

NOTE: When mechanical equipment is used, follow accompanying directions.
VARIATION: **Instant Coffee.** Dissolve 5 oz. (2½ c.) instant coffee in 2½ gal. boiling water.

Iced Coffee

Amount	Ingredient	Method
3 gal.	Water, boiling	Brew as for
2 lb.	Coffee	hot coffee
	Draw off coffee brew into a nonmetallic container. Cover. Cool at room temperature. Do not refrigerate.	

NOTE: Fill 12-oz. glass with ice, then add coffee.

● TEA

Tea is made by the process of infusion, in which freshly *boiling* water is poured over tea leaves or tea bags, and the mixture is allowed to stand until the desired concentration is reached. A nonmetallic container is preferable to a metal container for brewing tea.

Hot Tea

AMOUNT	INGREDIENT	METHOD
2 oz.	Tea	Place tea bag in a stainless steel, enamel, or earthenware container.
2 gal.	Add Water, boiling Steep for 3 min. Remove bag.	Yield: 2 gal.

NOTE: If bulk tea is used, tie loosely in a bag. The tea leaves may be placed in a sieve and boiling water poured slowly over them. The amount of tea to be used will vary with the quality.

Iced Tea

AMOUNT	INGREDIENT	METHOD
6 1-oz.	Tea bags	Place in stainless steel, earthenware, or enamel container.
3 qt.	Add Water, boiling Steep for 4–6 min. Remove bags.	
9 qt.	Pour into Water, cold Serve in ice-filled glasses.	Yield: 3 gal.

NOTE: Always pour the hot concentrate into the cold water. Do not refrigerate or ice the tea prior to service.

Spiced Tea

AMOUNT	INGREDIENT	METHOD
1½ gal.	Water, boiling	
1 lb. 8 oz.	Sugar	
¼ c.	Lemon juice and 1 rind, grated	Mix. Simmer
1 c.	Orange juice and 1 rind, grated	20 min.
4 t.	Cloves, whole	
8	Cinnamon sticks	
3 T.	Pour over Tea Strain and serve hot.	Let stand 5 min.
		Yield: Approximately 1½ gal.

VARIATION: **Russian Tea.** Use only 1¼ gal. water. After tea, spice and peels have simmered, add orange and lemon juice and 1 qt. grape juice. Strain and reheat to serve.

● COCOA AND CHOCOLATE

Hot Cocoa

Amount		Ingredient	Method
1 lb.	8 oz.	Sugar	} Mix
	8 oz.	Cocoa	
	½ t.	Salt	
		Add	
1 qt.		Water	} Mix until smooth. Heat to boiling point and boil 3 min. to form a thin sirup.
		Add to	
9 qt.		Milk, hot	Yield: Approximately 2½ gal.

NOTES: 1. Beat well with a wire whip just before serving and add 1 t. of vanilla. Add a marshmallow or 1 t. of whipped cream to each cup if desired; for a richer product, add 2 oz. of butter.
2. Cocoa sirup may be made in larger amounts and stored in the refrigerator. To serve, add 1 qt. cocoa sirup and 1 t. vanilla to 2 gal. hot milk.
VARIATION: 1. **Hot Chocolate.** Substitute 1 lb. of chocolate for cocoa.
2. **Instant Hot Cocoa.** Dissolve 2½ lb. instant cocoa powder in 2 gal. boiling water.

French Hot Chocolate

Amount		Ingredient	Method
1 lb.	2 oz.	Chocolate	} Combine and cook over direct heat 5 min., stirring constantly. Beat with a rotary beater until smooth.
	3 c.	Water, cold	
		Add	
2 lb.	8 oz.	Sugar	
	½ t.	Salt	
		Return to fire and cook over hot water 20–30 min. or until thick. Chill.	
		Carefully fold in	
	3½ c.	Cream, whipped	
		Place 1 rounded T. of chocolate mixture in each serving cup. Add hot milk to fill cup, stir well to blend.	

NOTES: 1. Serve as soon as mixed. (The chocolate mixture may be stored for a short time in refrigerator.)
2. Milk must be scalding hot when added to chocolate mixture.
3. 2½ gal. milk needed for 50 servings.

● PUNCH

The many frozen and canned juices now available are used as the base for most punch recipes and vegetable drinks prepared in institutional food services. Fruit juices, such as lemon, orange, pineapple, cranberry, and the several nectars, are combined in varying proportions to produce a drink of the desired flavor and concentration.

Lemonade (p. 53) or Foundation Punch (p. 54) may be used as a base for many other fruit drinks by the addition of fresh, frozen, or canned juices of the desired flavor. The amount of sugar needed will vary with the sugar concentration of the added juice, individual preference, and the total yield desired. Punch is usually served iced but may be served hot if desired. A carbonated beverage, such as ginger ale, enhances the flavor of most fruit drinks and should be added just before serving.

A ring mold of plain ice or one to which colorful fruits have been added before freezing provides an interesting touch to the punch bowl. To make such a mold, arrange fruit in one large or three small ring molds. Add water and freeze. Unmold and float in bowl of punch. Slices of lemon or orange, fresh strawberries, maraschino cherries, or sprigs of mint are also frequently used as garnishes for iced beverages.

Lemonade

Amount	Ingredient	Method
1¼ qt. 2 lb. 8 oz.	Lemon juice (approx. 30 lemons) Sugar	} Mix.
2¼ gal.	Add Water, cold Chill.	} Stir until dissolved.
		Yield: Approximately 2½ gal.

Notes: 1. Lemonade makes a good base for fruit punch.
2. Three 6-oz. cans frozen lemon juice concentrate may be substituted for fresh lemon juice. Increase water to 2½ gal.

Foundation Fruit Punch

AMOUNT	INGREDIENT	METHOD
2 lb. 8 oz. 3 c.	Sugar Water	} Mix. Bring to boil. Cool.
	Add	
4 6-oz. cans 4 6-oz. cans	Orange juice, concentrated, frozen Lemon juice, concentrated, frozen Water to make 2½ gal.	

NOTES: 1. If time does not permit making and cooling sirup, the sugar may be added and stirred until dissolved.

2. Ginger ale may be substituted for part or all of water. Add just before serving.

VARIATIONS: 1. **Golden Punch.** Reduce orange and lemon juices to 2 cans each. Add 2 46-oz. cans pineapple juice.

2. **Raspberry Punch.** Reduce orange and lemon juices to 3 cans each. Add 2 12-oz. packages frozen red raspberries.

3. **Sparkling Grape Punch.** Reduce orange and lemon juices to 2 cans each. Add 4 6-oz. cans frozen grape juice. Just before serving, add 2 qt. ginger ale.

Sparkling Apricot-Pineapple Punch

AMOUNT	INGREDIENT	METHOD
2 46-oz. cans 2 46-oz. cans 2 6-oz. cans 2 qt.	Apricot nectar Pineapple juice, unsweetened Frozen lemon or lime juice concentrate Water	} Mix and chill.
	Just before serving, add	
2 qt.	Ginger ale	
		Yield: 2½ gal.

Rhubarb Punch

AMOUNT	INGREDIENT	METHOD
10 lb. 4–5 lb. 1 gal.	Rhubarb, tender, pink Sugar Water	} Cook below boiling point and strain. (There should be 1¼ gal. of juice.) Chill.
	Just before serving, add	
1 pt. 1 qt.	Pineapple juice Ginger ale	
		Yield: Approximately 1½ gal.

NOTE: This punch should be a delicate pink color.

Cranberry Juice

Amount		Ingredient	Method
9 lb.		Cranberries	
9 qt.		Water	Cook and strain.
	2 T.	Cloves, whole	
		Add	
4 lb.	8 oz.	Sugar	Stir until dissolved. Chill.
		Just before serving, add	
	1 c.	Lemon juice	
		Chill.	
			Yield: Approximately 2½ gal.

VARIATION: **Cranberry Punch.** Use 3 qt. bottles cranberry juice cocktail in place of juice from cooked berries. Add 2 46-oz. cans pineapple juice, 2 6-oz. cans frozen lemon juice, and 1 qt. water. Just before serving, add 3 qt. ginger ale. 2 qt. cider may be substituted for 2 qt. cranberry juice.

Chilled Tomato Juice

Amount		Ingredient	Method
6 46-oz. cans		Tomato juice	
	¾ c.	Lemon juice	
	3 T.	Worcestershire sauce	Mix ingredients. Chill.
	½ t.	Tabasco sauce	
	3 T.	Celery salt	
			Yield: Approximately 2½ gal.

NOTE: Substitute 2 qt. of sauerkraut juice for 2 qt. of the regular tomato juice. Omit seasonings.

Hot Spiced Tomato Juice

Amount		Ingredient	Method
3 46-oz. cans		Tomato juice	
	8 oz.	Onions	
	3	Bay leaves	
	12	Cloves	Boil together 5 min. Strain.
	1 T.	Mustard, dry	
	6	Celery stalks	
	2 T.	Salt	
		Add	
1 gal.		Consommé	
		Serve hot.	
			Yield: Approximately 2½ gal.

Hot Spiced Cider

Amount	Ingredient	Method
2½ gal.	Cider	
	Add	
12 oz.	Sugar, brown	
	Add	
10	Cinnamon sticks	
2½ T.	Cloves, whole	
2½ T.	Allspice	
½ t.	Mace	Tied loosely in a bag.
1 t.	Salt	
f.g.	Cayenne	

Bring slowly to the boiling point. Boil 15 min.
Remove spices. Serve hot.

Yield: Approximately 2½ gal.

VARIATION: **Chilled Cider.** Omit spices; substitute 1 qt. each of orange and pineapple juice for an equal amount of cider. Chill. Garnish with thin slices of orange.

Christmas Wassail

Amount		Ingredient	Method
2 lb.	8 oz.	Sugar	
2½ qt.		Water	
	½ T.	Cloves, whole	Boil 10 min. Cover and let stand 1 hr. in a warm place. Strain.
	10	Cinnamon sticks	
	10	Allspice berries	
	5 T.	Ginger, crystallized, chopped	
		Add	
2 qt.		Orange juice, strained	
	5 c.	Lemon juice, strained	Mixed.
5 qt.		Cider, sweet	

When ready to serve, heat quickly to the boiling point.
Pour over crabapples or roasted apples in punch bowl.

Yield: 2½ gal.

breads

The addition of hot breads to a menu is an inexpensive way of adding interest to an ordinary meal. Many food services have established enviable reputations for food based largely on their biscuits, muffins, or rolls, served piping hot. The baking of hot breads should be so scheduled that freshly baked products are available throughout the serving period. In most cases, the entire amount of bread dough for a meal may be mixed at one time and baked as needed.

● QUICK BREADS

Quick breads are made with a leavening agent that acts quickly, thus enabling them to be baked at once. This type of bread includes biscuits, muffins, pan breads such as coffee cake and corn bread, loaf breads, and griddle cakes. Most quick breads should be mixed quickly, with as little handling as possible.

Baking Powder Biscuits

Amount		Ingredient	Method
5 lb.		Flour	
	5 oz.	Baking powder	Mix.
	2 T.	Salt	
		Add	
1 lb.	4 oz.	Fat	Blend with dry mixture. Mix low speed (3 min.).
		Add	
1¾–2 qt.		Milk	Mix low speed (1 min.).
		Place one-half of dough on floured board and knead lightly for one minute. Roll or pat to ¾-in. thickness and cut with a 2¼-in. cutter. Place on baking sheet. Repeat, using remaining dough.	

Bake 15 min. at 425°F.   Yield: 100 biscuits.

NOTE: Place biscuits ½ in. apart for crusty biscuits, just touching for softer biscuits.

Variations of Baking Powder Biscuits

Butterscotch Biscuits. Divide dough into 8 parts. Roll each part into a rectangular sheet ¼ in. thick. Spread with melted butter and brown sugar. Roll the dough and cut off slices ¾ in. thick. Bake 15 min. 375° F.

Cheese Biscuits. Use 4 oz. less fat and add 1 lb. dry grated cheese.

Cinnamon Biscuits. Proceed as for Butterscotch Biscuits. Spread with a mixture of 1 lb. sugar, 2 oz. cinnamon, and 1 lb. raisins.

Corn Meal Biscuits. Substitute 2 lb. corn meal for 2 lb. white flour.

Drop Biscuits. Add 1 qt. milk. Drop from spoon onto oiled baking sheet.

Filled Biscuits. Roll dough into a sheet ¼ in. thick. Cut dough with cutter 1¾ in. diameter. Cut out centers of half of the biscuits, using a ¾-in. cutter. Place biscuit ring on a whole biscuit; fill center of each with ½ oz. jam.

Nut Biscuits. Cut biscuit dough with fancy cutter; sprinkle with 2 c. finely chopped nuts and 1 c. sugar mixed.

Orange Biscuits. Proceed as for Butterscotch Biscuits. Spread with orange marmalade.

Raisin Biscuits. Use 6 oz. less fat and ½ c. less milk; add 4 whole eggs, 3 T. grated orange rind, 8 oz. sugar, and 8 oz. chopped raisins.

Shortcake. Add 8 oz. fat and 8 oz. sugar.

Whole Wheat Biscuits. Substitute 2 lb. whole wheat flour for 2 lb. white flour.

Plain Muffins

Amount		Ingredient	Method
2 lb.	8 oz.	Flour	
	2 oz.	Baking powder	
	3 T.	Salt	Mix.
	6 oz.	Sugar	
		Add	
	4	Eggs, beaten	Mixed. Blend 15 sec. (low
1½ qt.		Milk	speed).
		Add	
	8 oz.	Fat, melted	
		Stir only enough to mix ingredients slightly. Batter will still be lumpy. Use No. 16 dipper to fill oiled muffin tins.	

Bake 25 min. at 400°F.   Yield: Approximately 5 doz.

Notes: 1. Overmixing makes muffins more compact and inclined to form tunnels.
      2. When dipping muffins, always dip from the outside of the mixing bowl to avoid overmixing of batter. Muffins should be dipped at once, with as little handling as possible.
      3. After baking, remove muffins at once from pans, or tilt in pans to prevent steaming.

Variations of Plain Muffins

Apricot Muffins. Add 3 c. drained, chopped, cooked apricots to the liquid ingredients.
Bacon Muffins. Substitute 10 oz. chopped bacon, slightly broiled, and bacon fat for
the fat in recipe.
Blueberry Muffins. Carefully fold 1 lb. blueberries into the batter. Increase sugar to
10 oz.
Cherry Muffins. Add 2 c. well-drained cooked cherries to liquid.
Corn Meal Muffins. Substitute 1 lb. white corn meal for 1 lb. flour.
Cranberry Muffins. Sprinkle 4 oz. sugar over 1 lb. chopped raw cranberries. Fold into
batter.
Currant Muffins. Add 8 oz. chopped currants.
Date Muffins. Add 1 lb. chopped dates.
Graham Muffins. Substitute 12 oz. graham flour for 12 oz. white flour. Add 4 T.
molasses.
Jelly Muffins. Drop ¼ to ½ t. jelly on top of each muffin when placed in oven.
Nut Muffins. Add 10 oz. chopped nuts.
Raisin-Nut Muffins. Add 6 oz. chopped nuts and 6 oz. chopped raisins.
Spiced Muffins. Add 1½ t. cloves, 1 t. ginger, and 1 t. allspice to dry ingredients.

Honey Cornflake Muffins

Amount		Ingredient	Method
	8 oz.	Fat	Cream.
	11 oz.	Honey	
	4	Add Eggs, well beaten	
		Add milk alternately with flour mixture.	
1 qt.		Milk	
1 lb.	12 oz.	Flour	Mixed.
	2½ oz.	Baking powder	
	1 t.	Salt	
	8 oz.	Add Cornflakes	
		Stir only enough to mix slightly.	
		Use a No. 20 dipper to fill oiled muffin tins.	

Bake 20 min. at 400°F. Yield: 4 doz. muffins.

NOTE: All-Bran may be substituted for cornflakes. Soak All-Bran in the milk for 5 min.

Oatmeal Muffins

AMOUNT		INGREDIENT	METHOD
	14 oz.	Rolled oats, quick-cooking	Soak 1 hr.
1¼ qt.		Milk, sour	
		Add	
	5	Eggs	Mix lightly.
1 lb.	4 oz.	Sugar, brown	
		Add	
1 lb.		Shortening, melted, cool.	Mix to blend.
		Add	
1 lb.	4 oz.	Flour	
	5 t.	Baking powder	Sifted together.
	2½ t.	Salt	
	2½ t.	Soda	

Blend only enough to moisten dry ingredients. Fill oiled muffin pans ⅔ full, using No. 16 dipper.

Bake 15–20 min. at 400° F.   Yield: 5 doz. muffins.

All-Bran Muffins

AMOUNT		INGREDIENT	METHOD
1 lb.	8 oz.	All-Bran	
	3 c.	Molasses	Combine. Let stand 15 min.
2¼ qt.		Milk	
		Add	
	6	Eggs	Beat well.
	⅓ c.	Fat, liquid	
		Add	
1 lb.	8 oz.	Flour	
	1 T.	Salt	Sifted.
	2 T.	Soda	

Mix only until blended.
Use No. 16 dipper to fill muffin tins.

Bake 20 min. at 400° F.   Yield: 5 doz. muffins.

Griddle Cakes

Amount		Ingredient	Method
4 lb.	8 oz.	Flour, sifted	
	4 oz.	Baking powder	Sift together.
	2 T.	Salt	
	12 oz.	Sugar	

Add and mix only until dry ingredients are moistened.

Amount		Ingredient	Method
12		Eggs, beaten	
3½ qt.		Milk	Combined.
	12 oz.	Fat, melted, or oil	

Use a No. 16 dipper to place batter on hot griddle. Bake on one side until firm around edge and full of bubbles. Turn and finish baking.

Serving: 2 cakes, approximately 4-in. diameter.

NOTE: If a less bready product is desired, thin batter with milk.
VARIATIONS: 1. **Buttermilk Griddle Cakes.** Add 9 oz. dry buttermilk and 1 T. soda to dry ingredients. Substitute 3½ qt. water for milk.
2. **Blueberry Griddle Cakes.** Carefully add 1 lb. blueberries, well drained.

Waffles

Amount		Ingredient	Method
3 lb.		Flour	
	6 T.	Baking powder	
	2 T.	Salt	Sift together.
	4 oz.	Sugar	
		Add	
18		Egg yolks, beaten	
2¼ qt.		Milk	Combined.
		Add	
1 lb.		Fat, melted	Mix only until blended.
		Fold in	
18		Egg whites, beaten stiffly	

Bake on a hot waffle iron.   Yield: 1½ gal. batter.

NOTE: Serve immediately with sirup and butter or with creamed chicken.
VARIATIONS: 1. **All-Bran Waffles.** Add 4 oz. All-Bran.
2. **Bacon Waffles.** Add 1 lb. chopped bacon slightly broiled, and substitute bacon fat for the fat in recipe.
3. **Corn Meal Waffles.** Substitute 12 oz. fine corn meal for 8 oz. flour.
4. **Pecan Waffles.** Add 6 oz. chopped pecans.

Corn Bread

Amount		Ingredient	Method
1 lb.	11 oz.	Corn meal	
1 lb.	12 oz.	Flour	
	8 oz.	Sugar	Sift together.
	2 T.	Salt	
	3 oz.	Baking powder	
		Add	
1½ qt.		Milk	
	6	Eggs, well beaten	Mix only until dry ingredients are moistened.
	8 oz.	Fat, melted or oil	
		Pour into oiled baking pan 12 x 20 x 2 in.	

Bake 35 min. at 400° F.   Serving: Approximately 2 x 2½ in.

NOTE: Batter may be baked in corn stick or muffin pans. Reduce baking time to 15–20 min.

Bishop's Bread

Amount		Ingredient	Method
2 lb.	12 oz.	Sugar, brown	Cream 5 min. (medium speed).
	14 oz.	Fat	
		Add and blend	
2 lb.	8 oz.	Flour	
	1 T.	Cinnamon (optional)	Mixed.
	2 t.	Salt	
		Save 2½ c. of sugar-flour mixture to sprinkle on top.	
		Add	
1 lb.		Flour	
	4 t.	Baking powder	Mixed.
	2 t.	Soda	
		Add	
1¼ qt.		Milk, sour	
	4	Eggs, beaten	Mixed.
		Pour into 2 oiled pans 12 x 18 in. Sprinkle with sugar mixture.	

Bake approximately 25 min. at 400° F.   Yield: Approximately 72 2 x 3 in. pieces.

NOTE: 4½ oz. dry buttermilk and 1¼ qt. water may be substituted for sour milk.
        Use 1⅓ times recipe for pan 18 x 26 in.

Coffee Cake

Amount		Ingredient	Method
2 lb.		Flour	
	2⅔ T.	Baking powder	Mix.
1 lb.	4 oz.	Sugar	
	1 T.	Salt	
		Add	
	4	Eggs, beaten	Mix on medium speed until dry in-
	3 c.	Milk	gredients are just dampened.
		Add	
1 lb.		Fat, melted	Mix on medium speed for 1 min.
		Pour into oiled baking pan 12 x 20 in.	
		Sprinkle over batter	
	8 oz.	Butter or margarine	
1 lb.		Sugar	
	2½ oz.	Flour	Mix until crumbly.
	3 T.	Cinnamon	
	2 t.	Salt	

Bake 25 min. at 400° F.   Serving: 2 x 2½ in.

Notes: 1. Serve warm.
       2. For pan 18 x 26 in., use 1½ times recipe.

Blueberry Coffee Cake

Amount		Ingredient	Method
2 lb.	4 oz. 12 oz.	Sugar Shortening	} Cream.
		Add	
	6	Eggs	} Blend.
		Add alternately and mix	
	3 c.	Milk	
		and	
3 lb.		Flour	
	2 oz.	Baking powder	} Sifted together.
	1 T.	Salt	
		Fold in	
1 lb.	8 oz.	Blueberries, well drained	
		Spread in a baking pan 18 x 26 in.	
		Crumble evenly over the top	
	8 oz.	Sugar, brown	
	4 oz.	Sugar, granulated	
	4 oz.	Flour	} Mixed to a coarse
	2 t.	Cinnamon	crumb consistency.
	6 oz.	Butter, soft	

Bake 45 min. at 375° F.   Serving: 3 x 2½ in.

NOTE: When cake is baked, drizzle thin Powdered Sugar Glaze (p. 116) in a fine stream over the top to form an irregular design if desired.

Doughnuts

AMOUNT		INGREDIENT	METHOD
	3	Eggs, beaten slightly	
		Add	
	10 oz.	Sugar	} Blend well.
	1½ oz.	Fat, melted	
		Add alternately milk and flour mixture	
	1 pt.	Milk	
1 lb.	10 oz.	Flour	
	1 t.	Nutmeg	
	1¼ t.	Salt	} Mixed.
	⅛ t.	Ginger	
	3 T.	Baking powder	
	2 t.	Orange rind, grated	
		Chill. Roll ⅜ in. thick on floured board. Cut with 2½-in. cutter.	

Fry in deep fat approximately 3–4 min. at 350–375° F.   Yield: 4 doz. doughnuts.

NOTE: Add more flour if dough is too soft to handle. Sprinkle with sugar when partly cool.
VARIATION: **Chocolate Doughnuts.** Substitute 4 T. cocoa for 4 T. flour.

Boston Brown Bread

AMOUNT		INGREDIENT	METHOD
1½ qt.		Sour milk	} Mixed.
	2¼ c.	Molasses	
		Stir in	
1 lb.		Corn meal	
	12 oz.	Flour, graham	
	12 oz.	Flour, white	} Mixed.
	1 oz.	Salt	
	1½ T.	Soda	
		Fill oiled cans 3¼ x 4½ in.	

Cover and steam 2 hr.   Yield: 8 loaves.

Baked Brown Bread

Amount		Ingredient	Method
1 lb.	8 oz.	Sugar, brown	
	4	Eggs, beaten	} Mix.
	6 oz.	Fat, melted	
		Add alternately	
2 qt.		Milk, sour	
	2½ T.	Soda	} Mixed.
	1¼ c.	Molasses	
		and	
4 lb.		Flour, whole wheat	
	1 T.	Salt	
		Pour into oiled pans 4 x 9 in.	

Bake 45 min. at 375° F.   Yield: 7 loaves.

VARIATIONS: 1. **Pecan Brown Bread.** Add 12 oz. chopped pecans.
2. **Prune Brown Bread.** Add 1 lb. pitted prunes, chopped.
3. **Raisin Brown Bread.** Add 1 lb. raisins.

Nut Bread

Amount		Ingredient	Method
3 lb.		Flour	
	1 oz.	Baking powder	
1 lb.		Nuts, chopped	} Mix.
	1 T.	Salt	
1 lb.	8 oz.	Sugar	
		Add	
1½ qt.		Milk	} Combined.
	6	Eggs, beaten	
		Add	
	4 oz.	Fat, melted	} Mix only until blended.
		Pour into oiled pans 4 x 9 in.	Let stand 30 min.

Bake 1 hr. at 375° F.   Yield: 5 loaves.

Banana Bread

Amount		Ingredient	Method
	11 oz.	Shortening	} Cream.
1 lb.	6 oz.	Sugar	
		Add	
	8	Eggs	} Beat well.
		Add	
1 qt.		Bananas, mashed	} Blend.
		Add, and mix only until blended	
1 lb.	12 oz.	Flour, sifted	
	3 T.	Baking powder	} Sifted together.
	1 t.	Soda	
	2 t.	Salt	
	12 oz.	Nuts, coarsely chopped	
		Pour into 4 x 9 in. oiled loaf pans.	

Bake 50 min. at 350° F.   Yield: 4 loaves.

Cranberry-Nut Bread

Amount		Ingredient	Method
2 lb.	8 oz.	Flour	
2 lb.	4 oz.	Sugar	
	1 oz.	Baking powder	} Sift together.
	2 t.	Soda	
	2 t.	Salt	
		Add and blend	
	1½ c.	Orange juice	
	½ c.	Salad oil	
	3¾ c.	Water, boiling	
		and	
	5	Eggs, beaten	
		Add	
1 lb.		Nuts, chopped	} Mix only until
	7 oz.	Orange rind, ground	} ingredients are blended.
1 lb.	4 oz.	Cranberries, raw, coarsely ground	
		Pour into 4 x 9 in. oiled loaf pans.	

Bake 1 hr. at 350° F.   Yield: 5 loaves.

NOTE: Cool before slicing.

Date-Nut Bread

AMOUNT		INGREDIENT	METHOD
	3 oz.	Butter or margarine	} Cream thoroughly.
1 lb.	12 oz.	Sugar	
		Add	
	4	Eggs	} Blend.
	1½ T.	Vanilla	
		Add alternately	
2 lb.		Flour	} Mixed.
	1½ t.	Salt	
		and	
1 lb.	8 oz.	Dates	} Mixed and let stand 20 min.
	1½ T.	Soda	
	3¼ c.	Water, boiling	
		Add	
	8 oz.	Nuts, chopped	} Blend.
		Pour into 4 x 9 in. oiled loaf pans.	

Bake 70–75 min. at 300° F.

Yield: 4 loaves.

● YEAST BREADS

Although yeast breads and rolls require a longer preparation time than most quick breads, many food services find it possible to serve "homemade" rolls every meal. Scheduling is important, and it is advisable to limit the size of batches of dough to the amount the worker or workers can handle as the dough becomes ready. A refrigerator roll dough may be made and stored for 24 to 48 hours. Rolls may be made from a regular dough, shaped, and frozen for later baking; or they may be baked first, then frozen for future use.

A basic dough may be used for a variety of appetizing dinner rolls. Some managers use the same dough for sweet rolls; others prefer to use a regular roll dough for this purpose.

Plain Rolls

AMOUNT		INGREDIENT	METHOD
1¼ qt.		Milk	} Scald.
		Pour over	
	4 oz.	Sugar	
	3 T.	Salt	} Cool until lukewarm.
	6 oz.	Fat	
		Add	
	3 oz.	Yeast, compressed	
	1 c.	Water, lukewarm	} Softened in water.
	4	Eggs, beaten	
		Add	} Add flour to make a moderately soft
4 lb.	12 oz.	Flour (variable)	} dough. Mix until smooth and satiny.

1. Turn into oiled pan, cover, and let rise in a warm place until double in bulk.
2. Knead and let rise again.
3. Punch down, shape, and let rise.
4. Bake.

Bake 15–25 min. at 400°–425° F.   Yield: 100 rolls.

NOTES: 1. Requires 4 to 5 hr. for mixing and rising. For a quicker rising dough, increase yeast to 4 oz.
2. 5 oz. nonfat dry milk plus 1¼ qt. water may be substituted for milk. Mix dry milk with flour.

Variations of Plain Rolls

Bowknots. Roll dough ⅓ in. thick. Spread with melted butter or margarine. Cut into strips ½ in. x 9 in. Tie loosely into a single knot. (See Fig 1.)

Braids. Roll dough ¼ in. thick and cut in strips 6 in. long and ½ in. wide. Cross 3 strips in the middle and braid from center to end. Press ends together and fold under.

Butterhorns. When dough has doubled in bulk, roll to ¼-in. thickness. Cut 3-in. triangles of dough, brush with melted butter or margarine. Roll each triangle to the center, starting with wide side. Brush again with melted butter.

Caramel Crowns. Scale dough into balls 1½ oz. each. Roll in melted butter or margarine, then in a sugar and cinnamon mixture. Drop 18 into each of 5 oiled angel-food cake pans. Sprinkle each layer with nuts (and raisins if desired). The pan should be about ⅓ full. Let rise until double in bulk. Bake for 35–40 min. 350–375° F. Immediately loosen from pan with a spatula. Invert pan. After removing from pan, place whole maraschino or glacé cherries on top.

Cloverleaf Rolls. Shape small bits of dough into balls. Fit into oiled muffin pans, allowing 3 balls for each roll (See Fig. 2).

Fig. 1. Bowknots. (Courtesy of the Wheat Flour Institute.)

Fig. 2. Cloverleaf Rolls. (Courtesy of the Wheat Flour Institute.)

Crescents. Roll ⅛ in. thick. Cut into 4-in squares. Cut these into 2 triangles, brush top with melted fat. Begin at base, roll each triangles keeping point in middle of roll and bringing ends toward each other to form a crescent shape. Place on oiled baking sheet some distance apart. (See Fig. 3).

Dinner Rolls. Shape dough into small balls; place on well-oiled baking sheet. Cover. Let rise until light. Brush with mixture made of egg yolk and milk—1 egg yolk to 1 T. milk. (See Fig. 4).

Fan Tan Rolls. Roll out into very thin rectangular sheet. Brush with melted butter. Cut in strips about 1 in. wide. Pile six or seven strips together. Cut 1½-in. pieces and place on end in oiled muffin pans. (See Fig. 5).

Finger or Wiener Rolls. Divide dough into 2 portions. Roll each piece of dough into a strip 1½ in. in diameter. Cut strips of dough into pieces approximately 1 oz. each (1½ oz. for Wiener Rolls). Round pieces of dough; roll into pieces approximately 4½ in. long. Place in rows on oiled baking sheet ½ in. apart.

Half-and-half Rolls. Proceed as for Twin Rolls. Use 1 round plain dough and 1 round whole wheat dough for each roll.

Hot Cross Buns. Cut rounds ½ in. thick, 3 in. in diameter. Brush top with beaten egg. Score top of bun to make cross before baking or after baking make a cross on top with frosting. (See Fig. 7.)

Parkerhouse Rolls. When dough has doubled in bulk, roll to ⅓-in. thickness. Cut rounds 2 to 2½ in. in diameter or form 1½ oz. balls. Allow balls to stand for 10 min., then elongate with small rolling pin. Crease middle of each roll with dull edge of knife. Brush with melted butter, fold over, press together with palm of hand. (See Fig. 6).

Fig. 3. Crescents. (Courtesy of the Wheat Flour Institute.)

Fig. 4. Dinner or Pan Rolls. (Courtesy of the Wheat Flour Institute.)

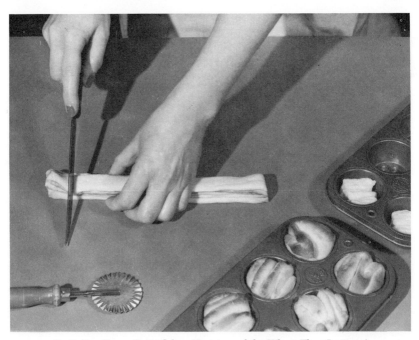

Fig. 5. Fan Tan or Butterflakes. (Courtesy of the Wheat Flour Institute.)

Fig. 6. Parkerhouse Rolls. (Courtesy of the Wheat Flour Institute.)

Poppy Seed Rolls. (1) Proceed as for Twists. Substitute poppy seeds for sugar and cinnamon.

(2) Proceed as for Cinnamon Rolls. Substitute poppy seed for sugar, cinnamon, and raisins.

Ribbon Rolls. Roll dough ¼ in. thick. Spread with melted butter. Place on top of this a layer of whole wheat dough rolled to the same thickness. Repeat, using the contrasting dough until 5 layers thick. Cut with a 1½-in. cutter. Place in oiled muffin pans with cut surface down.

Rosettes. Follow directions for Bowknots. After tying, bring one end through center and the other over the side.

Sandwich Buns. Divide dough into 2 portions. Roll each piece of dough into a strip 1½ in. in diameter. Cut strips into pieces approximately 2 oz. each. Round the pieces into balls. Place balls in rows on oiled baking sheet 1½ to 2 in. apart. Let stand 10 to 15 min.; flatten balls with fingers to desired thickness.

Sesame Rolls. Proceed as for Twin Rolls. Brush top with melted fat and sprinkle with sesame seeds.

Twin Rolls. Roll dough ⅝ in. thick. Cut rounds 1 in. in diameter. Place in well-oiled muffin pans, allowing 2 rounds for each roll.

Twists. Roll dough ⅓ in. thick, spread with melted butter, sugar, and cinnamon. Cut into strips ⅓ in. x 8 in., bring both ends together and twist dough.

Whole Wheat Rolls. Substitute 2 lb. 6 oz. whole wheat flour for 2 lb. 6 oz. white flour. Proceed as for Plain Rolls.

Quick Roll Dough

Amount		Ingredient	Method
	4 oz.	Compressed yeast	Stir until softened.
2 qt.		Water, lukewarm	
		Add	
12		Eggs	Mix.
	8 oz.	Fat, liquid	
		Add	
7 lb.	4 oz.	Flour (amount variable)	Mix 15 to 20 min. on low speed,
	7 oz.	Nonfat dry milk	until dough is smooth and elas-
	8 oz.	Sugar	tic and leaves side of bowl.
	3 T.	Salt	

Divide dough into 12 equal portions (approximately 1½ lb. each). Let rest a few minutes. Work with 1 portion at a time. This will be a rather soft dough. Shape and place rolls on oiled baking sheets and let rise.

Bake 15–25 min. at 400°–425° F.   Yield: Approximately 10 doz. rolls.

Variations: See pp. 69, 73.

Refrigerator Rolls

Amount		Ingredient	Method
1¼ qt.		Milk	Place in a pan and bring to the
	1½ c.	Potatoes, mashed	boiling point. Cool until luke-
	12 oz.	Sugar	warm.
	12 oz.	Fat	
	3 T.	Salt	
		Add	
	2 oz.	Yeast, compressed	Softened in water.
	1 c.	Water, lukewarm	
	½ T.	Soda	
	1 T.	Baking powder	
4 lb.		Flour. Add just enough to make a stiff batter.	

Let rise 15 min. Add remaining flour or enough to make a stiff dough. Knead and put in refrigerator for 24 hr. Remove from refrigerator, mold, let rise 1 to 1½ hr.

Bake 15 to 20 min. at 425° F.   Yield: 6 doz. rolls.

Variations: See pp. 69, 73.

Basic Sweet Roll Dough

Amount		Ingredient	Method
1 qt.		Milk	Scald.
		Add	
1 lb.		Sugar	
1 lb.		Fat	Mix. Cool to lukewarm.
	3 T.	Salt	
		Add	
	9	Eggs, beaten	
		Add and blend	
	4 oz.	Yeast, compressed	Softened in water.
	½ c.	Water, lukewarm	
		Add	
5–6 lb.		Flour (variable)	Mix to a smooth dough, approximately 5–6 min. on medium speed, if using a mixer. Care should be taken not to overmix. This should be a moderately soft dough.

1. The dough temperature just after mixing should be 78° to 82° F.
2. Place in lightly oiled bowl. Oil surface of dough lightly. Cover and let rise in warm place until double in bulk, about 2 hr. For a quicker rising dough, increase yeast to 6 oz.
3. Punch down and let rise again (about 1 hr.).
4. Punch down and divide into portions for rolls. Let rest 10 minutes.
5. Scale 2 oz. per roll. Shape and let rise until rolls are almost double in bulk.

Bake approximately 20–25 min. at 375° F.   Yield: Approximately 8 doz. rolls.

Note: 1. If using dry milk, mix 4 oz. nonfat dry milk with flour. Substitute 1 qt. water for the liquid milk.
2. Rolls may be shaped and frozen either before or after baking.

Variations of Sweet Rolls

Cherry-Nut Rolls. Add 1 t. nutmeg, 1 t. lemon extract, 1 lb. chopped glacé cherries, and 1 lb. chopped pecans to dough. Shape dough into 1 oz. balls. When baked, cover with glaze made of orange juice and powdered sugar.

Coffee Cake. Scale 4 lb. dough, roll out to size of sheet pan. Cover top of dough with melted butter or margarine and topping.

Butter Crunch Topping: Blend 1 lb. sugar, 1 lb. butter or margarine, ½ t. salt, 3 oz. honey, and 2 lb. flour together to form a crumbly mixture. Butter cinnamon topping: Cream 8 oz. butter or margarine, 1 lb. sugar, 3 T. cinnamon, ½ t. salt. Add 4 beaten eggs and 3 oz. flour'and blend. Fruit fillings may also be used.

Crullers. Roll dough ⅓ in. thick. Cut into strips ⅓ x 8 in. Bring 2 ends together and twist dough. Fry in deep fat after proofing. Frost with Powdered Sugar Glaze (p. 116) or dip in fine granulated sugar.

Danish Pastry. Roll a 4- or 5-lb. piece of dough into a rectangular shape about ¼ in. thick. Start at one edge and cover completely ⅔ of dough with small pieces of hard butter or margarine. Use from 2 to 5 oz. fat per lb. of dough. Fold the ⅓ portion of dough which is not buttered over an equal portion of buttered dough. Fold the remaining ⅓ buttered dough over the top to make 3 layers of dough separated by a layer of fat. Roll out dough ¼ in. thickness. This completes the first roll. Repeat folding and rolling two or more times. Do not allow fat to become soft while working with the dough. Let dough rest 45 min. Make into desired shapes.

Hot Cross Buns. Add to dough 8 oz. chopped glacé cherries, 8 oz. raisins, 2 T. cinnamon, ¼ t. cloves, and ¼ t. nutmeg. Shape into round buns, 1 oz. per bun. When baked, make a cross on top with powdered sugar frosting. (See Fig. 7.)

Kolaches. Add 2 T. grated lemon peel to dough. Shape dough into 1 oz. balls. Place on lightly oiled baking sheet. Let rise until light. Press down center to make cavity and fill with 1 t. filling. Brush with melted butter or margarine and sprinkle with chopped nuts. Suggested fillings: chopped cooked prunes and dried apricots with sugar and cinnamon, poppy seed mixed with sugar and milk, apricot or peach marmalade.

Fig. 7. Hot Cross Buns. (Courtesy of the Wheat Flour Institute.)

Long Johns. Roll out dough to a thickness of ½ in. Cut dough into rectangular pieces ½ x 4 in. Proof. Fry in deep fat.

Swedish Braids. Add to dough 1 lb. chopped candied fruit cake mix, 8 oz. pecans and ½ t. cardamon seed. Weigh dough into 1¾ lb. portions and braid. When baked, brush with Powdered Sugar Glaze made with milk (p. 116).

Cinnamon Rolls

Amount		Ingredient	Method
10 lb.		Plain Roll dough (p. 69) or Basic Sweet Roll dough (p. 75)	
2 lb.	12 oz.	Butter or margarine, melted	
		Sugar	Mixed.
	3 T.	Cinnamon	
		For each 1 doz. rolls, weigh	
1 lb.	4 oz.	Dough	
		Roll into rectangular strip 9 x 14 x ⅓ in. Spread with butter and sprinkle with 1 c. sugar-cinnamon mixture.	
		Roll as for Jelly Roll.	
		Cut into 1-in. slices. Place cut side down in oiled baking pans or muffin pans. (See Fig. 8.)	
		Let rise until doubled in bulk (¾ hr.).	

Bake 20–25 min. at 375° F.   Yield: Approximately 7–8 doz. rolls.

NOTE: After removing rolls from oven, spread top with mixture of 1 c. powdered sugar and ½ c. milk.

Variations of Cinnamon Rolls

Butterfly Rolls. Cut rolled dough into 1¼-in. slices. Press each roll across center at right angles to the cut side, with the back of a large knife handle. Press or flatten out the folds of each end. Place on oiled baking sheet 1½ in. apart. (See Fig. 9.)

Butterscotch Rolls. Use brown sugar and omit cinnamon, if desired. Cream 8 oz. butter or margarine, 1½ lb. brown sugar, and 1 t. salt. Gradually add 1 c. water, blending thoroughly. Spread 1 T. mixture into each oiled muffin pan cup. Place rolls cut side down in pans.

Cinnamon-Raisin Rolls. Use brown sugar and add 8 oz. raisins to filling.

Double Cinnamon Buns. Proceed as for Butterfly Rolls. Roll sheet of dough from both sides to form a double roll.

Glazed Marmalade Rolls. Omit cinnamon. Dip cut slice in additional melted butter and sugar. When baked, glaze with orange marmalade mixed with powdered sugar until of a consistency to spread. Apricot marmalade, strawberry jam, or other preserves may be used for the glaze.

Honey Rolls. Substitute honey filling for sugar and cinnamon. Whip 1 lb. butter or margarine and 1 lb. honey until light and fluffy.

Fig. 8. Cinnamon Rolls. (Courtesy of the Wheat Flour Institute.)

Fig. 9. Cinnamon Butterfly Rolls. (Courtesy of the Wheat Flour Institute.)

Orange Rolls. Omit cinnamon. Spread with mixture of 1½ lb. sugar and 1 c. grated orange rind. When baked, brush with glaze made of powdered sugar and orange juice. If desired, use a filling made by cooking 1½ lb. sugar and 6 c. ground whole oranges (about 9 medium-sized ones) until thickened. Cool. Spread on roll dough. A quick filling may be made by combining 12 oz. frozen orange juice and 1½ lb. sugar.

Pecan Rolls. Proceed as for Butterscotch Rolls. Add 12 oz. pecans to mixture placed in muffin pans. (See Fig. 10.)

Sugared Snails. Proceed as for Butterfly Rolls, rolling dough thinner before adding sugar filling. Cut rolled dough into slices ¾ in. thick. Place cut surface of each roll in granulated sugar. Place on oiled baking sheet ½ in. apart with sugared side up. Allow to stand 10 to 15 min., then flatten.

Fig. 10. Pecan Rolls. (Courtesy of the Wheat Flour Institute.)

Bran Rolls

AMOUNT		INGREDIENT	METHOD
1 lb.		Fat	
	1 pt.	Water, boiling	Mix. Stir until fat is melted. Let
	12 oz.	Sugar	stand until mixture is luke-
	1 T.	Salt	warm.
	4 oz.	All Bran	
		Add	
	2 oz.	Yeast, compressed	Softened in water.
	1 pt.	Water, lukewarm	
		Add	
	4	Eggs, beaten	
		Add	
3 lb.		Flour (more if necessary)	Beat thoroughly.

Cover and place in refrigerator until chilled. (May be held overnight in refrigerator.) Remove from refrigerator, form balls of dough to half fill oiled muffin tins. Let rise 2 hr.

Bake 15 min. at 425° F.   Yield: 6 doz. rolls.

Raised Muffins

AMOUNT		INGREDIENT	METHOD
1½ qt.		Milk	Scald.
		Pour over	
	3 T.	Salt	
	12 oz.	Sugar	Cool until lukewarm.
	9 oz.	Fat	
		Add	
	3 oz.	Yeast, compressed	Softened in water.
	1½ c.	Water, lukewarm	
		Add	
12		Eggs, beaten	
		Add	
2 lb.		Flour	Beat. Let rise in a warm place for 1½ hr.
		Add	
2 lb.	12 oz.	Flour (variable)	Beat.

Use a No. 20 dipper to fill oiled muffin tins. Let rise until double in bulk (approximately 1 hr.)

Bake 20 min. at 350° F.   Yield: 8 doz. muffins.

Butter Buns

Amount		Ingredient	Method
1 qt.		Milk	} Scald and cool until lukewarm.
		Add	
	4 oz.	Yeast, compressed	} Let stand to soften yeast.
		Add	
1 lb.		Sugar	
1 lb.	8 oz.	Butter or margarine	
		Add and mix thoroughly	
12		Eggs, beaten	
16		Egg yolks, beaten	
4 lb.	8 oz.	Flour	
	2 T.	Salt	
	4 t.	Lemon extract	
		Let rise until double in bulk. Use a No. 30 dipper to fill oiled muffin tins. Let rise 1 hr.	

Bake 15–20 min. at 400° F.   Yield: 9–10 doz. buns.

White Bread

AMOUNT	INGREDIENT	METHOD
10 oz.	Sugar	
5 oz.	Salt	Mix.
1 gal.	Water, lukewarm	
	Add	
4–5 oz.	Yeast, compressed	
1½ pt.	Water, lukewarm	Softened in water.
	Add	
12 oz.	Fat, melted	
	Add	
15 lb.	Flour	
14 oz.	Nonfat dry milk solids	Mixed.

Mix low speed (approximately 10 min.), or until dough is smooth and elastic.

1. Let rise approximately 2 hr., or until double in bulk. Knead.
2. Let rise approximately 1 hr. Knead and form into loaves; 16 loaves (26½ oz. raw dough per loaf will yield 1½ lb. loaf).
3. Let rise approximately 1 hr. 15 min., or until double in bulk.

Bake 30–40 min. at 400° F.   Yield: Approximately 16 1½ lb. loaves.

NOTE: 1. The temperature of the dough should be 88° to 90° F. when mixed.
2. Substitutes:
   (a) 1¼ gal. fresh liquid milk or reconstituted milk may be substituted for the water and powdered milk.
   (b) 2½ oz. active dry yeast may be substituted for 4¾ oz. compressed yeast.
3. Fat may be increased to 1 lb. and sugar to 12 oz. if a richer loaf is desired.

Variations of White Bread

Cinnamon Bread. After dough has been divided and scaled into loaves, roll in a rectangular sheet. Brush with melted fat; sprinkle generously with cinnamon and sugar. Brush bottom edge of dough with water. Roll as for jelly roll. Seal on bottom and place in greased baking pan. Sprinkle top with cinnamon and sugar.

Raisin Bread. Add 3 lb. of raisins to dough after mixing.

Whole Wheat Bread. Substitute whole wheat flour for ½ of white flour.

Butter Slices. Roll dough ⅓ in. thick. Cut with 3 in. biscuit cutter. Dip in melted butter or margarine and stand pieces on edge in 4 x 9 in. loaf pans (8 pieces per pan). Let rise and bake. Dough may be shaped into long roll and cut into slices.

Norwegian Christmas Bread

Amount	Ingredient	Method
1 qt.	Milk	} Scald.
	Add	
12 oz.	Sugar	} Cool to lukewarm.
2 T.	Salt	
	Add	
3 oz.	Yeast, compressed	} Softened in water.
1 pt.	Water, lukewarm	
	Add	
6	Eggs, beaten	
12 oz.	Fat, softened	
12 oz.	Mixed Glacé fruits and peels	} Mix to smooth stiff dough.
8 oz.	Pecans, chopped	
6 lb.	Flour	

Let rise until double in bulk.
　　Shape into 1¾ lb. loaves or make into braids. Place in oiled 5 x 9 in. loaf pans or oiled baking sheet, if dough is braided. Brush dough with melted butter or margarine. Let rise until double in bulk.

Bake 35–40 min. at 375° F.　　　　　　　　　Yield: 5 loaves or braids.

NOTE: May be frosted with Powdered Sugar Glaze (p. 116).

● MISCELLANEOUS BREADS

French Toast

Amount	Ingredient	Method
18	Eggs, beaten	
1½ qt.	Milk	} Mix.
1 T.	Salt	
½ c.	Sugar	
50	Bread slices	

Dip bread into mixture.

Fry in deep fat at 360° F. or on a well-oiled griddle until golden brown.
　　　　　　　　　　　　　　　　　　　　Serving: 1 slice.

NOTE: Bread slices may be dipped in thin batter (p. 32) and fried in deep fat.

Swedish Timbale Cases

AMOUNT	INGREDIENT	METHOD
3	Eggs, beaten	
1½ c.	Milk	} Mix.
1½ t.	Oil or melted fat	
	Add	
6 oz.	Flour	
1 t.	Salt	} Mixed.
1½ t.	Sugar	

Stir until smooth and let stand until air bubbles have come to the top. Dip timbale iron into batter and fry in deep fat.

Fry in deep fat 2–3 min. at 350°–365° F., until brown.

NOTE: This recipe may be used for either timbale cases or rosettes.
1. Serve timbale cases filled with creamed chicken or creamed peas.
2. Serve rosettes sprinkled with powdered sugar; heaped with fresh or preserved fruits and garnished with whipped or ice cream; or use the same as timbale cases.

Dumplings

AMOUNT		INGREDIENT	METHOD
2 lb.	8 oz.	Flour (variable)	
	3 oz.	Baking powder	} Mix.
	2 T.	Salt	
		Add	
	6	Eggs, beaten	} Combined.
	5½ c.	Milk	

Mix only until blended. Use a No. 24 dipper to drop on oiled trays. Do not cover trays.

Steam 15–18 min. under pressure.

NOTES: 1. Serve with meat stew.
2. Mixture may be dropped on meat or meat mixture in counter pans and steamed.

Cheese Straws

Amount	Ingredient	Method
6 oz.	Butter or margarine	} Cream.
	Add	
8 oz.	Cheese, grated	
	Add	
8 oz.	Flour	
1 t.	Salt	} Mixed.
2 t.	Baking powder	
¼ t.	Cayenne	
	Add	
3	Eggs, beaten	} Combine to form stiff dough. Chill.
2 T.	Water	
	Roll ¼ in. thick and cut into strips 4 in. long and 1 in. wide. Place on ungreased baking sheet.	

Bake 10–15 min. at 350° F.   Yield: Approximately 6 doz. straws.

desserts

● **CAKES**

Cakes are classified as butter cakes and sponge cakes. Butter cakes are usually leavened with baking powder or soda and an acid. True sponge cakes are leavened chiefly by air incorporated in beaten eggs, although modified sponge cakes may have baking powder added. Butter cakes are most often baked as sheet cakes, in layers, or as individual cup cakes; sponge cakes are baked in tube pans or sheets.

Essential to good cake making are a properly balanced formula, correct temperature of ingredients, accurate measurements, controlled mixing of ingredients, proper relationship of batter to pan, and correct oven temperature and baking time.

Angel Food Cake (Sara Jane's)

Amount		Ingredient	Method
	5 c.	Egg whites	} Beat on high speed until frothy.
		Add	
	1 t.	Salt	⎱ Continue beating until eggs are
	2 T.	Cream of tartar	⎰ just stiff enough to hold shape.
		Add, 1 T. at a time,	
1 lb.	8 oz.	Sugar	
		Add	
	1 T.	Vanilla	} Continue beating on high speed for 2 min.
		Add gradually, folding in lightly,	
	12 oz.	Sugar	⎱ Mixed, sifted 3 times.
	12 oz.	Flour, cake	⎰
		Continue folding 2 min. after last addition. Pour into 3 tube cake pans.	

Bake 50–55 min. at 325° F. or 35 min. at 400° F. Yield: 3 10-in. cakes.

NOTE: Either frozen or fresh egg whites may be used. The frozen egg whites should be approximately 70° F. when whipped.

VARIATIONS: 1. **Chocolate Angel Food Cake.** Substitute 1½ oz. cocoa for 1½ oz. flour.
2. **Tutti Frutti Angel Food Cake.** Add chopped candied fruits, dates, and nuts to cake batter.
3. **Orange-filled Angel Food Cake.** Cut cake into 3 slices. Spread Orange Filling (p. 120) between layers, and frost top and sides with Orange Frosting (p. 117).
4. **Gelatin-filled Angel Food Cake.** Cut a slice from top of cake. Remove some from inside, leaving a ¾-in. wall. Fill case with any gelatin mixture. Replace top of cake, cover with icing, and garnish with almonds and cherries.
5. **Frozen Filled Angel Food Cake.** Cut cake into 3 slices. Spread softened strawberry ice cream on first layer and cover with cake slice. Spread second slice with softened pistachio ice cream. Top with remaining slice. Frost top and sides with sweetened whipped cream and toasted coconut. Freeze. Other ice cream or sherbet variations may be used as filling.

Yellow Angel Food (Egg Yolk Sponge Cake)

Amount	Ingredient	Method
3 c.	Egg yolks, well beaten	
	Add	
2 c.	Water, boiling	Beat until very light,
1 t.	Salt	approximately 5 min.
	Add	
1 lb.	Sugar, sifted	1 T. at a time; beat well while adding.
	Add gradually, folding in lightly,	
12 oz.	Sugar	
12 oz.	Flour, cake	Mixed, sifted 3 times.
	Fold in gradually, alternately,	
4½ t.	Baking powder	
10 oz.	Flour, cake	Sifted together.
	and	
3 T.	Lemon juice	
1 T.	Lemon rind, grated	
	Add	
1 T.	Vanilla extract	
1½ t.	Lemon extract	Continue folding 2 min.
	Pour into 3 tube cake pans.	

Bake 30–45 min. at 350°–375° F.   Yield: 3 10-in. cakes.

Orange Chiffon Cake

Amount		Ingredient	Method
1 lb.	8 oz.	Flour, cake	
	1½ oz.	Baking powder	Sift together into
	2 t.	Salt	mixer bowl.
1 lb.	3 oz.	Sugar	
		Add	
	12 oz. (1½ c.)	Vegetable oil	Mix until smooth
1 lb. (2 c.)		Egg yolks, beaten	(medium speed).
	1½ c.	Water	
		Add gradually	Mix well after each
	1 c.	Orange juice	addition (avoid over-
	2 T.	Orange rind, grated	mixing).
		Fold gradually into	
1 lb.	4 oz. (2½ c.)	Egg whites	
	2 t.	Cream of tartar	Beaten until very stiff.
1 lb.	2 oz.	Sugar	
		Fold gently until just blended.	
		Pour into tube cake pans.	

Bake 45–50 min. at 350° F.   Yield: 3 10-in. cakes.

NOTE: Turn cake upside down as soon as removed from oven. Frost with Orange Frosting (p. 117).

VARIATIONS: 1. **Cocoa Chiffon Cake.** Omit orange juice and rind. Add 5 oz. cocoa to dry ingredients. Increase water to 2⅓ c. Add 1 T. vanilla.

2. **Walnut Chiffon Cake.** Omit orange juice and rind. Increase water to 2⅓ c. Add 2 T. vanilla and 12 oz. finely chopped walnuts. Frost with Burnt Butter Frosting (p. 118).

Plain Cake

Amount	Ingredient	Method

1 lb.   9 oz.
            10 oz.
            2½ T.
	Flour
	Fat
	Baking powder
		Mix 2 min. in mixer bowl (low speed). Scrape down bowl and mix 3 min. more.

	Add	

1 lb.   14 oz.
            1½ t.
            1¼ c.
	Sugar
	Salt
	Milk
		Mix 2 min. (low speed) and scrape down bowl; mix 3 min. more.

		Add ½ following mixture; mix 30 sec. Scrape down bowl; mix 1 min. Add remainder of mixture. Mix 1 min. Scrape down. Mix 2½ min.
5 1⅔ c. 1 T.	Eggs, whole Milk Vanilla	Mixed.
		Pour into oiled pan 12 x 20 in.

Bake 30–35 min. at 350° F.   Serving: 2 x 2½ in.

Note: 1. For 6 9-in. layer pans, use 1½ recipe.

Variations of Plain Cake

Banana Cake. Spread whipped cream or boiled frosting between layers of cake, and top with sliced bananas and frosting or whipped cream.

Boston Cream Pie. Bake plain cake in sheet pan or in layer pans. Spread with Custard Filling (p. 120). Sprinkle with chopped nuts and serve with whipped cream.

Chocolate Cake. Omit 6 oz. flour and add 6 oz. cocoa to the flour and fat.

Cottage Pudding. Cut cake into squares and serve with No. 20 dipper of Fruit Sauce or other sauce.

Dutch Apple Cake. After the cake batter is poured into baking pan, arrange in rows 2½ lb. pared sliced apples. Sprinkle over the top ½ c. sugar and 1 t. cinnamon, mixed.

Filled Cake. Spread jam or marmalade between thin layers of cake. Sift confectioners' sugar over top.

Lazy Daisy Cake. Mix 9 oz. butter, melted, 1 lb. brown sugar, 1 lb. coconut, and ¾–1 c. cream (enough to moisten to consistency for spreading). Spread over Plain Cake (baked) and brown under broiler or in oven.

Marble Cake. Divide batter into 2 portions after mixing. To 1 portion add 1 T. cocoa, 1 t. cinnamon, ½ t. cloves, and ½ t. nutmeg. Place spoonfuls of batters alternately in cake pans; mix slightly.

Praline Cake. Substitute chopped pecans for coconut in Lazy Daisy variation.

Shortcake. Cut cake into squares and serve with fresh, frozen, or canned fruit. Garnish with whipped cream.

Spice Cake. Add 1 T. cocoa, 2 t. cinnamon, ½ t. cloves, and 1 t. nutmeg.

Upside-down Cake. Place 1 No. 10 can of crushed pineapple (or tidbits), drained,
1 lb. butter or margarine, 1½ lb. brown sugar, and 8 oz. chopped nutmeats in
the bottom of the cake pan. Pour plain cake batter over the mixture. (2½ lb.,
A.P., cooked dried apricots may be substituted for the pineapple.)

Washington Cream Pie. Double the basic recipe and bake in 12 9-in. layers. Put the
layers together with cream or chocolate filling. Sift powdered sugar on top of
pie or cover with a thin Chocolate Frosting (p. 114).

White Cake

AMOUNT		INGREDIENT	METHOD
1 lb.	8 oz.	Flour	Mix 2 min. in mixer bowl (low speed).
	12 oz.	Fat	Scrape down bowl and mix 3 min.
	1 oz.	Baking powder	more.
		Add	
1 lb.	8 oz.	Sugar	
	1½ t.	Salt	Mix 2 min. (low speed) and scrape down
	1 c.	Milk	bowl; mix 3 min. more.
		Add ½ following mixture; mix 30 sec. Scrape down bowl; mix 1 min. Add remainder of mixture. Mix 1 min. Scrape down. Mix 2½ min.	
	8	Egg whites	
	1¼ c.	Milk	Mixed.
	1 T.	Vanilla	
		Pour into oiled pan 12 x 20 in.	

Bake 30–35 min. at 350° F.

NOTE: 1. Do not use this method if less than the above quantity is made.
    2. For 6 9-in. layer pans, use 1½ recipe.
VARIATIONS: 1. **Chocolate Chip Cake.** Add 4 oz. chocolate chips.
    2. **Poppy Seed Cake.** Add 4 oz. poppy seed.
    3. **Cup Cakes.** Increase flour to 1 lb. 14 oz. Use No. 20 dipper to portion.

Banana Cake

AMOUNT		INGREDIENT	METHOD
	12 oz.	Fat	
1 lb.	8 oz.	Sugar	Cream 10 min. (medium speed).
	1 T.	Vanilla	
		Add	
	3 c.	Bananas, crushed	Blend.
		Add	
	6	Eggs	Mix well 5 min.
		Add sour milk and flour mixture alternately (low speed)	
1 lb.	8 oz.	Flour, cake	
	1 t.	Salt	
	2½ T.	Baking powder	Mixed.
	½ T.	Soda	
		and	
	¾ c.	Milk, sour	

Bake 25–30 min. at 350° F.   Yield: 6 9-in. layers.

Applesauce Cake

AMOUNT		INGREDIENT	METHOD
	12 oz.	Fat, soft	Cream approximately 10 min.
1 lb.	8 oz.	Sugar	(medium speed).
		Add	
	6	Eggs	Beat 5 min.
	1½ t.	Salt	
		Add water and flour mixture alternately (low speed)	
	1 pt.	Water	
1 lb.	6 oz.	Flour, cake	
	2 t.	Cinnamon	
	2 t.	Cloves	
	½ t.	Soda	Mixed.
	1 t.	Nutmeg	
	2 T.	Baking powder	
		Add	
	1 pt.	Applesauce	
1 lb.		Raisins	
	8 oz.	Nuts, chopped	
		Pour into pan 12 x 20 in.	

Bake 35 min. at 350° F.   Serving: 2 x 2½ in.

NOTE: This cake is better if not baked in layers.

Fudge Cake

Amount		Ingredient	Method
2 lb.	12 oz.	Fat, soft	Cream approximately 10 min.
		Sugar	(medium speed).
	1 T.	Vanilla	
		Add	
	6	Eggs	Beat well.
		Add alternately	
	1½ pt.	Milk, sour	
		and	
	5 oz.	Cocoa	Mixed.
	1½ c.	Water, hot	
		and	
1 lb.	12 oz.	Flour, cake	Sifted together.
	1½ T.	Soda	
	1 t.	Salt	

Bake 25–30 min. at 350° F.   Yield: 6 9-in. layers.

VARIATIONS: 1. **Chocolate Sheet Cake.** Spread dough over 12 x 20 in. oiled pan.
             2. **Chocolate Cup Cakes.** Portion with No. 20 dipper into muffin pans.

German Sweet-chocolate Cake

Amount		Ingredient	Method
1 lb.		Fat	} Cream approximately 10 min.
2 lb.		Sugar	(medium speed).
		Add, one at a time	
	8	Egg yolks	} Beat after each addition.
		Add	
	8 oz.	German sweet chocolate	
	1 c.	Boiling water	} Melted and cooled.
	2 t.	Vanilla	
		Add alternately	
	2 c.	Buttermilk	
		and	
1 lb.	4 oz.	Flour, cake	
	2 t.	Soda	} Sifted together.
	1 t.	Salt	
		Fold in	
	8	Egg whites, beaten until stiff but not dry.	
		Pour into 9-in. oiled layer pans.	

Bake 35–40 min. at 350° F.   Yield: 6 9-in. layers.

When baked, frost top of cake and fill layers with the following:
   Combine 2 c. evaporated milk, 6 egg yolks, 1 lb. sugar, and 8 oz. butter, cooking mixture
   in double boiler until thickened. Remove from heat and add 12 oz. pecans finely chopped,
   12 oz. coconut flaked, and 2 t. vanilla. Cool, then beat well until thick enough to spread.

Pineapple Cashew Cake

Amount		Ingredient	Method
1 lb.	2 oz.	Butter or margarine	Cream 8 min. (medium speed).
1 lb.	14 oz.	Sugar	
		Add	
	10	Egg yolks	Add in 3 portions while creaming.
	1 t.	Vanilla	Mix 2 min.
		Add alternately (low speed)	
1 lb.	14 oz.	Flour, cake	Mixed.
	1½ oz.	Baking powder	
	1½ t.	Salt	
		and	
	2¼ c.	Milk	
		Carefully add	
1 lb.		Pineapple, crushed, drained	
		Fold in	
	10	Egg whites, beaten until stiff but not dry.	
		Pour into oiled layer pans.	

Bake 25–30 min. at 350° F.   Yield: 6 9-in. layers.

NOTE: After baking, ice cake with Pineapple Butter Frosting (p. 117) and sprinkle with 12 oz. toasted chopped cashew nuts.

Burnt Sugar Cake

Amount	Ingredient	Method
12 oz.	Fat	Cream approximately 6 min.
2 lb.	Sugar	(medium speed).
	Add	
6	Egg yolks	Mix 2 min.
	Add alternately (low speed)	
1½ c.	Milk	
1½ c.	Water	
9 T.	Sirup, burnt sugar	Mixed.
	(p. 32)	
1 T.	Vanilla	
	and	
1 lb. 10 oz.	Flour, cake	
2 T.	Baking powder	Mixed.
1 t.	Salt	
	Fold in	
6	Egg whites, beaten	

Bake approximately 25 min. at 375° F.   Yield: 6 9-in. layers.

Prune Cake

Amount	Ingredient	Method
2 lb.	Sugar	Cream 10 min. (medium speed).
1 lb. 8 oz.	Fat	
	Add, one at a time,	
12	Eggs, unbeaten	
	Add	
1 qt. (1½ lb. A.P.)	Prunes, cooked, pitted, mashed	
	Add alternately (low speed)	
2 c.	Cultured sour cream	
	and	
2 lb.	Flour, cake	
4 t.	Soda	
1 T.	Nutmeg	
1 T.	Cinnamon	Mixed.
1 T.	Allspice	
1 T.	Cloves	
1 t.	Salt	

Bake 25–30 min. at 360° F.   Yield: 6 9-in. layers.

NOTE: When cake is cooled, spread with Cream Cheese Frosting (p. 118).

Jelly Roll

Amount		Ingredient	Method
15		Eggs, whole	} Beat well.
		Add	
1 lb.	8 oz.	Sugar	} Mix well.
		Fold in	
	12 oz.	Flour, cake	⎫
	1 T.	Cream of tartar	⎬ Sifted together.
	2 T.	Baking powder	⎭
	1½ t.	Salt	
		Add	
	2 t.	Lemon juice	
		Pour into 3 12 x 20-in. pans lined with waxed paper.	

Bake 12 min. at 375° F.   Yield: 3 rolls.

Trim edges (if hard); turn onto cloth or heavy paper; remove waxed paper. Cover
with Custard Filling (p. 120), fruit jam, or jelly. Roll while hot.

VARIATION: **Apricot Roll.** Cover with Apricot Filling (p. 119) and roll. Cover outside with
sweetened whipped cream and toasted coconut.

Chocolate Roll

Amount		Ingredient	Method
24		Egg yolks, beaten	
		Add	
2 lb.	4 oz.	Sugar	} Mix.
		Add	
	12 oz.	Chocolate, melted	
	2 T.	Vanilla	
		Add	
	9 oz.	Flour, cake	
	1 T.	Baking powder	} Mixed.
	1½ t.	Salt	
		Fold in	
24		Egg whites, beaten	
		Pour on 2 bun pans 18 x 26 in. lined with waxed paper.	
		When baked, cut each cake in half.	

Bake 20 min. at 325° F. Yield: 4 rolls.

Trim edges; turn onto cloth; remove waxed paper. Cover with Custard Filling (p. 120) or with Fluffy Frosting (p. 115), plain or flavored with peppermint. Roll as Jelly Roll while hot.

NOTE: May be covered with Chocolate Frosting (p. 114).

Gingerbread

Amount	Ingredient	Method
14 oz.	Fat	Cream approximately 10 min.
14 oz.	Sugar	(medium speed).
	Add	
3½ c.	Sorghum	
	Add alternately flour mixture and water (low speed)	
2 lb. 3 oz.	Flour, cake	
3½ t.	Cinnamon	Mixed.
3½ t.	Cloves	
3½ t.	Ginger	
3½ c.	Water, hot	Combined.
2 T.	Soda	
1½ t.	Salt	
	Add	
7	Eggs, beaten	
	Pour into oiled baking pan 12 x 20 in.	

Bake approximately 40 min. at 350° F.   Serving: 2 x 2½ in.

NOTE: Sprinkle with powdered sugar and serve warm.

VARIATIONS: 1. **Almond Meringue Gingerbread.** Cover baked Gingerbread with meringue, sprinkle with almonds, and brown in a moderate oven.

2. **Praline Gingerbread.** Spread baked Gingerbread with topping of 9 oz. butter, melted, 1 lb. brown sugar, 1 lb. chopped pecans, ¾–1 c. cream. Brown under broiler, or return to oven and heat until topping is slightly browned.

Orange Cup Cakes

Amount		Ingredient	Method
	10 oz.	Fat	Cream approximately 10 min. (medium speed).
1 lb.	1 oz.	Sugar	
		Add	
	1 T.	Vanilla	Mix until smooth.
	5	Eggs, beaten	
		Add	
	7 oz.	Raisins, ground	
	3	Orange rinds, grated	
		Add alternately	
	1¾ c.	Milk, sour	
		and	
1 lb.	8 oz.	Flour, cake	
	¾ T.	Soda	Mixed.
	1½ oz.	Baking powder	
	¾ t.	Salt	

Mix only until smooth. Use No. 30 dipper to fill muffin tins.

Bake 25 min. at 375° F.

NOTE: 1. While cakes are hot, brush with 12 oz. sugar dissolved in 1½ c. orange juice, or frost with Orange Frosting (p. 117).
2. May be baked in loaves.

Fruit Cake

Amount		Ingredient	Method
	8 oz.	Fat	⎫ Cream approximately 8 min.
1 lb.		Sugar	⎭ (medium speed).
		Add	
	4	Eggs	⎬ Cream 5 min.
		Add (low speed)	
	8 oz.	Jelly	⎫
	2 t.	Cinnamon	
	2 t.	Cloves	
2 lb.		Raisins	
1 lb.		Currants	⎬ Mix only until fruit is coated with flour mixture.
1 lb.		Dates, coarsely cut	
	8 oz.	Nutmeats, coarsely chopped	
1 lb.	4 oz.	Flour, cake	⎭
		Add	
	2 t.	Soda dissolved in cold	⎫ Mix until blended.
	1½ c.	coffee infusion	⎭
		Pour into 4 pans 4 x 9 in., lined with double-thick waxed paper.	

Bake 2½ hr. at 300° F. or steam 4 hr.   Yield: 4 2-lb. cakes.

● COOKIES

Cookies may be classified as drop and bar cookies, made from a soft dough; and as rolled, refrigerator, pressed, and molded cookies, made from a stiff dough. Almost all cookie doughs may be made in large amounts and stored in the refrigerator or freezer and used as needed.

For drop cookies, use a No. 40 dipper. For a smaller, tea-size cookie, drop dough from the end of a teaspoon or use a No. 60 dipper, if available. Icebox cookies may be sliced with a meat slicer if they have been well chilled.

Avoid overbaking cookies, and always remove from baking sheet onto cooling racks immediately after taking pans out of oven.

Sugar Cookies

Amount	Ingredient	Method
8 oz.	Butter or margarine	Cream.
8 oz.	Sugar	
	Add	
2	Eggs	Mix.
2 t.	Vanilla	
	Add	
12 oz.	Flour	
1 t.	Salt	Mixed.
1 t.	Baking powder	
	Roll dough to ⅛ in. thickness on board lightly dusted with mixture of 1 c. flour and ½ c. sugar. Cut into desired shapes. Place on ungreased cookie sheet.	

Bake approximately 7 min. at 400° F.   Yield: Approximately 7 doz. 2-in. cookies.

NOTE: Dough may be rolled on lightly floured board. Sprinkle cookies lightly with sugar.

Variations of Sugar Cookies

Coconut Cookies. Cut rolled dough with a round cookie cutter. Brush each cookie with melted fat and sprinkle with shredded coconut.

Filled Cookies. Cut dough with a round cutter. Cover ½ with Fig or Date Filling (p. 119). Brush edges with milk, cover with remaining cookies. Press edges together with tines of a fork.

Pinwheel Cookies. Use ½ of Sugar Cookie recipe. Divide dough into 2 portions. Add 1 square melted chocolate to 1 portion. Roll each into ⅛-in. sheets the same size. Place the chocolate dough over the white dough and press together. Roll as for Jelly Roll. Chill thoroughly. Cut into thin slices.

Ribbon Cookies. Cut chocolate and plain dough into long strips 1¾ in. wide. Arrange chocolate and plain strips alternately, until 1¼ in. high. Press together. Chill thoroughly. Cut into thin slices.

Wreath Cookies. Cut rolled dough with a doughnut cutter. Brush with beaten egg and sprinkle with chopped nuts. For Christmas cookies, decorate with candied cherry rings and pieces of citron arranged to represent holly.

Butter Tea Cookies

AMOUNT	INGREDIENT	METHOD
8 oz.	Butter	} Cream.
4½ oz.	Sugar	
3	Add Egg yolks	} Mix well.
10 oz. ½ t.	Add Flour Vanilla Chill and shape with a cookie press onto an ungreased baking pan.	

Bake 10–12 min. at 400° F.   Yield: 50–75 cookies.

NOTE: Dough should be cold when shaped.

VARIATION: **Thimble Cookies.** Roll into 1-in. balls. Dip in egg white and roll in finely chopped pecans. Bake 3 min. at 325° F., then make indentation in center of cookies and fill with jelly. Bake 12–15 min. longer.

Chocolate Tea Cookies

AMOUNT	INGREDIENT	METHOD
8 oz.	Butter or margarine, creamed	
6 oz.	Add gradually Sugar	
1	Add Egg, unbeaten	
½ t. ⅛ t. 9 oz. 2 T.	Add gradually Baking powder Salt Flour, sifted Cocoa	} Mixed.
2 t.	Add Vanilla Chill and shape with a cookie press onto an ungreased baking pan.	

Bake 6–10 min. at 375° F.   Yield: 50–75 cookies.

Sandies

AMOUNT	INGREDIENT	METHOD
12 oz.	Butter or margarine	
3 oz.	Sugar	Cream until light and fluffy.
1 t.	Vanilla	
	Add and blend	
1 lb. 2 oz.	Flour	Sifted together.
1 t.	Salt	
	Add	
1 T.	Ice water	
8 oz.	Pecans, chopped	
	Chill and shape into small balls ¾ in. in diameter. This will be a crumbly mixture. If it will not stick together, add small amount of melted butter or margarine. Place on oiled baking sheet.	

Bake 20 min. at 325° F., or until lightly browned.

Yield: Approximately 8 doz. cookies.

Roll in confectioners' sugar while still hot.

Fudge Balls

AMOUNT	INGREDIENT	METHOD
12 oz.	Flour	
1 lb.	Sugar	Sift together.
1 t.	Salt	
	Add	
12 oz.	Shortening, soft	
4 oz.	Chocolate, melted	Beat until smooth.
½ c.	Coffee, cold	
	Fold in	
8 oz.	Rolled oats quick, uncooked	
	Shape dough into balls, 1 in. in diameter	
	Roll in	
6 oz.	Nuts, chopped	
	Place on ungreased baking sheet.	

Bake 10–12 min. at 350° F.   Yield: Approximately 6 doz. balls.

Butterscotch Pecan Cookies

Amount		Ingredient	Method
1 lb.	8 oz.	Butter or margarine Brown sugar	} Cream.
		Add	
	2 t. 2	Vanilla Eggs	} Beat well.
		Add	
	12 oz. 8 oz.	Flour Pecans	} Blend until all the flour is moistened.
		Drop onto oiled baking sheet, ⅔ oz. per cookie.	

Bake 10–12 min. at 375° F.   Yield: Approximately 6 doz. cookies.

Butterscotch Drop Cookies

Amount		Ingredient	Method
1 lb.	8 oz.	Sugar, brown Butter or margarine	} Cream.
		Add	
	4	Eggs	} Cream.
		Add, alternately,	
1 lb.	4 oz. 1 t. 2 t. 1 t.	Flour Baking powder Soda Salt	} Mixed.
		and	
	2 c.	Cultured sour cream	
		Add	
	2 t. 8 oz.	Vanilla Walnuts, chopped	
		Chill until dough is firm. Drop on oiled baking sheet, ½ oz. per cookie.	

Bake 10–15 min. at 400° F.   Yield: Approximately 8 doz. cookies.

NOTE: Cover with Burnt Butter Frosting (p. 118) while still warm.
VARIATIONS: 1. **Butterscotch Squares.** Spread batter in 12 x 26 in. pan. Bake 25 min. at 325° F.
2. **Chocolate Drop Cookies.** Add 4 oz. baking chocolate, melted, to creamed mixture.

Chocolate Chip Cookies

Amount	Ingredient	Method
6 oz.	Fat	
6 oz.	Sugar, white	} Cream.
4 oz.	Sugar, brown	
	Add	
2	Eggs, beaten	} Mix well.
	Add	
10 oz.	Flour	
1 t.	Salt	} Mixed.
1 t.	Soda	
	Add	
1 t.	Vanilla	
8 oz.	Nuts, chopped	
14 oz.	Chocolate chips	
	Drop on oiled baking sheet, ½ oz. per cookie.	

Bake 10–12 min. at 375° F.   Yield: Approximately 8 doz. cookies.

Oatmeal Drop Cookies

Amount	Ingredient	Method
8 oz.	Sugar, brown	
6 oz.	Fat	} Cream.
	Add	
2	Eggs, beaten	
	Add	
7 oz.	Rolled oats, quick, uncooked	
	Add alternately	
8 oz.	Flour	
2 t.	Baking powder	} Mixed.
1 t.	Salt	
	and	
5 T.	Milk	
½ t.	Soda dissolved in 1 T. water	
	Add	
6 oz.	Raisins, cooked, chopped	
1 t.	Vanilla	
	Drop on oiled baking sheet, ⅔ oz. per cookie.	

Bake approximately 12–15 min. at 375° F.

Yield: Approximately 5 doz. cookies.

Coconut Drop Cookies

Amount	Ingredient	Method
1½ c. 1 lb. 1 T. 8 oz.	Milk, condensed, sweetened Coconut, shredded Vanilla Nuts, chopped	} Mix.
	Drop on oiled baking sheet, ½ oz. per cookie.	

Bake 15–18 min. at 325° F.   Yield: Approximately 4 doz. cookies.

Cornflake Kisses

Amount	Ingredient	Method
4	Egg whites, beaten until frothy	
1 lb.	Add gradually Sugar, sifted	} Beat until sugar is dissolved.
4 oz. 8 oz. 3 oz. 1 t.	Fold in Cornflakes Nuts, chopped Coconut, shredded Vanilla	
	Drop on oiled baking sheet, ½ oz. per cookie.	

Bake 15 min. at 325° F.   Yield: Approximately 4 doz. small cookies.

Coconut Macaroons

Amount	Ingredient	Method
8	Egg whites, beaten until frothy	
12 oz. 12 oz. 2 t. ⅛ t.	Add gradually, and beat until stiff Sugar, granulated Sugar, powdered Vanilla Salt	
1 lb. 6 oz.	Fold in Coconut, shredded	
	Drop on oiled baking sheet, ⅔ oz. each.	

Bake 15 min. at 325° F.   Yield: Approximately 8 doz. macaroons.

NOTE: Do not enlarge this recipe.

Peanut Butter Cookies

AMOUNT	INGREDIENT	METHOD
8 oz.	Sugar	
5 oz.	Sugar, brown	} Cream together.
8 oz.	Fat	
	Add	
2	Eggs, beaten	
1 c.	Peanut butter	
	Add	
8 oz.	Flour	
1 t.	Soda	} Mixed and sifted.
½ t.	Salt	
	Add	
1 t.	Vanilla	

Form into balls and flatten with tines of fork.

Bake 8 min. at 375° F.   Yield: Approximately 8 doz. small cookies.

Crisp Ginger Cookies

AMOUNT		INGREDIENT	METHOD
	1 c.	Molasses	⎱ Boil together 1 min.
	8 oz.	Sugar	⎰ Cool.
		Add in order given	
	8 oz.	Fat	⎱ Mix well.
	2	Eggs, beaten	⎰
		Add	
	½ t.	Salt	
	1 t.	Soda	
	2 t.	Ginger	} Mixed.
1 lb.	12 oz.	Flour (or more)	

Form into a roll 2 in. in diameter. Chill thoroughly and slice.

Bake 8–10 min. at 375° F.   Yield: Approximately 8 doz. cookies.

NOTE: Dough may be rolled as any cookie dough and cut into fancy shapes.

Butterscotch Ice Box Cookies

Amount		Ingredient	Method
	8 oz.	Butter or margarine	
	8 oz.	Fat	Cream 5 min. (medium speed).
1 lb.		Sugar, brown	
	12 oz.	Sugar, white	
		Add	
	4	Eggs, beaten	Cream 5 min.
	2 t.	Vanilla	
		Add	
	2 t.	Cream of tartar	
	8 oz.	Nuts, chopped	
	2 t.	Soda	Mixed.
	8 oz.	Dates, chopped	
2 lb.		Flour	

Place dough on waxed paper, form into rolls. Wrap. Let stand overnight or longer in refrigerator. Cut into ⅛-in. slices.

Bake 8–10 min. at 400° F.   Yield: Approximately 8 doz. cookies.

Brownies

Amount		Ingredient	Method
1 lb.		Fat, melted	
2 lb.		Sugar	Mix.
12		Eggs, beaten	
		Add	
	12 oz.	Flour, cake	
	8 oz.	Cocoa	Mixed.
	4 t.	Baking powder	
	2 t.	Salt	
		Add	
	12 oz.	Nuts, chopped	
	4 T.	Vanilla	

Spread mixture ½ in. thick in oiled pan 12 x 20 in.

Bake 25–30 min. at 325° F. Should be soft to the touch when done.

Yield: 4 doz. 2 x 2½ in.

NOTE: 1. 3 squares chocolate may be substituted for the cocoa.
2. 2 lb. chopped dates may be added.
3. May be frosted with Mocha or Chocolate Frosting (p. 114), or with White Frosting (p. 114) with melted chocolate drizzled over top.

Butterscotch Squares

Amount		Ingredient	Method
	8 oz.	Butter or substitute, soft	Cream.
1 lb.	4 oz.	Sugar, brown	
		Add, one at a time,	
	5	Eggs, unbeaten	
		Add	
	12 oz.	Flour	
	1 T.	Baking powder	Sifted together.
	½ t.	Salt	
		Beat until smooth, add	
	2 t.	Vanilla	Blend.
	6 oz.	Pecans, broken (optional)	
		Spread on 12 x 18-in. baking pan to a thickness of ½ in.	

Bake 25 min. at 325° F.   Yield: Approximately 4 doz. 2 x 2¼-in. cookies.

Oatmeal Crispies

Amount		Ingredient	Method
	12 oz.	Flour	
	2 t.	Salt	Sift together.
	2 t.	Soda	
		Add	
1 lb.		Fat	
1 lb.		Sugar, brown	
1 lb.		Sugar, granulated	Beat until smooth, about 2 min.
	4	Eggs	
	2 t.	Vanilla	
		Fold in	
1 lb.		Rolled oats, quick, uncooked	Mix. Shape dough into rolls 2 in. in diameter. Wrap in waxed paper and chill overnight.
	8 oz.	Nuts, chopped	
		Slice ¼ in. thick and place on ungreased baking sheet.	

Bake 12–15 min. at 350° F.   Yield: Approximately 8 doz. cookies.

Oatmeal Fruit Bars

Amount		Ingredient	Method
	13 oz.	Fat	⎫ Cream in mixer for 20 min.
1 lb.	6 oz.	Sugar, brown	⎰ (medium speed).
		Add	
1 lb.		Flour	⎫
	12 oz.	Rolled oats, quick, uncooked	⎬ Mixed.
	4 t.	Soda	⎭
		Spread ⅔ of dough on oiled pan 12 x 20 in. Pat down by hand. Add Date Filling (p. 119) and spread evenly over entire surface. Cover with remainder of dough and pat down. Bake. Cut into bars.	

Bake 45 min. at 325° F.   Yield: 4 doz. 2 x 2½ in.

NOTE: Crushed pineapple or cooked dried apricots may be substituted for date filling.

Date Bars

Amount		Ingredient	Method
12		Egg whites	⎱ Beat until stiff.
		Fold in (in order given)	
12		Egg yolks, beaten	
2 lb.		Sugar	
1 lb.		Nuts, chopped	
2 lb.		Dates	
1 lb.		Flour	⎱ Mixed.
	1½ T.	Baking powder	⎰
		Spread 1 in. thick in oiled pan 18 x 26 in.	

Bake 25 min. at 350° F.   Yield: 96 1 x 2½-in. bars.

NOTE: Cut while hot and roll in powdered sugar, or serve with a rich custard sauce.

Coconut Pecan Bars

AMOUNT		INGREDIENT	METHOD
1 lb.	8 oz.	Butter or margarine	Blend together until
	12 oz.	Brown sugar	mixture resembles
1 lb.	4 oz.	Flour	coarse meal.

Press mixture into 18 x 26 in. bun pan and bake at 350° F. until light brown.

Cover with following topping:

		INGREDIENT	METHOD
	8	Eggs, beaten	
	4 oz.	Flour	
	1 T.	Baking powder	
	2 t.	Salt	Combine. Spread over
	8 oz.	Coconut, shredded	baked crust.
2 lb.	8 oz.	Brown sugar	
	1 T.	Vanilla	
	12 oz.	Nutmeats, chopped	

Bake 20–25 min. at 350° F.   Yield: 96 1 x 2½-in. bars.

Frost with Orange Frosting (p. 117), if desired.

Marshmallow Squares

AMOUNT	INGREDIENT	METHOD
6 oz.	Butter or margarine	Melt.
1 lb.	Marshmallows	

Add

1 t.	Vanilla	

Pour above mixture over

11 oz.	Rice Krispies	Mix well.

Press into oiled pan 12 x 20 in. to ½ in. thickness. Cool and cut.

Yield: 4 doz. 2 x 2½ in. squares.

VARIATION: **Chocolate Marshmallow Squares.** Cover squares with a thin rich chocolate frosting.

● FROSTINGS AND FILLINGS

The amount of frosting to use on a cake will depend on the kind of cake to be frosted and the individual preferences of the patrons. The following may serve as a guide:

1–1½ qt. for a 12 x 20 in. sheet cake
2¼–2½ qt. for 3 2-layer cakes
2–2½ qt. for 3 10-in. angel food cakes

Boiled Frosting

AMOUNT	INGREDIENT	METHOD
4 lb. 2½ c.	Sugar Water, hot	Stir until sugar is dissolved. Boil without stirring to soft ball stage (238° F.).
8	Egg whites, beaten	While beating, pour gradually over Continue beating until frosting is of consistency to spread.
2 T.	Vanilla	Add Spread on cake at once.
		Yield: Approximately 4½ qt.

VARIATIONS: See p. 114.

Ice Cream Frosting

Amount		Ingredient	Method
1 lb.	8 oz. 1 c.	Sugar, granulated Water, hot	Combine and boil until it spins a 3-in. thread (238° F.).
		Add slowly to	
	9 3 oz.	Egg whites, beaten Sugar, powdered	Combined and beaten until the con- sistency of meringue.
		Continue beating until mixture is thick and creamy.	
		Add	
	8 oz. 1 T.	Sugar, powdered, sifted Vanilla	
			Yield: Approximately 1 gal.

NOTE: Add more powdered sugar if necessary to make frosting hold its shape when spread. Can be kept several days in a covered container in the refrigerator.

Variations of Boiled or Ice Cream Frosting

Bittersweet Frosting. Melt 8 oz. bitter chocolate over water, gradually stir in 3 T. butter; when slightly cool, pour over white frosting to form a design.

Burnt Sugar Frosting. Add 1 lb. Burnt Sugar Sirup (p. 32) to the liquid.

Candied Fruit Frosting. Add 8 oz. chopped candied fruit.

Chocolate Frosting. Add 8 oz. melted chocolate.

Coconut Frosting. Frost cake, sprinkle with 4 oz. dry shredded coconut.

Creole Frosting. Substitute 1 lb. brown sugar for 1 lb. white sugar; add 4 oz. shredded coconut, toasted.

Lady Baltimore Frosting. Use 1¾ qt. Boiled Frosting. Add 1 t. orange juice, 4½ oz. macaroon crumbs, 5 oz. chopped almonds, and 1 c. chopped raisins.

Lemon Frosting. Reduce liquid ½ c. Add ½ t. lemon extract and ½ c. lemon juice. Omit vanilla.

Maple Nut Frosting. Flavor with maple flavoring; add 6 oz. chopped nuts.

Maraschino Frosting. Flavor with juice from Maraschino cherries; garnish with Maraschino cherries.

Peppermint Frosting. 1. Add a few drops of peppermint flavoring.
2. Add 8 oz. finely crushed peppermint candy.
3. Place large chocolate-coated peppermint patties on top of frosting while soft.

Fluffy Frosting

Amount		Ingredient	Method
2 lb.	8 oz. 1½ c. 5 T. ¼ t.	Sugar Water Corn sirup Salt	Boil together until mixture reaches the soft ball stage (238° F.).
		Add ½ of the mixture gradually to	
	10	Egg whites, beaten	Beating constantly.
		Add	
		Remainder of sirup	Cooked until it forms a hard ball (250° F.).
		Beat until it holds its shape.	
		Add	
	1 T.	Vanilla	
			Yield: 4¼ qt.

VARIATION: **Brown Sugar Frosting.** Substitute brown sugar for white sugar.

Creamy Frosting

Amount		Ingredient	Method
	12 oz.	Butter or margarine	Cream 1 min. (medium speed), or until soft.
		Add, gradually,	
	½ c.	Milk, evaporated	
	1 T.	Vanilla	Whip until mixture is smooth and creamy (medium speed).
2 lb.	8 oz.	Sugar, powdered	
	2 t.	Salt	
			Yield: Approximately 1½ qt.

NOTE: ½–¾ c. hot milk or cream may be substituted for evaporated milk.

VARIATIONS: 1. **Cocoa Frosting.** Increase liquid ¾ c.; add 6 oz. cocoa sifted with sugar.
2. **Lemon Butter Frosting.** Substitute ¼ c. lemon juice for an equal amount of milk, and 1½ T. grated lemon rind for the vanilla.
3. **Mocha Frosting.** Substitute cold coffee for liquid in Cocoa Cream Frosting.
4. **Orange Butter Frosting.** Substitute ½ c. orange juice for an equal amount of milk, and 1½ T. grated orange rind for the vanilla.

Powdered Sugar Glaze

AMOUNT	INGREDIENT	METHOD
2 lb.	Sugar, powdered, sifted	
	Gradually add	
¾ c.	Water, boiling	⎱ Beat until right consistency to ⎰ spread.
	Add	
2 t.	Vanilla	
		Yield: Approximately 1 qt.

NOTE: Use for frosting baked rolls or other products requiring a thin frosting.

Butter Cream Frosting

AMOUNT	INGREDIENT	METHOD
1 lb.	Sugar, powdered	⎱ Mix. Place over heat. Cook and beat
5	Eggs	⎰ until lukewarm.
	Remove from heat and add	
1 lb.	Butter, unsalted, creamed	
	Mix well.	
		Yield: Approximately 1 qt.

NOTE: Make several hours before using. May be used as frosting for petits fours.

Chocolate Butter Cream Frosting

AMOUNT	INGREDIENT	METHOD
2 lb.	Butter	⎱ Cream until light and fluffy.
	Add	
⅔ c.	Milk, evaporated	⎱ Mix well.
	Add	
2 lb.	Sugar, powdered	⎱ Mix well.
	Add	
6 oz.	Chocolate, unsweetened, melted	
1 t.	Vanilla	
		Yield: 3 qt.

NOTE: Keep in a cool place.

Pineapple Butter Frosting

Amount		Ingredient	Method
1 lb.		Butter or margarine	
2 lb.		Powdered sugar	Cream.
	½ t.	Salt	
		Add	
	2	Egg yolks	Cream until light and fluffy.
		Add	
	12 oz.	Crushed pineapple, drained.	
			Yield: Approximately 3 qt.

Mocha Frosting

Amount		Ingredient	Method
	1 c.	Coffee infusion	Mix together and bring to
	2 oz.	Butter or margarine	boiling point.
		Add	
	3 oz.	Cocoa	Mix well.
		Add	
	½ t.	Salt	
2 lb.		Sugar, powdered	Mix until smooth.
	½ t.	Vanilla	
			Yield: Approximately 1 qt.

NOTE: 1. Add more sugar if necessary to make frosting hold its shape.
2. If desired, use 2 T. instant coffee dissolved in 1 c. hot water.

Orange Frosting

Amount		Ingredient	Method
	8 oz.	Butter	Cream.
2 lb.	8 oz.	Sugar, powdered	
		Add	
	2 T.	Vanilla	
	½ t.	Salt	
	¼ c.	Orange juice	Beat until smooth.
	¼ c.	Lemon juice	
	1 t.	Orange rind, grated	
			Yield: Approximately 5 c.

Ornamental Frosting

Amount		Ingredient	Method
	8	Egg whites	} Beat until stiff.
1 lb.	8 oz.	Fold in Sugar, powdered Beat to the consistency of heavy cream if used for frosting; beat until it will retain its shape when drawn to a point if used for ornamenting.	
			Yield: 1 qt.

NOTE: 1. This frosting dries quickly when exposed to the air and should be covered with a damp cloth.
2. A few drops of lemon juice may be added for flavoring if desired.

Burnt Butter Frosting

Amount		Ingredient	Method
	9 oz.	Butter	} Melt and heat until golden brown.
1 lb.	8 oz.	Blend in Sugar, powdered	
	1 T.	Add Vanilla	} Beat until frosting is right con-
	½ c.	Water, hot (variable)	sistency to spread thinly.
			Yield: Frosting for 8 doz. 2½-in. cookies.

Cream Cheese Frosting

Amount		Ingredient	Method
2 8-oz. pkg.		Cream cheese	} Cream until light.
	¼ c.	Cream or milk	
1 lb.	12 oz.	Add gradually Sugar, powdered, sifted (variable)	
	1 T.	Vanilla Cream until smooth.	
			Yield: 4½ c.

NOTE: Use as frosting for Gingerbread (p. 99) and Spice Cake (p. 90).
VARIATION: **Orange Cheese Frosting.** Substitute 1 T. orange juice and 1 T. grated orange rind for vanilla.

Date Filling

Amount	Ingredient	Method
2 lb. (A.P.) 2¼ c. 12 oz.	Dates, chopped Water Sugar	} Cook until mixture is thick. Yield: Approximately 1½ qt.

NOTE: Cool and spread on cookies, or use as a cake filling.
VARIATIONS: 1. **Fig Filling.** Substitute figs for dates.
2. **Fruit Filling.** Omit ¼ c. water; add 6 oz. jelly or ¼ c. orange juice.

Chocolate Cream Filling

Amount	Ingredient	Method
6 pkg. 1 c. 8 oz.	Semisweet chocolate bits Orange juice or water sugar	} Melt over hot water. Cool.
	Fold in	
1½ qt.	Cream, whipped	
		Yield: 3 qt.

NOTE: Use as filling for Orange Cream Puffs (p. 152).

Prune Filling

Amount	Ingredient	Method
1 lb. ½ t. 1 oz.	Sugar Salt Flour	} Combine.
	Add to	
1 c. 2 oz. 4 1 pt.	Cultured sour cream Butter or margarine Eggs, beaten Prunes, cooked, pitted, and chopped Cook over hot water until thick.	
		Yield: Approximately 1 qt.

NOTE: 8 oz. chopped nutmeats may be added.
VARIATION: **Apricot Filling.** Substitute dried or canned apricots for prunes.

Custard Filling

Amount		Ingredient	Method
	6 oz.	Cornstarch	
1 lb.		Sugar	} Mix.
	½ t.	Salt	
		Add	
	1 pt.	Milk, cold	} Stir until smooth.
		Add	
2½ qt.		Milk, hot	} Stirring constantly.
		Cook over water until thick.	
		Add	
	10	Eggs, beaten	} Mix thoroughly. Cook 7 min.
		Remove from fire, add	
	2 t.	Vanilla	
			Yield: Approximately 3 qt.

NOTE: Use as a filling for Cream Puff (p. 152), Washington Cream Pie (p. 91), Chocolate Roll (p. 98), and Eclairs (p. 152).
To fill 3 9-in. layer cakes use ⅓ recipe.

Lemon Filling

Amount		Ingredient	Method
	3 c.	Water	} Heat.
1 lb.		Sugar	
		Add	
	2½ oz.	Cornstarch	} Blended.
	¾ c.	Water, cold	
		Cook until thickened and clear, stirring constantly.	
		Add	
	4	Egg yolks, beaten slightly	
		Cook 2 min. Add	
	¾ t.	Salt	
	2 t.	Lemon rind, grated	
	½ c.	Lemon juice	
	2 T.	Butter or margarine	
		Cool and spread between layers of cake, 1½ c. per cake.	
			Yield: Approximately 1 qt.

VARIATION: **Orange Filling.** Substitute orange juice for water and orange rind for lemon rind. Reduce lemon juice to 3 T.

Whipped Orange Topping

Amount	Ingredient	Method
10	Egg yolks	Combine. Cook over hot water until
8 oz.	Sugar	mixture thickens, 20 to 25 min.,
1¼ c.	Orange juice	stirring constantly. Cool.
	Fold in	
1¼ qt.	Orange pieces, cubed	
	Fold in	
1 pt.	Cream, whipped	
2 oz.	Sliced almonds, toasted	
	Serve with No. 16 dipper.	

Yield: Approximately 3 qt.

NOTE: Serve on cake, pudding, fruit, or ice cream.

● PASTRY AND PIES

The importance of serving good pies can hardly be overemphasized, since pie is a favorite dessert.

A good pie should have a tender, flaky crust and a filling that will just hold its shape. This type of product may be slightly more difficult to serve than a pie with a crust which does not break easily and a filling so stiff it could not possibly spread over the plate. However, the satisfaction of the patrons should justify the extra care in preparation and service of this popular American dessert.

Pies may be made with one or two crusts. One-crust pies may be baked before filling, as for chiffon and cream pies, or together with the filling, as for custard-type pies. Two-crust fruit pies are baked together with the filling. Pastry may be made as needed (Pastry I) or prepared in larger amounts (Pastry II) and stored in the refrigerator for several days.

To make a one-crust pie, roll pastry to ⅛-in. thickness and fit it loosely into pie pan, allowing ½ in. extra to build up the edge. For cream or chiffon pies, crimp edge and prick crust with fork; bake, cool, and fill. For custard pies, crimp edge but do not prick crust; add filling and bake.

To make a two-crust pie, roll pastry to ⅛-in. thickness. Place bottom crust in pan and trim. If desired, leave ½-in. crust around edge and fold over to fit pie pan, making a pocket of pastry to prevent fruit juices from running out. Add fruit filling and brush edge of bottom crust with water. Cover with top crust, in which slits or vents have been cut to allow the steam to escape. Trim, flute, and seal by pressing the two crusts together with the fingertips. Brush top crust with milk. Bake.

Pastry I

AMOUNT	INGREDIENT	METHOD
2 lb.	Flour	} Mix 1 min. (low speed).
1 lb. 8 oz.	Shortening	
	Add slowly (40 sec., low speed)	
1½–1¾ c.	Water, ice	} Combined.
1½ T.	Salt	
	Mix with minimum handling to form a dough. Scale 5 oz. for bottom crust and 4 oz. for top crust. Let stand 10 min. in refrigerator before rolling.	

Bake pie shell approximately 8–10 min. at 450° F.   Yield: 8 8-in. 2-crust pies.

Pastry II [1]

AMOUNT	INGREDIENT	METHOD
25 lb.	Flour	} Mix (low speed) until flour and
18 lb.	Shortening	fat are blended.
	Add	
3¾ qt.	Water, ice	} Combined.
12–14 oz.	Salt	
	Mix until dough will hold together.	
		Yield: Approximately 50 lb.

NOTE: 1. Pastry should be mixed several hours before it is to be used.
  2. This recipe is based on the use of hydrogenated shortening; if lard is used, reduce amount by ⅛.
  3. Use approximately 5 oz. for bottom crust and 4 oz. for top crust for 8-in. pie.

[1] Similar to recipe for Pastry I except for quantity. Pastry may be stored (covered) in refrigerator for several days.

Graham Cracker Crust

Amount		Ingredient	Method
1 lb.	5 oz.	Graham cracker crumbs	
	10 oz.	Sugar	Mix.
	10 oz.	Butter or margarine, melted	
	2 oz.	Flour	

Pat 8 oz. of crumb mixture into each pie pan. Bake. Chill several hours. Fill with Cream Pie Filling (p. 128) or a chiffon pie filling (pp. 132–136).

Bake approximately 12 min. at 375° F.   Yield: 8 8-in. pies.

NOTE: Vanilla wafers may be substituted for graham cracker crumbs.

VARIATION: **Ice Cream Pie.** Fill crust with softened ice cream of any desired flavor. Replace in freezer until serving time.

Pie Meringue

Amount		Ingredient	Method
16		Egg whites	Whip past frothy stage, approximately
	½ t.	Salt	1½ min. (high speed).

Add gradually, while beating,

| 1 lb. | Sugar, granulated |

Beat until the sugar has dissolved. The meringue should be stiff enough to hold peaks but not dry. Spread on pie to edge of crust.

Bake approximately 12 min. at 375° F.   Yield: Meringue for 8 8-in. pies.

Canned Fruit Pie

Amount	Ingredient	Method
1½ No. 10 can	Fruit, water pack	Drain. Measure juice and add water to make 1½ qt. liquid.
	Heat	
1 qt.	Fruit juice	
	Add, while stirring,	
1 pt.	Fruit juice	Mixed.
6 oz.	Cornstarch	
	Cook until thick and clear. While still hot, add	
3 lb.	Sugar	Mix thoroughly and bring to boiling point.
1 T.	Salt	
	Add drained fruit and mix carefully. Cool slightly. Measure 3 c. filling into each unbaked pie shell. Moisten edge of bottom crust with water. Cover with top crust. Trim and flute edges. Brush top crust with milk.	

Bake approximately 30 min. at 425° F.   Yield: 8 8-in. pies.

NOTE: May be used for all canned fruit fillings, such as apricot, blackberry, cherry, gooseberry, peach, or raspberry (sugar variable).

Frozen Fruit Pie or Cobbler

Guide in Using Frozen Fruit for Pies

Fruit (30 lb.)	Sugar °	Cornstarch °	Seasonings	Yield (Pies)
Apples	4–5 lb.	8 oz.	Salt, 1 T. Cinnamon, 2 T.	24 8-in.
Apricots	5–7 lb.	1 lb.	Cinnamon, 2 T.	24 8-in.
Berries	7–10 lb.	1 lb. 4 oz.	Lemon juice, ½ c. Salt, 1 T.	25 8-in.
Blueberries	7–9 lb.	1 lb.	Lemon juice, 3 pt.	23 8-in.
Blue plums	6–8 lb.	1 lb.	Salt, 1 T.	24 8-in.
Cherries	1–2 lb.	1 lb.	Salt, 1 T.	24 8-in.
Peaches	5–7 lb.	1 lb.	Salt, 1 T.	24 8-in.
Pineapple	6–8 lb.	1 lb.	Salt, 1 T.	24 8-in.
Rhubarb	5–7 lb.	1 lb. 6 oz.	Salt, 1 T.	24 8-in.

° The amount of sugar and cornstarch added to the fruit will vary according to the pack of the fruit and individual preferences of flavor and consistency. Frozen fruits packed without the addition of sugar are known as "dry pack." When sugar is added during the freezing process, the ratio is usually 3, 4, or 5 parts by weight of fruit to 1 part by weight of sugar.

Directions. Thaw fruit at room temperature in the unopened original container. When fruit is thawed, drain off the juice. Measure juice and figure the amount of cornstarch needed to thicken it, allowing 2½–3 oz. cornstarch for each quart of liquid. If fruit is lacking in juice, water may be added to bring the total liquid to 4–6 qt. for the 30 lb. fruit, according to the consistency desired. Bring liquid to boiling point. Add sugar and cornstarch, mixed, stirring constantly with a wire whip. Pour over fruit. Use 3 c. filling for each 8-in. pie. Bake 30–40 min. at 425° F.

For cobblers, follow the same procedure as for pies, using less cornstarch.

Fresh Apple Pie

Amount		Ingredient	Method
12 lb.		Apples, tart, sliced	} Arrange apples in 8 deep pie tins that have been lined with pastry.
		Sprinkle over the apples	
3 lb.	4 oz.	Sugar	}
	4 oz.	Flour	} Mixed.
	2 t.	Nutmeg	}
		Add	
	8 oz.	Butter or margarine, melted	
		Cover with pastry. Brush top with milk.	

Bake approximately 15 min. at 425° F.; then 30 min. at 350° F., or until apples are done.

Yield: 8 8-in. pies.

Variation: Apple Crumb Pie. Omit top crust. Sprinkle apples with Streusel Topping: Mix 1 lb. flour, 1 lb. 10 oz. sugar, 2 oz. nonfat dry milk, 1 t. salt, cut in 10 oz. butter or margarine and add 6 oz. chopped pecans. Use 1 c. per pie. Bake until apples are done and topping is brown.

Raisin Pie

Amount		Ingredient	Method
4 lb.		Raisins, washed	} Simmer until raisins are plump.
4½ qt.		Water, hot	}
		Add, while stirring,	
2 lb.	4 oz.	Sugar	}
	6 oz.	Cornstarch	} Mixed.
	2 t.	Salt	}
		Cook until thick.	
		Add	
	6 T.	Lemon juice	
	3 oz.	Butter or margarine	
		Pour into unbaked pie shells. Cover with pastry.	

Bake 15 min. at 425° F. and then 15 min. at 375° F.   Yield: 8 8-in. pies.

Note: A superior product is obtained if 3 qt. cream are substituted for 3 qt. water.

Dried Apricot Pie

Amount		Ingredient	Method
5 lb.		Apricots, dried	Wash and drain. Cover with water. Cook slowly without stirring until tender (approximately 45–60 min.).
		Add	
4 lb.		Sugar	
	2½ oz.	Cornstarch	Mixed.
	½ c.	Water	
		Continue cooking until juice is clear. Cool before pouring into unbaked pie shells. Cover with pastry.	

Bake 30 min. at 450° F.   Yield: 8 8-in. pies.

VARIATION: **Prune Pie.** 8 lb. prunes (cooked and pitted), 4 c. prune juice, 2 lb. sugar, 8 oz. butter, ½ oz. lemon juice, 4 oz. flour, and 1 t. salt.

Rhubarb Custard Pie

Amount		Ingredient	Method
4 lb.		Sugar	
	1 t.	Salt	
	4	Lemon rinds, grated	Mix.
	8 oz.	Flour	
		Add	
12		Eggs, beaten	
7 lb.	8 oz.	Rhubarb, cut fine	Mixed.
		Fill unbaked pie shells.	
		May be topped with meringue.	

Bake approximately 30 min. at 350° F.   Yield: 8 8-in. pies.

NOTE: May be covered with top crust of ⅜-in. pastry strips, arranged in lattice fashion.

VARIATION: **Fresh Rhubarb Pie.** Use 8–10 lb. fresh rhubarb. Combine 4 lb. 8 oz. sugar, 8 oz. cornstarch, 1 t. salt, 2 T. grated lemon rind and sprinkle over rhubarb in pie crusts. Cover with top crust. Bake 15 min. at 400° F. and then 30 min. at 350° F.

Strawberry Pie

Amount		Ingredient	Method
3 gal.		Strawberries, fresh	Wash and cap. Set aside ½ of the best berries and mash the rest.
		To mashed berries, add	
3 lb.	12 oz.	Sugar	Mixed.
	7½ oz.	Cornstarch	
		Cook 5–6 min. or until thick and clear.	
		Add	
	¾ c.	Lemon juice	
		Cool. Add reserved berries, whole or cut.	
		Pour into baked pie shells.	
		Top with sweetened whipped cream.	

Yield: 8 8-in. pies.

Cream Pie

Amount		Ingredient	Method
4 qt.		Milk	Heat to boiling point.
		Add, while stirring,	
2 lb.	4 oz.	Sugar	Mixed.
	11 oz.	Cornstarch	
	2 t.	Salt	
		Cook until thick and clear.	
		Add, while stirring,	
16		Egg yolks, beaten	Cook approximately 10 min.
		Add	
	4 oz.	Butter or margarine	Mix.
	2 T.	Vanilla	
		Pour into baked pie shells. Cover with meringue (p. 123).	

Bake 12 min. at 375° F.   Yield 8 8-in. pies.

Variations of Cream Pie

Banana Cream Pie. Slice 1 large banana in each pie shell before adding cream filling.

Chocolate Cream Pie. Add 6 oz. cocoa and 3 oz. sugar. Omit 1 oz. cornstarch.

Coconut Cream Pie. Add 10 oz. toasted coconut to filling and sprinkle 2 oz. coconut over meringue.

Pineapple Cream Pie. Add 3½ c. crushed pineapple, drained, to cooked filling.

Date Cream Pie. Add 3 lb. chopped, pitted dates to cooked filling.

Fruit Glazed Pie. Use frozen blueberries, strawberries, or cherries. Thaw 6 lb. frozen fruit and drain. Measure 1 qt. fruit sirup, adding water if needed to make that amount. Add slowly to a mixture of 4 oz. cornstarch, 6 oz. sugar, and ¾ c. lemon juice. Cook until thick and clear. Cool slightly. Add drained fruit. Spread over cream pies.

Fruit Tarts. Substitute 2 qt. cream for equal quantity of milk. Fill baked individual pastry shells ⅓ full of cream pie filling; add fresh, canned, or frozen fruits (blueberries, peaches, cherries). Cover with whipped cream.

Grapenut Cream Pie. Add ½ package Grapenuts and 2 oz. butter or margarine.

Nut Cream Pie. Add ½ c. chopped pecans or other nuts.

Butterscotch Cream Pie

AMOUNT		INGREDIENT	METHOD
1 lb.		Butter or margarine, melted	
		Add	
2 lb.	8 oz.	Sugar, brown	Mix thoroughly. Stir and cook over a
	1 T.	Salt	low heat to 220° F.
		Add slowly, while stirring,	
3 qt.		Milk, whole	Stir well.
		Heat above mixture to boiling point.	
		Add, while stirring,	
	6 oz.	Cornstarch	
	6 oz.	Flour	
1 qt.		Milk, warm	Thoroughly blended.
	5	Eggs, whole	
	10	Egg yolks	
		Cook until thick. Remove from heat.	
		Add	
	2 T.	Vanilla	
	4 oz.	Butter, in small pieces	
		Cool. Fill baked pie shells. Cover with meringue.	

Bake 12 min. at 375° F.   Yield: 8 8-in. pies.

NOTE: May be used for pudding. Omit flour, increase cornstarch to 8 oz.

Lemon Pie

AMOUNT		INGREDIENT	METHOD
2¼ qt.		Water	
	2 t.	Salt	Heat to boiling point.
	3	Lemon rinds, grated	
		Add slowly, stirring constantly,	
	12 oz.	Cornstarch	
	1½ pt.	Water	Cook until thickened.
		Add	
3 lb.	8 oz.	Sugar	
		Remove from heat.	
		Add slowly, stirring constantly,	
	1½ c.	Whole eggs, or 16 yolks, well beaten	
		Add	
	3 oz.	Butter	
		Add	
	1½ c.	Lemon juice	Mix well.
		Pour into baked pie shells. Cover with meringue.	

Bake 12 min. at 375° F.   Yield: 8 8-in. pies.

Custard Pie

AMOUNT		INGREDIENT	METHOD
24		Eggs, beaten slightly	
		Add	
1 lb.	8 oz.	Sugar	
	1 t.	Salt	
1 gal.		Milk, scalded	
	2 T.	Vanilla, if desired	
		Pour into unbaked pie shells.	
		Sprinkle over top	
	2 t.	Nutmeg	

Bake 15 min. at 450° F., then at 350° F. until knife inserted into side of filling comes out clean.

Yield: 8 8-in. pies.

VARIATION: **Coconut Custard Pie.** Omit nutmeg and add 1 lb. flaked coconut.

Pumpkin Pie

AMOUNT	INGREDIENT	METHOD
14	Eggs, beaten	Combine.
3 No. 2½ cans	Pumpkin	
	Add	
1 lb. 12 oz.	Sugar, white	
10 oz.	Sugar, brown	
½ T.	Ginger	Mixed.
1½ T.	Cinnamon	
1 T.	Salt	
	Add	
2¾ qt.	Milk	
	Pour into unbaked pie shells.	

Bake 15 min. at 450° F., then 25–30 min. at 325° F. until custard is firm.

Yield: 8 8-in. pies.

NOTES: 1. 1 lb. chopped pecans may be sprinkled over tops of pies after 15 min. baking. Continue baking.
2. 1 qt. cream may be substituted for 1 qt. milk.

Pumpkin Chiffon Pie

AMOUNT		INGREDIENT	METHOD
2½ qt.		Pumpkin	
	3 c.	Milk	
	2 t.	Salt	
2 lb.	8 oz.	Sugar, brown	
	½ T.	Ginger	Mix. Heat to boiling point.
	½ T.	Nutmeg	
	½ T.	Cinnamon	
	1 t.	Allspice	
		Add	
16		Egg yolks, beaten	Cook until mixture thickens.
		Pour over	
	3 oz.	Gelatin	Sprinkle gelatin over water.
	1 pt.	Water, cold	Soak 10 min.
		Add	
	2 oz.	Lemon rind, grated	Cool until mixture begins to
	¼ c.	Lemon juice	congeal.
		Fold in	
24		Egg whites, beaten until frothy	Beaten together to form
	8 oz.	Sugar, added gradually	meringue.

Pour into baked pie shells. Chill. Top with whipped cream and chopped nuts.

Yield: 8 8-in. pies.

Lemon Chiffon Pie

Amount		Ingredient	Method
21		Egg yolks	Beat well. Cook over water until the consistency of custard.
1 lb.	8 oz.	Sugar	
	2 t.	Salt	
	2½ c.	Lemon juice	
		Pour over	
	1½ oz.	Gelatin	Sprinkle gelatin over water. Soak 10 min.
	1¾ c.	Water, cold	
		Stir until dissolved, add	
	2 T.	Lemon rind	
		Place in refrigerator until mixture begins to congeal.	
		Fold in	
21		Egg whites, beaten until frothy	Beaten together to form meringue.
1 lb.	2 oz.	Sugar added gradually	
		Fill baked pie shells.	
			Yield: 8 8-in. pies.

NOTE: Just before serving, spread 1 c. whipped cream over the top of each pie.

VARIATIONS: 1. **Orange Chiffon Pie.** Substitute 2 c. orange juice for 2 c. lemon juice and 2 T. grated orange rind for 2 T. grated lemon rind.

2. **Frozen Lemon Pie.** Fold in 3 c. cream, whipped. Pile into pastry or graham cracker crust. Spread over tops of pies 1½ c. cream, whipped, sweetened with 3 T. sugar. Freeze.

Chocolate Chiffon Pie

AMOUNT		INGREDIENT	METHOD
	1½ oz. 1½ c.	Gelatin Water, cold	⎱ Sprinkle gelatin over water. ⎰ Soak 10 min.
		Add, stirring until dissolved,	
	1½ pt. 8 oz.	Water, boiling Chocolate	⎱ ⎰ Combined.
		Add	
24 1 lb.	 8 oz. 1½ t. 2 T.	Egg yolks, slightly beaten Sugar Salt Vanilla	⎱ Mixed. Cook until mixture ⎰ begins to thicken.
		Cool until gelatin begins to set.	
		Fold in	
24 1 lb.	 8 oz.	Egg whites, beaten until stiff Sugar	⎱ Beaten together to form ⎰ meringue.
		Pour into baked pie shells and chill. Spread whipped cream over the pies just before serving.	
			Yield: 8 8-in. pies.

VARIATIONS: 1. **Frozen Chocolate Chiffon Pie.** Fold in 3 c. cream, whipped. Pile into pastry or graham cracker crust. Spread over tops of pies 1½ c. cream, whipped, sweetened with 3 T. sugar. Freeze.
2. **Chocolate Peppermint Chiffon Pie.** Cover pie with whipped cream to which has been added 1 lb. crushed peppermint candy sticks.

Chocolate Sundae Pie

Amount	Ingredient	Method
1 lb.	Sugar	
1 oz.	Cornstarch	Combine.
½ t.	Salt	
	Add to	
3 qt.	Milk, scalded	Cook 5 min.
	Add	
22	Egg yolks, beaten slightly	Cook until thickened, stirring constantly.
	Add	
2 oz.	Gelatin	
1½ c.	Water, cold	Soaked 10 min.
	When cool, add	
1 T.	Vanilla	
2 t.	Almond extract	
	When custard starts to congeal, carefully fold in	
22	Egg whites	
12 oz.	Sugar	Beaten until stiff.
	Pour into baked pie shells. Chill until set, then cover with	
1 qt.	Cream, whipped	
¼ c.	Sugar	
	Sprinkle over top of pies	
8 oz.	Chocolate, grated	

Yield: 8 8-in. pies.

VARIATION: **Black Bottom Pie.** Add 8 oz. melted chocolate to 3 qt. custard. Pour 1½ c. into each baked pie shell. Let rest of custard start to congeal, then fold in beaten egg whites. Pour 2½–3 c. of this mixture over chocolate layer in crusts.

Mocha Almond Frozen Pie

Amount	Ingredient	Method
1 lb. 8 oz. 1 T. 7½ c. 18	Sugar Salt Coffee infusion Egg yolks, beaten	Mix. Cook over hot water until mixture coats spoon. Remove from heat.
	Add	
6 T. 1½ c.	Gelatin, softened in Water, cold	Stir until blended.
	Chill until mixture is consistency of unbeaten egg whites.	
18 1½ t. 1 lb. 8 oz.	Fold in Egg whites, beaten until frothy Cream of tartar Sugar, added gradually	Beaten together to form a meringue.
3 c. 3 c. 2 T.	Fold in Cream, whipped Almonds, toasted, chopped Vanilla Fill graham cracker crusts.	
1½ c. 3 T.	Cover with Cream, whipped Sugar Freeze.	
		Yield: 8 8-in. pies.

Pecan Pie

Amount	Ingredient	Method
4 lb. 4 oz. 1 T.	Sugar Butter Salt	Cream.
24	Add Eggs, beaten	Mix well.
1 qt. 2½ T.	Add Corn sirup, white Vanilla	Mix well.
1 lb.	Add Pecans Pour into unbaked pie shells.	

Bake 40 min. at 350° F.   Yield: 8 8-in. pies.

Sour Cream Raisin Pie

AMOUNT		INGREDIENT	METHOD
2½ qt.		Cultured sour cream	
2 lb.	12 oz.	Sugar	
	6 oz.	Flour	
21		Egg yolks, beaten	Mix and cook until thick.
	3 T.	Cinnamon	
	1½ T.	Cloves	
	2 T.	Nutmeg	
		Add	
3 lb.	8 oz.	Raisins, cooked.	
		Pour into baked pie shells. Top with meringue (p. 123).	

Bake 12 min. at 375° F.   Yield: 8 8-in. pies.

● PUDDINGS AND OTHER DESSERTS

Baked Custard

AMOUNT		INGREDIENT	METHOD
1 lb.	4 oz.	Sugar	
	½ t.	Salt	
20		Eggs	Beat until well mixed.
1 qt.		Milk	
		Add	
4 qt.		Milk, scalded	
	2 T.	Vanilla	
		Pour into custard cups.	
		Sprinkle over the top	
	2 t.	Nutmeg	
		Place cups in pans of hot water (water should not boil).	

Bake 45 min. at 325° F., or until firm when inserted knife tip comes out clean.

Serving: 4 oz.

VARIATIONS: 1. **Carmel Custard.** Add 8 oz. caramelized sugar (p. 32).
        2. **Rice Custard.** Use ½ of custard recipe, adding 1 lb. (A.P.) cooked rice, 1 lb. raisins, and 3 oz. melted butter.
        3. **Bread Pudding.** Pour liquid mixture over 1 lb. dry bread cubes and let stand until bread is softened. Add 1 lb. raisins if desired.

Floating Island

Amount	Ingredient	Method
4½ qt.	Milk	} Heat to boiling point.
	Add while stirring with whip	
1 lb.	Sugar	
4 oz.	Cornstarch	} Mixed.
½ t.	Salt	
	Cook until slightly thickened.	
	Add gradually to	
27	Egg yolks, well beaten	} Stir and cook until thickened. Do not overcook.
	Add	
2 T.	Vanilla	
	Dip into sherbet dishes, using No. 12 dipper. Chill. Top with meringue and garnish with a small sprinkling of nutmeg.	

Meringue for Topping

Amount	Ingredient	Method
8	Egg whites	} Beat until stiff.
8 oz.	Sugar	
	Drop by spoonful onto hot water and bake until set. Place 1 meringue on each serving of custard.	

Vanilla Cream Pudding

Amount		Ingredient	Method
4½ qt.		Milk	} Scald.
		Add, stirring constantly with wire whip,	
1 lb.	8 oz.	Sugar	
	7 oz.	Flour	
	2 t.	Salt	} Mixed.
	3 c.	Milk	
		Cook over hot water until smooth and thick, approximately 10 min.	
		Add, stirring constantly, a small amount of hot mixture to	
12		Eggs, beaten	
		Combine all ingredients. Cook 5 min. Cool.	
		Add	
	2 T.	Vanilla	
	4 oz.	Butter	
			Yield: 6 qt.

NOTE: 5 oz. cornstarch may be substituted for flour.

VARIATIONS: 1. **Banana Cream Pudding.** Use only ¾ of recipe. Add 4½ lb. (E.P.) sliced bananas to cold pudding.
2. **Chocolate Cream Pudding.** Add 6 oz. sugar and 8 oz. cocoa.
3. **Coconut Cream Pudding.** Add 8 oz. shredded coconut just before serving.
4. **Grapenut Pudding.** Add 8 oz. Grapenuts just before serving.
5. **Pineapple Cream Pudding.** Add 1 qt. grated pineapple, well drained.

Tapioca Cream

AMOUNT		INGREDIENT	METHOD
4 qt.		Milk	} Heat to boiling point.
	9 oz.	Add gradually Tapioca, Minute	} Cook until clear, stirring frequently.
1 lb.	8 2 t.	Add Egg yolks, beaten Sugar Salt	} Mixed.
		Cook 5 min. Remove from heat.	
	8 4 oz.	Fold in Egg whites beaten until frothy Sugar added gradually	} Beaten to form a meringue.
	2 T.	Add Vanilla	
		Serve with No. 10 dipper.	
			Serving: ½ c.

VARIATIONS: 1. **Chocolate Tapioca Cream.** Add 8 oz. melted chocolate.
2. **Caramel Tapioca Cream.** Add 8 oz. caramelized sugar (p. 32).
3. **Nut Tapioca Cream.** Add 6 oz. chopped nuts and fold in beaten egg whites last.
4. **Fruit Tapioca Cream.** Add 1 qt. chopped canned peaches or crushed pineapple, drained.

Chocolate Cream Pudding

AMOUNT		INGREDIENT	METHOD
1 gal.		Milk	} Heat to boiling point.
		Add gradually, stirring briskly with wire whip,	
	6 oz.	Flour	
	3 oz.	Cornstarch	
	1 t.	Salt	} Mixed.
2 lb.	6 oz.	Sugar	
	8 oz.	Cocoa	
		Cook until thickened.	
	8 oz. 2 T.	Add Butter or margarine Vanilla	
		Serve with No. 12 dipper.	
			Serving: ⅓ c.

Butterscotch Pudding

Amount		Ingredient	Method
3 qt.		Milk	} Heat.
		Add and cook until thickened	
1 lb.	2 oz.	Flour	
2 lb.	8 oz.	Brown sugar	} Mixed until smooth.
1½ qt.		Milk	
		Add	
18		Eggs, beaten	} Cook 4 min.
	1½ t.	Salt	
		Remove from heat, add	
	1 T.	Vanilla	
	12 oz.	Butter or margarine	
		Chill. Serve with No. 12 dipper.	
			Serving: ⅓ c.

Divinity Pudding

Amount		Ingredient	Method
3 qt.		Water, boiling	
		Pour over	
4 lb.	12 oz.	Sugar, brown	} Mixed together.
1 lb.		Cornstarch	
		Cook until mixture is thick and clear, approximately 40 min.	
		Pour slowly over	
16		Egg whites, beaten	} Beat until cool.
		Add	
	1 T.	Maple flavor	
	6 oz.	Nuts, chopped	
		Pour into a pan 12 x 20 in. Chill. Cut into squares.	
			Serving: 2 x 2½ in.

NOTE: Coconut may be substituted for nuts.

Lemon Snow

Amount		Ingredient	Method
	8 oz.	Cornstarch	
1 lb.	8 oz.	Sugar	Mix.
	½ t.	Salt	
		Add, while stirring,	
2 qt.		Water, boiling	Cook approximately 5 min. over hot water.
		Pour over	
16		Egg whites, beaten until stiff	Beating constantly.
	6 oz.	Sugar	
		Add	
	1 c.	Lemon juice	Mix well.
	2 T.	Lemon rind, grated	
		Pour into a pan 12 x 20 in. Chill.	

Serving: 2 x 2½ in.

NOTE: Cut and serve with chilled Custard Sauce (p. 286).

Apricot Whip

AMOUNT	INGREDIENT	METHOD
1½ oz. 1½ c.	Gelatin Water, cold	Soak 10 min.
1 c.	Add Water or apricot juice, boiling	Stir until dissolved.
1 lb. 4 T.	Add Sugar Lemon juice	
1 qt.	Add Apricot purée When mixture begins to congeal, place in mixer bowl and beat until light.	
12 12 oz.	Add Egg whites, beaten until frothy. Sugar added gradually Chill. Serve with No. 12 dipper.	Beaten to form a meringue.

Serving: ⅓ c.

NOTES: 1. Drain apricots, purée fruits, use juice for liquid.
2. To serve, garnish with whipped cream.
3. Raspberries, oranges, peaches, or strawberries may be substituted for apricots.
VARIATION: **Apricot Chiffon Pie.** Pour Apricot Whip into graham cracker crusts. Reserve 2 c. crumb mixture to sprinkle over top.

Prune Whip

AMOUNT	INGREDIENT	METHOD
15 8 oz.	Egg whites, beat until stiff Sugar	Combine.
2 lb.	Add Prunes	Cooked and pitted
2 T.	Add Lemon juice Chill. Serve with No. 12 dipper.	

Serving: ⅓ c.

NOTE: May be placed in custard cups, set in pans of hot water, and baked.

Date Pudding

Amount		Ingredient	Method
2 lb.		Sugar	
1 lb.		Flour	
	1½ oz.	Baking powder	Mix and pour into a well-oiled pan
	1½ t.	Salt	12 x 20 in.
	12 oz.	Nutmeats	
2 lb.	4 oz.	Dates, chopped	
	2¼ c.	Milk	
		Pour over above mixture	
1 lb.	14 oz.	Sugar, brown	
	2 oz.	Butter or margarine	Mixed and heated to boiling point.
2¼ qt.		Water, boiling	

Bake 45 min. at 350° F.   Serving: 3 oz.

Royal Rice Pudding

Amount		Ingredient	Method
1 lb.		Rice	Cook rice (p. 227). Drain and chill.
		When ready to serve add	
1 qt.		Pineapple, crushed, drained	
	8 oz.	Marshmallows, miniature	
	8 oz.	Nuts, chopped	Mixed.
1 lb.	12 oz.	Sugar, powdered	
	2 t.	Salt	
	1 c.	Cherries, maraschino, chopped	
		Fold in	
1 qt.		Cream, whipped	
		Serve with No. 12 dipper.	

Serving: ⅓ c.

Fudge Pudding

Amount		Ingredient	Method
1 lb.	2 oz.	Flour	
	1¼ oz.	Baking powder	
1 lb.	12 oz.	Sugar	} Mix.
	1 t.	Salt	
	2 oz.	Cocoa	
		Add	
	1 pt.	Milk	
	9 oz.	Butter or margarine, melted	} Mix until smooth.
		Add	
1 lb.		Nuts, chopped, 2 T. Vanilla	} Blend.
		Spread batter ¾ to 1 in. thick in well-oiled pan 12 x 20 in.	
		Pour over batter	
2 lb.	4 oz.	Sugar, brown	
	3 oz.	Cocoa	} Mixed.
2 qt.		Water, hot	

Bake 45 min. at 350° F.   Serving: 3 oz.

Lemon Cake Pudding

Amount		Ingredient	Method
3 lb.		Sugar	} Cream.
	6 oz.	Fat	
		Add	
	3 oz.	Flour	
	2 t.	Salt	
	2 c.	Lemon juice	
	5 T.	Lemon rind, grated	
		Add	
18		Egg yolks, beaten	} Combined.
3 qt.		Milk	
		Fold in	
18		Egg whites, beaten stiff	
		Pour in oiled pan 12 x 20 in. Place in pan of hot water.	

Bake 45 min. at 350° F.   Serving: 2 x 2½ in.

Date Roll

AMOUNT		INGREDIENT	METHOD
2 lb.		Dates, chopped fine	
2 lb.		Miniature marshmallows	Combine.
2 lb.	8 oz.	Graham crackers, ground	
	8 oz.	Nuts, chopped	
		Add	
	1 pt.	Milk	Mix only until ingredients are combined.

Form into 4 rolls; roll in powdered sugar. Place in refrigerator for 24 hr.

Serving: Approximately 2 oz.

NOTE: Cut in slices and serve with Hard Sauce (p. 287) or whipped cream.

Fruit Cobbler

AMOUNT		INGREDIENT	METHOD
2½ qt.		Fruit juice	Heat.
		Add, while stirring,	
	6 oz.	Cornstarch	Mixed.
	1 pt.	Water	
		Cook until thick.	
		Add	
2 lb.	8 oz.	Sugar	Mix thoroughly and bring to
	1 T.	Salt	boiling point.
		Add	
10 lb.		Fruit, drained	

Mix carefully. Cool at room temperature. Pour into oiled pan 12 x 20 in.

| | | Cover with | |
| 2 lb. | | Pastry (p. 122) | |

Bake 30 min. at 425° F.   Serving: 2 x 2½ in.

NOTE: Use cherries, berries, peaches, apricots, apples, or other fruit.

Baked Apples

Amount	Ingredient	Method
50	Apples, baking	} Wash and core. Place in baking pan.
	Add	
3 lb.	Sugar	
1½ pt.	Water	} Mixed.
1 t.	Salt	
1 T.	Cinnamon	

Bake approximately 45 min. at 375° F., basting occasionally with sirup.

Note: Use red apples of uniform medium size, suitable for baking. ½ c. red cinnamon candies may be substituted for cinnamon. Apple centers may be filled with chopped dates, raisins, nuts, cranberries, or mincemeat.

Applesauce

Amount	Ingredient	Method
15 lbs.	Apples	} Quartered. Cook until apples
1 qt.	Water	are transparent.
	Add	
4 lb. (variable)	Sugar. Stir until sugar is dissolved. Serve with No. 16 dipper.	

Note: Apples may be pared or unpared. Thin slices of lemon, lemon juice, or 1 t. cinnamon may be added. Peaches or pears may be substituted for apples.

Variation: **Apple Compote.** Combine sugar and water, and heat to boiling point. Add apples and cook until transparent.

Apple Crisp

AMOUNT		INGREDIENT	METHOD
10 lb.		Apples, sliced	Mix and arrange apples in
	8 oz.	Sugar	oiled pan 12 x 20 in.
¼ c.		Lemon juice	
		Cover with	
1 lb.	4 oz.	Butter or margarine, melted	
	12 oz.	Flour	Mixed until crumbly.
	12 oz.	Rolled oats, quick, uncooked	
2 lb.		Sugar, brown	

Bake 45–50 min. at 350° F.

NOTE: Serve with whipped cream, ice cream, or cheese.
VARIATIONS: 1. **Cherry Crisp.** Substitute frozen pie cherries for apples.
   2. **Peach Crisp.** Substitute sliced peaches for apples.

Apple Dumplings

AMOUNT		INGREDIENT	METHOD
5 lb.		Pastry	Roll and cut in 5-in. squares.
		Use No. 16 dipper to place on squares	
12 lb.		Apples (frozen), sliced	
		Fold corners of pastry to center on top of fruit and press edges together. Prick. Place in oiled baking pans.	
		Cover with mixture made of	
4 lb.		Sugar	
2 qt.		Water	
1 lb.		Butter or margarine	Heated until sugar is dissolved.
	2 t.	Cinnamon	
	2 t.	Nutmeg	

Bake 40–45 min. at 375°–400° F.

NOTE: Fresh or canned fruit (sugar variable) may be used.
VARIATION: **Peach Dumplings.** Substitute peaches for apples.

Apple Brown Betty

Amount		Ingredient	Method
12 lb. (A.P.)		Apples, pared and sliced	
3 qt.		Cake crumbs or bread crumbs	
		Arrange apples and crumbs in layers. 12 x 20-in. oiled pan.	
		Over each layer sprinkle	
	1 t.	Cinnamon	
	½ t.	Nutmeg	
1 lb.	8 oz.	Sugar, brown	Mixed.
2 qt.		Water (approximately)	
	2 T.	Lemon juice	
		Over the top pour	
	8 oz.	Butter or margarine, melted	

Bake 1 hr. (or longer) at 350° F.   Serving: Approximately 4 oz.

Notes: 1. The amount of water will vary according to the dryness of the crumbs used.
2. Serve hot with Lemon Sauce (p. 287) or cold with whipped cream.
3. Graham cracker crumbs may be substituted for cake crumbs. 8 oz. nutmeats may be added.

Pineapple Bavarian Cream

Amount		Ingredient	Method
	3 oz.	Gelatin	Soak 10 min.
1 qt.		Water, cold	
		Add	
1 No. 10 can		Pineapple, crushed	Heated to boiling point.
1 lb.	12 oz.	Sugar	
		Stir until gelatin is dissolved.	
		Add	
	2 oz.	Lemon juice	
		Chill. When mixture begins to congeal, fold in	
1 qt.		Cream, whipped	
		Pour into 50 individual molds or a 12 x 20-in. pan.	

Note: May be used for pie filling.
Variations: 1. Apricot. Substitute 3 lb. dried apricots (A.P.) or 6 lb. frozen apricots for crushed pineapple. (Cook and sieve dried apricots.) Fold 6 beaten egg whites into the whipped cream.
2. Strawberry Bavarian Cream. Substitute 6 lb. frozen sliced strawberries for pineapple.

Ice Box Dessert

Amount		Ingredient	Method
3 lb.	8 oz.	Sugar	} Cream.
	12 oz.	Butter or margarine	
		Add	
18		Egg yolks	} Cream.
		Add	
1½ qt.		Pineapple, crushed	
	1 c.	Cream	
		Cook over water until thick. Cool.	
		Add	
	4 oz.	Nuts, chopped	
	3 oz.	Cherries, maraschino, chopped	
3 lb.	8 oz.	Wafers, vanilla, crushed	

Place a thin layer of crushed wafers in the bottom of a pan 12 x 20 in. Fill pan with alternate thin layers of above mixture and crushed vanilla wafers.

Serving: Approximately 3 oz.

NOTES: 1. Store overnight in refrigerator; serve with whipped cream.
      2. Dry cake crumbs or sliced cake may be substituted for the wafers.
VARIATIONS: 1. Chocolate Ice Box Dessert. Use ⅔ Chocolate Chiffon Pie recipe (p. 134).
      2. Lemon Ice Box Dessert. Lemon Chiffon Pie recipe (p. 133).

English Toffee Dessert

Amount		Ingredient	Method
1 lb.	8 oz.	Vanilla wafers, finely crushed	
1 lb.		Nuts, finely chopped	} Mix.
	12 oz.	Butter or margarine, melted	

Cover bottom of 12 x 20-in. pan with approximately ⅔ of crumb mixture. Add filling, then remainder of crumb mixture. Place in refrigerator for several hours. Serve with whipped cream.

Amount		Ingredient	Method
		Filling	
1 lb.	4 oz.	Butter or margarine, soft	
3 lb.		Sugar, confectioners', sifted	
	8 oz.	Milk, dry, nonfat	} Beat until smooth and fluffy.
16		Egg yolks	
	8 oz.	Chocolate, melted	
	3 T.	Vanilla	
		Fold in	
16		Egg whites, beaten stiffly.	
			Serving: 2 x 2½ in.

NOTES: 1. Graham cracker crumbs may be used in place of vanilla wafers.
2. May be made in 8 8-in. pie tins.

Jellied Fruit Cup

Amount		Ingredient	Method
1 lb.	8 oz.	Gelatin, flavored	
		Add	
2 qt.		Water, boiling	} Stir until dissolved.
		Add	
2 qt.		Fruit juice, cold	
		Chill. When gelatin begins to congeal, pour over	
4–5 lbs.		Fruit, drained, arranged in 50 serving glasses or 12 x 20-in. pan.	

SUGGESTED COMBINATIONS: 1. Orange gelatin, orange sections, pineapple chunks, banana cubes.
2. Raspberry gelatin, frozen raspberries, sliced bananas.
3. Strawberry gelatin, frozen strawberries, sliced bananas, marshmallows.
4. Orange gelatin, peach slices, cantaloupe balls.
5. Lemon gelatin, cubed peaches, mandarin oranges, maraschino cherries.
6. Lime gelatin, canned pear pieces, canned pineapple chunks.

Cream Puffs

Amount		Ingredient	Method
1 lb. 1 qt.		Butter or margarine Water, boiling	} Melt butter in boiling water.
		Add	
	1 t.	Salt	} Beat vigorously.
1 lb.	3 oz.	Flour	

Remove from fire as soon as mixture leaves the sides of pan. Transfer to mixer bowl. Cool slightly.

		Add	
16		Eggs	} Add 1 egg at a time, beating after each addition.

Measure with No. 24 dipper and drop on an oiled baking sheet.

Bake 15 min. at 425° F., then 30 min. at 325° F.   Yield: 50 large puffs.

NOTES: 1. Fill puffs with Custard Filling (p. 120), using No. 16 dipper. Top with Chocolate Sauce (p. 284) if desired.
2. Fill with vanilla ice cream and serve with Chocolate Sauce (p. 284).
3. For tea service, small shells may be made with a pastry tube and filled with creamed chicken or chicken salad. Yield: Approximately 200 puffs.

VARIATIONS: 1. **Orange Cream Puffs with Chocolate Filling.** Add ½ c. grated orange rind and 2 c. chopped almonds to cream puff mixture. Bake. Fill with Chocolate Cream Pudding (p. 139) or Chocolate Cream Filling (p. 119).
2. **Butterscotch Cream Puffs.** Fill cream puffs with Butterscotch Pudding (p. 141). Top with Butterscotch Sauce (p. 283) if desired.
3. **Eclairs.** Shape cream puff mixture with pastry tube into 4½-in. strips. Bake. Split lengthwise. Proceed as in NOTE 1.

Christmas Pudding

AMOUNT		INGREDIENT	METHOD
1 lb.	4 oz.	Carrots, raw grated	
1 lb.	11 oz.	Potatoes, raw grated	
1 lb.	4 oz.	Raisins	
1 lb.	4 oz.	Dates, chopped	} Mix.
2 lb.		Sugar	
1 lb.		Butter or margarine	
	12 oz.	Nuts, chopped	
		Add	
	1⅓ T.	Soda	
	1 T.	Cinnamon	
	1 T.	Cloves	
	1 T.	Nutmeg	} Mixed.
	¼ t.	Salt	
1 lb.		Flour	
		Use No. 16 dipper to fill oiled muffin tins. Cover each filled tin with an empty tin.	

Steam 45 min. to 1 hr. under pressure.   Serving: Approximately 3 oz.

NOTE: Serve with Vanilla Sauce (p. 287) or Hard Sauce (p. 287).
VARIATION: **Flaming Pudding.** Dip sugar cube in lemon extract. Place on hot pudding and light just before serving.

Steamed Pudding

Amount		Ingredient	Method
	2½ oz.	Butter or margarine	
1 lb.	3 oz.	Sugar	
	5	Eggs	} Cream.
	2⅓ c.	Molasses	
		Add milk and flour mixture alternately.	
	2½ c.	Milk, sour	
	4½ oz.	Flour	
	1 T.	Soda	
	1 T.	Cloves	} Mixed.
	1½ T.	Cinnamon	
1 lb.	14 oz.	Crumbs, bread	
		Add	
	12 oz.	Raisins	
	8 oz.	Nuts, chopped	
		Use No. 16 dipper to fill oiled muffin tins. Cover with an empty tin.	

Steam 1 hr. under pressure.   Serving: 2½ oz.

Meringue Shells

Amount	Ingredient	Method
28 (3 c.)	Egg whites	} Beat until frothy.
1 t.	Salt	
1 t.	Cream of tartar	
	Add	
3 lb.	Sugar	
	½ c. at a time, beating between each addition until sugar is all dissolved and mixture will hold its shape (approximately 20–30 min.). Using No. 10 dipper, place on well-oiled and floured baking sheets. Shape into nests with spoon or pastry tube.	

Bake approximately 1 hr. at 275° F.

NOTE: Serve ice cream or fruit in center; or crush the shells and serve on ice cream.
VARIATION: **Meringue Sticks.** Force mixture through pastry tube to form sticks. Sprinkle with nuts.

meat

The quality of cooked meat will depend on the quality purchased, storage and handling of meat after delivery, and cooking methods. Federal inspection for wholesomeness is mandatory for all meat shipped in interstate or foreign commerce. This includes all processed meat products as well as fresh and frozen meats. Federal grading is on a voluntary basis. Grades of meat are based on composite evaluation of conformation, finish, and quality.

● PURCHASING MEAT

Meat for institutional food service is now available in carcass, wholesale cuts, fabricated roasts, and portion-ready items. The form in which meat is purchased depends on the policies and size of the institution, the type of service it offers, and its storage and meat-cutting facilities. Fabricated and portion-ready cuts require less storage space, eliminate skilled labor for cutting, and do away with waste. Costs are easily controlled, as the weight and price of each portion are predetermined and only the amount needed is ordered.

● STORING MEAT

Fresh meat should be unwrapped when delivered and stored on trays or hung on hooks at a temperature of 35° to 40° F., with relative humidity 80 to 90%. It should be used as soon after purchase as possible. The temperature should not fall below freezing, unless frozen meat is being stored.

Frozen meat requires a uniform holding temperature of 0° F. or below. It should be well wrapped to exclude air and to prevent drying.

155

Meat may be defrosted before unwrapping in the refrigerator at 30° to 35° F., at room temperature, in front of a fan, or under running water (in waterproof package). Defrosting in the refrigerator is preferred for large roasts and ground meat. It is not necessary to defrost special cuts, such as steaks and chops, unless they are to be coated for frying or baking.

Time Required to Defrost a 3-lb. Package of Meat by Different Methods[1]

METHOD	DEFROSTING TIME° (HR.)
In refrigerator	24 or longer
At room temperature	10–12
In front of a fan	5–6
Under running water (in waterproof package)	3–4

[1] Adapted from *Preserving Food by Freezing,* Circular 395, Kansas Agricultural Experiment Station (1958).

° The thawing times given here are only an approximation, since they will vary with the shape of package (especially thickness), composition of meat, exact thawing temperature, and other factors. For example, a 2-in. porterhouse steak in a refrigerator will thaw in about 20 hr., while a ½-in. steak will thaw in about 4 hr. A 1-in. steak in a room at 70° F. will thaw in 3½ hr., but will require 17 hr. in a refrigerator.

Any meat not cooked soon after thawing will spoil. Once thawed, raw meat should never be refrozen. However, cooked meat may be frozen provided it is frozen immediately after cooking.

Prepared or cured meat, such as ham and bacon, sausages, dried beef, and various kinds of canned meat, also require careful storage. These meats can be safely kept in their original container and stored in the refrigerator at 40° F. or less.

The limited keeping qualities of ham cannot be overemphasized. There are 3 types of ham on the market:

1. *Old-fashioned ham.* This has been fully cured but not cooked, and may be stored without refrigeration.

2. *Tenderized ham.* This has been partially cooked in the smoke house and must be kept under refrigeration.

3. *Ready-to-eat ham.* This has been cooked sufficiently so that it may be served without further processing, or it may just be heated before serving. It, too, must be kept under refrigeration.

Fully cooked hams require storage at refrigerator temperatures before and after heating, and must not be kept longer than 10 days. Canned hams also require refrigeration at all times. Commercially processed hams should indicate on the label which type they are or to what degree they have been cooked.

● COOKING METHODS

Meat is cooked either by dry or moist heat. The method used will depend on the grade and location of the cut. Tender cuts of high-grade meat (Prime, Choice, or Good) are usually cooked by dry heat (broiled or roasted). Moist heat is used for the less tender cuts from the upper grades, and for all lower-grade cuts that have a large amount of connective tissue. For these less tender cuts, pot roasting, stewing, and cooking under pressure are the preferred cooking methods. Dry-heat cookery does not improve tenderness, and under some conditions reduces it. Cooking with moist heat tends to make meat more tender. A low temperature, regardless of the method, is desirable to insure a minimum loss of juices. The degree of doneness also affects losses. The percentage loss is smaller in rare meat than in medium or well done meat provided other factors are the same.

Roasting

Meats may be completely or partially defrosted or frozen at the time the cooking process is begun. Roasts that have been partially defrosted before cooking often yield a more satisfactory cooked product than those that remain completely frozen up to the time they are put into the oven. However, when time is a factor, as it is in institutional food service, defrosting meat before cooking is usually the accepted method.

Place the meat to be roasted on a rack, fat side up, in an uncovered roasting pan, without the addition of water. Insert a meat thermometer in the roast so that the bulb rests in the center of the cut, but not in contact with bone. Cook at a constant temperature—350° F. for fresh pork; 300° F. for other meats, including cured meats—until the desired degree of doneness has been reached. Salt need not be added before cooking, as the salt does not penetrate more than 1 inch. Searing a roast is no longer considered necessary and may increase losses. Although flavor may be improved, only the surface of the meat is affected.

Cooking time has been used generally as a guide to the degree of doneness of roasts, but research studies have shown that measuring the

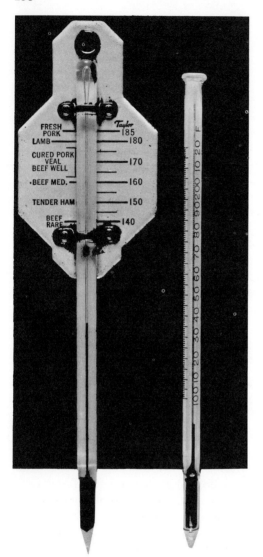

Fig. 11. Two types of meat thermometers used in testing the degree of doneness of meat.

internal temperature of the roast with a meat thermometer is the only accurate method (Fig. 11). The length of the cooking period depends on several factors: oven temperature, size and shape of roast, style of cut (boned or bone in), oven load, quality of meat, and the degree of doneness desired. Investigations indicate that the use of metal skewers in roasts shortens the cooking time.

Meat Thermometer Tests for Degree of Doneness in Roasts

MEAT	OVEN TEMPERATURE ° F.	DEGREE OF DONENESS	INTERNAL TEMPERATURE (° F.)	(° C.)	APPROXIMATE COOKING TIME PER POUND ° MINUTES
Beef	300	Rare	140	60	18–30
	300	Medium	160	71	22–40
	300	Well-done	170	77–80	27–50
Veal	300	Well-done	170	74	25–35
Lamb	300	Well-done	180	79–82	30–35
Pork, fresh	350	Well-done	185	85	30–50
Ham, cured, uncooked	300	Well-done	160	71	20–25
Ham, cured, partially cooked	300	Well-done	160	71	18–20
Ham, cured, fully cooked	300	Well-done	130–140	55–60	15–18

° For frozen meat, allow approximately double the cooking time here specified.

Meat Cuts for Roasting

BEEF U.S. PRIME, CHOICE, OR GOOD	VEAL	LAMB	PORK FRESH	SMOKED
Standing rib	Leg, bone in	Leg, bone in	Ham, bone in	Ham, whole
Rolled rib	Leg, boned and tied	Leg, boned and tied	Rolled ham	Ham, half
Sirloin butt	Loin	Rolled loin	Loin, bone in	Ham, boneless
Loin strip	Rib	Rolled shoulder	Loin, boneless	Rolled ham
Loin points	Rolled shoulder	Rolled breast	Regular pork strip	Picnic
Round Inside (top)			Canadian style pork strips	
Outside (bottom) °			Boston butt	Boneless butt
Sirloin tip or triangle			Picnic shoulder Boned and rolled Cushion style	
Rump°				

NOTE: For amount to buy, see p. 5.

° These cuts may be roasted satisfactorily if cooked at a low temperature for a long period of time.

Broiling

In institutions, steaks are usually broiled in a special broiler or sala-mander. If a broiling oven is used, turn the oven regulator to "broil" and preheat. Place the steaks on a rack 2 to 3 in. from tip of gas flame or from electric unit. Place 1-in. steaks or chops 2 in. from the heat, and 2-in. steaks or chops 3 in. from the heat. Brown on one side, season, then turn and brown on the opposite side and cook to the desired de-gree of doneness. The meat should be turned only once. Veal should not be broiled unless it is fairly mature and well marbled with fat, and then only loin chops or steaks. Fresh pork should never be broiled.

Pan-broiling

Place steak on a preheated ungreased griddle or heavy frying pan. When the meat is satisfactorily browned on one side, season, turn, and cook until the desired degree of doneness is reached. If the steak is a thick one, reduce the temperature after browning. Care should be taken not to puncture the meat with a fork while cooking. Neither water nor fat should be added, and excess fat should be drained off.

Time Table for Broiling°

Cut	Approximate Thickness (in.)	Approximate Cooking Time (min.)		
		Rare	Medium	Well-done
Beef				
Rib, club, T-bone,	1	15	20	30
porterhouse tenderloin,	1½	25	35	
or sirloin steak	2	35	50	
Ground beef patties	1 (4 oz.)	15	20	
Lamb				
Rib, loin, and	1		12	15
shoulder chops	1½		17	20
or steaks	2		20	25
Ground lamb patties	1 (4 oz.)		20	22
Pork, smoked				
Ham slice, uncooked	½			10–12
	1			16–20
Ham slice, cooked	½			5–6
	1			8–10
Bacon				4–5
Canadian-style bacon	¼			6–8

° For frozen meat, allow approximately double the cooking time here specified.

Braising

Season meat with salt and pepper, and dredge with flour if desired. Brown meat on all sides in fat in heavy utensil. Add a small amount of liquid, such as water, meat stock, tomato juice, or sour cream. Cover with a close-fitting lid. Cook slowly until tender. Vegetables may be added long enough before the meat is thoroughly cooked so as to be ready to serve with it. Pot roasts, Swiss steaks, veal or pork chops, and liver are examples of meats prepared by braising.

Time Table for Braising*

Cut	Average Weight or Thickness	Approximate Total Cooking Time (hr.)
Beef:		
Pot roast	3–5 lb.	3–4
Swiss steak	1½–2½ in.	2–3
Fricassee	2-in. cubes	1½–2½
Beef birds	½ in. (x 2 in. x 4 in.)	1½–2½
Short ribs	Pieces (2 x 2 x 4 in.)	1½–2½
Round steak	¾ in.	¾–1
Pork:		
Chops	¾–1½ in.	¾–1
Spareribs	2–3 lb.	1½
Tenderloin		
Whole	¾–1 lb.	¾–1
Fillets	½ in.	½
Shoulder steaks	¾ in.	¾–1
Lamb:		
Breast, stuffed	2–3 lb.	1½–2
Breast, rolled	1½–2 lb.	1½–2
Neck slices	¾ in.	1
Shanks	½ lb. each	1–1½
Shoulder chops	1 in.	¾–1
Veal:		
Breast, stuffed	3–4 lb.	1½–2½
Breast, rolled	2–3 lb.	1½–2½
Birds	½ in. (x 2 x 4 in.)	¾–1
Chops	½–¾ in.	¾–1
Steak or cutlets	½–¾ in.	¾–1
Shoulder chops	½–¾ in.	¾–1
Shoulder cubes	1–2 in.	¾–1

* Adapted from *Meat Recipe Rally*, National Live Stock and Meat Board.

Stewing

Brown meat if desired and cover with water. Season with salt and pepper. Herbs and spices, used wisely, add to the variety and flavor of stewed meats. Suggested seasonings are carrots, celery, onions, bay leaves, thyme, marjoram, and parsley. Cook in tightly covered heavy utensil below boiling point until tender.

Time Table for Cooking in Liquid [*]

Cut	Average Weight (lb.)	Approximate Cooking Time per Pound (min.)	Approximate Total Cooking Time (hr.)
Smoked ham (old-style and country-cured)			
Large	12–14	20	
Small	10–12	25	
Half	6–8	30	
Smoked ham (tendered)			
Shank or butt half	5–8	20–25	
Smoked picnic shoulder	4–8	45	
Fresh or corned beef	4–6	40–50	
Beef for stew			2½–3½
Veal for stew			2–3
Lamb for stew			1½–2

[*] Adapted from *Meat Recipe Rally,* National Live Stock and Meat Board.

● MEAT RECIPES

Swiss Steak

AMOUNT		INGREDIENT	METHOD
16 lb.		Beef, round, boneless, ⅝″ thick	
		Pound into steak	
1 lb.		Flour	
	¼ c.	Salt	} Mixed.
	2 t.	Pepper	
		Cut into serving portions and brown in	
1 lb.	4 oz.	Fat, hot	
		Place in roasting pan, or counter inset and add	
2 qt.		Water (or to cover bottom of pan)	
		Cover pan tightly with lid or aluminum foil.	

Bake approximately 1½ hr. at 350° F.   Serving: Approximately 5 oz.

NOTE: Cubed steaks, 4 or 5 oz. each, may be used in place of round steak. Add water in small amounts during cooking if necessary.

Variations of Swiss Steak

Spanish Steak. Add Spanish Sauce (p. 293) in place of water.

Steak with Vegetables. Roll each portion of thin cut steak around ¼ raw carrot strip and secure with a toothpick. Place in roasting pan after browning. Add 1 c. chopped onion and 2 c. chopped celery. Proceed as for Swiss Steak.

Country Fried Steak. Use beef round cut ⅜ in. thick. Cut steak into portions, dip each in flour mixture, proceed as for Swiss Steak.

Smothered Steak with Onions. Proceed as for Swiss Steak. Add 3 lb. sliced onions lightly browned, and substitute 3 qt. gravy for water.

Stroganoff Steak. Proceed as for Swiss Steak. Add 2 qt. cultured sour cream in place of water.

Pot Roast of Beef

Amount	Ingredient	Method
20 lb.	Beef, boneless, chuck, round or rump.	
	Dredge with	
5 oz.	Flour	
½ t.	Pepper	
1½ T.	Salt	
	Brown in fat.	
	Place meat in roaster or steam-jacketed kettle. Add 2 qt. water. Cover closely and cook slowly about 4 hr., or until tender. Add water as necessary.	

Serving: 3 oz. cooked meat.

Beef Stew

Amount		Ingredient	Method
12 lb.	8 oz.	Beef, cut into ½-in. cubes	} Dredge meat with flour.
	6 oz.	Flour	
		Brown in	
	8 oz.	Fat, hot	
		Place in kettle. Add	
3 qt.		Water (more as necessary)	} Cover and simmer 2 hr.
		Add	
2 lb.		Potatoes, cubed	
2 lb.		Carrots, sliced	
1 lb.		Onion, cubed	
1 lb.	8 oz.	Celery, diced	} Cook until tender.
	¼ c.	Salt	
	1 t.	Pepper	
		Thicken liquid with	
	2 oz.	Flour	

Serving: Approximately 6 oz.

NOTE: Veal may be substituted for beef.

VARIATIONS: 1. **Beef Pot Pie.** Omit potatoes and add 1 40-oz. package frozen peas. Place cooked stew in well-oiled baking pan or casseroles. Cover with Pastry (p. 122) or Batter Crust (p. 190). Bake 20–25 min. at 450° F.

2. **Beef Stew with Biscuits.** Place cooked stew in baking pan. Just before serving, completely cover with hot Baking Powder Biscuits (p. 57).

3. **Beef Stew with Dumplings.** Drop Dumplings (p. 84) on meat mixture and steam 15–18 min.

Hungarian Goulash

Amount		Ingredient	Method
10 lb.		Beef, raw, in cubes	
1 lb.	8 oz.	Onion, chopped	Brown.
1 clove		Garlic, chopped	
	8 oz.	Fat	
		Add	
	1 T.	Mustard, dry	
	¼ c.	Paprika	
	⅛ t.	Pepper, cayenne	
	¼ c.	Salt	
	5 oz.	Sugar, brown	Combined.
	1½ c.	Worcestershire sauce	
	2 T.	Vinegar	
1 qt.		Catsup	
3 qt.		Water	
		Simmer in a covered container 2½–3 hr., or until meat is tender.	
		Thicken liquid from meat with	
1 qt.		Water, cold	Combined.
	10 oz.	Flour	
		Serve over	
4 lb.		Broad noodles, cooked, (p. 229).	

Serving: ½ c. goulash, ½ c. noodles.

Meat Loaf

Amount	Ingredient	Method
8 lb.	Beef, ground	
2 lb.	Pork, ground	
10 oz.	Crumbs, bread	
12	Eggs, beaten	
2 qt.	Milk (variable)	
¼ c.	Salt	
2 oz.	Onion, chopped finely (optional)	
1 t.	Pepper	
f.g.	Cayenne	
	Mix ingredients lightly. Do not overmix. Place in 5 loaf pans 4 x 9 in.	

Bake 1½ hr. at 300° F.   Serving: 4 oz.

VARIATIONS: 1. **Pork Meat Loaf.** Substitute ½ veal and ½ pork for beef.
2. **Veal Meat Loaf.** Substitute veal for beef.
3. **Vegetable Meat Loaf.** Add 2 c. catsup; 8 oz. each raw carrots, onions, and celery; and 4 oz. green peppers. Grind vegetables. Pour a small amount of tomato juice over loaf before baking.
4. **Sour Cream Meat Loaf.** Add 1 qt. of chopped stuffed olives to meat mixture. Cover the unbaked loaf with 1 qt. of cultured sour cream.
5. **Meat Balls.** Measure with No. 8 dipper and shape into balls. Proceed as for Swedish Meat Balls (p. 168), or Meat Balls and Spaghetti (p. 167).

Meat Balls and Spaghetti

Amount	Ingredient	Method
8 lb.	Ground beef	
4 lb.	Ground pork	Mix, measure with No. 24 dip-
6 slices	Bread, crumbled	per onto baking sheet. Brown
1 pt.	Milk	in oven approximately 20
2 T.	Salt	min. at 400° F.
2 t.	Pepper	

Remove to deep counter pan or roaster.

Add sauce made of

Amount	Ingredient	Method
7 10-oz. cans	Tomato soup	
7 8-oz. cans	Tomato paste	
3½ qt.	Water, boiling	
2 T.	Mustard, prepared	
2 T.	Paprika	Simmered 1½–2 hr.
½ c.	Worcestershire sauce	
2 T.	Sugar	
2 c.	Parsley flakes, dried	
4 cloves	Garlic	
8 oz.	Onions, chopped	

Serve over
5 lb.   Spaghetti (p. 229)

Serving: 3 meat balls, 5 oz. spaghetti.

NOTE: If desired, mix cooked spaghetti with tomato sauce and place in baking pan. Arrange meat balls over top and bake 20–30 min. at 375° F.

Swedish Meat Balls

Amount		Ingredient	Method
2 lb.	8 oz.	Bread	Soak bread in milk 1 hr.
1½ qt.		Milk	
		Add	
3 lb.		Beef, ground	
2 lb.	8 oz.	Veal, ground	
2 lb.	8 oz.	Pork, ground	
1 lb.	4 oz.	Potato, raw, grated	Mixed.
	12 oz.	Onion, minced	
	3 T.	Salt	
	2 t.	Pepper	
		Shape into balls with a No. 16 dipper. Place in baking pan; brown in oven at 400° F. approximately 20 min. Make 3 qt. gravy from meat drippings and pour over meat balls.	

Bake 1 hr. at 300° F.   Serving: 2 2½-oz. balls.

NOTE: Beef may be substituted for pork and veal.

Spanish Meat Balls

Amount		Ingredient	Method
12 lb.		Meat, ground	
12		Eggs, beaten	
	2 oz.	Onion, grated	Combine. Measure with No. 8 dipper and form into balls. Place in roaster or counter pan.
	2 T.	Salt	
1 lb.	2 oz.	Rice, partially cooked	
1 lb.		Potatoes, mashed	
	4 oz.	Pepper, green	
		Pour over balls	
3 qt.		Tomato purée	Mixed.
2 qt.		Water	
		Cover tightly. Add more moisture if necessary.	

Bake approximately 2½ hr. at 325° F.   Serving: 1 4-oz. ball.

NOTE: Spanish Sauce (p. 293) may be substituted for tomato purée mixture.

Corned Beef and Cabbage

Amount	Ingredient	Method
20 lb.	Corned beef	Cover with water and simmer until tender, 4–5 hr.
12 lb.	Serve with Cabbage, cut in wedges	Cooked in corned beef stock.
		Serving: 3 oz. cooked meat.

Breaded Veal

Amount		Ingredient	Method
15 lb.		Veal, round, sliced	Cut into 50 portions.
		Dredge each piece in	
	8 oz.	Flour	Mixed.
	3 T.	Salt	
		Egg and crumb (p. 32)	
		Brown in	
1 lb.	8 oz.	Fat, hot	
		Place meat in roaster or counter pan. Add 1 qt. water. Cover with lid or aluminum foil.	

Bake 2 hr. at 300° F.   Serving: 4–5 oz.

NOTE: Veal cutlets, 4 oz. each, may be used.

Veal in Sour Cream

Amount		Ingredient	Method
50		Veal chops, cut 3/1	
		Dredge with	
	8 oz.	Flour	
	3 T.	Salt	} Mixed.
	1 t.	Pepper	
		Brown in	
1 lb.	8 oz.	Fat, hot	
		Place in baking pan.	
		Add	
2 qt.		Cultured sour cream	
2 qt.		Water	} Mixed.
		Cover with lid or aluminum foil.	

Bake 2 hr. at 300° F.   Serving: Approximately 5 oz.

NOTE: Veal cutlets, 3 or 4 per lb., may be used.

Veal Birds

Amount		Ingredient	Method
12 lb.	8 oz.	Veal, round, ¼ in. thick, boneless	} Cut into 50 oblong pieces.
		(1) Place No. 16 dipper of dressing on each piece of meat. ½ recipe, p. 190.	
		(2) Roll and fasten each with a round toothpick.	
		(3) Roll in	
	8 oz.	Flour	
	3 T.	Salt	} Mixed.
		Brown in	
1 lb.	8 oz.	Fat, hot	
		Place in roaster or counter pan. Add 1 qt. water.	
		Cover with lid or aluminum foil.	

Bake 2 hr. at 300° F.   Serving: 4 oz.

NOTE: Veal or pork cutlets, 4 per lb., may be substituted for veal round.

Veal Fricassee

Amount		Ingredient	Method
15 lb.		Veal, 1-in. cubes.	
	8 oz.	Flour	Dredge in
1 lb.		Salt pork or other fat	Brown floured veal in
4 qt.		Water	Add
	3 T.	Salt	
		Simmer 2 hr. or until meat is tender.	
			Serving: Approximately 4 oz.

VARIATIONS: 1. **Curried Veal.** Add 2 oz. curry powder when water is added.
2. **Veal Paprika with Rice.** Add ½ c. paprika to flour. Cook 12 oz. minced onions with veal. Add 2 qt. cultured sour cream the last few minutes of cooking. Serve with hot rice. Veal cutlets may be used in place of veal cubes.

Veal Patties

Amount		Ingredient	Method
12 lb.		Veal, ground	
2 lb.		Salt pork, ground	
	8 oz.	Crumbs, bread	
12		Eggs, beaten	Mix.
	3 T.	Salt	
	2 t.	Pepper	
	1 oz.	Onion, grated	
	1 c.	Milk	
		Measure with No. 10 dipper. Form into patties.	

Bake approximately 30 min. at 350° F.

NOTE: Wrap with a strip of bacon and fasten with a toothpick if desired.
VARIATIONS: 1. **Lamb Patties.** Substitute 14 lb. ground lamb for veal and salt pork. Wrap each pattie with a strip of bacon. Bake approximately 30 min.
2. **Stuffed Meat Cakes.** Place thin slice of onion and tomato between 2 thin meat patties. Press edges together and fasten with a toothpick. Bake approximately 30 min.

Braised Tongue

AMOUNT	INGREDIENT	METHOD
20 lb.	Tongue	Wash tongues. Cover with water and simmer until tender, approximately 3–4 hr. Remove skin.
	Place in pan, add	
4 oz.	Onions	
5 oz.	Carrots	Diced fine.
4 oz.	Celery	
	Add	
3 qt.	Broth, hot	
10 oz.	Fat, melted	
5 oz.	Flour	Made as white sauce.
3 T.	Salt	
2 t.	Pepper	
	Simmer 2 hr., turning meat occasionally.	
		Serving: Approximately 4 oz.

NOTE: Cut tongue into thin slices; pour sauce over slices and serve.

VARIATION: **Spiced Tongue.** Substitute 5 t. allspice, 1 T. cloves (whole), and 10 bay leaves for vegetables. Serve cold.

Liver with Spanish Sauce

AMOUNT	INGREDIENT	METHOD
10 lb.	Liver, sliced, 5/1	
	Dredge with	
8 oz.	Flour	
3 T.	Salt	Mixed.
2 t.	Pepper	
	Brown liver in	
1 lb. 8 oz.	Fat, hot	
	Place in a roaster or counter pan, cover with Spanish Sauce (p. 293), and bake until tender.	

Bake approximately 1½ hr. at 350° F.   Serving: Approximately 3½ oz.

NOTE: Soaking liver in milk before cooking improves the flavor.

VARIATIONS: 1. **Liver and Onions.** Cover browned liver with 4 lb. onions, sliced, and 2 qt. water. Bake until tender.
2. **Liver and Bacon.** Dredge liver with flour and fry in bacon fat. Top each serving with 1 slice crisp bacon.
3. **Braised Liver.** Cover with sauce used for Braised Tongue (p. 172).

Baked Heart with Dressing

Amount	Ingredient	Method
20 lb.	Heart, beef	} Wash, split large hearts.
	Add	
8 oz.	Onion	
4 T.	Peppercorns	Simmer until almost tender. Drain. Remove membranes and surplus fat. Slice. Place in roaster.
6	Bay leaves	
2 gal.	Water	
	Cover with	
⅔ recipe	Bread Dressing (p. 190).	

Bake 1 hr. at 300° F. Serving: 3 oz. cooked meat, 3 oz. dressing.

NOTE: If dressing is baked separately, use full recipe. Serve 1 No. 10 dipper of dressing with each serving of meat. Cover with gravy made from broth.

Sweetbread Cutlets

Amount	Ingredient	Method
12 lb. (A.P.)	Sweetbreads	Soak 30 min. in cold water. Boil gently in acidulated water (2 T. vinegar, 1 t. salt to 1½ qt. water), for 20–30 min. Drain and plunge into cold water. Remove connective membrane. Chop coarsely.
	Add	
8 oz.	Mushrooms, chopped	
3 T.	Salt	
1 t.	Pepper	
5 T.	Lemon juice	
½ t.	Nutmeg	
	Add	
2 qt.	Thick White Sauce (p. 295)	} Mix well.
8	Eggs, slightly beaten	
	Measure with No. 12 dipper. When cool, shape and egg and crumb (p. 32). Chill in refrigerator at least 2 hr. Remove ½ hr. before frying.	

Fry in deep fat 3–4 min. at 375° F.

NOTE: Cutlets may be served on toast points with Hollandaise Sauce (p. 289).
VARIATION: Chicken Cutlets. Substitute cooked chicken for sweetbreads.

Mock Drum Sticks

AMOUNT	INGREDIENT	METHOD
10 lb. 7 lb. 50	Veal, 1 in. cubes Pork, fresh, 1 in. cubes Skewers	Place meat cubes on skewers, alternating veal and pork pieces—2 pork and 3 veal on each skewer.
	Dredge in	
8 oz. 3 T.	Flour Salt	Mixed.
	Egg and crumb (p. 32)	
	Brown in	
1 lb.	Fat, hot	
	Place in a roaster or counter pan. Add ½ qt. water. Cover with lid or aluminum foil.	

Bake approximately 2 hr. at 350° F.   Serving: Approximately 4 oz.

NOTE: 1 fresh mushroom may be placed at each end of skewer before cooking.
VARIATION: **Barbecued Kabobs.** Arrange meat on skewers as above. Dredge in flour and brown in hot fat. Cover with Barbecue Sauce (p. 293). Bake 2 hr. at 350° F.

Glazed Baked Ham

Amount	Ingredient	Method
20 lb.	Ham, whole, cured	Trim if necessary. Place fat side up on a rack in an open roasting pan.

Bake about 4½ hr. at 325° F. (see time table, p. 159). (If ready-to-eat ham is used, omit this step).

Remove ham from oven about ½ hr. before it is done. Drain off drippings and trim thin layer of browned fat from entire surface.

Score (diamond-cut) ham and stud with whole cloves.

Cover with

8 oz.	Sugar, brown	
2 T.	Cornstarch	Mixed until smooth.
¼ c.	Corn sirup	
2 T.	Juice, pineapple	

Return to hot oven and bake until done.

Bake approximately 30 min. at 400° F.   Serving: Approximately 3 oz. cooked meat.

VARIATIONS: 1. **Apricot Glaze.** 1 c. apricot jam and ¼ c. fruit juice or enough to cover ham.
2. **Brown Sugar Glaze.** 1 c. brown sugar, 1½ t. dry mustard (or 3 T. prepared mustard), and ¼ c. vinegar.
3. **Cranberry Glaze.** 1¼ c. strained cranberry sauce, or enough to cover.
4. **Honey Glaze.** 1 c. honey, ½ c. brown sugar, and ¼ c. fruit juice. Baste with fruit juice or ginger ale.
5. **Cinnamon Candy Glaze.** Add ½ c. redhots (cinnamon candy) to ¾ c. honey, ¼ c. water, and 1 T. lemon juice. Bring to a boil and simmer until candy dissolves.
6. **Orange Glaze.** 1 c. orange marmalade and ¼ c. spiced peach or orange juice.

Baked Ham Slices

AMOUNT	INGREDIENT	METHOD
18 lb.	Ham, cured, center cut	} Sliced ½ in. thick.
	Rub over surface of meat	
14 oz.	Sugar, brown	}
2⅔ T.	Mustard, dry	} Mixed.
	Place in baking pan.	
	Pour around the ham slices.	
1 c.	Pineapple, spiced fruit	}
	juice or vinegar	} Mixed.
2 qt.	Water	}
	Cover tightly.	

Bake approximately 2 hr. at 325° F.   Serving: Approximately 2½ oz. cooked meat.

NOTES: 1. Sliced ham roll may be used.
      2. Milk may be substituted for fruit juice.
VARIATIONS: 1. **Baked Ham Slices with Pineapple Rings.** When ham is tender, cover with pineapple
rings, bake until pineapple is browned.
      2. **Baked Ham Slices with Orange Sauce.** Arrange ham slices in counter pan and
cover with Orange Sauce. Cover with aluminum foil and bake.

Pork Chops with Dressing

AMOUNT	INGREDIENT	METHOD
17 lb.	Pork chops, 3/1	
	Brown chops in	
8 oz.	Fat, hot	
	Arrange chops in roaster or counter pan. Sprinkle chops with	
2 oz.	Salt	
	Place 2 oz. dressing on each chop.	} Use ⅔ Bread Dressing recipe (p. 190).
	Pour over chops	
3 qt.	Milk	
	Baste frequently with the milk.	

Bake 1½ hr. at 350° F.   Serving: Approximately 5 oz.

NOTE: Dressing may be spread in pan and pork chops placed on top.
VARIATION: **Stuffed Pork Chops.** Cut pocket in each chop. Fill with dressing and proceed as above.

Deviled Pork Chops

Amount		Ingredient	Method
17 lb.		Pork chops, 3/1	
		Dip each chop in sauce	
1½ qt.		Chili sauce	
	3 c.	Water	
	1 t.	Mustard, dry	Combined to form a sauce.
	3 T.	Worcestershire sauce	
	3 T.	Lemon juice	
	2 t.	Onion, grated	
		Place chops on bun pan and sprinkle with salt and pepper.	

Bake 1½ hr. at 350° F.   Serving: Approximately 5 oz.

NOTE: Chops may also be placed on edge, close together, with fat side up. Bake 2–2½ hr.
VARIATION: **Barbecued Pork Chops.** Brush each chop with Barbecue Sauce (p. 293). Pour remaining sauce over chops. Bake.

Barbecued Spareribs

Amount		Ingredient	Method
25 lb.		Pork spareribs or loin back ribs	Brown in oven and pour off fat.
		Add	
	3 qt.	Barbecue Sauce (p. 293)	

Bake 2 hr. at 350° F.   Serving: 8 oz.

VARIATIONS: 1. **Barbecued Lamb.** Substitute lamb shanks for spareribs.
2. **Barbecued Shortribs.** Substitute beef or veal shortribs for spareribs.
3. **Sweet-Sour Spareribs.** Make sauce by combining 2 c. vinegar, 2 c. water, 8 oz. sugar, 1 T. salt, and ¼ c. soy sauce. Bring to a boil. Add 4 oz. cornstarch made into a paste with 1 c. cold water. Cook until clear. Add 8 oz. onion, 6 oz. celery and 6 oz. green pepper, chopped and sautéed in fat for 5 min.; then add 1 No. 10 can pineapple tidbits. Brown spareribs for 30 min. in 400° F. oven, or simmer in water 1 hr. Drain and cover with sauce. Bake in 350° F oven until meat is done. Serve with Steamed Rice or Fried Rice with Almonds (p. 228).

Ham Loaf

AMOUNT	INGREDIENT	METHOD
4 lb.	Fresh pork, ground	
8 lb.	Cured ham, ground	
1 lb.	Bread crumbs	
1 qt.	Milk	Mix only until ingredients are blended.
12	Eggs, beaten	
1 t.	Pepper	
	Mold into 5 oiled loaf pans 4 x 9 in.	

Bake 2 hr. at 350° F.   Serving: Approximately 5 oz.

NOTE: Use ⅓ veal, ⅓ fresh pork, and ⅓ cured ham if desired.

VARIATIONS: 1. **Glazed Ham Loaf.** Cover top of loaves with a mixture of 1½ lb. brown sugar, 1 c. vinegar, and 1½ T. dry mustard.
2. **Glazed Ham Balls.** Measure with No. 8 dipper and shape into balls. Place on baking pans. Brush with glaze and bake.
3. **Ham Patties with Pineapple.** Measure with No. 8 dipper and shape into patties. Top with slice of pineapple and clove. Pour pineapple juice over patties and bake.
4. **Ham Patties with Cranberries.** Spread pan with Cranberry Sauce (p. 258). Place ham patties on sauce and bake.

Cheese-stuffed Wieners

AMOUNT		INGREDIENT	METHOD
8 lb.	4 oz.	Wieners, 12 per lb.	Split wieners lengthwise, but do not cut into halves.
3 lb.		Cheese, Cheddar, cut into strips about 3½ in. long.	Place strip cheese and ½ T. relish in each wiener.
1 qt.		Pickle relish	
4 lb.	4 oz.	Bacon, 24 to 26 slices per lb.	Wrap slice bacon around each wiener.

Bake 30 min. at 350° F.   Serving: 2 wieners.

VARIATIONS: 1. **Barbecued Wieners.** Leave wieners whole. Place in counter pans. Cover with Barbecue Sauce (p. 293) and bake about 30 min. at 400° F. Add more sauce as necessary.
2. **Wieners and Sauerkraut.** Steam wieners or cook in boiling water. Serve with sauerkraut seasoned with bacon or ham.

NOTE: For additional recipes containing meat, see p. 201.

poultry

● PURCHASING POULTRY

Poultry usually is purchased in the eviscerated or ready-to-cook state. Whether it is cut up or whole, frozen or fresh, will depend on the class of poultry concerned and the preferences of the buyer. Fryers are available cut up, halved or quartered, and whole. Other classes of poultry are usually purchased whole. The ready-to-cook birds require no further processing except washing. All poultry sold in interstate commerce must have been examined for wholesomeness under United States Government supervision in officially approved processing plants. Most of the poultry in market channels is graded, and all classes are available in U. S. Grades A, B, and C. Grade A birds present the best appearance, but the grade to purchase will depend upon the use and price differential.

There is a trend toward purchasing custom-cut, ready-for-the-pan chicken parts, such as whole or half breasts, legs, or thighs. Many institutions find it advantageous to purchase chicken parts, although there is some price differential between custom-cut pieces and whole poultry. Each portion in the package is of identical weight; there is no waste, and the cost of each portion is easily determined. Such a method of purchase makes it possible to order only the amount needed.

Turkeys range in size from 8 to 30 lb. ready-to-cook weight. Larger birds yield more meat in proportion to bone weight than do smaller ones.

Cut-up turkey, bone in and boned, and turkey rolls are becoming increasingly popular in institutional food service. A cut-up turkey has the advantage of saving ⅓ to ½ the time required to roast a whole turkey, and ½ the stove and storage space. These pieces may be braised, fried, roasted, broiled, or stewed. Turkey rolls or logs, a combination of breast and thigh meat, about 60% white and 40% dark meat, may be purchased cooked or raw in 8- to 10-lb. rolls. It is also available in all white meat. Turkey in this form tends to assure portion control and requires a minimum of labor for preparation and service.

179

Frozen birds may be of the same high quality as unfrozen. Freezing does not change the original quality but maintains it. In young birds and broilers, the freezing temperature may darken the bones; but other than appearance, there are no detrimental effects as a result of freezing. The purchase of fresh or frozen poultry depends on the preference of the buyer, the facilities of the institution, and the availability of poultry in local markets.

Complete defrosting before cooking is recommended; but if cooking is started in the frozen state, it will take approximately 1½ times the total time allowance for defrosted poultry. Once defrosted, poultry may be kept safely no longer than 24 hours at 38° F. before cooking. It should never be refrozen. To defrost frozen poultry, use one of the following procedures:

1. Place unwrapped in a refrigerator. Allow about 1 hr. per pound for a heavy turkey.

2. Place in original wrap, under a stream of cold water 4–5 hours. Never use warm water.

● COOKING METHODS

Recommended cooking methods for the various classes of poultry are given in the following table:

Cooking Methods for Poultry

Kind of Poultry	Class	Average Ready-to-cook Weight (lb.)	Cookery Method	Per Capita Allowance Ready to Cook
Chicken	Broiler or fryer	1½–3	Barbecue, fry, or broil	¼–½ bird
	Capon	5–7	Roast	¾–1 lb.
	Roaster	3–5	Roast	¾–1 lb.
	Fowl or hen	3–5	Stew or fricassee	½–¾ lb.
Turkey	Fryer	4–6	Barbecue, fry, or broil	¼–½ bird
	Hen or tom	8–20	Roast	½–1 lb.
	Roll, raw	8–10	Bake	4½–5 oz.
	Roll, cooked	8–10	Heat in broth	2½–3 oz.
Duck		4–6	Roast	¾–1 lb.
		6–10	Roast	¾–1 lb.

NOTE: For cooked yields, see p. 184.

Broiling

Only young tender chickens, 2½ lb. or under, or 3–5 lb. ready-to-cook turkeys should be broiled. Split each bird in half lengthwise, or into quarters, depending on size. Fold wing tip back onto cut side with the thick part around the shoulder joint. Brush with melted butter or margarine. Season each piece with salt and pepper, and place, skin side down, on broiler. Place broiler 7–9 in. below source of heat, as chicken and turkey should broil slowly. Turn and brush with fat while broiling in order to brown and cook evenly. The time required to cook chicken varies from 50 to 60 min., and 1 to 1¼ hr. for turkey.

Deep-fat Frying

Cut 1¾–2-lb. broiler-fryers into pieces of desired serving size. Roll chicken in seasoned flour; or dredge in flour, dip in egg and water mixture, then roll in crumbs (p. 32). Fry in deep fat 12–15 min. at no more than 330° F.

Pan-frying

Cut 2–2½-lb. broiler-fryers into pieces. Dip chicken in milk, dredge in seasoned flour (1 lb. flour, 2 T. salt, 1 T. paprika or poultry seasoning) and brown in a skillet containing ½ in. of hot fat. Reduce heat, cover tightly, and cook slowly until tender—usually about 45–60 min. Cooking time depends on size of pieces. Turn once or twice to assure even browning and doneness.

Oven-frying

Melt 1 lb. fat on bun pan. Combine 1 lb. flour, 2 c. dry milk, 1–2 t. paprika, and 2 T. salt. Dredge each chicken part in flour mixture and roll in fat on pan. Place pieces close together, skin side down, in 1 layer. Bake 1 hr. at 350° F. This method should result in browning with no turning.

Stewing

Cover fowl with boiling water and add 2 t. salt for each 4–5 lb. bird. Cover kettle closely and simmer fowl until tender, approximately 2½ hr. For additional flavor, when meat is to be used in jellied loaves, salads, or creamed dishes, add to cooking water 1 carrot, 1 medium onion, 1 stalk of celery, 2 or 3 cloves, and 2 whole peppercorns for each bird. For cooking in a steamer, place whole or parts of birds in solid steamer pans and steam at 5-lb. pressure until tender, 1½–2 hr.

If cooked fowl is to be held it must be cooled immediately and kept below 38° F. This applies to the broth as well as to the meat. Better flavor and less drying result if the meat is covered with broth during storage. The carcass may be dismantled to save refrigerator space. Cooked poultry should not be used later than the second day after it is cooked.

Roasting

For large-quantity cookery, it is usually recommended that poultry be roasted unstuffed and that dressing be baked separately. If turkey is to be stuffed, mix the stuffing just before it is needed. Do not prepare dressing or stuff the bird in advance. Follow this order of procedure in preparing a roaster:

1. Prepare bird. Remove pin feathers and singe if necessary. Wash well inside and out.

2. Salt inside and outside of bird.

3. Cover bird with cheesecloth dipped in fat, or rub with flour and fat paste (4 oz. flour to 6 oz. fat).

4. Place bird on rack in roasting pan, breast up. Turn when half cooked if necessary for even browning.

5. Baste with fat and hot water (4 oz. fat to 1 qt. hot water) as needed. Drippings may also be used for basting.

6. Roast at 250–300° F. to an internal temperature of 190° F. Insert meat thermometer in center of inside thigh muscle (Fig. 12). Allow approximately 15–18 min. per lb. for a 20-lb. unstuffed turkey. Allow approximately 30 min. per lb. for a 5-lb. chicken. If thermometer is not available, test doneness by moving drumstick. It moves easily at the thigh joint when done.

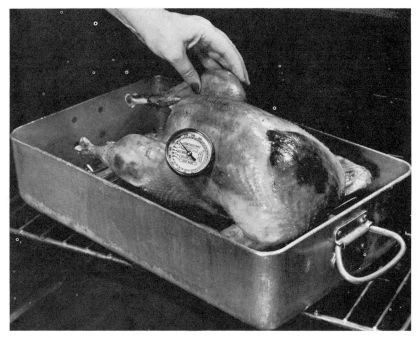

Fig. 12. The proper placement of a thermometer in a turkey for roasting. (Courtesy of the National Turkey Federation and the Kansas Turkey Federation.)

Timetable for Roasting Unstuffed Birds[1]

Weight of Turkey	Oven Temperature (° F.)	Cooking Time Min. per Lb.	Hr. per Bird
8–10	250	25–30	3–3½
10–14	250	18–20	3½–4
14–18	250	15–18	4–4½
20–30	250	12–15	5–6

[1] Turkey, *Care and Cookery in the Restaurant,* National Turkey Federation.

The yield of fowl and turkey is influenced by the method of preparation and service, and the size of portions desired. A fowl weighing 4 to 4½ lb. ready to cook will yield approximately 1 qt. (1¼ lb.) cooked edible meat. The following table can be used as a guide in estimating the probable yield of a turkey:

Yield and Standard Portion Sizes of Turkey[1]

READY-TO-COOK WEIGHT (LB.)	COOKED YIELD (LB.)	NUMBER OF PORTIONS		
		2 OZ.	3 OZ.	5 OZ.
10.3–12	5½	44	29	17
12–13.7	6½	52	34	21
13.7–15.6	7¾	62	41	25
15.6–17.4	8¾	70	46	28
17.4–19.2	9¾	78	52	31
19.2–21.1	11	88	58	35
26.9–28.6	16	128	85	51

[1] Turkey, *Care and Cookery in the Restaurant,* National Turkey Federation.

● POULTRY RECIPES

Chicken à la Maryland

AMOUNT	INGREDIENT	METHOD
35 lb. (8 4–4½ lb. hens) 2 T. 12 oz.	Chicken Salt Flour	Cut into desired pieces. Roll in seasoned flour.
1 lb.	Brown in Fat, hot	
3 qt.	Place in roaster and cover with Thin cream	
Bake 2½–3 hr. at 325° F.		Serving: Approximately 3 oz. cooked meat.

Barbecued Chicken

AMOUNT	INGREDIENT	METHOD
35 lb. (13 2–2½ lb. fryers)	Chicken	Cut into quarters or pieces as desired.
2 T.	Season with Salt	
1 lb.	Brown in oven in Fat, hot	
	Pour Cooked Barbecue Sauce (p. 293). 1 recipe, over chicken.	
Bake 1½–2 hr. at 325° F.		Serving: Approximately 3 oz. cooked meat.

Brown Fricassee of Chicken

AMOUNT	INGREDIENT	METHOD
35 lb. (8 4-lb. hens) 2 T. 1 t.	Chicken Salt Pepper	Cut into desired pieces. Season with salt and pepper.
12 oz.	Dip each piece in Flour	
1 lb.	Brown chicken in Fat, hot	

Remove to roasting pan or steam kettle and cover with boiling water. Cook slowly. When tender remove from stock and make gravy in pan in which chicken was browned, using 10 oz. fat, 5 oz. flour, and 3 qt. liquid in which chicken was cooked.

Serving: Approximately 3 oz. cooked meat.

NOTE: Serve with Mashed Potatoes (p. 319), Steamed Rice (p. 227), or Dumplings (p. 84).

VARIATION: **White Fricassee of Chicken.** Stew chicken until tender, without browning, and remove from liquid. Boil liquid until concentrated. Add milk or cream to make 1½ gal., thicken to make a medium white sauce. Beat constantly while pouring sauce gradually over 10 beaten egg yolks. Season to taste.

Chicken Tahitian

AMOUNT	INGREDIENT	METHOD
35 lb. (13 2–2½ lb. fryers) 12 oz.	Chicken, cut into quarters Fat	Sauté until lightly browned.
	Place in baking pan in single layer.	
4 6-oz. cans 1 lb. 2 T. 2 T.	Brush with Orange concentrate, undiluted Butter or margarine Ginger Soy sauce	Combined and heated until blended.

Place chicken in oven and baste with orange mixture every 15 min. until chicken is glazed.

Bake 35–40 min. at 350° F.   Serving: ¼ fryer.

NOTE: Serve with Steamed Rice (p. 227) and garnish with slivered almonds and avocado wedges.

Creamed Chicken

Amount		Ingredient	Method
	3½ c.	Chicken fat	
1 lb.		Flour	Make as Medium White
3¼ qt.		Chicken stock, hot	Sauce (p. 295).
	2 T.	Salt	
		Add	
2 qt.		Milk or chicken stock, hot	
5 lb. (4 4½-lb. hens)		Chicken, cooked, cubed	

Cook until thoroughly heated.   Serving: Approximately 5 oz.

VARIATION: **Chicken à la King.** Add 12 chopped hard-cooked eggs, 8 oz. pimiento, shredded, and 1 lb. mushrooms if desired.

Chicken Cutlets

Amount		Ingredient	Method
6 lb. (5 4½–5-lb. fowls)		Chicken, cooked, cut fine	
		Add	
1 qt.		Broth	
	1 pt.	Milk	Make as Thick White Sauce
	12 oz.	Fat, chicken or other	(p. 295).
	6 oz.	Flour	
	2 T.	Salt	
		When thickened, add	
	8	Eggs, beaten	

Measure with No. 12 dipper. Shape. Dip in egg and crumbs (p. 32). Chill at least 2 hr. before frying.

Fry in deep fat 3–4 min. at 360°–375° F.

Scalloped Chicken

Amount	Ingredient	Method
5 lb. (4 4½–5-lb. fowls)	Chicken, cooked, cubed	
2 c.	Fat, chicken, melted	
8 oz.	Flour	Make as Medium White
4 qt.	Broth, hot	Sauce (p. 295).
1½ T.	Salt	

When thick and smooth add

12 · Eggs, well beaten · } Stirring constantly.

Place a layer of Bread Dressing (p. 190, ⅔ recipe) in baking pan 12 x 20 in., a layer of sauce, a layer of chicken, then another layer of sauce. Cover with buttered crumbs.

Bake 30–40 min. at 350° F. · Serving: Approximately 6 oz.

Chicken Turnovers

Amount	Ingredient	Method
4 lb. (3 4½–5-lb. fowls)	Chicken, cooked, cubed	
	Add	
1 qt.	Chicken broth	
4 oz.	Flour	Make as Thick White Sauce
6 oz.	Fat, chicken or other	(p. 295).
1 T.	Salt	

Place a No. 20 dipper of mixture on

50 (approximately 5 lb.) · Pastry rounds, 6 in. in diameter

Fold rounds over and seal. Perforate top.

Bake approximately 25–30 min. at 400° F.

NOTE: Serve with chicken gravy (1 gal.).

Chicken Soufflé

Amount	Ingredient	Method
3¾ qt.	Milk	
2½ c.	Broth, chicken	
1 lb.	Butter or margarine	Make as Thin White
4 oz.	Flour	Sauce (p. 295).
1½ T.	Salt	
1 t.	Pepper	
	Add, in order given	
1 lb.	Bread crumbs	
24	Egg yolks, beaten	Mix well.
5 lb. (4 4½–5-lb. hens)	Chicken, cooked, diced	
	Fold in	
24	Egg whites, stiffly beaten	
	Pour into 2 pans 12 x 20 in.	

Bake approximately 1 hr. at 325° F., or until set.

NOTE: Serve with Béchamel Sauce (p. 294) or Mushroom Sauce (p. 296). Veal or turkey may be substituted for chicken.

Chicken Loaf

Amount	Ingredient	Method
7 lb. (6 4½–5-lb. fowls)	Chicken, cooked, diced	
	Add	
1 lb.	Rice	} Cook (p. 227).
	Add	
6 oz.	Pimiento, chopped	
2 oz.	Onion, grated	
16	Eggs, beaten	
1½ T.	Salt	
1 t.	Pepper	
2 qt.	Broth, chicken, cold	
	and	
1 qt.	Milk	} Combined.
1 lb.	Bread crumbs, soft	
	Mix only until ingredients are well blended. Place in oiled baking pan, 12 x 20 x 4 in., or in 5 4 x 9 in. loaf pans.	

Bake approximately 1½ hr. at 325° F.   Serving: Approximately 5 oz.

NOTES: 1. Serve with chicken gravy or Mushroom Sauce (p. 296).
       2. Turkey or tuna may be used in place of chicken.

Chicken Pie

Amount	Ingredient	Method
5 lb. (4 4½–5-lb. fowls)	Chicken, cooked, cubed	
3 lb. 8 oz.	Potatoes, partially cooked, cubed	
2 lb.	Peas, fresh or frozen	
1 gal.	Chicken gravy	
	Place in each of 50 8-oz. baking dishes	
	5 potato cubes	
	1 T. peas	
	Approximately 1 oz. chicken	
	Add	
	⅓ c. chicken gravy	
	Cover each with ½ c. Batter Crust (p. 190).	

Bake 12–15 min. at 450° F.

Batter Crust for Chicken or Meat Pot Pies

AMOUNT		INGREDIENT	METHOD
2 lb.	4 oz.	Flour	
	1½ oz.	Baking powder	
	1 T.	Salt	Mix.
	2 oz.	Sugar	
		Add	
2 qt.		Milk	
18		Egg yolks, beaten	
	4 oz.	Butter or margarine, melted	
		Stir only enough to mix.	
		Fold in	
18		Egg whites, beaten	
		Pour ½ c. batter over contents of each individual casserole. Pour around edges and then in center to form a thin covering over meat or chicken mixture.	

Bake 12–15 min. at 450° F.   Yield: 6 qts.

NOTE: Batter may be refrigerated until needed. Thin mixture with cold milk if it is too thick.

Bread Dressing or Stuffing

AMOUNT		INGREDIENT	METHOD
6 lb.		Bread, dry, cubed	
	1 t.	Pepper	
	1 oz.	Sage	Mix.
	1½ T.	Salt	
	2 oz.	Onion, minced	
		Add	
2½ qt.		Water or broth	
	6 oz.	Fat, melted (chicken or other)	Mix lightly.
	3	Eggs, beaten	
		Place in oiled baking pan.	

Bake 30 min. at 350° F.   Serving: 2½–3 oz.

NOTES: 1. The amount of liquid (water, stock, or milk) will depend on the dryness of the bread.
      2. Do not use whole wheat bread.
      3. Approximately 4–5 lb. stuffing is required for a 20-lb. turkey.

Variations of Bread Dressing

Almond Stuffing. Add 1 lb. diced celery browned in 4 oz. melted fat, 1 lb. chopped almonds, and 1 pt. evaporated milk.

Apple Stuffing. Substitute 12 oz. finely chopped apples for 6 oz. bread crumbs. Add 4 oz. chopped celery.

Celery Stuffing. Substitute 12 oz. finely chopped celery for 6 oz. bread crumbs.

Chestnut Stuffing. Substitute 1¼ lb. cooked chestnuts, chopped, and 8 oz. chopped celery for 6 oz. bread crumbs. Substitute milk for water.

Corn Bread Stuffing. Substitute 4½ lb. corn bread crumbs for 4½ lb. bread crumbs. Add 6 oz. minced onion, 6 hard-cooked eggs, chopped, and 12 oz. chopped celery. Omit sage.

Giblet Stuffing. Add cooked giblets, chopped.

Mushroom Stuffing. Substitute 2 lb. mushrooms fried in butter for 6 oz. bread crumbs. Omit sage.

Onion Stuffing. Add 1 lb. minced onion and 1 c. of chopped celery tops.

Oyster Stuffing. Substitute 1½ lb. oysters for 6 oz. bread crumbs. Add 1 lb. cooked ham, minced, and ½ bay leaf, minced.

Raisin Stuffing. Add 1 lb. washed seedless raisins.

Rice Stuffing. Substitute 5 lb. cooked rice for bread crumbs. Add giblets, cooked and chopped, and 8 oz. diced celery.

Sausage Stuffing. Substitute 2 lb. sausage for 8 oz. bread crumbs. Add 1 lb. tart apples, chopped, and 3 oz. green pepper, minced.

NOTE: For additional recipes containing Poultry, see p. 213–214.

fish

● SELECTION AND COOKING OF FRESH FISH

Fish may be obtained fresh or frozen in most markets during all seasons of the year. The most common forms available are whole (undrawn), drawn (entrails removed), dressed (scaled and eviscerated), steaks (cross-sectional slices of larger fish), fillets (boneless side of fish cut lengthwise), butterfly fillets (two sides of fish corresponding to two single fillets held together by uncut flesh), and sticks (pieces of fish from fillet blocks cut into uniform portions). Many kinds of fish are available in breaded portion-ready form. Shellfish, clams, crabs, lobsters, and oysters also add variety and interest to the institutional menu.

Fish usually is, but need not be, completely thawed before cooking. Pieces frozen together, such as fillets, should be thawed just enough so that they can be separated. This may be done by allowing the unopened and unwrapped packages of frozen fish to stand at room temperature until thawing begins. Cook immediately after defrosting. If cooking is started while the fish is frozen, additional cooking time must be allowed.

Fish may be cooked in many ways, but some methods are more suitable for certain varieties than others. The following chart shows not only the preferred method of cookery, but also the usual market forms in which fish may be purchased.

Fish Buying and Cooking Chart[1]

COOKING METHOD

FISH	TYPE	BAKE	BOIL OR STEAM	BROIL	FRY	MARKET FORMS
Bass, sea	Lean	Good		Best	Good	Whole, drawn, fillet
Bluefish	Lean	Best		Good	Fair	Whole, drawn
Catfish	Lean	Fair			Best	Whole, dressed
Cod	Lean	Best	Fair	Good	Good	Drawn, dressed, steaks or fillets
Flounder	Lean	Good		Good	Best	Whole, fillets
Haddock	Lean	Good	Fair	Best	Good	Drawn, fillets
Halibut	Lean	Good	Fair	Best	Good	Drawn, steaks, fillets
Herring	Fat	Fair		Best	Good	Whole
Mackerel	Fat	Good	Fair	Best		Whole, drawn, fillets
Pike	Lean	Good		Fair	Best	Whole, dressed, fillets
Pompano	Fat	Good		Best	Fair	Whole
Salmon	Fat	Best	Fair	Good		Drawn, dressed, steaks, fillets
Shad	Fat		Best		Good	Whole, drawn
Smelts	Fat			Good	Best	Whole
Snapper, red	Lean	Best	Good	Good		Drawn, dressed, fillets
Sole	Lean	Fair		Good	Best	Whole, fillets
Swordfish	Lean	Good		Best		Dressed, steaks
Trout	Fat	Fair		Good	Best	Drawn, dressed, fillets
Whitefish	Fat	Good		Best	Fair	Whole, drawn, dressed, fillets
Whiting	Lean		Good	Good	Best	Whole, drawn, dressed, fillets

[1]Adapted from *Basic Fish Cookery*, Test Kitchen Series No. 2, Fish and Wildlife Service, United States Department of the Interior, Washington, D.C., 1959.

Poached or Steamed Fish

Place fillets or thick slices of fish in a flat baking pan and cover with liquid. This may be acidulated water, court bouillon, fish stock, milk, or milk and water. Cover with parchment or oiled paper. Cook in a moderate oven (350° F.) or in a steamer until fish loses its transparent appearance or until bones may be removed easily. Drain. Allow about 10 min. per pound for cooking whole fish or 10 min. for cooking fillets cut 4 to the pound. Avoid overcooking. Serve with a sauce.

Acidulated water. Use 1 T. salt and 3 T. lemon juice or vinegar for each quart of water.

Court bouillon. Add to 1 gal. of water, ¾ c. chopped carrots, ¾ c. sliced onions, ¾ c. chopped celery, 3 T. salt, ½ c. vinegar, 2 or 3 bay leaves, 6 peppercorns, 9 cloves, and 3 T. butter or margarine. Boil gently for 20–30 min. Strain to remove spices and vegetables.

Broiled Fish

Wipe fish fillets or steaks as dry as possible. Season with salt and pepper. Place in a well-oiled broiler. Broil, turning skin side up just long enough to crisp and brown. Serve with melted butter and chopped parsley.

Fried Fish

Use small whole fish, fillets, or steaks. Season with salt and pepper, roll in flour or corn meal, or a combination of both, and cook in a small amount of fat. Dip in egg and crumbs (p. 32) if fish is to be fried in deep fat. Fry 4–6 min. at 375° F. Fried fish should be served at once while crisp. If it must be held, arrange fish in counter pans and place uncovered in 250° F. oven until serving time.

Oven-fried Fish

Dip individual servings of fish in egg and crumbs (p. 32) and place on well-oiled baking pans. Pour melted fat over fish and bake in 500° F. oven for approximately 10–12 min.

● SELECTION AND COOKING OF SHELLFISH

Clams. If purchased in the shell, clams should be alive. Wash the shells well and rinse if the clams are to be cooked in the shell. To open a clam, hold it in the palm of the hand and insert a slender strong knife into the shell; pry open the shell and cut the muscle. The skin of the razor and soft clam should be removed before cooking.

Soft-shell crabs should be alive at the time they are cooked. To prepare them, place top shell down, turn back taper points of the shell about halfway, and remove the spongy substance which is found next to the shell. After the tail or apron has been removed, wash the crab thoroughly. It is then ready to cook. Soft-shell crabs are usually dipped in egg and crumbs (p. 32) and fried in deep fat, or they may be pan-fried.

Lobsters. Lobsters should be alive when the cooking process begins. If the lobster is to be boiled, plunge the live lobster head down in the boiling salted water and simmer for 20 to 30 min. Drain and place lobster on its back. Then with a sharp knife, cut in half lengthwise and remove the stomach and intestinal vein. If the lobster is to be broiled, place it on its back and kill it by inserting a sharp knife to cut the spinal cord. Split the body open on the underneath side, being careful not to cut the stomach, which is the sac just back of the head. Remove stomach and intestine which run the length of the body. Crack the claws and lay the opened lobster shell side down as flat as possible on the broiler. Brush with butter, and add salt and pepper. Broiling time will vary with the size of the lobster, but it is usually 25–30 min. Serve with melted butter and lemon.

Oysters. Oysters are not ordinarily washed before using. If washing seems necessary, care should be taken to remove the oysters from the water quickly, so that they do not become soaked or waterlogged. They should be inspected and any bits of shell removed. When making oyster stew, add butter to oysters and heat only until edges begin to curl, then add to hot milk. Serve at once. To fry, dip oysters in egg and crumbs (p. 32) before frying.

Shrimp, raw or green, should be washed carefully. Cover with water and bring to a boil. Let simmer 3 min. in water to which have been added 1½ t. salt to each quart, 2 bay leaves, and mixed spice. Drain. Remove shell and dark vein from the center back of each shrimp. To fry, dip peeled and cleaned raw or cooked shrimp in batter, or egg and crumb (p. 32). Fry in deep fat 3–5 min. at 350–365° F. Cooked shrimp may be purchased either in the shell or peeled and cleaned ready to use.

Guide to Purchasing Shellfish[1]

Fish	Count or Weight per Unit of Measure	Usual Market Form	Purchase Unit
Clams, hard-shell	80 per bushel	In shell, live	Per 100 or bu.
	100–125 per gal.	Shucked, fresh or frozen	Per gal. or lb.
Clams, soft-shell	45 per bushel	In shell, live	Per 100 or bu.
	350–500 per gal.	Shucked	Per 100 or bu.
Crabs, all kinds	4 oz.-20 lb. (varies with kind)	Live, frozen, or fresh-cooked	Per lb. or doz.
Crabmeat, cooked E.P.			
Blue	1-lb. tins	Fresh or frozen	Per lb.
Dungeness	5-lb. tins	Fresh or frozen	Per lb.
King	1- and 5-lb. cartons	Frozen	Per lb.
Lobster	1¼-2 lb. each	Whole, live	Per lb.
Lobster tails, Australian or South African	5-24 oz. each	In shell Frozen raw	Per lb.
Oysters (Eastern)			
Counts	160 or less per gal.	Shucked, fresh or frozen	Per gal.
Extra select	161–210 per gal.		
Select	211–300 per gal.		
Standard	301–500 per gal.		
Shell oysters			
Half shell	800–900 per barrel	Live	Per 100 or barrel
Contuit	600–700 per barrel		
Scallops, bay	150–200 per gal.	Fresh or frozen	Per lb. or gal.
Deep-sea	18–25 per gal. (8 lb. per gal.)		
Shrimp, in shell, headless	Under 15 per lb.	Frozen raw	Per lb.
Jumbo	15–20 per lb.		
Large	21–25 per lb.		
Large-medium	26–30 per lb.		
Medium	31–42 per lb.		
Shrimp, peeled and deveined			
Jumbo	15–20 per lb.	Frozen raw	Per lb.
Large	21–25 per lb.		
Large-medium	26–30 per lb.		
Medium	30–50 per lb.		
Shrimp, cooked, peeled, and deveined			
Jumbo	35–40 per lb.	Fresh or frozen	Per lb.
Large	40–50 per lb.		
Medium	50–60 per lb.		
Shrimp, breaded	15–20 per lb.	Frozen raw	Per lb.
Fantail or round	21–25 per lb.		

[1]Adapted from *Fresh and Frozen Fish Buying Manual,* Fish and Wildlife Service, Circular No. 20, United States Department of the Interior, Washington, D.C., 1954.

● FISH RECIPES

Baked Fish Fillets

Amount		Ingredient	Method
15 lb.		Fish fillets	} Cut into 50 portions.
		Dip each fillet in	
1 lb.		Fat, melted	
	1 T.	Salt	
	1 t.	Pepper, white	} Mixed.
	½ c.	Lemon juice	
		Dredge with	
	14 oz.	Flour	

Place close together in oiled baking pan. Pour over the top 2 oz. of melted butter or margarine in ¾ c. milk.

Bake approximately 25 min. at 400° F.   Serving: Approximately 4–4½ oz.

Scalloped Oysters

Amount		Ingredient	Method
3 qt.		Cracker crumbs	
1 lb.		Butter or margarine, melted	
	1½ T.	Salt	} Mix.
	½ t.	Paprika	
	½ t.	Pepper	
6 qt.		Oysters	} Drain and remove any bits of shell.

Spread ⅓ crumbs over the bottom of an oiled baking pan 12 x 20 in. Cover with ½ oysters; repeat with crumbs and oysters.

		Pour over the top of oysters	
1 qt.		Milk or cream	
	1½ pt.	Oyster liquor or water	

Cover with remaining crumbs.

Bake 30 min. at 400° F.   Serving: 5 oz.

Note: 2 c. finely chopped celery may be added.

Deviled Crab

Amount	Ingredient	Method
12 6½-oz. cans	Crabmeat, flaked (or 5 lb. fresh crabmeat)	
	Add	
4 T.	Lemon juice	
1½ T.	Salt	
2 t.	Pepper	Mix.
f.g.	Cayenne	
5	Eggs, beaten	
1 T.	Worcestershire sauce	
	Add	
12 oz.	Butter or margarine	
2 qt.	Milk	Made into a Thick White Sauce
8 oz.	Flour	(p. 295).
1½ t.	Mustard, prepared	
	Mix lightly; fill individual casseroles or shells and cover with	
1 qt.	Crumbs, buttered	

Bake 15 min. at 400° F.   Serving: Approximately 2 oz.

Creole Shrimp with Rice

Amount		Ingredient	Method
5 lb.		Shrimp, cooked	
4 lb.	8 oz.	Rice	Cook (p. 227).
		Prepare sauce	
	6 oz.	Onions, chopped	
	12 oz.	Celery, chopped	
		Brown in	
	3 oz.	Fat	
		Add	
	3 T.	Flour	
	1½ T.	Salt	Cook 15 min.
	1 pt.	Water	
		Add	
1½ qt.		Tomatoes	
	6 T.	Vinegar	
	2 T.	Sugar	
		Add cooked shrimp to sauce. Serve over No. 8 dipper of cooked rice.	
		Serving: 3 oz. shrimp creole, ½ c. rice.	

Note: If raw shrimp are used, purchase 10 lb. Cook as directed on page 195.

Salmon Loaf

Amount		Ingredient	Method
3 c.		Milk	} Scald.
1 lb.		Add Bread cubes, soft	} Mix.
8 lb.		Add Salmon	
	1½ T.	Salt	
	1 t.	Paprika	
	2	Lemon rinds, grated	} Mix lightly.
	½ c.	Lemon juice	
15		Eggs, beaten	
		Place in 5 oiled pans 4 x 9 in. Set pans in hot water.	

Bake 1¼ hr. at 325° F.   Serving: Approximately 3½ oz.

NOTE: For a lighter-textured product, beat egg whites separately and fold into salmon mixture.

Scalloped Salmon

Amount		Ingredient	Method
1 lb.		Butter or margarine	
	12 oz.	Flour	
	1½ T.	Salt	} Make as Medium White Sauce
	½ t.	Pepper	(p. 295).
1 gal.		Milk	
	¼ c.	Add Parsley, chopped	
	2 t.	Onion juice	
	1 t.	Celery salt	
10 lb.		Arrange in alternate layers, sauce and Salmon, flaked	
	8 oz.	Bread, crumbs	
	4 oz.	Cover with Crumbs	
	4 oz.	Butter or margarine	} Combined.

Bake 25 min. at 375° F.   Serve with a No. 10 dipper.

VARIATION: Scalloped Tuna. Substitute tuna for salmon.

Tuna-Cashew Casserole

Amount	Ingredient	Method
8 lb.	Tuna	
8 oz.	Celery, chopped	
6 oz.	Onion, chopped	Arrange in layers in oiled casse-
7 3-oz. cans	Chinese noodles	roles or baking pans, with
1 lb. 8 oz.	Cashews	noodles as top layer.
9 10-oz. cans	Cream of mushroom soup	

Bake approximately 1 hr. at 350° F.

VARIATION: **Chicken-Cashew Casserole.** Substitute diced cooked chicken for tuna.

Garnishes for Fish

1. Parsley, chopped or sprig.
2. Small center lettuce cup filled with cole slaw or cranberry sauce.
3. Spiced whole apricot or crabapple.
4. Cubes of tomato aspic or other colorful gelatin and a bit of watercress or other greens.
5. Lemon wedges, plain or with edges dipped in paprika or chopped parsley.
6. Thin slices of lemon or orange, plain or notched.
7. Celery hearts or celery curls and radish roses.
8. Black, green, or stuffed olives and a bit of salad green.
9. Carrot curls or strips, onion ring, green onions, or pickled onions.
10. Tomato slices, wedges, or small whole cherry tomato and parsley sprig.
11. Cucumber slices, peeled and fluted, or unpeeled and accented with pimiento strips.
12. Slices of hard-cooked egg, chopped egg, riced egg yolk, or ½ stuffed egg.
13. Latticed pickled beets.
14. Lemon butter balls. Mint leaves.
15. Sprig of frosted white grapes or sprigs of green or red grapes.
16. Blanched toasted almonds.
17. Sautéed button mushrooms.
18. Small green pepper cups with tartar sauce.
19. Toasted croutons.
20. Kumquats and parsley sprig, avocado slice, or melon balls.

NOTE: For additional recipes containing fish, see p. 215–p. 217.

luncheon dishes

High-protein foods combined with bland foods, such as rice, spaghetti, or noodles, and bound by a white sauce or a well-seasoned tomato sauce, are often classified as luncheon dishes. Ground or chopped meat, chopped chicken or turkey, flaked fish, cheese, and eggs are all used effectively in these entrées. These foods may be served as an alternate to the main entrée on a multiple-choice menu or as the main dish for luncheon or supper in hospitals, nursing homes, and similar food services.

● MEAT DISHES

Ham and Egg Scallop

Amount	Ingredient	Method
4 lb.	Ham, minced	Fill oiled baking pans with alternate layers of ham, eggs, and white sauce.
36	Eggs, hard-cooked, sliced	
4 qt.	Medium White Sauce (p. 295)	
	Cover with	
12 oz.	Bread crumbs	Mixed together.
3 oz.	Butter or margarine, melted	

Bake 30–40 min. at 400° F.   Serving: Approximately 5 oz.

VARIATION: **Ham and Sweetbread Casserole.** Cut ham into cubes. Substitute 4 lb. sweetbreads, cooked and cubed, for eggs.

201

Creamed Ham

AMOUNT	INGREDIENT	METHOD
1 lb. 8 oz. 1 gal.	Butter or margarine Flour Milk	Made into a Medium White Sauce (p. 295).
	Add	
6 lb.	Ham, cooked	Cut into cubes.

Salt to taste. Heat slowly over hot water for approximately 20 min. Serve over biscuits, spoon bread or cheese soufflé.

Serving: Approximately ½ c.

VARIATION: **Creamed Ham and Celery.** Substitute 2 lb. chopped celery for 2 lb. ham.

Creamed Beef

AMOUNT	INGREDIENT	METHOD
10 lb. 1	Beef, ground Onion, small, chopped (may omit)	Cook beef in own fat, in heavy pan.
	Add	
3 pt. 3 pt. 6 oz. 12 oz. 3 T. 1 t.	Stock, hot Milk, hot Flour Fat, melted Salt Pepper	Made into a Medium White Sauce (p. 295).

Serving: Approximately ½ c.

NOTE: Serve with No. 8 dipper on toast, biscuit, or baked potato.

Creamed Chipped Beef

Amount		Ingredient	Method
2 lb.	8 oz.	Chipped beef	
1 lb.		Fat, hot	Brown lightly in
5 qt.		White Sauce, Medium (p. 295).	Add and blend
		Season to taste, omitting salt.	
		Serve with No. 8 dipper.	

Serving: Approximately ½ c.

NOTE: Serve on toast or with baked potato.
VARIATIONS: 1. **Creamed Chipped Beef and Peas.** Reduce beef to 2 lb. and add 1 40-oz. package frozen peas, cooked, just before serving.
2. **Chipped Beef and Noodles.** Add 2 lb. cheese, ground. Combine with 2 lb. noodles, cooked. Top with buttered crumbs and bake 30 min.

Baked Hash

Amount		Ingredient	Method
10 lb.		Beef, cooked	
8 lb.		Potatoes, cooked	Chop together.
1 lb.		Onions	
		Add	
	1 t.	Pepper	
	¼ c.	Salt	Mix.
2 qt.		Meat stock or gravy	
		Pour into an oiled pan 12 x 20 in.	

Bake 1¼ hr. at 350° F.   Serving: 6½ oz.

NOTE: Corned beef may be substituted for cooked beef. Decrease salt to 2 T.

Meat Croquettes

AMOUNT	INGREDIENT	METHOD
10 lb. 2 oz. 1 qt. 1½ T.	Meat, cooked, ground Onions, finely chopped White Sauce, Thick (p. 295) Salt	} Combine.
	Measure with No. 12 dipper. Shape, egg and crumb, using	
6 1 c. 12 oz.	Eggs Milk Crumbs, bread Chill at least 2 hr. before frying.	

Fry in deep fat 3–4 min. at 350–375° F.   Serving: 3½ oz. croquette

NOTES: 1. If desired, croquettes may be baked 1 hr. at 375° F.
        2. Consommé may be substituted for part of milk in white sauce.
        3. Serve with Mushroom Sauce (p. 296) or Tomato Sauce (p. 292).

Stuffed Peppers

AMOUNT	INGREDIENT	METHOD
9 lb.	Meat, cooked, ground	
4 oz. 4 oz.	Add Green pepper trimmings Onion, chopped Fat	} Sautéed 3 min.
1½ T. 6 1 pt.	Add Salt Eggs, beaten Milk	} Mixed well.
50	Fill Green pepper halves	
4 oz. 4 oz.	Sprinkle over top Bread crumbs Fat, melted	} Mixed.
2 qt.	Pour around peppers Tomato juice	

Bake 1 hr. at 350° F.   Serving: Approximately 5 oz.

NOTES: 1. To shorten cooking time, peppers may be parboiled or steamed until partially
        cooked.
        2. Corn, rice, or spaghetti may be substituted for part of the meat.
        3. Corned beef hash or salmon loaf mixture may be used for stuffing.

Meat Roll

AMOUNT		INGREDIENT	METHOD
2 lb.	8 oz.	Flour	
1 qt.		Milk	Mix as for Biscuits (p. 57). Divide
	2½ oz.	Fat	dough into 4 portions. Roll each
	2 oz.	Baking powder	portion ¼ in. thick.
	1½ T.	Salt	
		Spread over dough	
7 lb.		Meat, cooked, ground, well seasoned	Mixed.
	3 c.	Gravy, cold	
		Roll as for jelly roll. Slice into pieces 1 in. thick. Place on oiled baking sheet.	

Bake 15 min. at 450° F.   Serving: 5 oz.

NOTE: Serve with a hot meat gravy or Mushroom Sauce (3 qt.). (p. 296).
VARIATIONS: 1. **Ham Biscuit Roll.** Substitute ground cooked ham for meat. Serve with Mushroom Sauce (p. 296).
  2. **Tuna or Salmon Biscuit Roll.** Substitute tuna or salmon for meat and combine with Thick White Sauce (p. 295). Serve with Cheese Sauce (p. 296).
  3. **Chicken or Turkey Biscuit Roll.** Substitute cooked poultry for meat. Serve with Mushroom Sauce (p. 296).

American Pizza

Amount		Ingredient	Method
3 lb.	10 oz.	Flour	
	1½ t.	Salt	} Mix.
	3 T.	Sugar	
		Add	
	1 oz.	Yeast, dissolved in	
	2⅔ c.	Water, lukewarm	} Mix to form dough.
	3 T.	Fat	

Knead until smooth and elastic. Cover and let rise 2 hr. Punch down and let rest 45 min. Divide into 2 portions and roll out as thin as possible, stretching to desired shape. Put dough into 2 oiled 18 x 26-in. bun pans; trim and seal edges.

Amount		Ingredient	Method
		Cover with mixture of	
1 qt.		Tomato paste	
1 qt.		Tomato purée	
	2 t.	Thyme or oregano	
	1 T.	Salt	} Mixed.
	½ t.	Cumin, ground	
	1	Garlic clove, crushed	
	2 T.	Chili powder	
2 lb.	8 oz.	Sausage	} Partially cooked and drained
2 lb.	8 oz.	Ground beef	of excess fat.
		Top with	
2 lb.	8 oz.	Mozzarella cheese, sliced	

Bake 10–15 min. at 450° F.   Serving: 3 x 4 in. approximately 5 oz.

NOTE: Processed Cheddar cheese may be substituted for Mozzarella. Sweet basil may be sprinkled over top.

Chili Con Carne

Amount	Ingredient	Method
3 lb. 1 gal.	Beans, kidney Water, boiling	Wash beans. Pour boiling water over beans. Cover and let soak 1 hr. or longer. Cook until tender, approximately 1½ hr.
	Add	
9 lb. 8 oz.	Beef, ground Onion, chopped	Browned.
	Add	

1½ qt.
2 oz.
3–4 oz.
3 T.
	Tomato purée
	Chili powder
	Cumin seed, ground
	Salt
	Water to make a total
	   volume of 3 gal.
	      Let simmer about 3 hr.	

	Add, while stirring	
5 oz. 2 c.	Flour Water, cold Heat until flour is cooked.	Made into a paste.
		Serving: Approximately 1 c.

NOTE: Pinto or red beans may be substituted for kidney beans. If canned beans are used, substitute 1 No. 10 can.

VARIATION: **Chili Spaghetti.** Use only 5 lb. ground beef. Proceed as for Chili Con Carne. Cook 1½ lb. spaghetti and add to chili mixture just before serving.

Tamale Pie

AMOUNT		INGREDIENT	METHOD
2 lb.	8 oz.	Corn meal	
	3 T.	Salt	Make a stiff mush.
7 qt.		Water	
		Pour half of hot mush into oiled baking pan.	
		Cover with	
8 lb.		Ground beef, cooked	
3 qt.		Tomatoes	
	4 oz.	Onions, minced	
	1 clove	Garlic	Mixed.
	1½ T.	Salt	
	2 oz.	Chili powder	
		Pour remaining mush over meat mixture.	

Bake 40 min. at 350° F.   Serving: Approximately 6 oz.

NOTES: 1. Meat mixture may be poured into a well-oiled pan, covered with corn bread batter and baked 35 min. at 400° F.
2. 3 c. chopped ripe olives may be added.

Sausage Rolls

AMOUNT		INGREDIENT	METHOD
12 lb.	8 oz.	Sausage, link	
2 lb.	8 oz.	Flour	Make a biscuit dough (p. 57). Divide
	3 oz.	Baking powder	dough into 2 portions. Roll each por-
	1½ T.	Salt	tion to ½-in. thickness and cut into
1 lb.		Fat	rectangles 3 x 4 in.
1 qt.		Milk	
		Place two partially cooked link sausages in the center of each piece of dough and fold over.	

Bake 20 min. at 400° F.   Serving: 1 roll, ¼ c. gravy.

NOTE: Serve with sausage gravy (3 qt.).
VARIATION: **Pigs in Blankets.** Substitute wieners for link sausages. Serve with Cheese Sauce (p. 296).

Beef and Pork Casserole

Amount		Ingredient	Method
4 lb.		Pork, ground	Cook until well done and brown. Drain excess fat.
4 lb.		Beef, ground	
1 lb.		Onion, ground	
		Add	
1 lb.	12 oz. A.P.	Noodles, cooked (p. 229)	Mix.
2 lb.		Cheese, Cheddar, grated	
1½ qt.		Tomato soup	
1½ qt.		Water	
	1 T.	Salt	
	1 t.	Pepper	
		Pour into 2 pans 12 x 20 in.	
		Cover with	
1 lb.	2 oz.	Crumbs, bread	Combined.
	5 oz.	Butter or margarine, melted	

Bake 30 min. at 300° F. Serving: Approximately 5 oz.

Spaghetti with Meat Sauce

Amount		Ingredient	Method
8 lb.		Beef, ground	Brown.
		Add	
1 qt.		Water	Cook slowly, stirring frequently, until thickened, approximately ½ hr.
5 qt.		Tomatoes or purée	
	7 c.	Catsup	
1 lb.		Onions, chopped	
	2	Bay leaves	
	1 t.	Thyme	
	1 clove	Garlic	
	¼ c.	Worcestershire sauce	
	2 t.	Cayenne pepper	
	1½ T.	Salt	

Serving: Approximately 6 oz.

NOTE: To serve dip with 4 oz. ladle over freshly cooked spaghetti, 4 lb. A.P. (p. 229).

Creole Spaghetti

Amount		Ingredient	Method
5 lb.		Beef, ground	
	6 oz.	Onion, finely chopped	Sauté.
1 lb.		Green pepper, chopped	
		Add	
3 qt.		Tomato purée	
		Add	
3 lb.		Spaghetti	Cook (p. 229).
		Pour into an oiled baking pan.	
		Sprinkle over the top	
1 lb.	8 oz.	Cheese, ground	

Bake approximately 45 min. at 325° F.   Serving: Approximately 6 oz.

NOTE: Tomatoes may be substituted all or in part for tomato purée.

Chop Suey

Amount		Ingredient	Method
5 lb.		Veal or beef, ½-in. cubes	
5 lb.		Pork, ½-in. cubes	Brown.
	6 oz.	Fat	
		Add	
	¼ c.	Salt	Simmer until tender.
1 gal.		Water	
		Add	
	4 oz.	Green peppers, cut fine	
	8 oz.	Onions, chopped	Cook approximately 30 min.
5 lb.		Celery, diced	
		Add	
	8 oz.	Flour	Smoothed to a paste.
	1 pt.	Water	
		Add	
3 (No. 2) cans		Bean sprouts	
	1–1½ c.	Soy sauce	
		Serve with No. 10 dipper on mounds of	
3 lb.		Rice	Steamed (p. 227).
		Garnish with	
3 (No. 2½) cans		Chinese noodles	

Serving: 4 oz. Chop Suey, ½ c. rice.

NOTE: 2 No. 2 cans chop suey vegetables may be added.
VARIATION: **Chicken Chow Mein.** Substitute cubed cooked chicken or turkey for veal.

Scrapple

Amount		Ingredient	Method
8 lb.		Pork, fresh	Boil until the meat falls to pieces.
6 qt.		Water	(Add water as necessary.)
	¼ c.	Salt	

(1) Remove the meat and bones from the liquid.
(2) Remove any bones or gristle from the meat.
(3) Chop meat fine and return to liquid. (There should be 1¼ gal. of boiling liquid.)

		Add slowly	
3 lb.		Corn meal, yellow	Stirring constantly.

Boil 5 min., then place in steamer and cook 3 hr. Turn into 5 4 x 9 in. loaf pans to mold. Cut into ½-in. slices, dip in flour, and fry until brown and crisp on both sides.

NOTE: 8 lb. pork sausage may be substituted for fresh pork. Cook in 1½ gal water, skim excess fat, then add corn meal and cook.

● POULTRY DISHES

Turkey may be substituted for chicken in any of the following recipes.

Chicken Timbales

Amount	Ingredient	Method
1 lb.	Butter or margarine }	Melt.
	Add	
12 oz.	Bread crumbs }	Cook 5 min., stirring constantly.
2½ qt.	Milk }	
	Add	
5 lb. 6 oz.	Chicken, cooked, chopped	
(4 4½–5-lb. fowls)		
3 T.	Parsley, chopped (may omit)	
32	Eggs, beaten slightly	
1½ T.	Salt	
1 t.	Pepper, white	
	Pour into 50 custard cups and bake as custard in pans of water.	

Bake 30 min. at 350° F., or until firm.

NOTE: Serve with Béchamel Sauce (p. 294). Garnish with riced egg yolk.
VARIATIONS: 1. **Ham Timbales.** Substitute ham for chicken; omit 2 t. salt.
2. **Vegetable Timbales.** Substitute 3 qt. finely chopped or puréed vegetables for chicken. Serve with Cheese Sauce (p. 296).

Chicken and Rice Casserole

AMOUNT		INGREDIENT	METHOD
4 lb.		Rice	} Cook (p. 227).
	4 oz.	Fat, chicken or other	
	4 oz.	Flour	Make as Medium White Sauce
2½ qt.		Milk	(p. 295).
2 qt.		Broth	
		Add	
5 lb. (4 4½–5-lb. fowls)		Chicken, cooked, diced	
	2 T.	Salt	
		Arrange in layers in oiled pans or casseroles	
		Rice, chicken, and	
1 lb.	12 oz.	Mushrooms	
	8 oz.	Almonds, shredded	
	4 oz.	Pimiento	
		Cover with sauce. Sprinkle with buttered crumbs.	

Bake 1 hr. at 350° F.   Serving: Approximately 6 oz.

Chicken Croquettes

AMOUNT		INGREDIENT	METHOD
1 lb.	8 oz.	Rice	} Cook rice in broth.
3 qt.		Chicken stock	
		Add	
	1 T.	Lemon juice	
	2 T.	Onion juice	
	3 T.	Salt	
	1 t.	Celery salt	
		Add	
	6 oz.	Flour	Made into a thick sauce by combining flour with 1 pt. cold stock. Add to
1 qt.		Chicken stock	1 pt. boiling stock. Cook until thick.
		Add	
5 lb. (4 4½–5-lb. fowls)		Chicken, cubed	} Mix well.
		Measure with No. 12 dipper. Cool. Shape, egg, and crumb (p. 32). Chill at least 2 hr. before frying.	

Fry in deep fat 3–4 min. at 360–375° F.   Serving: 1 3-oz. croquette.

Chicken and Noodles

Amount	Ingredient	Method
2 lb. 8 oz. 2 gal.	Noodles Chicken stock	⎫ ⎬ Cook until noodles are tender. ⎭ Remove from stock and place in oiled baking pan.
5 lb. (4 4½–5-lb. hens)	Add Chicken, cooked, cubed	
10 oz. 6 oz. 3 qt. 1 T. 1 t.	Cover with Fat, chicken Flour Chicken stock or milk Salt Pepper	⎫ ⎬ Made into a sauce. ⎭

Bake approximately 30 min. at 350° F.   Serving: Approximately 4 oz.

Variation: **Pork and Noodle Casserole.** Substitute 10-lb. pork shoulder, diced and cooked, for
chicken.

● FISH DISHES

Salmon and Potato Chip Casserole

Amount	Ingredient	Method
8 lb.	Salmon, flaked	
2 lb. 8 oz.	Potato chips, coarsely crushed	
8 10-oz. cans.	Cream of mushroom soup	
8 oz.	Butter or margarine	} Make into a sauce.
5 oz.	Flour	
	Arrange in layers in casseroles or counter pan.	

Bake 20 min. at 375° F.   Serving: Approximately 5 oz.

Variation: **Tuna and Potato Chip Casserole.** Substitute tuna for salmon.

Salmon Croquettes

Amount	Ingredient	Method
12 oz.	Fat	
9 oz.	Flour	} Make a thick white sauce. Cool.
1½ qt.	Milk	
	Add	
8 lb.	Salmon	} Bones and skin removed. Flaked.
	Add	
6 oz.	Cornflakes	
3 T.	Onion juice	} Mix. Chill thoroughly.
7 oz.	Pimiento, chopped	
	Measure with a No. 30 dipper. Shape, egg and crumb (p. 32).	
8	Eggs	
2 c.	Milk	
1 lb. 8 oz.	Crumbs, bread	

Fry in deep fat about 4 min. at 375° F.   Serving: 2 croquettes.

Note: Serve with Egg Sauce (p. 296) or creamed peas.

Codfish Balls

AMOUNT	INGREDIENT	METHOD
8 lb. (A.P.)	Potatoes	} Cook and mash.
	Add	
5 lb.	Codfish, salt	} Cooked until tender and boned.
5 oz.	Fat, melted	
12	Eggs, beaten	
	Form into balls 1½ in. in diameter. Egg and crumb (p. 32) and fry.	
		Serving: 1 3½-oz. ball.

NOTES: 1. If codfish is very salty, some soaking may be needed.
2. Serve with parsley, cream, or tomato sauce.
3. Any cooked fish may be substituted for codfish; add 1 T. salt and 1 lb. onion finely chopped.

Tuna and Noodles

AMOUNT	INGREDIENT	METHOD
2 lb.	Noodles	} Cook, drain, and wash.
	Add	
5 lb.	Tuna, flaked	
	Add	
2 qt.	Milk	
1½ T.	Salt	Made into a Medium
4 oz.	Flour	White Sauce (p. 295).
8 oz.	Butter or margarine	
	Place in oiled baking pan 12 x 20 in. Bake 30 min.	
	Sprinkle over the top	
1 lb.	Cheese, ground.	
	Bake 15 min. longer.	

Bake 45 min. at 300° F.   Serving: 5½ oz.

VARIATION: **Tuna and Rice.** Substitute 2 lb. cooked rice for the noodles.

Creamed Tuna

AMOUNT		INGREDIENT	METHOD
	12 oz.	Butter or margarine	Make a Medium
	6 oz.	Flour	White Sauce (p. 295).
4 qt.		Milk	
		When thickened, add	
	6 T.	Worcestershire sauce (may omit)	
	¼ t.	Cayenne	
	1 T.	Salt	
		Add	
	9	Eggs, hard cooked, chopped	
	6 oz.	Green pepper, chopped	
	6 oz.	Pimiento, chopped	
		When ready to serve pour over	
5 lb.		Tuna, flaked, hot	
			Serving: Approximately 4 oz.

NOTE: Serve on toast or biscuit. Other cooked fish may be substituted for tuna.
VARIATIONS: 1. **Creamed Tuna and Celery.** Substitute 1 lb. diced cooked celery for 1 lb. tuna.
2. **Tuna Rarebit.** Use 4 lb. tuna; add 1½ lb. ground cheese.
3. **Creamed Salmon.** Substitute salmon for tuna.

● CHEESE DISHES

Cheese Balls

AMOUNT		INGREDIENT	METHOD
4 lb.	8 oz.	Cheese, grated	
	4 oz.	Flour	Mix.
	1 T.	Salt	
	f. g.	Cayenne	
		Fold in carefully	
24		Egg whites beaten stiff	
		Shape into balls 1–1¼ in. diameter or dip with No. 30 dipper.	
		Egg and crumb (p. 32).	
		Chill for several hours before frying.	

Fry in deep fat 2–3 min. at 360° F.   Yield: 150 balls.

NOTES: 1. Serve 3 balls in center of hot buttered pineapple ring.
2. For serving as first-course accompaniment, use half the recipe and shape into balls ½–¾ in. in diameter. Yield: 150 balls.

Cheese Croquettes

AMOUNT	INGREDIENT	METHOD
8 oz. 8 oz. 2 qt.	Fat, melted Flour Milk	Make a Thick White Sauce (p. 295).
	Add	
32 2 lb. 1½ T. 1 T.	Egg yolks, beaten Cheese, diced Salt Paprika Chill several hours.	Stir until cheese is melted. Measure with No. 16 dipper. Cool. Shape.
16 1 lb.	Bread each croquette, using Egg whites and 8 T. water, beaten Crumbs Place in a wire basket.	

Fry in deep fat 3–4 min. at 360° F.   Serving: 1 croquette.

Cheese Fondue

AMOUNT	INGREDIENT	METHOD
4½ qt. 4 oz. 1½ t. 1 T. f.g.	Milk, scalded Fat, melted Mustard Salt Cayenne	Mix together.
3 lb. 8 oz.	Pour over Bread cubes, soft, stale	
4 lb. 8 oz.	Cool slightly and add Cheese, ground	
24	Add Egg yolks, beaten	Mix until blended.
24	Fold in Egg whites, beaten until stiff Pour into 3 oiled pans 10 x 12 in. Set pans in hot water.	

Bake 50–60 min. at 350° F.   Serving: Approximately 4 oz.

Cheese Soufflé

Amount	Ingredient	Method
2½ qt.	Milk, hot	
	Add	
10 oz.	Tapioca, Minute	} Stirring constantly.
2 T.	Salt	
	Cook in steamer 15 min. Stir frequently during first 5 min.	
	Add	
3 lb.	Cheese, ground	
24	Egg yolks, beaten	
	Fold in	
24	Egg whites, beaten	
	Pour into 3 oiled pans 10 x 12 in. Set pans in hot water.	

Bake 50 min. at 350° F.   Serving: Approximately 2½ oz.

NOTE: Serve with Spanish Sauce (p. 293), Shrimp Sauce (p. 296), or Creamed Ham, (p. 202).
VARIATION: **Mushroom Soufflé.** Add 1 lb. chopped mushrooms and 5 oz. chopped green peppers to uncooked mixture. Serve with Béchamel Sauce (p. 294).

Macaroni and Cheese

Amount		Ingredient	Method
2 lb.	8 oz.	Macaroni	} Cook (p. 229).
		Add	
3 lb.		Cheese, ground	
		Pour macaroni into an oiled pan 12 x 20 x 4 in.	
		Add	
	8 oz.	Butter or margarine	
	6 oz.	Flour	} Made as Medium White Sauce (p. 295).
	2 T.	Salt	
3 qt.		Milk	
		Sprinkle over the top	
	12 oz.	Bread crumbs	} Mixed.
	4 oz.	Fat, melted	

Bake 35 min. at 350° F.   Serving: Approximately 5 oz.

NOTES: 1. Cheese may be added to white sauce.
2. Fresh tomato and green pepper or pimiento may be added.

Scalloped Macaroni

AMOUNT		INGREDIENT	METHOD
2 lb.	8 oz.	Macaroni	} Cook (p. 229).
		Add	
2 lb.		Cheese, cubed	} Mix.
1 lb.	2 oz.	Bread, fresh, cubed	
		Pour into an oiled pan 12 x 20 in. Pour over the macaroni.	
	6	Eggs, beaten	
	8 oz.	Fat, melted	} Mixed.
	3 T.	Salt	
3 qt.		Milk	

Bake 45 min. at 350° F.   Serving: Approximately 5 oz.

● EGG DISHES

Directions for Cooking Eggs

Method	Directions	Cooking Time
Hard-cooked:		
Steamer I	Place eggs in solid steamer pan or counter pan. Cover with cold water. Steam at 5-lb. pressure. Plunge at once into cold water.	25–30 min.
Steamer II	Place eggs in shallow perforated pans. Steam at 5-lb. pressure. Plunge at once into cold water.	15–18 min.
Kettle	Place eggs in wire baskets. Lower into kettles of boiling water. Simmer.	30 min.
Soft-cooked:		
Kettle	Place eggs in kettle, cover with cold water. Bring to full rolling boil. Remove eggs from boiling water. Run cold water over eggs for a few seconds.	
Poached:		
Steamer	Break eggs into water in shallow counter pans. Steam at 5-lb pressure.	3–5 min.
Top of range	Break eggs one at a time into sauce dishes. Line up dishes on trays. Carefully slide eggs into boiling water in skillets or shallow pans. Keep water at simmering temperature. Remove eggs with slotted spoon or turner.	5–7 min.
Fried:		
Top of range	Break eggs into sauce dishes. Slide carefully into hot fat in skillets or on griddle. Cook over low heat, carefully basting eggs until of desired hardness. If eggs are to be served on hot counter, drain well before removing to counter pans.	
Oven	Heat fat in counter pans or skillets. Carefully slide eggs into fat. Bake at 400° F.	5–7 min., or until of desired hardness.

Scrambled Eggs

AMOUNT	INGREDIENT	METHOD
75	Eggs	} Break into bowl. Beat slightly.
	Add	
1½ qt.	Milk, hot	} Combine.
2 T.	Salt	
	Pour into skillets or steam-jacketed kettle in which has been melted 8 oz. butter or margarine. Cook until desired consistency, stirring occasionally. Serve with No. 10 dipper.	

NOTES: 1. **Steamer Method.** Melt 4 oz. butter or margarine in each of two steamer or counter pans. Pour egg mixture into pans. Steam for 6–8 min. at 5-lb. pressure. Stir and return to steamer until desired degree of hardness has been reached.
2. **Oven Method.** Melt 4 oz. butter or margarine in each of 2 counter or baking pans. Pour egg mixture into pans. Bake approximately 20 min. at 350° F., stirring once after 10 min. of baking.

VARIATIONS: 1. **Scrambled Eggs and Cheese.** Add 1 lb. grated Cheddar cheese.
2. **Scrambled Eggs and Ham.** Add 1 lb. 4 oz. chopped cooked ham.
3. **Scrambled Eggs and Chipped Beef.** Add 1 lb. chopped chipped beef.

Omelet

AMOUNT	INGREDIENT	METHOD
12 oz.	Butter or margarine, melted	
8 oz.	Flour	Make a Thick White Sauce
3 qt.	Milk, hot	(p. 295). Cool.
2 T.	Salt	
½ t.	Pepper, white	
	Add	
24	Egg yolks, beaten	} Mix well.
	Fold in	
24	Egg whites, beaten until stiff	
	Pour into 2 oiled pans 12 x 20 in. Set pans in hot water.	

Bake approximately 45 min. at 325° F.   Serving: Approximately 3 oz.

VARIATIONS: 1. **Bacon Omelet.** Fry 1½ lb. diced bacon; substitute bacon for butter in white sauce. Add the diced bacon to the egg mixture.
2. **Cheese Omelet.** Add 12 oz. grated cheese before placing pans in oven.
3. **Ham Omelet.** Add 3 lb. finely diced cooked ham.
4. **Jelly Omelet.** Spread 2 c. tart jelly over cooked omelet.
5. **Spanish Omelet.** Serve with Spanish Sauce (p. 293).

Chinese Omelet

AMOUNT	INGREDIENT	METHOD
1 qt.	White Sauce, Medium (p. 295).	
	Add	
1 lb.	Cheese, ground	
	Add	
24	Egg yolks, beaten	
1 t.	Mustard	
2 T.	Salt	} Mixed.
1 t.	Paprika	
	Add	
2 lb. A.P.	Rice	} Cook (p. 227).
	Fold in	
24	Egg whites, beaten until stiff	
	Pour into 3 oiled pans 10 x 12 in.	

Bake 45 min. at 325° F.   Serving: Approximately 4 oz.

NOTE: Serve with Cheese Sauce (p. 296) or Tomato Sauce (p. 292).

Potato Omelet

AMOUNT	INGREDIENT	METHOD
50	Bacon slices	Arrange bacon close together in meat pans and bake in oven until crisp. Remove from pans.
	Add to bacon fat	
9 lb. (E.P.)	Potatoes, cooked, diced	} Brown slightly.
	Remove to 2 baking pans 12 x 20 in. Pour over the potatoes.	
36	Eggs, beaten	
3 T.	Salt	
1 t.	Pepper, white	} Beaten until light.
f.g.	Cayenne	
3 qt.	Milk, hot	

Bake 1 hr. at 325° F.   Serving: Approximately ½ c.

NOTE: Lay crisp bacon slices on top of omelet when removed from oven. Serve at once.
VARIATION: **Potato-Ham Omelet.** Omit bacon. Add 4 lb. diced cooked ham to potatoes.

Creamed Eggs

Amount	Ingredient	Method
1 lb. 8 oz. 4 qt.	Butter or margarine Flour Milk, hot	} Make as Medium White Sauce (p. 295).
	Add	
1½ T. ¼ t.	Salt Pepper, white	} Mixed.
75	When ready to serve pour over Eggs, hard-cooked, sliced	
		Serving: Approximately 6 oz.

NOTE: 1 qt. stock may be substituted for 1 qt. milk.

VARIATIONS: 1. **Curried Eggs.** Substitute chicken broth for milk and add 2 T. curry powder. May be served with steamed rice or chow mein noodles.

2. **Eggs à la King.** Substitute chicken stock for milk and add 1 lb. mushrooms that have been fried in the fat, 12 oz. shredded green peppers, and 8 oz. shredded pimiento.

3. **Scotch Woodcock.** Add 1 lb. sharp cheese to white sauce and blend. Cut eggs in half lengthwise and place in pans. Pour sauce over eggs. Cover with buttered crumbs. Bake until heated through and crumbs are brown.

4. **Goldenrod Eggs.** Reserve 25 egg yolks to mash or rice, and sprinkle over top of creamed eggs.

Egg Cutlets

Amount	Ingredient	Method

12 oz.
    10 oz.
    3 T.
2 qt.
	Butter or margarine
	Flour
	Salt
	Milk
		} Make a Very Thick
		    White Sauce (p. 295).

48	Add sauce to
	Eggs, hard-cooked, coarsely ground
	    Mix well. Measure cutlets with No. 12 dipper. Cool 3 hr.
	    or longer. Shape and bread.	

Fry in deep fat approximately 3 min. at 370° F.   Serving: 1 3-oz. cutlet.

NOTE: May be served with Mushroom Sauce (p. 296) or Creamed Ham (p. 202).

Deviled Eggs

AMOUNT	INGREDIENT	METHOD
50	Eggs, hard-cooked	} Peel and cut in half lengthwise. Remove yolks and mash thoroughly.
	Add	
½ c.	Milk, hot	} Mix.
	Add	
1½ c.	Mayonnaise or cooked dressing	
1 T.	Salt	} Mix thoroughly.
¾ T.	Mustard, dry	
½ c.	Vinegar	

Refill whites with mixture, using approximately 1½ T. filling for each half of egg white.

NOTES: 1. Pastry bag may be used to fill egg whites.
2. 6 oz. finely chopped celery or pimientos may be added to yolk mixture.

Hot Stuffed Eggs

AMOUNT	INGREDIENT	METHOD
50	Eggs, hard-cooked	} Cut eggs lengthwise and remove yolks.
	To mashed yolks, add	
3 oz.	Butter or margarine, melted	
2 t.	Salt	} Mix thoroughly and refill the whites. Arrange in baking pans.
⅛ t.	Cayenne	
1 T.	Mustard, prepared	
1 lb.	Ham, minced	
	Pour over eggs	
1 gal.	White Sauce, Medium (p. 295).	
	Sprinkle over the top	
¼ c.	Parsley, chopped	

Bake 30 min. at 325° F.

NOTE: May be served on toast or en casserole. Tuna may be substituted for ham.

Egg and Noodle Casserole

Amount		Ingredient	Method
4 lb.		Noodles } Cook (p. 229). Drain. Place in 2 oiled baking pans	
		Add ½ following mixture:	
1 lb.	4 oz.	Butter or margarine ⎫	
1 lb.	2 oz.	Flour	
1 gal.		Milk	
	1½ T.	Salt ⎬ Made as Cheese Sauce (p. 296).	
	1 t.	Pepper	
4 lb.		Cheese, Cheddar, grated ⎭	
50		Place in a layer over noodles. Eggs, deviled (p. 225), omitting vinegar. Cover with remaining cheese sauce and sprinkle with buttered crumbs.	

Bake approximately 20 min. at 350° F.   Serving: Approximately 5 oz.

Baked Eggs and Bacon Rings

Amount		Ingredient	Method
50		Eggs ⎫	Arrange bacon around inside of 50 baking cups (or muffin tins), fat side up.
2 lb.	8 oz. (approximately)	Bacon, sliced ⎬	
		Place bacon in hot oven until fat is clear. Remove from oven. In each cup place 1 egg. Return to oven.	

Bake approximately 25 min. at 350° F., or until firm.   Serving: 1 egg, with bacon.

VARIATION: **Oven-cooked Bacon.** Lay strips of bacon on bun pans or skillets. Bake at 400–425° F., without turning. Remove from oven when bacon is crisp. Drain on paper towels.

Baked Eggs with Cheese

Amount		Ingredient	Method
50		Eggs	⎱ Break and drop into oiled muffin tins ⎰ or custard cups.
			On top of each egg, place, in order given, the following,
	4 t.	Salt	
1 lb.	8 oz.	Cheese, grated or ground	
	6½ c.	Cream or Thin White Sauce (p. 295)	
	8 oz.	Crumbs, buttered	
			Set cups in pan of hot water.

Bake approximately 25 min. at 350° F., or until firm.   Serving: 1 egg.

Note: 1 thin slice raw tomato may be placed in bottom of each cup.

● MISCELLANEOUS DISHES

Rice

Amount		Ingredient	Method
1 gal.		Water, boiling	Pour boiling salted water over rice and fat or oil. Stir and cover tightly. Cook according to preferred method:
		Add	
	2 T.	Salt	
	¼ c.	Fat or oil	*Top-of-range method.* Cook over low heat approximately 15 min.
3 lb.	8 oz.	Rice	
			Steamer method. Pour ingredients in 2 12 x 20-in. counter pans. Steam at 5-lb. pressure approximately 25 min.
			Oven method. Pour ingredients into shallow pans. Cover with tight lid or aluminum foil and cook 25-30 min. at 350° F.
			Remove from heat and let stand covered 5–10 min.
			Yield: Approximately 7 qt. cooked rice.

Notes: 1. Addition of fat or oil is optional. It tends to prevent foaming.
    2. 1 lb. uncooked rice yields approximately 2 qt. cooked rice.

Variations of Plain Rice

Green Rice: Cook 3 lb. rice. Add 6 lb. finely chopped raw spinach, 3 T. onion juice, and 2 qt. Medium White Sauce (p. 295). Bake 30–40 min. at 325° F.

Fried Rice with Almonds: Cook together for 5 min. 4 oz. chopped onion and 4 oz. chopped green pepper in 1 c. salad oil. Add 6 qt. cooked rice (3 lb. before cooking), 1 T. pepper, 1 t. garlic salt, salt to taste, ½ c. soy sauce, 2 lb. blanched slivered almonds. Mix and bake until thoroughly heated.

Curried Rice: Cook 12 oz. minced onion in 12 oz. butter or margarine. Add 4 lb. rice and stir until fat is absorbed. Add 3–4 T. curry powder, 2 T. salt, and 4 qt. boiling water. Boil 10 min. Add 3 qt. hot milk and cook over water until rice is tender. Serve with Veal Stew (p. 164), Creamed Chicken (p. 186), Creamed Eggs (p. 224), or Creamed Tuna (p. 217).

Rice Croquettes

Amount		Ingredient	Method
3 lb.		Rice	} Wash with cold water.
		Add to	
3 qt.		Milk, hot	
2 qt.		Water, hot	} Cook until tender.
	2 oz.	Salt	
		Add	
18		Eggs, beaten	} Cook until eggs are done.
	2 oz.	Fat	
		Measure with No. 12 dipper. Cool 2 hr. Shape. Egg and crumb.	

Fry in deep fat approximately 3–4 min. at 375° F.   Serving: 1 croquette.

Note: Serve with Cheese Sauce (p. 296), Creamed Ham (p. 202), or Creamed Chicken (p. 186).

Spanish Rice

Amount		Ingredient	Method
2 lb.	4 oz.	Rice	} Cook (p. 227).
		Add	
1 gal.		Tomatoes	
1 lb.	4 oz.	Green pepper, chopped	
	2½ oz.	Pimiento, chopped	
	3 T.	Salt	
		Add	
1 lb.	4 oz.	Bacon, chopped	} Sautéed together.
1 lb.		Onion, chopped	
		Pour into oiled pan 12 x 20 in.	

Bake 1 hr. at 350° F. Serving: 5 oz.

NOTE: May omit bacon and green pepper and add 5 lb. beef, ground.

Spaghetti

Amount		Ingredient	Method
3 gal.		Water	} Heat to boiling point.
	¼ c.	Salt	
		Add	
4 lb.		Spaghetti	
		Reheat to boiling temperature. Cook approximately 20 min. or until tender, stirring occasionally. Drain. Rinse with hot water to remove excess starch.	
			Serving: 5 oz.

NOTES: 1. To cook in steamer, place 2 lb. spaghetti in each of 2 counter pans or solid steamer pans. Add 1½ gal. hot water, 2 T. salt, and 2 T. oil to each.
2. Addition of oil is optional. It tends to prevent foaming.
3. 1 lb. uncooked spaghetti yields 2½ qt. cooked spaghetti.

VARIATIONS. 1. **Macaroni.** Proceed as for spaghetti. Allow 4 lb. for 50 5-oz. servings.
2. **Noodles.** Proceed as for spaghetti. Allow 5 lb. noodles for 50 5-oz. servings.

Noodle Ring

Amount		Ingredient	Method
1 lb.	12 oz.	Noodles	
6 qt.		Water or broth	Cook until tender. Drain and wash.
	2 T.	Salt	
		Add and mix	
	8 oz.	Bread, soft crumbs	
	4 oz.	Onion	
	2 oz.	Green pepper	Chopped fine.
	3 oz.	Pimiento	
	2 t.	Parsley	
12		Eggs, beaten	
1 qt.		Milk	
	1 t.	Paprika	
		Pour into oiled molds (50 individual or 4 large). Place molds in pan of hot water.	

Bake 30 min. at 350° F.

Note: Fill baked rings with creamed chicken or ham.
Variations: 1. **Rice Ring.** Substitute 1 lb. of rice for noodles.
2. **Noodle Casserole.** Cook noodles in chicken broth. Add 5 lb. large-curd cottage cheese, 4 oz. grated onion, ⅓ c. Worcestershire sauce, 2½ c. dry bread crumbs, 1 T. salt, and 1½ qt. cultured sour cream. Place in oiled pan, cover with 2½ c. grated Parmesan cheese, and bake 30–35 min. at 350° F.
3. **Poppy Seed Noodles.** To 5 lb. noodles, cooked, add 1 lb. butter or margarine, melted, ½ cup poppy seeds, and 1 lb. chopped toasted almonds. Mix lightly.

Spoon Bread

Amount		Ingredient	Method
5¾ qt.		Milk	} Scald.
		Add	
1 lb.	12 oz.	Corn meal	
	3 T.	Salt	} Mix and cook approximately 10 min.
		Add slowly	
25		Eggs, beaten	
	6 oz.	Fat, melted	
	2 oz.	Baking powder	
		Pour into 2 oiled pans 12 x 20 in., or 8 casseroles (1¾ lb. to each). Place in pans of hot water.	

Bake 1 hr. at 350° F.   Serving: 4½ oz.

Note: Serve with crisp bacon, Creamed Chicken (p. 186), or Creamed Ham (p. 202).

Mushroom Puff

Amount		Ingredient	Method
1 lb.	8 oz.	Mushrooms, chopped	
	4 oz.	Onions, chopped	Sauté.
	12 oz.	Butter or margarine	
		Add	
	2 oz.	Flour	
	1½ T.	Salt	Made as Very Thick
	½ T.	Pepper	White Sauce (p. 295).
	¾ c.	Milk	
50		Place No. 24 dipper of mixture on each of Bread triangles arranged in baking pan Cover each piece with another triangle.	
		Pour over bread the following mixture	
6 qt.		Milk	
25		Eggs, beaten	
	1½ T.	Salt	

Bake 45 min. at 300° F.   Serving: 5 oz.

VARIATION: **Cheese Puff.** Make sandwiches with bread and cheese slices. Place in baking pan and cover with egg and milk mixture. Bake 40 min. at 325° F. Serve with jelly.

Fritters

Amount		Ingredient	Method
4 lb.		Flour	
	1 T.	Salt	
	4 oz.	Baking powder	Sift together.
	2 oz.	Sugar	
		Add	
	12	Eggs, beaten	
2 qt.		Milk	Mixed.
	6 oz.	Fat, melted	
		Mix, measure with No. 24 dipper (scant).	

Fry in deep fat approximately 2–5 min. at 375° F.   Serving: 2 fritters.

VARIATIONS: 1. **Apple Fritters.** Add 1 lb. raw apple, peeled and finely chopped.
             2. **Corn Fritters.** Add 2 qt. corn, drained.
             3. **Fruit Fritters.** Add 1 qt. fruit: banana, peach, or pineapple.

Hot Potato Salad

AMOUNT	INGREDIENT	METHOD
1 lb.	Bacon	} Dice and fry. Drain.
1½ qt.	Add Mayonnaise	
15 lb. (E.P.)	Add Potatoes	} Diced and steamed until tender.
3 oz. 6 oz. 16	Add Onion Green pepper, chopped Eggs, hard-cooked Combine all ingredients just before serving.	
		Serving: Approximately 6 oz.

NOTES: 1. Bacon may be omitted.
   2. Hot Vegetable Sauce (p. 292) may be substituted for mayonnaise.

Corn Rarebit

AMOUNT	INGREDIENT	METHOD
4 oz. 6 oz.	Onions Fat	} Brown onions in fat.
1 qt.	Add Milk	} Heat to boiling point.
	Add gradually, stirring constantly	
1 pt. 6 oz. 2 T. f.g.	Milk Flour Salt Cayenne	} Blended.
1 lb. 8 oz. 3 oz.	Add Cheese, sharp, ground Green pepper, chopped	} Cook over water until cheese is melted.
1 No. 10 can	Add Corn (whole grain) hot, drained Measure with No. 8 dipper. Serve immediately on split toasted buns.	
		Serving: 3½ oz.

VARIATION: **Hot Corn Sandwich.** Substitute 1 qt. tomato purée for milk and pimiento for green pepper. To hot cheese-corn mixture, add 2 c. beaten egg yolks. Continue cooking, stirring constantly, until yolks are cooked. Serve immediately on split toasted buns.

Baked Beans

Amount	Ingredient	Method
5 lb. 1½ gal.	Beans, navy Water, boiling	Wash beans. Add boiling water and let stand 1 hr. or longer. Cook in same water until tender (about 1 hr.).
	Add	
4 oz.	Salt	
6 oz.	Sugar, brown	
1 t.	Mustard, dry	
2 T.	Vinegar	
8 oz.	Molasses	
2½ c.	Catsup (optional)	
1 lb.	Salt pork, cubed	
	Pour into baking pan.	

Bake 5–6 hr. at 350° F. Serving: Approximately 5 oz.

NOTE: If necessary more hot water may be added to beans while cooking.
VARIATION: **Boston Baked Beans.** Omit catsup and bake in oven the entire cooking time.

Baked Lima Beans

Amount		Ingredient	Method
6 lb. 1 gal.		Beans, lima Water, boiling	Wash beans. Add boiling water. Cover and let stand 1 hr. or longer. Cook beans in same water until tender (about 1 hr.).
		Add to beans	
4 oz.		Pimiento, chopped	
8 oz.		Fat, bacon	Mixed.
1½ T.		Salt	
1 c.		Molasses	
		Pour beans into a baking pan.	
		Place on top of beans	
1 lb.	8 oz.	Salt pork, sliced	
		Bake until tender and brown.	

Bake approximately 2 hr. at 350° F. Serving: Approximately 5 oz.

VARIATIONS: 1. **Baked Lima Beans with Sausage.** Omit salt pork and bacon fat. Place 6 lb. link sausages on top of beans.
2. **Boiled Lima Beans and Ham.** Omit salt pork and seasonings. Add 5 lb. cured ham, diced, to beans and simmer until tender.

Ranch Style Beans

Amount	Ingredient	Method
5 lb.	Beans, red	Soak beans overnight; drain off water.
	Add	
	Water, cold, to cover	
2 lb. 8 oz.	Salt pork, 1-in. cubes	Cook slowly until tender.
	Add and continue cooking	
2 qt.	Tomatoes, cooked	
8 oz.	Onions, sliced	
1½ T.	Salt	
1 T.	Pepper	
f.g.	Cayenne	
2 buttons	Garlic, chopped	
	Add	
3–4 pods	Chili pepper	Soaked in warm water and pulp removed from pods.

Cook additional 5 hr., or bake 6–8 hr. at 300° F.   Serving: Approximately 5 oz.

Note: If chili peppers are not available, 1 oz. chili powder may be used.

salads

● SELECTION OF SALAD INGREDIENTS

Salad ingredients must be clean, fresh, tender, chilled, and crisp. They must form simple and palatable combinations harmonizing in flavor and color with the food they accompany. Salads should be colorful and should offer a contrast in texture with the food they accompany.

● PREPARATION OF SALAD INGREDIENTS

Fresh Fruit

Apples. Wash, pare, core, remove bruises and spots. If the skins are tender and the desired color, do not pare.

To dice, cut into rings and dice with sectional cutter. Drop diced pieces into salad dressing, lemon, pineapple, or other acid fruit juice to prevent discoloration. If diced apple is placed in fruit juice, drain before using in a salad.

To section, cut into uniform pieces, so the widest part of the section is not more than ½ in. thick. Remove core from each section. If the peeling has not been removed, score it in several places to facilitate cutting when it is served. Prevent discoloration by the same method as for diced apples, only do not use salad dressing.

Apricots. Cut into halves or sections and remove seed. Remove skins if desired.

Avocados. If hard, ripen at room temperature. Peel, cut into halves or quarters, and remove seed. Slice, dice, or cut into balls. Dip into French dressing or lemon juice to prevent discoloration. Peel shortly before serving.

Bananas. Remove skins and soft or discolored parts. Cut into strips, sections, wedges, or slices. Dip each piece into pineapple, other acid fruit juice, or salad dressing to prevent discoloration.

Cantaloupes and Other Melons. Pare, dice, cut into balls with a French vegetable cutter, or cut into uniform wedges or strips.

Cherries and Grapes. Wash, drain, halve, and remove seeds. To frost, brush with slightly beaten egg white. Sprinkle with sugar. Let dry before using.

Grapefruit. For sections, select large grapefruit, wash and dry. Cut off a thick layer of skin from the top and bottom. Place grapefruit on cutting board, start at the top, and cut toward the board. Always cut with a downward stroke and deeply enough to remove all the white membrane. Turn grapefruit with the left hand. When paring is completed and pulp is exposed, remove sections by cutting along the membrane of one section to the center of the fruit. Turn the knife and force the blade along the membrane of the next section to the exterior of the fruit. Repeat for each section.

Oranges. Pare, section as grapefruit, or slice or dice.

Peaches. Peel or submerge in boiling water for a few minutes and remove skins. Chill. Cut into halves, wedges, or slices. Remove skins only a short time before using. Drop into acid fruit juice to prevent discoloration.

Pears. Pare and remove core and seeds a short time before serving. Cut into halves, wedges, or slices.

Pineapple. Cut off top; pare and cut out eyes. Cut into 4 sections. Remove hard center and cut sections into ¼-in. pieces or into cubes. Sprinkle with sugar. Let stand overnight or at least a few hours before using.

Canned Fruit

Select whole pieces uniform in size and shape and with a firm appearance. Drain. If cubes or sections are desired, cut into pieces uniform in size and shape with well-defined edges. Pieces should not be too small.

Dried Fruit

Prunes. Use size 20–30. Wash, add to hot water, and simmer until tender. Remove seeds. Chill before stuffing.

Raisins. Add hot water and let stand until cool. Wash, drain well. Add to salad ingredients or dressing.

Gelatin Salads (See pp. 249–253).

Meat, Fish, Chicken, Eggs, Cheese, and Nuts

Meat. Cut cooked meat into ⅓-in. cubes. Mix just before serving.

Fish. Cook, remove skin and bones. Flake.

Chicken. Cook, remove skin, gristle, and bone. Cut into ⅓-in. cubes. Mix with dressing and other ingredients just before serving.

Eggs. Hard-cook (p. 221). Use whole, halved, sliced, or sectioned. Slice or mince whites. Force yolks through ricer.

Cheese. Grate, cut in tiny cubes, or put through a ricer or pastry tube.

Nuts. Heat in hot oven to freshen if desired. Use whole, shredded, or chopped. To blanch almonds, shell, cover with boiling water, and let stand until skins will slip. Drain. Cover with cold water and rub off skins. Place skinned almonds between dry clean towels to remove water. Toast blanched nuts in oven or prepare as for salted nuts.

Vegetables

Whether used raw or cooked, strive to preserve shape, color, flavor, and crispness of vegetables.

Asparagus. Cook and marinate tips.

Beans, dry. Soak, cook, keep whole.

Beans, green. Leave whole or cut lengthwise. Wash, cook, and marinate.

Beets. Wash, cook, peel, remove any blemishes. Cut into desired shape and marinate.

Cabbage. Remove outer leaves. Wash heads, cut into 4–6 pieces. Remove center stalk. Shred remaining portions as desired with a long sharp knife or shredder. Crisp in ice water 15–30 min.

Carrots. Pare and remove blemishes. Cut into wedges, rounds, or strips. Grind, shred, or cook; then cut into desired shapes and marinate. For carrot curls, see Relishes, p. 237.

Cauliflower. Remove all leaves and cut away dark spots. Separate into flowerets, leaving 1 in. stem. Soak in salt water (1 oz. salt or ⅓ c. vinegar per gal.). Cauliflower may be cooked and marinated, or it may be marinated and served raw.

Celery. Separate outer stalks from heart. (Outer stalks may be used for soup.) Wash, trim, and remove strings, bruised, and blemished parts. To dice, cut lengthwise. Several stalks may be cut at one time. Place on a board and cut crosswise with a French knife. For celery curls, see p. 237.

Celery Cabbage. Remove outer leaves and wash. Shred as lettuce or cut into 1–2-in. slices.

Chives. Remove roots and any objectionable portions. Wash. Drain. Cut leaves crosswise with a sharp knife or scissors.

Cucumbers. Wash and pare, or score lengthwise with a fork. Crisp and let stand in salted ice water 15 min. Cut into slices or wedges.

Green Peppers. Wash, remove seeds and stems. Cut into rings or strips; dice or chop.

Onions. Pour water over onions to cover. Under water, remove wilted leaves, outer layer of the bulb, firm root end, and all bruised or decayed parts. Cut as desired.

Peas. Shell. Cook and marinate. Drain before using.

Potatoes. Pare in electric peeler. Remove remaining skin, eyes, and bruised parts by hand. Cut into ½-in. cubes and cook; or wash, cook with skins on, peel, and dice. Marinate 2 hr. before using.

Tomatoes. Wash and peel. If skins are difficult to remove, place in a wire basket and dip in boiling water until the skins begin to loosen. Then dip in cold water and remove skins. Chill.

Turnips. Remove tops, wash, pare by hand. Shred or cut into fine strips.

Relishes

Carrot Curls. Cut long, paper-thin slices. Roll each strip around finger, fasten with toothpick, and chill in ice water for several hours.

Carrot Sticks. Cut carrots into thin strips. Chill in ice water for several hours.

Celery Curls or Fans. Cut celery into 2½-in. lengths. Make lengthwise cuts ⅛ in. apart and about 1 in. in length on one or both ends of celery strips. Place in ice water about 2 hr. before serving.

Celery Rings. Cut celery into 2-in. lengths and then into pieces ⅛ in. thick. Place in ice water for several hours. Each strip of celery will form a ring.

Green Pepper Rings. Remove stem and seeds. Cut into thin slices.

Green Pepper Sticks. Cut pepper lengthwise into narrow strips.

Radish Roses. Cut off root end of radish with sharp knife. Leave an inch or two of the green stem. Cut 4 or 5 petal-shaped slices around the radish from cut tip to center. Place radishes in ice water, and petals will open.

Radish Accordions. Cut long radishes not quite through into 10 to 12 narrow slices. Place in ice water. Slices will fan out accordion-style.

Salad Greens

Chicory. See Endive.

Endive. Wash, remove objectionable portions. Drain, place in plastic bag, and refrigerate.

Escarole. See Endive.

Head Lettuce. Remove ragged and objectionable leaves from head. For a garnish, cut out stem end or core. Hold inverted head under running cold water until the leaves are loosened. Turn heads right side up to drain. Separate the leaves, and stack 6 or 7 leaves in a nest. Invert the nest and pack in a covered container or plastic bag. Place in refrigerator 2 hr. or more to complete crisping.

Leaf Lettuce. Wash, drain, place in plastic bag and refrigerate.

Romaine. See Leaf Lettuce.

Spinach. Remove tough stems. Examine leaves and discard all dry, yellow, wilted, or slimy leaves. Wash first in warm, then in cold water, as many times as necessary to remove sand. Crisp and use as a salad green.

Watercress. See Endive.

● MAKING THE SALAD

1. Use only clean, cold, and crisp salad greens. Vegetables most often used for salad garnish are head lettuce, leaf lettuce, endive, chicory, escarole, parsley, romaine, spinach, and watercress. Red and green cabbage, celery, celery cabbage, carrot, and green pepper may also be used in salad green mixtures.

2. Cut fruits and vegetables into generous wedges, slices, or cubes for an attractive salad.

3. Drain fruit or any ingredients surrounded by liquid.

4. Marinate, when desired, each ingredient separately with a well-seasoned French dressing.

5. Drain and toss ingredients lightly together, if a mixed salad. Place on individual chilled salad plates or bowls.

6. Set up salads as follows:

(*a*) Arrange chilled plates on large trays or in rows on the table. Select china, if possible, that will add to the attractiveness of the salad.

(*b*) Place salad green on plates. Place a lettuce cup so that the frilly edge is at the back and top of the salad. The leaf should not extend over the edge of the plate.

(*c*) Build from the back to the front, with the salad green as a base. To give height, chopped lettuce may be placed in the lettuce cup under such salad ingredients as fruit or vegetable slices, asparagus tips, or gelatin ring molds.

(*d*) Top salad lightly with some material that will give accent in color and flavor, if desired.

(*e*) Select a dressing that will enhance the flavor of the salad ingredients. Add salad dressing just before serving, or pass for individual service. For a green salad, add only enough dressing to flavor.

● SERVING THE SALAD

Salads may be used:

1. As a first course in a dinner menu: fruit or sea food.

2. As a main course of a luncheon: meat, fish, poultry, cheese.

3. As an accompaniment to the main course of a dinner or luncheon: salad greens with vegetables, fruit, or combination.

4. As a second course in a dinner menu: fruit or vegetable.

Accompaniments for Salads Used as a Separate Course

1. *Breads:*

Hot breads, buttered: biscuits, rolls, muffins.

Crisp breads: bread sticks, cracker, Melba toast, hard rolls.

Sandwiches (small): rolled, ribbon, or open face; banana, date, nut, or orange bread.

2. *Cheese:*

Cream cheese balls, plain or rolled in nuts or parsley.

Toasted cheese crackers, cheese straws.

3. *Miscellaneous Crisp Materials:*

Celery curls, celery hearts, stuffed celery, or radish roses.

Olives, plain, stuffed, or ripe.

Pickles, sweet, sour, dill, burr gherkins, fans, rounds.

Potatoes, chips or latticed, shoestring.

Salted nuts.

● FRUIT SALADS

Apple-Celery Salad

Amount	Ingredient	Method
1 pt.	Mayonnaise or Cooked Salad Dressing (p. 263).	} Mix.
½ c.	Whipped cream (may omit)	
	Add	
8 lb. (E.P.)	Apples, tart (unpeeled)	} Dice. Add each apple to dressing as soon as diced.
	Add	
2 lb. (E.P.)	Celery, chopped	
1½ T.	Salt	
6 oz.	Sugar (may omit)	
	Serve with No. 12 dipper.	
		Serving: ⅓ c.

Note: Add 8 oz. of cut marshmallows to dressing for additional flavor.

Variations: 1. **Waldorf Salad.** Add 8 oz. chopped walnuts just before serving.
2. **Apple-Fruit Salad.** Use 3 lb. diced apples. Add 3 lb. cubed pineapple and 2 lb. cubed oranges, sliced peaches, or grapes.
3. **Apple-Date Salad.** Substitute 2 lb. cut dates for celery.
4. **Apple-Carrot Salad.** 6 lb. diced apples, 3 lb. shredded carrots, and only 1 lb. chopped celery.
5. **Apple-Cabbage Salad.** 6 lb. diced apples and 4 lb. crisp shredded cabbage. Omit celery.

Spiced Apple Salad

Amount	Ingredient	Method
50 (approximately 12 lb.)	Apples	} Core and peel apples and leave whole.
		Place apples in a flat pan. Pour over them a thin sirup made from
6 lb.	Sugar	
2 qt.	Water	
1 c.	Vinegar	
½ t.	Coloring, red	
1 oz.	Cinnamon (tied in a bag) or a few drops of oil of cinnamon	
1 oz.	Cloves, whole	
	Cook on top of range; turn while cooking.	
		Serving: 4 oz.

Note: When cool, fill centers of apples with a mixture of 8 oz. celery, 4 oz. English walnuts, ½ t. salt, and 6 oz. mayonnaise; or with a mixture of cream cheese and chopped pecans.

Fruit Salad

Amount	Ingredient	Method
6 lb.	Pineapple, cubed	
2 lb.	Cherries, Royal Anne, seeded	
6 lb.	Peaches, cubed	
12	Oranges, diced	
	Combine with as few motions as possible. Serve with No. 12 dipper.	
		Serving: ⅓ c.

NOTE: Drain all fruit well. Other fruit combinations may be used (see pp. 242–243).

Grapefruit-Orange Salad

Amount	Ingredient	Method
16 (size 40)	Grapefruit	Pare. Remove white membrane. Cut into sections.
17 (size 56)	Oranges	Pare. Remove white membrane. Cut into 6 uniform sections.
	For each salad use 2 sections of orange and 3 sections of grapefruit arranged alternately on garnish.	

NOTE: For other citrus fruit combinations, (see pp. 242–243).

Frozen Fruit Salad

Amount		Ingredient	Method
	1 oz.	Gelatin, plain	Sprinkle gelatin over water. Soak 10 min.
	½ c.	Water, cold	
		Add	
	1¾ c.	Orange juice, hot	
	1¾ c.	Pineapple juice, hot	
		When cold and slightly congealed, add	
	1 c.	Mayonnaise (p. 261).	Folded together.
	1 pt.	Cream, whipped	
		Fold in	
1 lb.	12 oz.	Pineapple, canned, diced, drained	
1 lb.	8 oz.	Orange sections, cut in halves	
1 lb.	8 oz.	Peaches, sliced, drained	
2 lb.		Bananas, diced	
	8 oz.	Marshmallows, diced	
	12 oz.	Pecans, chopped	
	8 oz.	Cherries, Maraschino	
		Pour into molds and freeze.	Yield: 4½ qt.

Fruit Salad Combinations[1]

1. Apples, celery, Malaga grapes. Chantilly Dressing.
2. Apples, pineapple, cucumber, or celery. Pimiento garnish. Mayonnaise Dressing.
3. Apples, grapes, bananas, pineapple. Fruit Dressing.
4. Apples, bananas, pineapple. Mayonnaise Dressing.
5. Apples, celery, dates. Combination Dressing.
6. Apples, pineapple, Tokay grapes. Chantilly Dressing.
7. Apples, grapes, bananas, pineapple, oranges, lemon juice. Chantilly Dressing.
8. Apples, oranges, dates, marshmallows. Combination Dressing.
9. Apples, celery, grapefruit. Mayonnaise Dressing.
10. Apple wedges, orange slices, pineapple, sliced strawberries. Celery Seed Dressing.
11. Apple, orange, and pear sections arranged alternately. French Dressing.
12. Apple, orange, and pear mixed with Mayonnaise.
13. Avocado half, filled with Waldorf Salad or Tomato Aspic.
14. Red-skin apple wedges, grapefruit or orange sections, and avocado arranged alternately on leaf lettuce. Thick French Dressing.
15. Waldorf salad served on a slice of pineapple, garnished with Maraschino cherry and sprig of parsley.
16. Bananas, grapes, pineapple chunks, marshmallows. Fruit Dressing.
17. Cubed bananas, tangerines, pineapple. Whipped Cream Dressing.
18. Diced banana, pineapple chunks, pear, and peach. Whipped Cream Dressing.
19. Banana sliced lengthwise, orange, and grapefruit sections. Celery Seed Dressing.
20. Banana and orange sections arranged alternately on Bibb lettuce. French Dressing.
21. Banana cut in thirds crosswise and lengthwise, rolled in thin cooked dressing and chopped nuts or cornflakes. Arrange with thin slices of orange.
22. Layer of sliced bananas marinated, topped with apricot half, on shredded lettuce. Whipped Cream Dressing.
23. Grapefruit sections arranged alternately with orange or apple sections. French Dressing.
24. Grapefruit sections arranged alternately with tomato sections and ½ slice pineapple. French Dressing.
25. Grapefruit sections arranged on watercress like spokes of a wheel with 4 shrimp or stuffed prune in the center. Mayonnaise and paprika garnish.
26. Grapefruit, orange, and pear sections, with strips of red and green pepper placed alternately between slices of fruit. Poppy Seed Dressing.
27. Grapefruit, fresh pear, and orange sections arranged on lettuce, radiating from center; cream cheese in center, topped with cherry. French Dressing.
28. Five grapefruit sections arranged on endive and garnished with pomegranate seeds. Celery Seed Dressing.
29. Three sections of grapefruit and orange placed on a lettuce leaf, garnished with avocado. Poppy Seed Dressing.
30. Grapefruit sections and avocado wedges, garnished with fresh strawberries. French Dressing.

[1] See pp. 261 to 267 for Salad Dressing recipes.

31. Cantaloupe circles filled with cottage or whipped cream cheese, garnished with fresh red raspberries. French Dressing.

32. Honeydew cantaloupe wedges garnished with watermelon balls. Honey-Fruit Dressing.

33. Cranshaw honeydew on fresh pineapple slice, garnished with watercress. Poppy Seed Dressing.

34. Casaba spear, orange slices, garnished with small cluster of grapes. French Dressing.

35. Orange slices, Bermuda onion rings, cream cheese balls rolled in chopped nuts. French Dressing.

36. Orange, grapefruit, celery, nuts, peach slices. Mayonnaise.

37. Orange and avocado sections, halves of Ribier grapes. French Dressing.

38. Diced orange sections, peaches, pears, pineapple, and pistachio nuts. Whipped Cream Dressing.

39. Orange and pineapple cubes mixed with Mayonnaise and chopped nuts on a lettuce leaf, garnished with alternate sections of orange, avocado, and grapefruit.

40. Thin orange slices on shredded lettuce, garnished with stuffed fig. Mayonnaise Dressing.

41. Three orange sections and 2 half slices of pineapple arranged alternately and sprinkled with minced green pepper. French Dressing.

42. Orange sections arranged on bed of lettuce like spokes of wheel, with ripe olive or cream cheese ball in center. French Dressing.

43. Large cooked prunes stuffed with cream cheese or orange sections. Mayonnaise or Celery Seed Dressing.

44. Peach half stuffed with cream cheese balls, cottage cheese, chopped dates, stuffed prunes, Waldorf Salad, or toasted slivered almonds.

45. Peach half, filled with blueberries, garnished with mint sprig. French Dressing.

46. Peach slices alternated with other fruit slices or wedges. French Dressing.

47. Pear stuffed with cream cheese, cottage cheese, Cheddar, or shredded cheese.

48. Spiced canned pear halves substituted for pear halves in salads.

49. Pear half on orange slice, topped with lime gelatin and Maraschino cherry.

50. Pear half stuffed with diced apple and celery mixed with Whipped Cream Dressing.

51. Diced pear, pineapple, and apricots mixed with Whipped Cream Dressing.

52. Pear half, with frosted blueberries in center, fresh plum-slice garnish.

53. Pear half, round side up, sprinkled lightly with granulated red gelatin.

54. Diced pineapple, marshmallows, white grapes, and nuts. Fruit Dressing.

55. Diced pineapple, celery, almonds. Mayonnaise Dressing.

56. Diced pineapple, celery, white grapes. Whipped Cream Dressing.

57. Eight strips of dates, radiating from center of slice of pineapple.

58. Pineapple slice with cream cheese ball in center. French Dressing.

59. Pineapple slice topped with small, quartered, ripe tomato. Cream Cheese Dressing.

60. Two sections of orange and 2 of pear arranged on slice of pineapple, garnished with cream cheese rosettes.

61. Four slices of banana arranged around pineapple slice, garnished with black cherry halves. Chantilly Dressing.

62. A pineapple slice, orange slice, and apricot half arranged in pyramid style, garnished with Maraschino cherry. Celery Seed Dressing.

63. Fresh pineapple, honeydew, and cantaloupe wedges, garnished with whole fresh strawberries. Celery Seed Dressing.

64. Fresh pineapple and banana wedges, tangerine sections, garnished with black cherries. Honey-Orange Fruit Dressing.

● VEGETABLE SALADS

Tossed Green Salad

AMOUNT	INGREDIENT	METHOD
6 lb.	Head lettuce	Break or cut into pieces.
3 lb.	Leaf lettuce or Bibb lettuce	
	Endive, spinach, or chicory	
1¼ qt.	Just before serving, toss lightly with French Dressing (p. 264).	
		Serving: 1 c.

NOTE: Any combination of salad greens may be used. Serve in individual salad bowls.

Variations of Tossed Green Salad

Green Salad Bowl. Add 4 sliced cucumbers, 3 bunches sliced radishes to 7 lb. of Tossed Green Salad. Garnish with 6 lb. tomato wedges, 2 wedges per salad. Serve with French, Roquefort, or Thousand Island Dressing.

Combination Fresh Vegetable Salad. To 5 lb. Tossed Green Salad, add 1 lb. cauliflowerets; 3 bunches radishes and 2 cucumbers, sliced; 2 lb. red cabbage, shredded; 1 lb. celery, 4 oz. green peppers, and 1 lb. celery cabbage, coarsely chopped. Serve with French, Roquefort, or Thousand Island Dressing.

Salad Greens with Grapefruit. Serve 8 lb. Tossed Green Salad in individual bowls. Garnish each with 3 sections pink grapefruit. Serve with Poppy Seed or French Dressing.

Hawaiian Tossed Salad. To 8 lb. Tossed Green Salad, add sections from 8 grapefruit, 8 oranges, 4 avocados, and 1 fresh pineapple, cubed. Serve with Honey-Orange Dressing.

Chef's Salad Bowl. Place 6 lb. mixed salad greens in bowls. Arrange 6 lb. meat (turkey, tongue, ham) and 3 lb. Cheddar cheese, cut Julienne or in cubes, over top of salad. Garnish with green pepper ring, carrot curl, and tomato wedges. Serve with French or Roquefort Dressing.

Russian Salad. Mix 4 lb. head lettuce, 2 bunches sliced radishes, and 1 lb. crisp, clean spinach leaves broken into pieces. Fill individual salad bowls ⅔ full. Top each salad with 1 oz. ham or luncheon meat, 2 oz. turkey, and 1 oz. Cheddar cheese, cut into strips. Garnish with quarters of hard-cooked egg and tomato wedges. Serve with Thousand Island Dressing.

Head-lettuce Salad. 6 heads well-trimmed lettuce, cut into 8 wedges. Serve with Chiffonade, Thousand Island, or Garden Dressing.

Cabbage Salad

AMOUNT	INGREDIENT	METHOD
7 lb. (E.P.) 1 qt. 1½ T.	Cabbage, shredded Cooked Salad Dressing (p. 263) Salt Serve with No. 12 dipper.	} Combine.
		Serving: ⅓ c.

NOTE: Thin dressing with cream if too thick.

VARIATIONS: 1. **Cabbage-Apple Salad.** Use 4 lb. shredded cabbage. Add 3 lb. diced unpeeled red apples.

2. **Cabbage-Carrot Salad.** Substitute 2 lb. shredded carrots for 2 lb. shredded cabbage.

3. **Cabbage-Pineapple-Marshmallow Salad.** Add 2 lb. diced pineapple, 1 lb. diced marshmallows, 1 pt. whipped cream, and 1 pt. mayonnaise. Omit Cooked Salad Dressing.

4. **Cole Slaw.** Add 3 c. sugar and 3 c. vinegar mixed. Omit salad dressing. 1 T. celery seed may be added.

5. **Creamy Cole Slaw.** Use 2 c. mayonnaise, 2 c. sweet or sour cream, ½ c. vinegar, ½ c. sugar.

6. **Red Cabbage-Celery Salad.** Use 4 lb. shredded cabbage. Add 1 lb. diced celery and Sour Cream Dressing (p. 266). Omit Cooked Salad Dressing.

Carrot-Raisin Salad

AMOUNT	INGREDIENT	METHOD
6 lb. 8 oz. 8 oz. 1 T. 1 qt.	Carrots, coarsely ground or shredded Raisins Salt Mayonnaise Serve with No. 12 dipper.	} Combine.
		Serving: ⅓ c.

NOTE: Marinate 1 hr. before serving.

VARIATIONS: 1. **Carrot Coconut Salad.** 1 lb. toasted coconut may be substituted for raisins.

2. **Carrot-Celery Salad.** Omit raisins. Use 5 lb. ground carrots. Add 2 lb. chopped celery and 2 oz. sugar.

3. **Carrot-Celery-Apple Salad.** Substitute 3 lb. diced apples for 2 lb. ground or shredded carrots.

4. **Carrot-Celery-Cucumber Salad.** Use 4½ lb. shredded carrots, 1½ lb. chopped celery, and 1½ lb. chopped cucumbers.

Carrifruit Salad

Amount		Ingredient	Method
4 lb.	8 oz.	Carrots, shredded	
	9 oz.	Marshmallows, cut	
2 lb.	12 oz.	Pineapple tidbits, drained	Mix together lightly.
	8 oz.	Coconut, flaked	
		Add, mix carefully	
	2¼ c.	Mayonnaise	Blended.
	¾ c.	Cream	
		Serve with No. 12 dipper.	
			Serving: ⅓ c.

Stuffed Tomato Salad

Amount		Ingredient	Method
50 (approximately 12½ lb.)		Tomatoes	Peel tomatoes. Remove core and part of pulp from each.
		Add tomato pulp to	
1 lb.		Cabbage, chopped fine	
1 lb.		Celery, chopped fine	
	8 oz.	Pickle, sweet, chopped	Combined.
	8 oz.	Mayonnaise	
	1 T.	Salt	
		Sprinkle in the cavity of the tomatoes	
	1½ T.	Salt	
		Stuff each tomato with approximately 2 T. of vegetable mixture.	

NOTES: 1. Tomatoes may be cut into fourths to within ½ in. of bottoms. Spread apart. Sprinkle with salt and fill with salad mixture.
2. Fish, egg, or chicken salad may be substituted for vegetable mixture.
VARIATIONS: 1. **Tomato-Shrimp Salad.** Fill tomato cups with Shrimp Salad (p. 255). Omit lettuce.
2. **Tomato-Cottage Cheese Salad.** Substitute 6 lb. cottage cheese, seasoned, for vegetable mixture. Fill tomato cups with No. 20 dipper.

Sliced Cucumber and Onions in Sour Cream

Amount		Ingredient	Method
	3 c.	Sour cream, cultured	Blend well.
	3 c.	Mayonnaise	
	1½ t.	Salt	
	3 T.	Sugar	
	¾ c.	Vinegar	
		Add to	
4 lb.	4 oz.	Cucumbers, sliced	Mix lightly.
	9 oz.	Onions, sliced	
		Serve with a No. 16 dipper.	
			Serving: ⅓ c.

NOTE: Sour Cream Dressing (p. 266) may be served on lettuce.

Potato Salad

Amount		Ingredient	Method
15 lb. (E.P.)		Potatoes	Cook and dice.
		Marinate with	
	2 c.	Salad dressing, French	
	1½ T.	Salt, or more	
	½ c.	Vinegar, mild (optional)	
		Add	
12		Eggs, hard-cooked, diced	
	4 oz.	Peppers, green, chopped	
	6 oz.	Pimiento, chopped	
1 lb.		Celery, diced	
	2 c.	Mayonnaise	
	8 oz.	Onions, chopped	
	8 oz.	Pickles, chopped	
		Combine carefully. Serve with No. 10 dipper.	
			Serving: Approximately ½ c.

Brown Bean Salad

Amount		Ingredient	Method
2 No. 10 cans		Beans, brown or kidney	
		Add	
18		Eggs, hard-cooked, diced	
1 lb.		Pickles, minced	
	4 oz.	Onion, minced	
	½ c.	Vinegar	
	3 T.	Salt	
1 lb.	4 oz.	Celery, diced	
	4 oz.	Pepper, green, chopped	
1 qt.		Salad dressing	
		Marinate before serving. Serve with No. 12 dipper.	

Serving: ⅓ c.

NOTE: 4 lb. dried beans, cooked, may be substituted for canned beans.

Vegetable Salad Combinations[1]

1. Three asparagus tips through a ring of green pepper placed on a slice of tomato. Bibb lettuce garnish. Mayonnaise Dressing.
2. Asparagus tips on shredded lettuce, garnished with sliced hard-cooked egg and pimiento strip.
3. Cooked green beans mixed with diced marinated carrots, celery, parsley, and green pepper. Combination Dressing.
4. Cooked green beans mixed with chopped small green onions and thinly sliced radishes. Thick French Dressing.
5. Cooked green beans, peas, lima beans, cauliflower and carrot strips, marinated. Chiffonade Dressing.
6. Marinated whole green beans, garnished with pimiento strips. French Dressing.
7. Sliced pickled beets and hard-cooked eggs arranged on lettuce. Mayonnaise Dressing.
8. Sliced marinated beets, overlapping each other, in a circle on lettuce, with a mound of julienne celery in center, watercress garnish. French Dressing.
9. Julienne beets and celery on endive. French Dressing.
10. Sliced cooked beets, Bermuda onion rings, quartered hard-cooked eggs, arranged on shredded lettuce. French Dressing.
11. Cucumbers cut in thin slices and placed on watercress in a half circle, garnished with paprika. French Dressing.
12. Thin slices of cucumber on slices of tomato, arranged on a lettuce leaf. Tarragon Dressing.
13. Thin slices of cucumber and Bermuda onion marinated. Vinaigrette Dressing.

[1] See pp. 261 to 267 for salad dressing recipes.

14. Diced cucumber and celery with Thousand Island Dressing, combined lightly with endive, garnished with chopped hard-cooked eggs.

15. Cooked peas, diced cheese, celery, pickle, and pimiento. Combination Dressing.

16. Raw spinach, chopped, combined with hard-cooked eggs, garnished with crumbled crisp bacon. Tarragon Dressing.

17. Whole tomato stuffed with fresh pineapple balls or cubes, garnished with 3 small cream cheese balls and watercress. Thick French Dressing.

18. Tomato sections arranged around a pimiento cheese ball, garnished with green pepper. French Dressing.

19. Cream cheese, green pepper, and onion mixture placed between 2 slices of tomato, garnished with chopped green pepper. Mayonnaise Dressing.

20. Tomato and avocado slices, arranged alternately on endive. French Dressing.

21. Tomato sections and marinated broccoli spears. French Dressing.

22. Tomato sections garnished with watercress. French Dressing.

23. Molds filled with alternate layers of chopped green pepper, shredded cabbage, and diced tomatoes mixed with mayonnaise. Chill before removing from molds. French Dressing.

24. Tomato sections with carrot rings and marinated cauliflowerets. French Dressing.

• GELATIN SALADS

Fruit Gelatin Salad

AMOUNT		INGREDIENT	METHOD
1 lb.	8 oz.	Gelatin, flavored	Stir until dissolved.
2 qt.		Add Water, boiling	
2 qt.		Add Fruit juice or water, cold	
4–5 lb.		Chill. When gelatin begins to congeal, pour over Fruit, drained, in 12 x 20 in. pan. Place in refrigerator to congeal	
			Yield: 48 2 x 2½ in. servings.

NOTES: 1. For quick preparation, dissolve 24 oz. flavored gelatin dessert in 1½ qt. boiling water. Measure 2½ qt. chipped or finely crushed ice, then add enough cold water or fruit juice to cover ice. Add to gelatin and stir constantly until ice is melted. Gelatin will begin to congeal at once. Speed of congealing depends on proportion of ice to water and size of ice particles.

2. One or more canned, frozen or fresh fruits, cut into desired shapes and sizes, may be used. Fresh or frozen pineapple must be cooked before adding to gelatin salad.

3. Fruit juice may be used for part or all of the liquid.

4. If unflavored granulated gelatin is used, soak 2½ oz. plain gelatin for 10 min. in 1 pt. cold water. Add 3½ qt. boiling fruit juice and 1 lb. sugar.

Variations of Fruit Gelatin Salad

Jellied Vegetable Salad. Substitute vegetables for fruit. Add 1 t. salt and substitute ½ c. vinegar for ½ c. fruit juice. Use water or vegetable juice for remainder of liquid. If unflavored gelatin is used, add 1 T. salt and 1 c. vinegar or lemon juice.

Applesauce Mold. Add 24 oz. lime gelatin to 3 qt. boiling hot applesauce and stir until dissolved. Add 1 qt. gingerale and pour into salad molds or 12 x 20-in. pan.

Autumn Salad. Dissolve 24 oz. orange gelatin in 2 qt. hot water. Add 2 qt. cold liquid, 2½ lb. sliced fresh peaches and 2½ lb. fresh pears.

Cabbage Parfait. Dissolve 24 oz. lemon gelatin in 2 qt. hot water. Blend in 1 qt. mayonnaise, 1 qt. cold water, 1 c. vinegar, 2 t. salt. Chill until mixture is partially congealed, then beat until fluffy. Add 2 qt. finely shredded cabbage, 1 qt. radish slices, 1 qt. diced celery, 1 c. chopped green pepper, and ½ c. minced onion.

Cherry Gelatin Salad. Dissolve 24 oz. cherry gelatin in 2 qt. hot water. Add 2 qt. cold fruit juice, 2½ lb. Bing cherries, seeded and drained, and 1½ lb. sliced bananas.

Cranberry Ring Mold. Dissolve 24 oz. cherry or raspberry gelatin in 2 qt. hot water. Add 3 lb. fresh or frozen cranberry relish, 1 lb. chopped apples, and 1 lb. crushed pineapple or 1 No. 10 can whole cranberry sauce and 6 oranges, ground. Pour into individual ring molds or 12 x 20-in. pan.

Frosted Cherry Salad. Dissolve 24 oz. cherry gelatin in 2 qt. hot water. Add 2 qt. cold fruit juice, 3 lb. drained, pitted red cherries and 2 lb. crushed pineapple. When congealed, frost with cream cheese and chopped toasted almonds.

Frosted Lime Mold. Dissolve 24 oz. lime gelatin in 2 qt. hot water. Add 2 qt. cold fruit juice and when mixture begins to congeal, add 2 qt. crushed pineapple, 2½ lb. cottage cheese, 8 oz. diced celery, 4 oz. chopped pimiento, and 4 oz. nutmeats. When congealed, frost with mixture of 4 lb. cream cheese blended with ½ c. mayonnaise.

Molded Grapefruit Salad. Dissolve 24 oz. lime gelatin in 2 qt. hot water. Add 2 qt. cold fruit juice, sections from 15 grapefruit, or 2 3-lb. cans frozen grapefruit sections.

Jellied Citrus Salad. Dissolve 24 oz. lemon or orange gelatin in 2 qt. hot water. Add 2 qt. cold water, sections from 15 oranges and 8 grapefruit; or 4 No. 2 cans mandarin oranges and 3-lb. can frozen grapefruit sections.

Jellied Waldorf Salad. Dissolve 24 oz. raspberry or cherry gelatin in 2 qt. boiling water. Add 1 c. red cinnamon candies and stir until dissolved. Add 2 qt. cold liquid. When mixture begins to congeal, add 2 qt. diced apple, 3 c. finely diced celery, 2 c. chopped pecans.

Molded Pear Salad. Dissolve 24 oz. lime gelatin in 2 qt. hot water. Add 2 qt. cold fruit juice and 50 pear halves.

Molded Pineapple-Cheese Salad. Dissolve 24 oz. lemon gelatin in 2 qt. hot liquid. Add 2 qt. cold fruit juice, 1 lb. grated Cheddar cheese, 3 lb. drained crushed pineapple, 3 oz. chopped green pepper or pimiento, and 4 oz. finely chopped celery.

Molded Pineapple-Cucumber Salad. Dissolve 24 oz. lime gelatin in 2 qt. hot liquid. Add 2 qt. cold fruit juice, 3 lb. drained crushed pineapple, 1½ lb. diced cucumber, and 4 oz. finely chopped pimiento.

Molded Pineapple Relish. Dissolve 24 oz. lemon gelatin in 2 qt. hot liquid. Add 2 qt. cold fruit juice, 4 lb. pineapple tidbits, and 1½ c. pickle relish.

Molded Pineapple and Rhubarb Salad. To 4 lb. frozen rhubarb, add 2 lb. sugar and 1 qt. water. Cook 5 min. Add 4 lb. pineapple tidbits and 24 oz. strawberry gelatin dissolved in juice from rhubarb and pineapple. Add enough water to make 4 qt.

Raspberry Ring Mold. Dissolve 24 oz. raspberry gelatin in 2 qt. hot liquid. Add 2 qt. cold raspberry juice, 3 lb. frozen raspberries and 2 lb. cantaloupe or watermelon balls. Pour into individual ring molds.

Spicy Apricot Mold. To sirup drained from 2 No. 10 cans peeled apricot halves, add 1 c. vinegar, 6 pieces stick cinnamon, and 1 T. whole cloves. Simmer 10 min. Remove spices and add enough hot water to make 1 gal. liquid. Combine with 24 oz. orange gelatin and congeal. Sliced peaches may be substituted for apricots.

Sunshine Salad. Dissolve 24 oz. lemon gelatin in 2 qt. hot liquid. Add 2 qt. cold fruit juice, 3 lb. drained crushed pineapple, and 8 oz. grated raw carrot.

Ribbon Gelatin Salad. Dissolve 24 oz. raspberry gelatin in 1 gal. hot water. Divide into 3 equal parts. Pour ⅓ into 12 x 20-in. pan and chill. Add 1 lb. cream cheese to another third and whip to blend; pour on the first part when it is congealed. Return to the refrigerator until it too is congealed, then top with remaining portion.

Swedish Green-top Salad. Dissolve 24 oz. lime gelatin in 1½ qt. boiling water. Pour into 12 x 20-in. pan. Dissolve 12 oz. orange gelatin in 1 qt. boiling water and stir until dissolved. While mixture is still hot, add 1½ lb. marshmallows and stir until melted. When cool, add 12 oz. cream cheese, 1½ c. mayonnaise, and ½ t. salt. Fold in 1 pt. cream, whipped. Pour over congealed lime gelatin and return to refrigerator to chill.

Under-the-sea Salad. Dissolve 24 oz. lime gelatin in 1 gal. hot water. Divide into two parts. Pour one part into a pan and chill. When it begins to congeal, add 3 c. sliced pears or drained crushed pineapple. To the remaining gelatin mixture, add 1 lb. cream cheese, whipping until smooth. Pour over first portion.

Ginger Ale Fruit Salad

Amount	Ingredient	Method
1 lb. 8 oz.	Gelatin, lemon flavored	
	Add	
2 qt.	Water, boiling	} Stir until gelatin is dissolved.
	When cold, add	
2 qt.	Ginger ale	
	When liquid begins to congeal, add	
1 lb.	Grapes (or white cherries)	
12 oz.	Celery, cut fine	
1 lb. (E.P.)	Apples, cubed	
1 No. 10 can	Pineapple, diced	
¼ c.	Lemon juice	
	Pour into pan 12 x 20 in., or into individual molds.	
		Yield: 48 2 x 2½-in. servings.

Bing Cherry Salad

Amount	Ingredient	Method
1 lb. 8 oz.	Gelatin, raspberry or cherry flavored	Dissolve gelatin in hot water. Cool.
1 qt.	Water, boiling	
	Add	
3½ qt.	Water and cherry juice	Chill.
2 drops	Coloring, red	
	When gelatin mixture begins to thicken, add	
2 No. 2½ cans	Cherries, Bing	Seeded and stuffed with nuts.
12 oz.	Nuts	
3 c.	Olives, stuffed, sliced	
	Pour into 50 individual molds or a pan 12 x 20 in.	

Yield: 48 2 x 2½-in. servings.

Tomato Aspic

Amount	Ingredient	Method
1 qt.	Water, cold	Sprinkle gelatin over water. Soak 10 min.
4 oz.	Gelatin, plain	
	Add	
4 qt.	Tomato juice	
2	Onions, small	
2	Bay leaves	
4	Celery stalks	Boiled 5 min. and strained.
8	Cloves, whole	
2 t.	Mustard, dry	
14 oz.	Sugar	
1 T.	Salt	
	Stir until gelatin is dissolved.	
	Add	
2 c.	Vinegar or lemon juice	
	Pour into pan 12 x 20 in. Place in a refrigerator to congeal.	

Yield: 48 2 x 2½-in. servings.

NOTE: If ring molds are used, recipe will yield approximately 75 servings. Centers may be filled with cole slaw or cottage cheese.

Perfection Salad

Amount	Ingredient	Method
3–3¼ oz.	Gelatin, plain	⎫ Sprinkle gelatin over water.
1 pt.	Water, cold	⎭ Soak 10 min.
	Add	
3 qt.	Water, boiling	⎬ Stir until gelatin is dissolved.
	Add	
1 c.	Vinegar, mild	⎫
1 c.	Lemon juice	⎪
1½ T.	Salt	⎬ Stir until sugar is dissolved.
1 lb.	Sugar	⎭
	Chill. When liquid starts to congeal, add	
1 lb. 8 oz. (E.P.)	Cabbage, chopped	
10 oz. (E.P.)	Celery, chopped	
4 oz.	Pimientos, chopped	
4 oz.	Pepper, green, chopped	
1 T.	Paprika	
	Pour into a pan 12 x 20 in. Place in refrigerator to congeal.	
	Yield: 48 2 x 2½-in. servings.	

Note: 1 lb. 10 oz. lemon gelatin may be substituted for gelatin and cold water.

Jellied Beet Salad

Amount	Ingredient	Method
1 lb. 8 oz.	Gelatin, lemon flavored	
	Add	
2 qt.	Water, boiling	⎬ Stir until dissolved.
	Add	
1 qt.	Beet juice	⎫
1 c.	Vinegar, mild	⎪
2 T.	Salt	⎬ Chill.
3 T.	Onion juice	⎭
	When mixture begins to congeal, add	
6 T.	Horseradish	
2 lb. 8 oz.	Celery, finely diced	
2 lb. 8 oz.	Beets, diced	
	Pour into a pan 12 x 20 in. Place in refrigerator to congeal.	
	Yield: 48 2 x 2½-in. servings.	

● LUNCHEON SALADS

Chicken Salad

AMOUNT	INGREDIENT	METHOD
5 lb. (4 4½–5-lb. fowls)	Chicken, cooked	Cook and let stand in broth overnight. Remove skin and cut chicken meat into ½-in. cubes.
	Add	
12	Eggs, hard-cooked, diced	
3 lb.	Celery, diced	
2 T.	Salt	
1 t.	Pepper, white	
3 c.	Mayonnaise	
	Season, combine and add mayonnaise. Serve in lettuce cup (with No. 10 dipper).	
		Serving: Approximately ½ c.

NOTES: 1. The marinating of cubed chicken with ⅔ c. French Dressing (p. 264) for 2 hr. will improve the flavor. May add just before serving, 8 oz. toasted almonds, white cherries, ripe olives, pineapple chunks, sweet pickle or cucumbers.

2. Turkey may be substituted for chicken.

VARIATION: **Chicken Salad in Cranberry or Raspberry Ring Mold.** Fill center of individual cranberry or raspberry ring molds (p. 250, 251) with chicken salad.

Shrimp Salad

Amount		Ingredient	Method
6 lb. (E.P.)		Shrimp, cooked and cut into ½ in. pieces	
2 lb.		Celery, diced	Mix lightly.
1 lb.		Cucumber, diced	
	1 head	Lettuce, chopped (optional)	
		Add	
2 T.		Lemon juice	
2 t.		Salt	
1 t.		Paprika	Mixed.
2 t.		Mustard, prepared	
3 c.		Mayonnaise	
		Serve with No. 10 dipper in a lettuce cup.	
			Serving: Approximately ½ c.

NOTES: 1. 1 doz. hard-cooked eggs, coarsely chopped, may be added; reduce shrimp to 5 lb.
2. May be garnished with tomato wedges or served in a tomato cup.

Crabmeat Salad

Amount		Ingredient	Method
10 6½-oz. cans		Crabmeat, flaked (or 4 lb. fresh crab meat)	
30		Eggs, hard-cooked	
1 lb.		Almonds, blanched, shredded	
2 lb.		Celery, chopped	
	1 pt.	Olives, ripe, sliced	
		Add	
1 qt.		Mayonnaise	
		Chill. Serve with No. 10 dipper.	
			Serving: Approximately ⅓ c.

NOTE: If desired, omit mayonnaise and marinate with French Dressing (p. 265).
VARIATION: Lobster Salad. Substitute lobster for crabmeat.

Tuna Salad

Amount		Ingredient	Method
8 lb.		Tuna, flaked	
1 lb.	8 oz.	Celery, chopped fine	
1 lb.	8 oz.	Cucumbers, diced	} Combine.
12		Eggs	
1 qt.		Mayonnaise	
		Serve with No. 10 dipper.	
			Serving: Approximately ½ c.

VARIATIONS: 1. **Tuna Apple Salad.** Substitute tart, diced apples for cucumbers.
     2. **Salmon Salad.** Substitute salmon for tuna.

Macaroni Salad

Amount		Ingredient	Method
2 lb.	8 oz.	Macaroni	} Cook in boiling salted water and wash in hot water. Drain. Chill.
		Add	
2 lb.		Cheese, Cheddar, diced or shredded	
1 lb.	8 oz.	Pickle, chopped	
18		Eggs, hard-cooked, chopped	
2 lb.		Celery, chopped fine	
1 qt.		Mayonnaise	
	1½ T.	Salt	
		Mix carefully. Serve with No. 12 dipper.	
			Serving: ⅓ c.

NOTE: Spaghetti or shell macaroni may be substituted for macaroni.

Cottage Cheese Salad

Amount		Ingredient	Method
6 lb.		Cheese, cottage, dry	
3 lb.		Tomatoes, raw, peeled, diced	
	4 oz.	Peppers, green, chopped	
1 lb.		Celery, diced	
1 lb.		Cucumber, diced	
	8 oz.	Radishes, diced	
	3 T.	Salt	
	1½ pt.	Mayonnaise (less if cream in cheese)	
		Combine carefully. Serve with No. 12 dipper.	
			Serving: ⅓ c.

Salad Plate Combinations

1. Cottage cheese surrounded by peach slices, mixed fruits molded in red gelatin, banana chunks rolled in mayonnaise and coconut.

2. Fruit gelatin mold, 3 slices honeydew melon, cut ¾ in. thick, cantaloupe and watermelon balls, cluster of white grapes.

3. One half avocado filled with chopped fruit, 1 slice pineapple, 3 prunes stuffed with cream cheese.

4. Grapefruit and orange sections, avocado slices arranged alternately on romaine, ½ cantaloupe ring with 2 canned or fresh figs.

5. Cantaloupe ring with dipper of sherbet, surrounded by fresh pear slices, mandarin oranges, white grapes, fresh strawberries.

6. Frozen fruit salad, cantaloupe ring with cottage cheese, honeydew sections, fresh strawberries.

7. Tuna or salmon salad, tomato wedges, deviled eggs, garnished with ripe olive, carrot curls and midget sweet pickle.

8. Tomato stuffed with shrimp salad, cucumber slices, potato chips.

9. Ham rolls, stuffed tomato salad, deviled eggs, ripe olives.

10. Cold sliced turkey and baked ham, cranberry gelatin mold, cheese stuffed celery and carrot curls.

11. Chicken salad in cranberry ring mold, celery curls, ripe olives.

12. Sliced cold roast pork, molded peach and cream cheese salad, potato salad, radish rose.

13. Tomato aspic ring with cottage cheese, tuna salad, stuffed olives, celery curls.

14. Avocado half filled with chicken or shrimp salad, spiced peach, sliced tomatoes.

15. Molded meat or fish salad, frosted grapes, pineapple slice, honeydew melon wedges, fresh plum.

For salad plate accompaniments, see p. 239.

● RELISHES

Cranberry Relish (Raw)

Amount	Ingredient	Method
4 (size 72)	Oranges	
4 lb.	Cranberries, raw	Grind.
6 lb.	Apples (remove cores)	
	Add	
3 lb.	Sugar	
	Chill 24 hr. before using. Serve with No. 16 dipper.	
		Serving: ¼ c.

NOTE: May be used as salad if drained before using.

Cranberry Sauce

AMOUNT	INGREDIENT	METHOD
4 lb.	Sugar	
1 qt.	Water	Cover, boil gently until skins burst.
4 lb.	Cranberries	
	Serve with No. 16 dipper.	
		Serving: ¼ c.

NOTES: 1. Overcooking makes cranberries bitter.
       2. Make sauce at least 24 hr. before using.
       3. Cranberries may be puréed before adding sugar.

Royal Cranberry Sauce

AMOUNT		INGREDIENT	METHOD
2 lb.		Cranberries	
2 lb.		Sugar	Cover and simmer until tender. Cool.
	1 pt.	Water	
		Add	
	2	Oranges, large, chopped	
1 lb.		Apples, tart, chopped	
1 lb.		White grapes, seeded	
1 lb.		Pineapple, diced	
	4 oz.	Pecans, chopped	
		Serve with No. 24 dipper.	
			Serving: 2½ T.

NOTE: The sauce will keep for several weeks if placed in a covered jar in a cool place.

Apples (Buttered)

Amount	Ingredient	Method
13 lb. (E.P.)	Apples	Cut apples into sections. Remove core. Arrange in pan.
	Add	
8 oz.	Butter or margarine	
1 pt.	Water, hot	Mixed.
1 lb. 8 oz.	Sugar	
1½ T.	Salt	
	Cover and let simmer until apples are tender, approximately 1 hr.	
		Serving: 4 oz.

NOTES: 1. A more attractive product is obtained if apple sections are arranged in a serving pan and steamed until tender, butter or margarine and sugar sprinkled over the top, and then bake for 15–20 min.
2. Hot buttered apples are often served in place of a vegetable.

VARIATIONS: 1. **Cinnamon Apples.** Cut apples into rings. Add cinnamon drops (redhots) for flavor and color.
2. **Apple Rings.** Cut rings of unpared apples, steam until tender, add sugar and butter or margarine and bake 15 min.

Cabbage Relish

Amount	Ingredient	Method
9 oz.	Peppers, green	
1 lb. 12 oz.	Carrots	Grind.
6 lb.	Cabbage	
	Add	
1 qt.	Cultured sour cream	
2 T.	Salt	Mixed.
9 oz.	Sugar	
1 c.	Vinegar	
	Serve with No. 12 dipper.	
		Serving: ⅓ c.

VARIATION: **Cucumber Relish.** Substitute 8 lb. finely diced cucumber for cabbage, carrots, and peppers. Season with salt, pepper, and lemon juice. Fold in sour cream and chill. Serve in lettuce cup; garnish with thin slice of red radish or sprig of parsley.

Beet Relish

Amount	Ingredient	Method
1 qt. (2 No. 2½ cans)	Beets, cooked, chopped	⎫
12 oz.	Cabbage, raw, shredded	⎬ Combine.
	Add	
1 lb.	Sugar	⎫
1 t.	Salt	
1 c.	Horseradish	⎬ Combined.
4 oz.	Onion, chopped fine	
2 c.	Vinegar	⎭
	Chill 24 hr. Serve as relish with meat.	

Serving: Approximately 1 T.

Pickled Beets

Amount	Ingredient	Method
2 qt.	Vinegar, mild	⎫
1 lb.	Sugar, brown	
8 oz.	Sugar, white	
1 t.	Salt	Mix. Heat to boiling point.
½ t.	Pepper	⎬ Boil 5 min.
1 t.	Cinnamon	
1 t.	Cloves	
1 t.	Allspice	⎭
	Pour over	
10 lb.	Beets, cooked, sliced	

Serving: Approximately 3 oz.

NOTE: Prepare 24 hr. before using. Add onion rings if desired.

salad dressings

Mayonnaise Dressing

Amount	Ingredient	Method
8	Egg yolks (or 4 whole)	
3 T.	Salt	Mix well.
2 t.	Paprika	
2 T.	Mustard, dry	
	Add	
¼ c.	Vinegar	
	Add slowly	
2 qt.	Salad oil	
	Add oil very slowly, beating steadily until an emulsion is formed. (Oil may then be added in amount of ½ c. and later 1 c. at a time, beating well after each addition.)	
	Add	
¼ c.	Vinegar	Beat well.
	Add	
2 qt.	Salad oil	Continue beating until oil is emulsified.

Yield: 1 gal.

Mayonnaise Dressing with Cooked Base

Amount	Ingredient	Method
1 lb.	Cornstarch	} Make a smooth paste.
2 c.	Water, cold	
	Add	
2 qt.	Water, boiling	} Stirring constantly. Cook until clear.
	Place in bowl of electric mixer. Beat until cool.	
	Add, ¼ at a time, while beating,	
20 (or 12 whole eggs)	Egg yolks	} Mix well.
	Add	
3 T.	Salt	
¼ c.	Mustard	} Mix well.
2 t.	Paprika	
	Add	
2 c.	Vinegar	
	Add slowly, beating constantly,	
1 gal.	Salad oil	
	Add	
2 c.	Vinegar	
	Add slowly, beating constantly,	
1 gal.	Salad oil	

Yield: 3 gal.

Variations of Mayonnaise Dressing

Blue Cheese Dressing. Mix 6 oz. blue cheese with 3 c. Mayonnaise Dressing and ¼ c. cream or milk. Add a few drops Tabasco sauce.

Campus Dressing. Combine 3 T. chopped parsley, 2 T. chopped green pepper, and ¼ c. finely chopped celery with 4 c. Mayonnaise Dressing.

Chantilly Dressing. Whip ¾ c. heavy cream and fold into 3 c. Mayonnaise Dressing.

Cranberry Dressing. Blend 2½ c. Mayonnaise Dressing and 2 c. jellied cranberries, beaten until smooth. Fold in 1 c. whipped cream just before serving.

Egg Dressing. Chop 4 hard-cooked eggs and combine with 4 c. Mayonnaise Dressing.

Egg and Green Pepper Dressing. Combine 6 chopped, hard-cooked eggs, 2 T. finely chopped green pepper, 1 T. onion juice, and a few grains cayenne with 3½ c. Mayonnaise Dressing.

Garden Dressing. Add 1 qt. cultured sour cream, ¼ c. sugar, 1 T. salt, f.g. pepper, 1 c. minced green onions, 1 c. sliced radishes, 1 c. chopped cucumbers, 1 c. minced green peppers to 2 c. Mayonnaise Dressing.

Honey-Cream Dressing. Blend 1 oz. cream cheese, ⅔ c. strained honey, ¼ c. lemon or pineapple juice, ¼ t. salt. Fold in 3½ c. Mayonnaise Dressing.

Roquefort Dressing. Add 1 c. French Dressing, 4 oz. Roquefort cheese, and 1 t. Worcestershire sauce to 3 c. Mayonnaise Dressing.

Russian Dressing. Add 1 c. chili sauce, 1 T. Worcestershire sauce, 1 t. onion juice, f.g. cayenne to 1 qt. Mayonnaise Dressing.

Sour Cream-Roquefort Dressing. Add 1 c. cultured sour cream, 2 T. lemon juice, 2 t. grated onion, ½ t. salt, 4 oz. Roquefort cheese, crumbled fine, to 2 c. Mayonnaise Dressing.

Thousand Island Dressing. Add 1½ oz. minced onion, 3 oz. chopped pimiento, 1¾ c. chili sauce, 10 chopped hard-cooked eggs, ½ c. chopped pickles or olives, f.g. cayenne to 7 c. Mayonnaise Dressing.

Cooked Salad Dressing

Amount		Ingredient	Method
3 lb.		Sugar	
1 lb.	8 oz.	Flour	Sift together.
	6 oz.	Salt	
	3 oz.	Mustard, dry	
		Add	
1 qt.		Water	Stir until a smooth paste is formed.
		Add	
4 qt.		Milk, hot	Stir continuously while adding.
2 qt.		Water, hot	Cook in steamer 20 min.
		Add	
1 lb.		Butter or margarine	Mixed.
3 qt.		Vinegar, hot	
		Add very slowly to	
50 (2 lb. 12 oz.)		Egg yolks, beaten	Stir briskly while adding.
		Cook in steamer 7 min. Remove from fire and cool.	
			Yield: 3 gal.

NOTE: 25 whole eggs may be substituted for egg yolks, and hot water for hot milk.

VARIATIONS: 1. **Combination Dressing.** Combine 2 c. Cooked Salad Dressing and 2 c. Mayonnaise (p. 261)

2. **Egg Dressing.** Add 4 chopped hard-cooked eggs, ⅓ c. chopped pimiento and ¼ c. chopped pickles to 1 qt. Cooked Dressing.

3. **Whipped Cream Dressing.** Add 1 pt. cream, whipped, to 1 qt. Cooked Salad Dressing.

French Dressing

Amount	Ingredient	Method
3 T.	Salt	
2 T.	Mustard, dry	
2 T.	Paprika	Mix.
1 T.	Pepper	
	Add	
2 qt.	Oil	
1 qt.	Vinegar	
4 t.	Onion juice	

Put into a jar and shake vigorously just before serving, or beat well with a Dover beater.

Yield: 3 qt.

NOTE: An egg white beaten into each quart of dressing just before using will keep it from separating.

Variations of French Dressing

California Dressing. Add 2 c. mashed avocado, 2 T. lemon juice, and 1 t. salt to 3 c. French Dressing.

Catsup Dressing. Blend 1 c. catsup with 3 c. French Dressing.

Chiffonade Dressing. Add 4 t. chopped parsley, 1 oz. chopped red pepper or pimiento, 1 oz. chopped onion, 1½ oz. chopped green pepper, and 4 chopped hard-cooked eggs to 3 c. French Dressing.

Chive Dressing. Add 1 c. cultured sour cream, 3 T. finely chopped chives to 3 c. French Dressing.

Cream Dressing. Add 1 c. heavy cream, beaten or unbeaten, to 3 c. French Dressing.

Cucumber Dressing. Add 3 oz. finely chopped cucumber to 4 c. French Dressing.

Curry Dressing. Add ½ t. curry powder and 8 diced hard-cooked eggs to 4 c. French Dressing.

Fruit Dressing. Use French Dressing recipe and omit onion. Substitute orange, pineapple, lime or grapefruit juice, or a combination of these for vinegar in the recipe.

Honey-Orange Dressing. Add ½ c. honey, ½ c. orange juice to 3 c. French Dressing.

Mexican Dressing. Add 2½ oz. chopped green pepper, ¾ c. chili sauce, and 1 oz. chopped onion to 3 c. French Dressing.

Piquante Dressing. Add 2 t. mustard, ½ t. Worcestershire sauce, 2 t. onion juice to 4 c. French Dressing.

Roquefort Cheese Dressing. Add slowly, 3 c. French Dressing to 4 oz. Roquefort cheese, finely crumbled. Whip dressing slowly into cheese. May also mix 1 c. heavy cream with cheese before adding French Dressing.

Tomato Dressing. Add 4 oz. sugar, 1 t. onion juice, and 1½ c. tomato soup to 3 c. French Dressing.

Vinaigrette Dressing. Add ¾ c. chopped pickle, ½ c. chopped green olives, 6 T. chopped parsley, 1 t. onion juice, 2 T. capers, to 3 c. French Dressing.

Thick French Dressing

Amount	Ingredient	Method
1¼ t.	Onion juice	
2 T.	Salt	
4 t.	Mustard, dry	Mix.
2 T.	Paprika	
2 lb.	Sugar	
	Add	
1⅓ c.	Vinegar	Mix well.
	Add gradually	
1 qt.	Salad oil	Stirring constantly.
		Yield: Approximately 5 c.

NOTE: If a dressing of the usual consistency is desired, use only 8 oz. sugar.
VARIATIONS: 1. **Poppy Seed Dressing.** Add ½ c. poppy seed.
2. **Celery Seed Dressing.** Add ½ c. celery seed.

French Dressing, Semipermanent

Amount	Ingredient	Method
4 t.	Mustard, dry	
4 t.	Paprika	
3 T.	Sugar	Mix.
f.g.	Pepper, red	
2 T.	Salt	
	Add slowly	
1 qt.	Salad oil	Beating continuously.
	Add slowly	
1 c.	Vinegar	Beat vigorously 5 min.
	Add	
4 t.	Gelatin	The gelatin should be previously soaked
4 T.	Water, cold	in the cold water and dissolved in the
½ c.	Water, boiling	hot water and chilled.
		Yield: Approximately 5 c.

Celery Seed Fruit Dressing

Amount		Ingredient	Method
1 lb.	8 oz.	Sugar	
	⅓ c.	Cornstarch	
	2 T.	Mustard, dry	Mix.
	2 T.	Salt	
	2 T.	Paprika	
		Add	
	2 c.	Vinegar	Cook until thickened and clear. Cool to room temperature.
		Add	
	1 t.	Onion juice, optional	
		Add, slowly while beating	
1 qt.		Oil, salad	
		Add	
	2 T.	Celery seed	
		Serve with any fruit salad combination.	
			Yield: 2 qt.

NOTE: Poppy seed may be used in place of celery seed.

Sour Cream Dressing

Amount		Ingredient	Method
1 qt.		Cream, cultured sour	Mix.
16		Eggs, beaten	
		Add to	
2 lb.		Sugar	
	1½ oz.	Flour	Mixed.
	1 c.	Water	
		Add	
	1 pt.	Vinegar	Stir and cook until thick.
			Yield: Approximately 2 qt.

NOTES: 1. Dressing may be stored several days in refrigerator.
   2. 1 pint cream, whipped, may be added before serving.
VARIATION: **Sweet-Sour Cream Dressing.** Combine 1 qt. cultured sour cream, ½ c. sugar, 2 t. salt and ½ c. vinegar. May be combined with shredded cabbage or served over tomatoes, cucumbers, or any fruit combination.

Fruit Salad Dressing

Amount		Ingredient	Method
	5 oz.	Cornstarch	} Mix.
2 lb.		Sugar	
			While stirring constantly with wire whip, add to
1 qt.		Pineapple juice	
	1½ pt.	Orange juice	} Mixed and heated to the boiling point.
	1 pt.	Lemon juice	
16		Eggs, well beaten	
		Cook until thick.	
		Cool and add	
	1 pt.	Cream, whipped	
			Yield: 5 qt.

NOTE: Serve with Fruit Salad (p. 241).

sandwiches

Sandwiches may be hearty and substantial, approximating a meal, or light and dainty, as an accompaniment to tea. They are made of one or more slices of bread, spread with one or more kinds of filling. The closed sandwich is made by spreading one slice of bread with a filling and covering it with a second slice. The open-faced sandwich is made by spreading a slice of bread with filling and decorating it.

● SANDWICH INGREDIENTS

1. *Bread.* Any kind may be used with a suitable filling. Cracked wheat, graham, whole wheat, white, or rye are most often used for the substantial type of sandwich. Nut, orange, raisin, date, banana, or rolled oat bread are most often used for plain tea sandwiches.

For most sandwiches, the bread should be a Pullman or sandwich loaf. The bread should be sliced ⅛- to ¼-in. thick, depending upon the type of sandwich to be made.

2. *Butter or Margarine.* Butter should be softened so that it is soft and pliable. It is best creamed by placing it in the bowl of the electric mixer, and allowing it to stand at room temperature, until soft enough to mix with the mixer. (A half cup of milk or boiling water per pound of butter may be added to increase the volume.) Mix first on low speed and then whip on second and high speed until fluffy. Butter or margarine need not always be used on sandwiches when a rich filling is used. However, butter helps to prevent fillings from soaking into the bread and improves the flavor. Minced cucumber, spices, onion, or other ingredients may be added to change the flavor of the butter.

3. *Fillings.* Sandwich filling may be made of chopped meats, poultry, fish, cheese, vegetables, jellies, nuts, or fruits. One of these ingredients or a combination of them is usually mixed with mayonnaise, cooked dressing, or cream.

Soft mixed fillings should be measured with a spoon or small dipper to insure a uniform amount in each sandwich.

If slices of meat or cheese are used for filling, the slices should be even in thickness and the same size as the bread upon which they are to be placed.

4. *Garnishes.* The garnishes to be used depend upon the type of sandwich. Lettuce, parsley, watercress, and other salad greens, olives, pickles, pimiento, green peppers, and radishes are most often used. Nuts, paprika, cheese, and mayonnaise are also often used as garnishes for various types of sandwiches.

● MAKING SANDWICHES

Plain Sandwiches

1. Have filling, garnish, and butter prepared.
2. Allow plenty of work space.
3. Arrange the slices of bread in rows.
4. Spread butter or filling with a pie server or short spatula, having enough butter on spatula to cover 2 or 3 slices.
5. Spread all bread with butter before spreading with filling. Do not pick up bread to spread.
6. Spread from back row of bread to front row.
7. Use dipper or spoon and place a uniform amount of filling on alternating slices of bread.
8. Spread the filling evenly and to the edge of the bread.
9. Cover each slice with corresponding slice of bread.
10. Place another row of bread slices over the first layer of made sandwiches and repeat steps 4–9. After the stack has reached 4 or 5 layers of made sandwiches, cut down through the middle with 1 stroke of the knife. Stack on a tray and cover with a wet cloth (or wrap in wax paper) to prevent drying.

Simple sandwiches may be made more attractive by cutting into rounds, triangles, or small squares.

Tea Sandwiches

Checkerboard Sandwiches (Fig. 13):

1. Cut 2 slices white and 2 slices whole wheat bread about ½ in. thick.
2. Spread 1 slice white bread with a thin spread, place a slice of whole

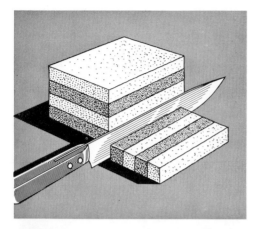

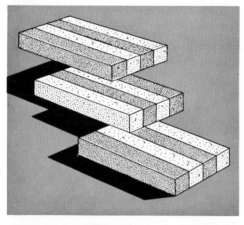

1. For each stack, alternate 2 slices whole wheat and 2 slices enriched wheat bread, filling as for Ribbon Sandwiches.

2. Cut each stack in ½-in. slices. Then put 3 alternating slices together as shown, using a "butter" or spread as filling.

3. Chill for several hours. Remove from refrigerator, and with sharp knife immediately slice into checkerboard slices, ½ in. thick.

Fig. 13. Checkerboards. (Courtesy Good Housekeeping Institute, "Sandwich Manual," 1951.)

wheat bread on this and spread with butter, and top with another slice of white bread.

3. Use remaining 2 whole wheat slices and 1 of white bread to make another stack.

4. Wrap in a damp cloth, place under a light weight, and put in a cool place until firm and cooled.

5. Trim, and cut each pile into 3 slices.

6. Spread these slices and combine them crosswise, white and whole wheat squares alternating.

7. Repeat weighting and cooling process for a few hours. When ready to serve, cut in ¼- to ½-in. slices.

Ribbon Sandwiches:

Proceed as for checkerboard sandwich to step 5, then slice each pile into desired thickness (Fig. 14).

Open Sandwiches:

Cut slices of bread ¼ in. thick into rounds, hearts, stars, diamonds, crescents, squares, or any desired shape. Spread with creamed butter, then with filling. Decorate. The filling may be ham and sliced cheese, lettuce and hard-cooked egg, chicken salad, shrimp, lobster, or crab salad, minced tongue and sliced tomato, sliced cucumber and lettuce, cottage cheese and sliced tomatoes, jam, olives, chopped parsley and pimiento, hard-cooked eggs. (Cut the bread a little thicker and use a little thicker filling than for the simple sandwich.) A few suggestions for open sandwiches follow:

1. Place a thin slice of tomato on a round of buttered bread. Garnish with mayonnaise and a sprig of parsley, or butter the edges of the bread and roll in chopped parsley.

2. Spread bread cut into diamond shapes with butter and cream cheese. Garnish with pimiento or green peppers.

3. Place thin slices of American cheese on crisp crackers. Add a dash of salt and pepper and place under the broiler until the cheese has melted. Garnish with paprika and serve hot.

4. Spread bread cut in heart shapes with a mixture of chopped almonds, Maraschino cherries, and whipped cream.

5. Mix chopped walnuts, candied ginger, and mayonnaise. Cut bread into tiny squares and garnish with a half walnut and bit of paprika.

6. Mix ground American cheese, butter, lemon juice, Worcestershire sauce, paprika, cayenne, and onion juice. Spread on rounds of rye bread. Garnish with stuffed olive slices.

For additional sandwich spreads, see pp. 276–277.

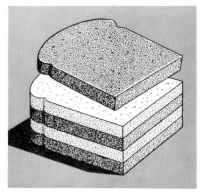

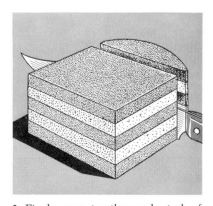

1. Using fresh or day-old bread, stack alternately 3 slices whole wheat and 2 enriched white bread, filling with one or more spreads (pp 276–277).

2. Firmly press together each stack of slices. Then with sharp knife, using a sawing motion, slice crusts from all sides of each stack.

3. Arrange stacks in shallow pan; cover with waxed paper and moist cloth. Chill for several hours. Cut in ½-in. slices.

4. Cut each slice into thirds, halves, or triangles, as shown above. Arrange on plates.

Fig. 14. Ribbon Sandwiches. (Courtesy Good Housekeeping Institute, "Sandwich Manual," 1951.)

Rolled Sandwiches:

1. Slice a sandwich loaf of bread lengthwise into 6 slices. Run rolling pin over each slice, starting at narrow end.

2. Spread each slice with creamed butter or margarine and then with a thin filling of cream cheese, or other spread.

3. Place a thin strip of pimiento, and chopped parsley, or stuffed olives across the end of each slice and roll bread around pimiento as you would a jelly roll.

4. Wrap each roll in wax paper or aluminum foil, twisting ends securely. Chill several hours or overnight, or freeze.

5. When ready to serve, slice thin.

Pinwheel Sandwiches (Fig. 15):

1. Remove crusts from half an unsliced Pullman loaf of bread and cut into lengthwise slices ¼-in. thick.

2. Spread slices with creamed butter and then with pimiento cream cheese or other spreads.

3. Roll like a jelly roll.

4. Cover with a very damp cloth and place in the refrigerator until set.

5. Slice into ¼-in. slices.

Two-tone Sandwiches:

1. Cut whole wheat and white bread into 2½-in. rounds.

2. Spread with butter or cream cheese or other thin fillings.

3. Use a doughnut cutter and remove the center from half of the whole wheat and half of the white bread.

4. Place the whole wheat round on the white bread and vice versa; fit the white rounds into the whole wheat circles and vice versa.

Freezing Sandwiches

When making sandwiches to be frozen for later use, certain precautions need to be taken. Bread should be spread with butter or margarine, rather than mayonnaise or salad dressing. Fillings such as minced chicken, meat, egg yolks, fish, or peanut butter freeze well, but sliced cooked eggs and some vegetables, such as tomatoes and parsley, should not be frozen.

Wrap large closed sandwiches individually. Pack tea-sized closed sandwiches in layers in freezer boxes; or place in any suitable box and over-wrap with moisture-vapor-proof material. Place open-faced sandwiches on cardboard or trays, wrap as for closed sandwiches. Wrap ribbon, rolled or other loaf sandwiches, uncut.

Sandwiches will thaw in 1–2 hr., open-face most quickly. Outer wrapping should not be removed until sandwiches are partly thawed. If sandwiches are not served immediately after thawing, they should be held in the refrigerator until serving time.

Grilled and Toasted Sandwiches

Many ingredients may be combined to make suitable fillings for toasted or grilled sandwiches. For a grilled sandwich, the outside is

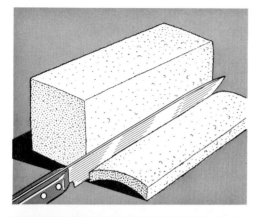

1. Place loaf of fresh or day-old unsliced, enriched white bread on cutting board; then with long, sharp knife (or bread knife) slice off all crusts except bottom one.

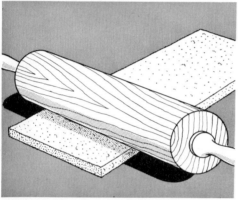

2. With crust side of loaf to the left, cut into lengthwise slices, ⅛ to ¼ in. thick, as shown above. Now run rolling pin over each slice, starting at narrow end. This makes the bread easy to handle, less likely to crack.

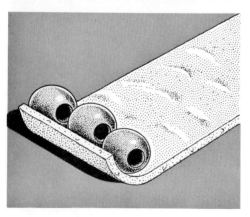

3. Spread each slice to the edge with softened butter or margarine; then cover with one of spreads on page 276. If desired, place 3 stuffed olives or gherkins, a frankfurter, or 2 Vienna sausages across short end.

Fig. 15. Pinwheels. (Courtesy Good Housekeeping Institute, "Sandwich Manual," 1951.)

4. Starting at the end with the stuffed olives or other filler mentioned above, roll up each slice tightly as for jelly roll, being careful to keep sides in line. Tight rolling makes for easier slicing and neat pinwheels with distinct markings.

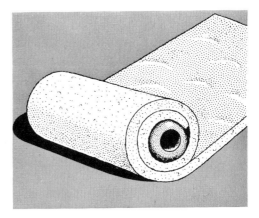

5. Wrap rolls individually in waxed paper or aluminum foil, twisting ends securely. Chill several hours or overnight. Rolls may be made ahead of time, then wrapped and frozen. Let thaw for about 45 min. before slicing.

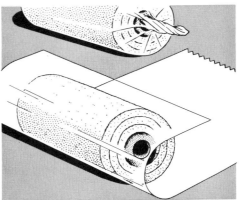

6. Cut chilled rolls into ¼- to ½-in. slices. Lift with broad spatula onto serving plate or trays. Cover with waxed paper, then moist cloth, and chill for use later. May be toasted just before serving.

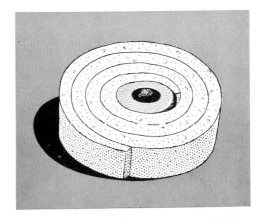

Fig. 15. Pinwheels. (Courtesy Good Housekeeping Institute, "Sandwich Manual," 1951.)

brushed with butter or margarine and the sandwich grilled after the filling has been added. Bread for toasted sandwiches may be toasted before or after filling is added, although a crisp ingredient like lettuce is added after the sandwich is toasted. Toasted sandwiches may be either closed or open faced. A few suggestions for toasted sandwiches follow:

1. Thinly sliced tomato, broiled bacon, lettuce, and salad dressing.
2. Chicken livers, mashed, crisp bacon, and salad dressing.
3. Sweetbreads and mushrooms browned in butter.
4. Sardine and hard-cooked eggs, mayonnaise, and slice of tomato.
5. Sweetbreads, hard-cooked eggs, mayonnaise, and lemon juice.
6. Goose liver, mayonnaise, and onion.
7. Sliced cheese, sliced ham, and prepared mustard.
8. Sliced cheese, tomato, and mayonnaise.
9. Chicken salad.
10. Sliced Cheddar or Swiss cheese.
11. Sliced corned beef, Swiss cheese, lettuce, on rye bread.

● SANDWICH FILLING SUGGESTIONS

1. Dates, figs, raisins, orange, ground.
2. Peanut butter and Cheddar cheese, mixed.
3. Peanut butter, finely shredded cabbage and carrot.
4. Hard-cooked eggs and olives, chopped.
5. Hard-cooked eggs and olives, chopped, grated cheese and mayonnaise, mixed.
6. Hard-cooked eggs and pickles, chopped, tuna and mayonnaise, mixed.
7. Hard-cooked eggs and pimiento, chopped, sweet relish and mayonnaise, mixed.
8. Sliced cold boiled tongue and mayonnaise.
9. Stuffed olives, sliced, and Neufchâtel cheese.
10. Cucumber, chopped and mixed with creamed butter.
11. Dates, lemon juice, and nuts, minced.
12. Raspberry jelly or jam and cream cheese.
13. Sliced tomato and mayonnaise.
14. Cream cheese, minced dried beef, mixed with mayonnaise and seasoned with horseradish, grated onion, and mustard.
15. Cream cheese, chopped red and green peppers, mixed.
16. Cream cheese and chopped dates, mixed.
17. Cream cheese and chopped chives.
18. Cream cheese, chopped preserved ginger, mixed.
19. Cabbage and carrot, chopped fine, mixed with salad dressing.
20. Grated carrots, chopped nuts, and mayonnaise, mixed.
21. Chopped celery, nuts, and salad dressing, mixed.
22. Chopped celery, nuts, olives, and salad dressing, mixed.
23. Mashed baked beans, sliced tomato, and lettuce.
24. Cottage cheese, nuts, mixed.
25. Cottage cheese and chopped green onions on rye bread.
26. Nuts and olives chopped and salad dressing, mixed.
27. Sardines and olives, minced, butter, catsup, and lemon juice, mixed.

● SANDWICH RECIPES

Chicken Sandwiches

Amount	Ingredient	Method
4 lb.	Chicken, chopped	
4 oz.	Almonds, chopped, toasted	
2 t.	Salt	
8 oz.	Celery, chopped fine	Combine.
¼ c.	Vinegar	
1 c.	Mayonnaise	
100 slices	Bread	
2–3 heads	Lettuce	
	Portion with No. 24 dipper.	

Tuna Sandwiches

Amount	Ingredient	Method
4 lb.	Tuna, flaked	
6	Eggs, hard cooked	
¼ c.	Lemon juice	
1 t.	Onion juice	Combine.
1 c.	Cooked Salad Dressing	
1 c.	Mayonnaise	
100 slices	Bread	
2–3 heads	Lettuce	
	Portion with No. 20 dipper.	

NOTE: 1 c. chopped pickle may be added.

Meat Sandwiches

Amount	Ingredient	Method
4 lb.	Meat, cooked, finely chopped	
4 oz.	Celery, chopped fine	
8 oz.	Olives or pickles, chopped	
1 c.	Mayonnaise	
¼ c.	Vinegar	Combine.
1 c.	Cooked Salad Dressing	
1 t.	Salt	
100 slices	Bread	
2–3 heads	Lettuce	
	Portion with No. 20 dipper.	

Hot Meat Sandwich

Amount	Ingredient	Method
8 lb.	Roast beef or pork, cooked	} Cut into thin slices.
50 slices	Arrange on Bread	
2½ qts.	Cover with Gravy	

NOTE: Meat may be covered with additional slice of bread if desired. Then cover entire sandwich with gravy.

VARIATION: **Hot Turkey Sandwich.** Substitute roast turkey or turkey roll for meat.

Ham Salad Sandwiches

Amount	Ingredient	Method
4 lb.	Ham, cooked, coarsely ground	
8 oz.	Pickles, chopped	
2 oz.	Pimientos, chopped	} Combine.
1 c.	Cooked Salad Dressing	
1 c.	Mayonnaise	
100 slices	Bread	
2–3 heads	Lettuce	
	Portion with No. 20 dipper.	

NOTE: 6 hard-cooked eggs, chopped, may be added.

Egg Salad Sandwiches

Amount	Ingredient	Method
3 doz.	Eggs, hard cooked	} Peel and chop.
	Add	
2 c.	Mayonnaise	
2 c.	Pickle relish	
2 t.	Salt	} Combine.
½ c.	Pimiento, chopped	
100 slices	Bread	
2–3 heads	Lettuce	
	Portion with No. 24 dipper.	

Peanut Sandwiches

Amount		Ingredient	Method
2 lb.		Peanuts, shelled	} Grind.
	6 oz.	Add Butter or margarine, soft Mix well.	
	1 c.	Add Cream, whipped	
	1 c.	Mayonnaise	} Mixed.
	1 T.	Salt	
2 heads		Lettuce Place a piece of lettuce in each sandwich.	
100 slices		Bread, cracked wheat Portion with No. 24 dipper.	

VARIATION: **Peanut Butter Sandwiches.** Substitute 4 lb. peanut butter for peanuts. Omit cream.

Cheese Sandwiches

Amount		Ingredient	Method
3 lb.	8 oz.	Cheese, ground	
	1 pt.	Salad dressing or cream	
	2 t.	Salt	} Mix well.
	f.g.	Cayenne	
	4 oz.	Butter or margarine, soft	
100 slices		Bread Portion with No. 24 dipper.	

VARIATION: **Pimiento Cheese Sandwiches.** Add 1 c. chopped pimientoes.

Grilled Cheese Sandwiches

Amount		Ingredient	Method
100		Bread slices	} Make sandwiches.
3 lb.	2 oz.	Cheese, 1 oz. slices	
		Brush both sides of sandwiches with	
1 lb.		Butter or margarine, melted	
		Grill sandwiches on hot griddle or toast in hot oven until golden brown.	

NOTES: 1. Cheese may be ground and the following ingredients added to make a spread: 2 T. prepared mustard, ½ c. chili sauce, 1 c. Mayonnaise.
2. Salad mixtures such as chicken, ham salad, tuna, and egg salad are satisfactory fillings for grilled sandwiches.
VARIATION: **French Fried Cheese Sandwiches.** Dip in batter (p. 32) and fry in deep fat 1–2 min. at 375° F.

Tomato and Bacon Sandwiches

Amount		Ingredient	Method
4 lb.		Bacon, sliced	} Place slices in rows in a baking pan. Cook in oven until crisp and brown.
7 lb.		Tomatoes, sliced	
	1 c.	Mayonnaise	
100 slices		Bread	
	8 oz.	Butter or margarine	
2–3 heads		Lettuce	
		Spread 50 slices of bread with mayonnaise, place bacon slices, thin slices of tomato, and a piece of lettuce on each. Top with remaining 50 slices of bread, spread with whipped butter or margarine.	

Oven-baked Hamburgers

AMOUNT		INGREDIENT	METHOD
12 lb.		Beef, ground	
	3	Eggs, beaten	
	2 c.	Milk	
	2 c.	Bread crumbs, soft	} Combine.
	2 T.	Salt	
	2 t.	Pepper	
	4 oz.	Onion, chopped	

Measure with No. 10 dipper and flatten into patties. Place on lightly oiled baking sheet.

Bake 15–20 min. at 400° F. Yield: 50 4-oz. patties.

NOTE: Serve on hot hamburger buns.

VARIATION: **Barbecued Hamburgers.** Place browned hamburgers in baking pans. Pour Barbecue Sauce (p. 293) over patties. Cover with aluminum foil and bake 20–25 min.

Western Sandwiches

AMOUNT		INGREDIENT	METHOD
10 lb.		Beef, ground	} Sauté
	8 oz.	Onions, chopped	
		Add	
1 qt.		Tomato purée	
	2 T.	Salt	
	2 t.	Paprika	
	2 t.	Dry mustard	
	2 T.	Worcestershire sauce	
	2 t.	Chili powder	

Simmer 20–30 min. Serve with No. 10 dipper on a hot bun.

Serving: Approximately 4 oz.

Hot Chipped Beef and Cheese Sandwiches

Amount	Ingredient	Method
12 oz. 1 oz. 2 c.	Butter or margarine Flour Milk	} Make a Medium White Sauce (p. 295).
2 lb.	Add Beef, chipped, shredded	} Cook 2 min.
¼ c. 1 T.	Add Horseradish Mustard	} Blend.
50	Place a No. 30 dip of mixture on each of Bread slices, toasted and buttered	
3 lb. 2 oz.	Cover with Cheddar cheese, sliced	

Bake 3–5 min. at 350° F.

Hot Tuna Bun Sandwiches

Amount	Ingredient	Method
4 lb.	Tuna	
1 lb. 8 oz.	Cheddar cheese, shredded	
18	Eggs, hard cooked, chopped	
½ c.	Green pepper, chopped	
¼ c.	Onion, chopped	} Combine.
¾ c.	Stuffed olives, chopped	
¾ c.	Sweet pickle, chopped	
3 c.	Mayonnaise	
50	Hamburger or coney buns	
	Fill buns, using No. 16 dipper. Place in counter pan, cover with aluminum foil.	

Bake 15–20 min. at 350° F.

Variation: **Hot Luncheon Sandwiches.** Substitute any ground prepared luncheon meat for tuna, omitting green pepper and olives, and adding ½ c. prepared mustard.

sauces

Sauces, if chosen to complement the foods with which they are served, are valuable adjuncts that add variety in flavor to many common foods. Spicy, pungent sauces are served with meat, poultry, fish, and eggs; sweet sauces, with desserts, and well-seasoned cream sauces, with vegetables.

● Dessert Sauces

Butterscotch Sauce

AMOUNT	INGREDIENT	METHOD
1 lb.	Sugar, brown	Cook until a soft ball forms
1⅓ c.	Corn sirup	(238° F.).
⅔ c.	Water	
	Add	
6 oz.	Butter or margarine	Stir until melted.
8	Marshmallows	
	Cool, then add	
1⅓ c.	Milk, evaporated	
		Yield: Approximately 5 c.

Chocolate Sauce

Amount	Ingredient	Method
2 oz.	Cornstarch	
12 oz.	Sugar	Mix.
1 t.	Salt	
3 oz.	Cocoa	
	Add slowly to make a paste	
1 c.	Water, cold	
	While stirring, add	
3½ c.	Water, boiling	Boil 5 min., or until thick.
	Remove from heat, add	
6 oz.	Butter or margarine	Mix well.

Yield: 6 c.

NOTE: Serve hot or cold on pudding, cake, or ice cream.

Hot Chocolate Sauce

Amount		Ingredient	Method
	8 oz.	Butter or margarine, soft or melted	Cream over hot water.
1 lb.	8 oz.	Sugar, powdered	
	1¼ c.	Add Milk, evaporated	Cook slowly 30 min.
	8 oz.	Add Chocolate, melted	Blend.

Yield: Approximately 5 c.

NOTES: 1. Serve on vanilla or peppermint ice cream.
2. This sauce may be stored in refrigerator. Then heat over hot water before serving.

Hot Mincemeat Sauce

Amount	Ingredient	Method
1½ qt. 3 lb.　　8 oz. 　　　　2 T.	Water Sugar Orange rind, grated	Boil to soft ball stage (240° F.).
1 No. 10 can 　　　　½ c.	Add Mincemeat Orange juice	Boil about 10 min.
	Serve hot over vanilla ice cream.	
		Yield: 5 qt.

NOTE: Sirup may be omitted and hot well-seasoned mincemeat served on the ice cream.

Oriental Sauce

Amount	Ingredient	Method
2 lb. 　　　1½ pt.	Sugar Water	Cook and stir until sugar is dissolved.
2 T. 1 ¼ c. 1	Add Lemon juice Lemon rind, cut into 　long, thin strips Orange juice Orange rind, cut into 　long, thin strips	Cook until clear.
6 oz.	Add Ginger, candied	Cook to 234° F.
4 oz.	Remove from heat, add Almonds, blanched, slivered	
		Yield: Approximately 1 qt.

NOTE: Serve cold with vanilla ice cream.

Melba Sauce

Amount	Ingredient	Method
2½ qt.	Raspberries, red, frozen and juice	
¼ c.	Sugar	Mix and cook until clear.
3½ T.	Cornstarch	
	Add	
2½ c.	Currant jelly	
		Yield: 2½ qt.

NOTE: Peach Melba is made by pouring 3 T. of this sauce over a scoop of vanilla ice cream in the center of a canned or fresh peach half. It also may be served over sherbet.

Custard Sauce

Amount	Ingredient	Method
14 oz.	Sugar	
2 oz.	Cornstarch	Mix.
½ t.	Salt	
	Add	
1 pt.	Milk, cold	Stir until smooth.
	Add	
3 qt.	Milk, hot	Stirring constantly.
	Add	
10	Egg yolks, beaten	Blend well.
	Cook over hot water	
2 T.	Vanilla	
		Yield: 5 qt.

NOTE: Cool and serve with pudding or over cubed oranges.

Lemon Sauce

AMOUNT		INGREDIENT	METHOD
2 lb.		Sugar	
	3 oz.	Cornstarch	} Mix.
	½ t.	Salt	
		Add	
2 qt.		Water, boiling	} Cook until clear.
		Add	
	5 oz.	Lemon juice	
		Add	
	2 T.	Butter or margarine	
			Yield: 2 qt.

NOTE: Serve hot with Steamed Pudding (p. 154), Bread Pudding (p. 137), or Rice Pudding (p. 144).

VARIATIONS: 1. **Vanilla Sauce.** Omit lemon juice and reduce sugar to 1¼ lb. Add 2 T. vanilla.
2. **Nutmeg Sauce.** Omit lemon juice and reduce sugar to 1 lb. Add ¾ t. nutmeg.

Hard Sauce

AMOUNT		INGREDIENT	METHOD
	8 oz.	Butter	} Cream well.
		Add	
	2 T.	Water, boiling	} Stir until creamy.
		Gradually add	
1 lb.	3 oz.	Sugar, powdered	
	½ t.	Lemon extract	
			Yield: 3⅓ c.

NOTE: Serve with Christmas Pudding (p. 153).

VARIATIONS: 1. **Strawberry Hard Sauce.** Omit lemon extract and water. Add ¾ c. fresh or frozen strawberries.
2. **Cherry Hard Sauce.** Add ½ c. chopped Maraschino cherries.

Brown Sugar Hard Sauce

Amount		Ingredient	Method
	12 oz.	Butter, creamed	
1 lb.	4 oz.	Sugar, light brown, sifted	Add sugar gradually. Cream well.
		Fold in	
	¾ c.	Cream, whipped	
	2 t.	Vanilla	
			Yield: Approximately 4 c.

NOTE: Serve with Christmas Pudding (p. 153) or Steamed Pudding (p. 154).

Brown Sugar Sirup

Amount		Ingredient	Method
5 lb.		Sugar, brown	
5 lb.	8 oz.	Sugar, granulated	
	1 c.	Corn sirup	Combine and heat until dissolved.
2½ qt.		Water	
	4 oz.	Butter or margarine	
			Yield: Approximately 2 gal.

NOTE: Serve hot or cold on griddle cakes, fritters or waffles.

● MEAT AND VEGETABLE SAUCES

Hollandaise Sauce

AMOUNT	INGREDIENT	METHOD
2 oz.	Butter	
	Add	
1½ T.	Lemon juice	⎱ Place over hot water (not boiling) and
3	Egg yolks	⎰ cook slowly, beating constantly.
	When first portion of butter is melted, add	
2 oz.	Butter	⎱ Continue cooking and beating until mix-
		⎰ ture thickens.
	Add, beating constantly,	
2 oz.	Butter	
	Remove from heat, add	
f.g.	Salt	
f.g.	Cayenne	
	Serve immediately.	
		Yield: 12 servings.

Serve with fish or green vegetables, such as asparagus or broccoli.

NOTES: 1. Recommend making this sauce only in small quantity.
2. If sauce tends to curdle, add hot water, a teaspoon at a time, stirring vigorously.

Mock Hollandaise Sauce

AMOUNT		INGREDIENT	METHOD
1½ qt.		Milk, hot	⎫
	6 oz.	Butter, melted	⎪
	3 oz.	Flour	⎬ Make a White Sauce (p. 295).
	1 t.	Salt	⎪
	½ t.	Pepper	⎪
	f.g.	Cayenne	⎭
		Add	
12		Egg yolks, unbeaten	⎱ Add 1 egg at a time, a little butter,
1 lb.		Butter	⎬ and a little lemon juice until all
	½ c.	Lemon juice	⎰ are added. Beat well.
			Yield: Approximately 2 qt.

Tartar Sauce

Amount	Ingredient	Method
1 qt.	Mayonnaise	
1 c.	Pickles, chopped	
4 T.	Green pepper, chopped	
4 T.	Parsley, chopped	
1 c.	Green olives, chopped	
½ c.	Vinegar or lemon juice	} Mix.
1 T.	Onion, minced	
4 T.	Pimiento, chopped	
Few drops	Worcestershire sauce	
Few drops	Tabasco sauce.	

Yield: 7 c.

NOTE: Serve with fish.

Cucumber Sauce

Amount	Ingredient	Method
2 c.	Cucumber	} Peel, remove seeds and grate.
	Add	
1 T.	Onion, grated	
1 T.	Vinegar	
1½ T.	Lemon juice	
1 c.	Sour cream, cultured	
½ t.	Salt	
Dash	Pepper, red	

Yield: 2¾ c.

NOTE: Serve cold with fish.

Mustard Sauce

Amount	Ingredient	Method
2 T.	Sugar	
½ t.	Salt	} Mix.
2 t.	Mustard, dry	
	Add	
2	Eggs, beaten	
2 T.	Water	} Mixed.
4 T.	Vinegar	
	Cook over water until thick.	
	Add	
1 oz.	Butter or margarine	} Stir until melted.
	When cold, fold in	
1 pt.	Cream, whipped	
		Yield: Approximately 2½ c.

NOTE: Serve cold with pork, beef, or ham roasts.

Apple-Horseradish Sauce

Amount	Ingredient	Method
1 c.	Applesauce, sieved	
1 c.	Horseradish	} Mix.
1 c.	Mayonnaise	
		Yield: 3 c.

NOTE: Whipped cream may be substituted for Mayonnaise if served at once.
      Serve with ham.

Cocktail Sauce

Amount	Ingredient	Method
1 qt.	Chili sauce	
1 pt.	Catsup	
1 c.	Lemon juice	
2 T.	Onion juice	
2½ c.	Celery, chopped fine	} Mix all ingredients and chill.
5 t.	Worcestershire sauce	
6 T.	Horseradish	
f.d.	Tabasco sauce	
		Yield: Approximately 2 qt.

NOTE: Serve with clam, crabmeat, lobster, oyster, or shrimp cocktail.

Hot Vegetable Sauce

Amount		Ingredient	Method
1 lb.		Bacon, cubed (or butter)	} Fry crisp.
	4 oz.	Add Flour	} Stir until smooth and flour browned.
1 lb.	4 oz.	Add Sugar	
	¼ c.	Salt	
	1½ pt.	Vinegar, mild	} Mixed and boiled 1 min.
	1½ pt.	Water	
		Cook over water.	

Yield: 2½ qt.

NOTE: Use to wilt lettuce or spinach, or with hot potato salad or shredded cabbage.

Tomato Sauce

Amount		Ingredient	Method
	6 oz.	Butter or margarine, melted	} Blend.
	4 oz.	Flour	
2 qt.		Add Tomato juice	
	4 oz.	Onion, finely chopped	
	2 T.	Sugar	
	1 t.	Salt	} Simmer for 20 min.
	¼ t.	Pepper	
	1 t.	Worcestershire sauce	

Yield: 2 qt.

Spanish Sauce

AMOUNT	INGREDIENT	METHOD
4 oz.	Onion, chopped	Sauté.
4 oz.	Fat	
	Add	
2 qt.	Tomatoes, canned	
1 lb.	Celery, diced	
8 oz.	Green pepper, chopped	Simmer until all vegetables are tender.
6 oz.	Pimiento, chopped	
1 T.	Salt	
½ t.	Pepper	
f.g.	Cayenne	
		Yield: 2½ qt.

NOTE: May be served with meat, fish, and cheese luncheon dishes.

Uncooked Barbecue Sauce

AMOUNT	INGREDIENT	METHOD
3 c.	Vinegar	
12 oz.	Sugar	
1 No. 10 can	Catsup	Mix.
4 oz.	Salt	
4 oz.	Onion, grated	
		Yield: Approximately 4 qt.

NOTE: Pour over spareribs, shortribs, chops, or lamb shanks. Bake.

Cooked Barbecue Sauce

AMOUNT	INGREDIENT	METHOD
1 No. 10 can	Catsup	
3 qt.	Water	
2 c.	Vinegar	
2 T.	Salt	
1 t.	Pepper	
½ c.	Sugar	
1 t.	Chili powder	Combine. Simmer 10 min.
¼ c.	Worcestershire sauce	
1 T.	Tabasco sauce	
½ c.	Grated onion	
2	Lemons, sliced	
		Yield: Approximately 1½ gal.

NOTES: 1. Baste chicken or meat with sauce during cooking.
2. May also be used for barbecued hamburgers, beef, pork, or ham sandwiches.

Hot Mustard Sauce

Amount	Ingredient	Method
2 qt.	Beef broth	} Heat.
	Add gradually, stirring constantly,	
2 t.	Salt	
½ t.	Pepper	
5 oz.	Cornstarch	} Blended.
1 oz.	Sugar	
½ c.	Water	
	Cook until thick, add	
2 oz.	Mustard, prepared	
4 oz.	Horseradish	
2 T.	Vinegar	
1 oz.	Butter or margarine	
	Stir until blended.	

Yield: Approximately 2 qt.

NOTE: Serve hot with boiled beef, fresh or cured ham, or fish.

Béchamel Sauce

Amount	Ingredient	Method
1½ qt.	Stock, chicken	Cook together 20 min. Strain.
4	Onion slices	(There should be 1 qt. of
2 T.	Peppercorns	liquid.) Use in the prepara-
3 oz.	Carrots, chopped	tion of sauce.
1	Bay leaf	
8 oz.	Butter or margarine, melted	
4 oz.	Flour	
1 qt.	Liquid (prepared above)	Use same procedure as for
1 qt.	Milk, hot	White Sauce (p. 295).
½ t.	Salt	
½ t.	Pepper, white	
f.g.	Cayenne	

Yield: Approximately 2 qt.

NOTE: Serve with meat or chicken timbales or soufflés.
VARIATION: **Mornay Sauce:** Add gradually to 6 c. of hot Béchamel Sauce a few grains of cayenne pepper, 1 c. each of grated Parmesan and Swiss cheese. Let sauce remain over heat until cheese is melted; then remove and gradually beat in 1 c. of butter or margarine. Serve with fish and egg dishes.

Raisin Sauce

Amount		Ingredient	Method
4 oz.		Sugar	Bring to boiling point.
1 pt.		Water	
		Add	
1 lb.		Raisins, cooked	
	⅓ c.	Vinegar	
	2 oz.	Butter or margarine	
	1 T.	Worcestershire sauce	
	1 t.	Salt	Simmer 5 min., or until jelly is
	¼ t.	Pepper, white	dissolved.
	½ t.	Cloves	
	⅛ t.	Mace	
1 lb.		Currant jelly	

Yield: 5 c.

NOTE: Red coloring may be added. Serve with ham.

White Sauce

	Ingredients				
Consistency	Milk	Flour	Butter or Margarine	Salt	Uses
Very thin	4 qt.	2 oz.	8 oz.	1½ T.	Cream soup made from starchy foods
Thin	4 qt.	4 oz.	8 oz.	1½ T.	Cream soup made from nonstarchy foods
Medium	4 qt.	8 oz.	1 lb.°	1½ T.	Creamed dishes, gravies
Thick	4 qt.	12–16 oz.	1 lb.°	1½ T.	Soufflés
Very thick	4 qt.	1 lb. 4 oz.	1 lb. 4 oz.°	1½ T.	Croquettes

Method 1. Melt butter or margarine, remove from heat. Add flour; stir until smooth. Add salt, then hot milk gradually, stirring constantly. Cook and stir as necessary, until smooth and thick (15–20 min.).

Method 2.° Reduce butter or margarine to 8–10 oz. in Medium, Thick, and Very Thick White Sauce. Combine flour with ¼ milk. Add flour-milk paste to remainder of milk (hot). Cook to desired consistency, then add fat and salt.

Method 3. This method is used for making large quantities (more than 4 qt.). Add ¼ milk to the fat-flour mixture; beat until smooth. Add mixture to remaining milk.

Method 4. This method uses a steamer. Make a paste of flour and butter or margarine. Add cold milk until mixture is the consistency of cream. Heat remaining milk; add flour and fat mixture, stirring constantly with wire whip. Place in steamer until flour is cooked; if necessary, stir once during cooking.

White Sauce Variations

Sauce à la King. Add 12 oz. chopped green pepper and 12 oz. sliced mushrooms, sautéed, and 1 lb. chopped pimiento to 1 gal. Medium White Sauce. Combine with cubed cooked chicken, meats, vegetables, or eggs.

Bacon Sauce. Add 1½ lb. cooked chopped bacon to 1 gal. Medium White Sauce. Use bacon fat in making the sauce. Combine with eggs or vegetables in scalloped dishes.

Cheese Sauce. Add 3 lb. sharp Cheddar cheese (grated or ground), 2 T. Worcestershire sauce, f.g. cayenne pepper to 1 gal. Medium White Sauce. Serve on fish, egg dishes, soufflés, and vegetables.

Egg Sauce. Add 20 chopped hard-cooked eggs and 2 T. prepared mustard to 1 gal. Medium White Sauce. Serve with cooked fish or croquettes.

Golden Sauce. Add 2 c. slightly beaten egg yolks to 1 gal. Medium White Sauce. Serve on fish, chicken, or vegetables.

Mushroom Sauce. Add 1½ lb. sliced mushrooms and 4 oz. minced onion, sautéed in 4 oz. butter or margarine, to 1 gal. Medium White Sauce. Serve over egg, meat or poultry dishes or vegetables.

Pimiento Sauce. Add 1¼ lb. finely chopped pimiento and 2 c. finely chopped parsley to 1 gal. Medium White Sauce. Serve with poached fish, croquettes, or egg dishes.

Shrimp Sauce. Add 4 lb. cooked shrimp, 2 T. prepared mustard, and 2 T. Worcestershire sauce to 1 gal. Medium White Sauce. Serve with fish, eggs, or cheese soufflé.

Brown Sauce

Amount	Ingredient	Method
10 oz.	Flour, browned	Blend.
1 lb.	Fat, hot	
	Add, stirring constantly,	
1 gal.	Meat stock	
8 oz.	Onion, thinly sliced	Simmered 10 min. Strained.
1½ T.	Salt	
½ t.	Pepper	
	Cook until sauce is thickened.	

Yield: Approximately 1 gal.

Brown Sauce Variations

Jelly Sauce. Add 2 c. currant jelly, beaten until melted, 2 T. tarragon vinegar, and 4 oz. sautéed minced onions to 2 qt. Brown Sauce. Serve with lamb or game.

Mushroom Sauce. Add 1 lb. sliced mushrooms and 2 oz. minced onions, sautéed, to 2 qt. Brown Sauce. Serve with steak.

Olive Sauce. Add 1 c. chopped stuffed olives to 2 qt. Brown Sauce. Serve with meat or duck.

Piquante Sauce. Add 2 oz. minced onions, 2 oz. capers, ½ c. vinegar, ¼ c. sugar, ¼ t. salt, ¼ t. paprika, and ½ c. chili sauce or chopped sweet pickle to 2 qt. Brown Sauce. Serve with meats.

Savory Mustard Sauce. Add ½ c. prepared mustard and ½ c. horseradish to 2 qt. Brown Sauce. Serve with meats.

Drawn Butter Sauce

Amount		Ingredient	Method
2 qt.			Make as White Sauce (p. 295). Cook 5 min.
	4 oz.	Water, hot	
	2 oz.	Flour	
		Butter	
		When ready to serve, add	
	1 t.	Salt	Beat well.
	6 oz.	Butter, cut	
			Yield: 2 qt.

NOTE: Serve with green vegetables, fried or broiled fish, or egg dishes.

VARIATIONS: 1. **Almond Butter Sauce.** Add 4 T. lemon juice and 1 c. toasted slivered almonds just before serving.

2. **Lemon Butter Sauce.** Add 1 T. grated lemon rind and 4 T. lemon juice just before serving. Serve with fish, new potatoes, broccoli, or asparagus.

3. **Maitre D'Hotel Sauce.** Add 4 T. lemon juice, 4 T. chopped parsley, and 8 egg yolks, well beaten.

4. **Parsley Butter.** Add 1½ c. minced parsley just before serving. Serve with fish, potatoes, or other vegetables.

Meuniere Sauce

AMOUNT		INGREDIENT	METHOD
1 lb.	4 oz.	Butter or margarine	} Heat until lightly browned.
	2 oz.	Add Minced onion	} Brown slightly.
	½ c. 1 T. 1 T. 1 t.	Add Lemon juice Worcestershire sauce Grated lemon rind Salt	
10 lb.		Serve hot over Cooked asparagus, broccoli, Brussels sprouts, green beans, spinach, or cabbage.	

NOTE: ½ c. toasted sliced almonds may be sprinkled over the top.

Mushroom Sauce

AMOUNT		INGREDIENT	METHOD
4 lb.	8 oz.	Mushrooms, sliced Butter or margarine	} Sauté
	4 oz.	Add Flour	} Blend.
2 qt.	1 pt.	Add, while stirring Chicken stock, hot Cream or milk Salt to taste	} Cook until thick and smooth.

VARIATIONS: 1. **Mushroom and Almond.** Add 1 lb. slivered toasted almonds. Serve over rice as an entrée.
2. **Mushroom and Cheese.** Add 1 lb. grated Cheddar cheese. Serve over asparagus or broccoli.

Pan Gravy

AMOUNT	INGREDIENT	METHOD
8 oz.	Fat (meat drippings), hot	
	Add	
8 oz.	Flour	} Stir until smooth.
	Add	
1 T.	Salt	
1 t.	Pepper	
	Add gradually, stirring constantly	
1 gal.	Water or meat stock	
	Cook until smooth and thick.	

VARIATIONS: 1. **Brown Gravy.** Use 10 oz. flour and brown in the fat.
2. **Cream Gravy.** Substitute milk for water or stock.
3. **Giblet Gravy.** Use chicken drippings for fat and chicken broth for liquid. Add 1 qt. cooked giblets, chopped.
4. **Onion Gravy.** Lightly brown 1 lb. thinly sliced onions in fat before adding flour.
5. **Vegetable Gravy.** Add 1 lb. diced carrots, 4 oz. chopped celery, and 12 oz. chopped onion, cooked in water or meat stock.

soups

There are few people who do not enjoy a bowl of homemade soup. This is especially true of patients in hospitals and nursing homes, and of regular restaurant and cafeteria clientele. Soups may be classified as stock soups, cream soups, and thick soups or chowders. Soup stock is broth made from meat or poultry, or water in which vegetables have been cooked. A thin white sauce is usually the base for cream soup. Chowders are thick vegetable or fish soups made with or without milk.

● SOUP RECIPES

Beef Stock

AMOUNT	INGREDIENT	METHOD
15 lb.	Beef shank, lean	
	Add	
6 gal.	Water, cold	} Bring to boiling point.
	Add	
8 oz.	Onions, chopped	
8 oz.	Celery, chopped	
8 oz.	Carrots, chopped	Simmer until meat leaves bone
1 T.	Peppercorns	(about 4 hr.)
2	Bay leaves	
3 oz.	Salt	

Remove meat, strain, cool, and skim off fat.

Yield: 3–4 gal.

VARIATIONS: 1. **Brown Stock.** Allow 10 lb. beef shank to stand 30 min. in cold water. Heat slowly to boiling point. Simmer 2 hr. Add vegetables which have been browned with remaining meat. Add seasonings. Simmer 3 hr.
2. **Chicken Stock.** Substitute 4 4–4½ lb. hens, cut up, for beef shank.

Variations of Beef Stock

Alphabet Soup. To 3 gal. Beef Stock, add 2 T. celery salt, ¼ t. pepper, 4 oz. grated onions, 6 oz. grated carrots, and 10 oz. alphabet noodles. Cook until added ingredients are tender. Serving: 1 c.

Barley Soup. To 3 gal. Beef Stock, add 1¾ lb. barley. Cook until barley is done. Serving: 1 c.

Beef Soup. To 3 gal. Beef Stock, add 3 lb. freshly ground beef, 5 oz. chopped celery, 5 oz. chopped carrots, 3 oz. chopped onions, 12 oz. peas, and 8 oz. rice (if desired). Cook until ingredients are tender. Serving: 1 c.

Creole Soup. To 2¼ gal. Beef Stock, add 1 No. 10 can tomatoes, 1 lb. shredded green peppers, 1 lb. chopped onions, 1 lb. cooked shell macaroni, 2 oz. salt (may vary), ¼ t. pepper, and 4 bay leaves. Cook until ingredients are tender. Serving: 1 c.

French Onion Soup. To 3 gal. Beef Stock, add 8 lb. onions, thinly sliced and sautéed in 12 oz. fat; 3 oz. flour, blended with fat and onions; 3 T. Worcestershire sauce; salt and pepper to taste. Cook until onions are tender. Serving: 1 c. To serve, pour over toasted bread cubes or strips and sprinkle with grated Parmesan cheese.

Julienne Soup. To 3 gal. Beef Stock, add 2 T. celery salt; 1 lb. carrots, 1 lb. green beans, and 12 oz. celery, cut long and thin; 2 oz. chopped onions; 2 oz. salt (may vary). Cook until vegetables are tender. Serving: 1 c.

Minestrone Soup. To 3 gal. Beef Stock, add 1 No. 2 can kidney or brown beans, 12 oz. spaghetti, 1 lb. chopped onions, 1 lb shredded potatoes, 1¾ lb. carrot strips, and 1 oz. chopped parsley. Cook until ingredients are tender. Serving: 1 c.

Noodle Soup. To 3 gal. Beef Stock, add 1½ lb. (A.P.) noodles. Cook until noodles are tender. Serving: 1 c.

Rice Soup. To 3 gal. Beef Stock, add 1½ lb. (A.P.) rice. Cook until rice is done. Serving: 1 c.

Spaghetti or Vermicelli Soup. To 3 gal. Beef Stock, add 1½ lb. (A.P.) spaghetti or vermicelli and cook till tender. Serving: 1 c.

Vegetable-Beef Soup

AMOUNT		INGREDIENT	METHOD
15 lb.		Beef shank, with meat	Bring to boiling point. Simmer 3–4 hr. Remove meat from bones and chop.
4 gal.		Water, cold	
	2	Bay leaves	
	2 oz.	Salt	
		Add	
1 lb.	8 oz.	Carrots, cubed	
1 lb.	8 oz.	Celery, chopped	
1 lb.		Onion, chopped	Simmer 30–40 min.
2 lb.		Potato, cubed	
	¼ c.	Salt	
	1 t.	Pepper	
			Yield: 3 gal.
			Serving: 1 c.

Bouillon

AMOUNT	INGREDIENT	METHOD
8 lb.	Beef, lean, seared	
	Add	
4 lb.	Bone, cracked	} Let stand 1 hr.
4 gal.	Water, cold	
	Simmer for 3–4 hr. Replace water as necessary.	
	Add	
8 oz.	Carrots, diced	
8 oz.	Celery, chopped	
8 oz.	Onion, chopped	Cook 1 hr. Strain. Chill overnight.
1	Bay leaf	Remove fat.
1 T.	Peppercorns	
¼ c.	Salt	
	To clear the broth, add	
3	Egg shells, crushed	
3	Egg whites, beaten	
	Bring slowly to the boiling point, stirring constantly.	
	Boil 15–20 min. without stirring. Strain through a cloth.	
		Yield: Approximately 3 gal.
		Serving: 1 c.

VARIATIONS: 1. **Chicken Bouillon.** Substitute 4 4–4½ lb. hens, cut up, for the beef and bone. Do not sear chicken.
2. **Tomato Bouillon.** To 1½ gal. bouillon, add 4 46-oz. cans tomato juice, 1 oz. chopped onion, 2 oz. sugar, 3 T. salt (may vary), ½ t. pepper, ½ t. cloves, 2 bay leaves, ½ T. peppercorns, ½ t. soda.

Tomato-Rice Soup

AMOUNT	INGREDIENT	METHOD
2 gal.	Soup stock	
1 gal.	Tomato purée	} Heat to boiling point.
1½ T.	Salt	
	Add	
2 oz.	Onions, chopped	
4 oz.	Green peppers, chopped	Cook until rice is tender.
8 oz.	Rice	
	Add	
6 oz.	Butter or margarine, melted	} Mix.
3 oz.	Flour	
		Yield: Approximately 3 gal.
		Serving: 1 c.

VARIATIONS: **Tomato-Barley Soup.** Add 1 lb. barley in place of rice.

Pepper Pot Soup

Amount		Ingredient	Method
	2 oz.	Onions, chopped fine	
	8 oz.	Peppers, green, chopped fine	
	6 oz.	Celery, chopped	Sauté 15 min.
3 lb. (E.P.)	8 oz.	Potatoes, diced	
	12 oz.	Butter or margarine	
		Add	
	5 oz.	Flour	Stir until well blended.
		Add	
2¼ gal.		Stock, hot	
1 qt.		Milk, hot	Keep just below boiling point 30 min.
	1½ T.	Salt	
	2 T.	Pepper, red, chopped	
			Yield: Approximately 3 gal. Serving: 1 c.

Note: Serve with Spatzels (p. 310).

Rice Soup

Amount		Ingredient	Method
4½–5 qt.		Beef or chicken stock (p. 300)	
		Add	
	12 oz.	Rice	Cooked in 6 qt. boiling water.
		Add	
1 gal.		Milk, hot	
	1 t.	Onion juice	
	3 T.	Salt	
	1 t.	Pepper	
	¼ c.	Parsley, chopped	
			Yield: Approximately 3 gal. Serving: 1 c.

Note: Garnish with toast rings sprinkled with chopped parsley and Parmesan cheese.

Split Pea Soup

Amount	Ingredient	Method
4 lb. 2 gal.	Peas, split Water	} Wash and soak overnight.
1	Add Ham bone (or 2 lb. salt pork or bacon ends, sliced) Cook in water in which peas were soaked. Cook 4–5 hr. or until peas are soft. Remove bone. Add water to make 2½ gal.	
4 oz. 2 oz. 4 oz. 2 T. ½ t. 2 qt.	Add to peas Fat, melted Flour Onion, chopped Salt Pepper Milk, hot Bring to boiling point. Serve at once.	} Made as a Thin White Sauce (p. 295).
		Yield: Approximately 3 gal. Serving: 1 c.

NOTES: 1. It may be necessary to add more salt. If soup becomes too thick, add hot milk to
bring to proper consistency.
2. If a smoother soup is desired, remove bone and meat and pureé peas.

Spanish Bean Soup

Amount	Ingredient	Method
5 lb. 12 oz. 4½ gal.	Beans, kidney or garbonza Onions, chopped Water	} Cook until beans are tender. Strain. Add water to make 1½ gal.
6 oz. 2 oz. 2 oz.	Add Onions, chopped Green peppers Butter or bacon fat	} Fried until onions are slightly browned.
1½ gal. ¼ c. 1¼ T.	Add Tomato purée Salt Pepper Cook 5 min. to blend thoroughly the ingredients.	} Heat about 10 min. Add to bean purée.
		Yield: Approximately 3 gal. Serving: 1 c.

NOTES: 1. Baked-bean purée may be substituted for kidney bean purée.
2. Ham stock may be used in place of tomato purée. 2 t. saffron may be added if
desired.

Navy Bean Soup

Amount	Ingredient	Method
3 lb. 1½ gal.	Navy beans Water, boiling	Wash beans. Add boiling water and let stand 1 hr. or longer.
	Add	
5 lb.	Ham shanks	Simmer until beans are cooked. Remove ham bones. Chop meat.
	Add	
4 oz. 8 oz.	Onion, chopped Celery, diced Water to make a total volume of 3 gal. Ham, chopped Salt and pepper to taste	Cook 30 min.
		Yield: 3 gal. Serving: 1 c.

Basic Cream Soup

Amount	Ingredient	Method
9 qt. 12 oz. 6 oz. 3 T. ½ t.	Milk, hot Butter or margarine, melted Flour Salt Pepper, white	Make as Thin White Sauce (p. 295).
		Yield: 2½ gal.

Variations of Cream Soup

Cream of Asparagus Soup. To 2½ gal. Cream Soup, add 6½ lb. asparagus, puréed. Serving 1 c.

Cream of Celery Soup. To 2½ gal. Cream Soup, add 1½ lb. chopped celery, 8 oz. diced carrots, and 2½ oz. chopped onions cooked in 1 gal. water about 1 hr. Serving 1 c.

Cream of Corn Soup. To 2½ gal. Cream Soup, add 3 qt. corn, cream style, and 1 oz. chopped onions. Serving: 1 c.

Cream of Pea Soup. To 2½ gal. Cream Soup, add 3 qt. pea purée, 2 oz. minced onions, and 1 oz. sugar. Serving: 1 c.

Cream of Potato Soup. To 2½ gal. Cream Soup, add 12 lb. diced potatoes, 6 oz. chopped onions, and 8 oz. chopped celery which have been cooked in 3 qt. water until soft. Potatoes may be mashed or puréed if desired.

Cream of Spinach Soup. To 2½ gal. Cream Soup, add 2½–3 qt. spinach purée and 2 oz. grated onions (optional). Serving: 1 c.

Cream of Vegetable Soup. To 2½ gal. Cream Soup, add 1 lb. chopped celery, 4 oz. chopped onions, 1 lb. diced carrots, 2 lb. diced potatoes, cooked in 1 gal. water, seasoned with 3 T. salt, until soft.

Vegetable Chowder. To Cream of Vegetable Soup, add 2 No. 2 cans whole kernel corn, 5 oz. green pepper, and 1 lb. diced cooked bacon or salt pork.

Corn Chowder

Amount	Ingredient	Method
1 lb.	Salt pork or bacon, cubed	} Fry until crisp.
12 oz.	Add Onions, chopped	} Cook slowly 5 min.
5 lb. (E.P.) 1 No. 10 can	Pour into kettle Potatoes, cubed, cooked Corn, whole kernel	
4 oz. 2 gal. 3 T.	Add Fat, fried from pork Flour Milk Salt	} Made as a Thin White Sauce (p. 295).
		Yield: Approximately 3 gal. Serving: 1 c.

VARIATION: **Potato.** Omit corn and increase potatoes to 8 lb.

Cream of Tomato Soup

Amount		Ingredient	Method
1½ gal.		Tomato juice	
	1 oz.	Onion, chopped	Heat to boiling point.
	½	Bay leaf	
		Add	
	1 T.	Soda	Mix well.
		Just before serving, pour slowly into	
1½ gal.		Milk, hot	
	10 oz.	Butter or margarine, melted	
	3 oz.	Flour	Made as Very Thin White Sauce (p. 295).
	3 T.	Salt	
	1 t.	Pepper	
	4 oz.	Sugar	
			Yield: Approximately 3 gal.
			Serving: 1 c.

NOTE: Chopped parsley and 1 t. whipped cream may be used as a garnish for each serving.

Cream of Chicken Soup

Amount		Ingredient	Method
	8 oz.	Fat, chicken	
	3 oz.	Flour	Make as Very Thin White Sauce (p. 295).
1 gal.		Milk	
	1½ T.	Salt	
		Add	
2 gal.		Chicken stock	
	2 t.	Celery salt	
	¼ t.	Pepper, white	
1 lb.	8 oz.	Chicken, cooked, chopped	
			Yield: Approximately 3 gal.
			Serving: 1 c.

NOTE: 1 lb. cooked rice or noodles may be added.

Cheese Soup

Amount	Ingredient	Method
8 oz. 8 oz.	Butter Onion, chopped	} Sauté until lightly browned.
	Add	
4 oz. 2 oz.	Flour Cornstarch	} Blend. Cook 3–4 min.
	Add	
1 t. 2 T. 1 t.	Paprika Salt Pepper, white	} Blend.
	Add slowly, while stirring	
1 gal. 1½ gal.	Milk Stock, chicken	} Cook until thickened.
	Add	
3 c. 3 c.	Carrots, diced, cooked Celery, diced, cooked	
	Just before serving, add	
1 lb.	Cheese, sharp Cheddar, diced	} Blend.
	Garnish with chopped parsley as served.	
		Yield: 3 gal. Serving: 1 c.

Orange Soup (Ch'en Tzu Keng)

Amount	Ingredient	Method
2 c. 6 oz. 1 t.	Water Sugar Salt	} Heat to boiling point.
	Add	
2 oz. ½ c.	Cornstarch Water, cold	} Made into a paste.
	Cook until clear, add	
6 qt. 2 oz.	Orange juice Butter	
	Heat and serve at once.	
		Yield: Approximately 1¾ gal. Serving: ½ c.

Clam Chowder

Amount	Ingredient	Method
1 gal. fresh, or 4 (15 oz.) cans	Clams	⎱ Clean. Steam until tender. ⎰ Drain and chop (save juice).
	Add	
2 oz.	Onions, chopped	⎱ Sautéed 5 min.
4 oz.	Salt pork or bacon, cubed	⎰
	Add	
6 lb. (E.P.)	Potatoes, cubed, cooked	
1 T.	Salt	
1 t.	Pepper	
	Add	
8 oz.	Butter or margarine	⎱ Made into Very Thin White
2 oz.	Flour	⎰ Sauce (p. 295).
2 gal.	Milk	
		Yield: Approximately 3 gal. Serving: 1 c.

NOTE: Juice drained from clams may be substituted for an equal quantity of the milk in white sauce. Heat and add just before serving.

Oyster Stew

Amount	Ingredient	Method
2½ gal.	Milk	⎱ Scald.
	Add, 10 min. before serving	
2½ qt.	Oysters	⎱ Heated until edges of oysters
8 oz.	Butter or margarine	⎰ begin to curl.
	Add	
3 T.	Salt	
½ t.	Pepper	
	Serve immediately	
		Yield: 3 gal. Serving: 1 c.

NOTES: 1. Care should be taken not to overcook oysters.
2. Serve at once to avoid curdling.

● ACCOMPANIMENTS AND GARNISHES FOR SOUP

Accompaniments for Soup

Celery	Dumplings	Potato Chips
Cheese sticks	Julienne vegetables	Radishes
Cheese, grated on toast	Melba toast	Spatzels (see below)
Crackers, toasted	Nuts	Sandwiches, small
Crisped bread	Olives	Toast sticks
Croutons	Pickles	

Garnishes for Soup

Cream Soups:
  Almonds, shredded, toasted
  Bacon, broiled, diced
  Cheese, grated
  Chives, chopped
  Fresh mint
  Hard-cooked egg white, finely chopped
  Hard-cooked egg yolk, riced
  Paprika
  Parsley, finely chopped
  Pimiento, minced, in whipped cream

Stock Soups:
  Cheese, grated
  Egg dumplings (see below)
  Lemon, thin slices
  Lime, thin slices
  Onion rings
  Parsley, finely chopped
  Popcorn
  Vegetables, diced or
    shredded

Egg Dumplings (Spatzels)

Amount		Ingredient	Method
1 lb.	4 oz.	Flour, sifted	
	1 t.	Baking powder	Combine.
	1½ t.	Salt	
		Add, all at once	
	3 c.	Milk	Combined.
	6	Eggs, whole	

Mix to form a soft dough. Drop small bits or press through a colander into 3 gal. of hot soup. Cook approximately 5 min.

NOTE: Soup must be very hot in order to cook dumplings.

vegetables

● COOKING VEGETABLES

Great care should be given to the preparation of fresh vegetables before cooking or serving raw. This procedure, as well as the cookery, influences the nutritive value, attractiveness, palatability, and color of the finished product. All leafy and stem vegetables should be washed thoroughly and crisped before they are cooked or used raw. Details of preparation of vegetables are given on pp. 313–316.

Fresh or frozen vegetables may be cooked by boiling, steaming, baking, pan- or deep-fat frying. The method used will depend largely on the quality of the product, the amount to be cooked, and the equipment available. To insure a high-quality product, it is important that vegetables be cooked in as small an amount of water as is practicable and as quickly as possible. Water should be brought to a second boil immediately following the addition of vegetables. Add no soda to cooking water.

Vegetables should be cooked in as small a quantity at one time as is feasible for the type of service. The needs of most food services can be met by the continuous preparation of vegetables in small quantities. A small steam-jacketed kettle, if time and pressure are carefully controlled, is highly satisfactory for cooking both fresh and frozen vegetables. It is usually large enough to prevent crowding; it will·bring water to a boil quickly after vegetables are added; and it will cook a large or small amount equally well. When a steam-jacketed kettle is not available, top-of-stove cookery is preferred for all vegetables except potatoes and carrots, which may be successfully cooked in a pressure steamer. However, other vegetables also may be cooked with satisfactory results under pressure if cooked in small quantities and arranged in thin layers in shallow pans. Here, too, the time and temperature must be carefully controlled. Whatever the method used, cook vegetables only until tender. Do not overcook.

Vegetables should be served as soon as possible after cooking and handled carefully to prevent breaking.

311

Fresh Vegetables

1. Prepare vegetables according to the directions given in the time table on pp. 313–316.

2. Cook in lots no larger than 10 lb. of prepared raw vegetable. Cook until just tender, no longer than necessary to give a palatable product. For a given vegetable, cooking time will differ according to the method of cookery, variety and maturity of the vegetable, length of time and temperature at which it has been held since harvesting, and its size or the size pieces into which it is cut. See time table for approximate cooking time.

3. Cook green and strongly flavored vegetables without a cover.

4. Drain and add 8 oz. butter or margarine for each 10 lb. of vegetable. For a creamed vegetable, add 2–3 qt. Thin or Medium White Sauce. For other serving suggestions, see pp. 327–330.

A 10-lb. lot of prepared raw vegetable makes about 50 3-oz. portions when cooked, drained, and seasoned. To determine as purchased weights, see p. 23 for preparation losses.

Time Table for Cooking Fresh Vegetables[1]

VEGETABLE	PREPARATION	BOILING			STEAMING	
		Amount of boiling water	Amount of salt	Approximate cooking time (min.)	Type of container and fill	Approximate cooking time 5-lb. steam pressure (min.)
Artichokes	Cut off stem close to leaves and 1 in. from top.	1–1½ gal.	1 T.	30–60		
Asparagus	Cut off tough parts of stems. Wash and thoroughly clean remaining portions. Asparagus may be tied in bundles of 1–2 lb. each, for boiling.	1–1½ gal.	1 T.	10–12	Counter pans (in rows not more than 2 in. deep).	8–10
Beans, Lima	Shell. (Scald pods to make shelling easier.) Wash.	2½ qt.	1 T.	20–25	Solid (½ full)	15–20
Beans, snap or wax	Wash. Trim ends and remove strings. Cut or break beans into 1 in. pieces.	2½ qt.	1 T.	30–40	Solid (⅓ full) Perforated (⅔ full)	20–30 20–30
Beets	Remove tops, leaving 2-in. stem on beets. Wash. Do not peel or remove root.	To cover	None	60–90	Solid (full) Perforated (full)	60–75 60–75

[1] Adapted from *Recipes for Quantity Service*, Home Economics Research Report No. 5, United States Department of Agriculture, Washington, D.C., 1958.

Time Table for Cooking Fresh Vegetables (Continued)

VEGETABLE	PREPARATION	BOILING			STEAMING	
		Amount of boiling water	Amount of salt	Approximate cooking time (min.)	Type of container and fill	Approximate cooking time 5-lb. steam pressure (min.)
Broccoli	Cut off tough stalk ends and wash broccoli. Soak in salted water for ½ hr. if insects are present. Drain. Peel stalks. Cut broccoli lengthwise if thick, to speed cooking.	3 qt.	1 T.	10–20	Single layer in shallow pan (2–2½ lb. per pan)	7–10
Brussels Sprouts	Remove withered leaves and wash thoroughly.	1½ gal.	1 T.	10–15	Shallow counter pan (¼ full)	15–20
Cabbage, coarsely shredded	Remove wilted outside leaves. Wash, quarter, and core cabbage. Crisp in cold water, if wilted. Shred.	1½ gal.	2 T.	10–15	Solid (½ full) Perforated (⅔ full)	10–12 5–10
Carrots	Wash; scrape or pare. Slice if desired.	3 qt.	1 T.	Sliced, 15–20 Whole, 20–30	Solid (½ full) Perforated (½ full)	20–30 15–20
Cauliflower	Remove outer leaves and stalks. Break cauliflower into flowerets. Wash. Soak in salted water for ½ hr. if insects are present. Drain.	1½ gal.	2 T.	15–20	Solid (⅓ full) Perforated (¼ full)	10–12 8–10

Vegetable	Preparation	Water	Salt	Time	Steamer	Time
Celery, Pascal	Wash, trim. Cut into 1-in. pieces.	1 gal.	1 T.	15–20	Solid (filled to depth of 1½ in.) / Perforated (filled to depth of 2½ in.)	12–15 / 10–12
Chard, mustard and turnip greens	Sort. Cut off tough stems. Wash greens at least 5 times, lifting them out of water each time.	Only water clinging to leaves	1 T.	15–25	Solid (¾ full)	15–25
Collards	Sort and trim. Strip leaves from coarse stems. Wash at least 5 times, lifting out of water each time. Stir occasionally while cooking.	1 gal.	1½ T.	20–35	Solid (½ full) / Perforated (½ full)	20–30 / 15–20
Corn on cob	Husk. Remove silks. Wash. Do not allow to stand in water.	1¼ gal. or to cover	1½ T.	10–15	Perforated (25 portions)	8–10
Kale	Sort. Strip leaves from coarse stems. Wash at least 5 times, lifting out of water each time. Stir occasionally while cooking.	1 gal.	1½ T.	25–45	Solid (¼ full) / Perforated (¼ full)	25–35 / 15–20
Onions	Peel and wash. Quarter if large.	1½ gal.	2 T.	20–35	Perforated (⅓ full)	20–25
Parsnips	Wash and pare. Quarter lengthwise and cut in 3-in. pieces.	1¼ gal.	1½ T.	20–30	Perforated (¼ full)	15–20
Potatoes	Scrub. Cut large potatoes to serving size. Peel and remove eyes.	1¼ gal.	1½ T.	30–50	Solid (¾ full) / Perforated (¾ full)	30–45 / 30–35
Rutabagas	Wash and pare. Cut into 1-in. cubes.	3 qt.	1 T.	20–30	Solid (½ full) / Perforated (½ full)	20–30 / 15–25

Time Table for Cooking Fresh Vegetables (Continued)

VEGETABLE	PREPARATION	BOILING			STEAMING	
		Amount of boiling water	Amount of salt	Approximate cooking time (min.)	Type of container and fill	Approximate cooking time 5-lb. steam pressure (min.)
Spinach	Sort and trim. Cut off coarse stems and roots. Wash leaves at least 5 times, lifting out of water each time.	Only water clinging to leaves	1 T.	10–20	Solid (½ full) / Perforated (½ full)	6–8 / 4–6
Squash, Hubbard	Wash. If peel is hard and tough, soften it by steaming or boiling whole squash for 10 min. Cut, remove seeds, fiber, and peel. Cut squash into pieces.	1¼ gal.	1½ T.	15–20	Solid (½ full) / Perforated (½ full)	15–20 / 12–15
Squash, summer	Wash and trim. Cut unpeeled squash into 1-in. pieces or thin slices.	2 qt.	2 t.	10–20	Solid (¾ full) / Perforated (⅓ full)	15–20 / 8–12
Sweet potatoes	Select potatoes of uniform size. Scrub.	1¼ gal.	None	35–50	Solid (¾ full) / Perforated (¾ full)	30–40 / 20–30
Turnips	Wash, pare, and cut into 1-in. cubes.	3 qt.	None	15–20	Perforated (½ full)	10–15

Frozen Vegetables

Frozen vegetables should never be served raw. To insure uniform cooking, tightly packed vegetables should be thawed until they can be easily separated. Loosely packed vegetables need not be thawed before cooking.

Frozen vegetables may be cooked covered in boiling salted water on top of the range or in a steam-jacketed kettle, steamer, or pressure saucepan. The amount of water needed depends on the vegetable to be cooked, the method of cookery, and the utensils used. The approximate time for cooking frozen vegetables is about half as long as for fresh vegetables, but will vary with the quality of the vegetable and the degree of thawing, (see p. 318).

Boiling:

1. Add 1 t. salt to each quart of water.

2. Add vegetable to boiling water, cover pan and quickly bring back to boiling.

3. Start timing when water returns to boil. Cook for the time indicated in the time table.

4. Drain and add 8 oz. butter or margarine for each 10 lb. of vegetable. For a creamed vegetable, add 2–3 qt. Thin or Medium White Sauce. For other serving suggestions, see pp. 327–330.

Steaming:

1. Place vegetables in 5-lb. lots in solid steamer pans. Leave uncovered, unless otherwise specified. Mashed winter squash should be covered with aluminum foil to prevent water from collecting in the pans.

2. Steam in a compartment steamer for the time indicated in the time table.

3. Drain and add 8 oz. butter or margarine for each 10 lb. vegetable. Add salt, if desired, using 2 T. for each 10-lb. lot.

NOTE: A 10-lb. lot of frozen vegetable makes about 50 3-oz. portions when cooked, drained, and seasoned.

Canned Vegetables

1. Pour off half the liquid; use for soups, gravies, and sauces.

2. Heat vegetables and remaining liquid in kettle on top of the range only long enough to bring to serving temperature; or heat in covered counter pans in the steamer approximately 3–5 min.

3. Add 4 oz. butter or margarine or 1–1½ qt. Thin or Medium White Sauce for each No. 10 can of vegetables. Season to taste.

NOTE: Two No. 10 cans of vegetables will make approximately 50 portions.

Time Table for Cooking Frozen Vegetables[1]

	BOILING		STEAMING
VEGETABLE	Amount of boiling water (qt.)	Approximate cooking time (after liquid begins to boil) (min.)	Approximate cooking time (min.)
Asparagus, cuts and tips	1½	7–10	5–10
Beans, blackeye (blackeye peas, cowpeas)	1	25–30	15–25
Beans, Lima, baby	2	12–15	10–15
Beans, Lima, large	2	6–12	12–20
Beans, snap, green	1	5–30	10–15
Broccoli, chopped	1½	8–20	15–20
Broccoli, spears	1½	10–12	4–5
Brussels sprouts	1	5–8	3–5
Cauliflower	1½	10–12	4–5
Collards	1½	30–40	15–40
Corn, cut	1½	5–10	5–10
Kale	2	20–30	20–30
Okra	1	3–5	3–5
Peas, green	1	5–10	3–5
Peas and carrots	1	8–10	3–5
Squash, Hubbard (in double boiler)	none	35–40	20–25
Succotash	2	6–15	12–20
Turnip greens	2	25–30	18–20
Vegetables, mixed	1	20–25	15–20

[1] Adapted from *Recipes for Quantity Service,* Home Economics Research Report No. 5, United States Department of Agriculture, Washington, D.C., 1958.

Dried Vegetables

Wash. Cover vegetable with boiling water. Cover kettle and let stand 1 hr. Cook in same water until tender (about 1 hr.); or cover with cold water and soak overnight.

● VEGETABLE RECIPES

Mashed Potatoes

Amount		Ingredient	Method
12 lb. (E.P.)		Potatoes	} Cook (p. 315).
		Mash and add	
2–2½ qt.		Milk, hot	
	8 oz.	Butter or margarine	
	3 T.	Salt	
		Whip until light and creamy.	
			Serving: Approximately 5 oz.

NOTES: 1. Potato water may be substituted for part of milk.
  2. 8 oz. nonfat dry milk, sprinkled over potatoes before mashing, plus 2–2½ qt. water may be substituted for liquid milk.
  3. 2–2½ lb. instant mashed potatoes may be substituted for 12 lb. raw potatoes. Follow processor's instructions for preparation.
VARIATION: **Mashed Sweet Potatoes.** Use 15 lb. (E.P.) sweet potatoes. Add ½ t. nutmeg.

Scalloped Potatoes

Amount		Ingredient	Method
12 lb. (E.P.)		Potatoes, pared	⎱ Slice. Place in 2 12 x 20-in.
	3 T.	Salt	⎰ baking pans.
		Pour over potatoes	
	8 oz.	Butter or margarine	
	8 oz.	Flour	Made as White Sauce (p. 295).
1 gal.		Milk	
	1½ T.	Salt	
		Cover potatoes with	
	6 oz.	Bread crumbs	Mixed.
	2 oz.	Butter or margarine, melted	

Bake approximately 2 hr. at 350° F.   Serving: 5 oz.

NOTE: Potatoes may be steamed until tender and Medium White Sauce added.
VARIATIONS: 1. **Scalloped Potatoes with Onions.** Before baking, cover potatoes with shredded cheese and onion rings.
  2. **Scalloped Potatoes with Ham.** Add 5 lb. cubed cured ham to white sauce.
  3. **Scalloped Potatoes with Pork Chops.** Brown chops, season, place on top of potatoes before baking.

Variations in Potato Preparation

Au Gratin Potatoes. Cube boiled potatoes (or dice before cooking). Add 1 gal. Medium White Sauce (p. 295) and 2 lb. grated cheese. Place in oiled baking pan; top with buttered crumbs. Bake approximately 25 min. at 400° F.

Baked Potatoes. Scrub potatoes of uniform size and remove blemishes. Bake approximately 1 hr. (or until tender) at 400°–450° F. Potatoes may be wrapped in aluminum foil. May be served with sour cream and chives or with cheese sauce and chopped green onions.

Cottage Fried Potatoes. Add sliced cold boiled potatoes to fat in hot frying pan. Add salt and pepper. Stir as needed and fry until browned.

Duchess Potatoes. Add melted butter or margarine, a small amount of milk, and beaten egg to mashed or riced potatoes. Mix well. Pile mixture lightly into an oiled baking pan. Bake in a moderate oven until set.

Franconia Potatoes. Cook pared uniform potatoes approximately 15 min.; drain and place in pan in which meat is roasting. Bake approximately 40 min., or until tender and lightly browned, basting with drippings in pan or turning occasionally to brown all sides. Serve with roast.

French Baked Potatoes. Select small uniform potatoes and pare. Roll potatoes in melted fat, then in cracker crumbs or crushed Cornflakes. Place in shallow pan and bake.

Hashed Brown Potatoes. Add finely chopped boiled potatoes to fat in hot frying pan. Add salt and pepper. Stir occasionally and fry until browned.

Lyonnaise Potatoes. 1. Cook onion slowly in fat without browning. Add seasoned, cut, boiled potatoes and cook until browned. 2. Cut potatoes as for French fries. Steam until tender, place in oiled baking pan. Cover top with fat and onions. Place in oven and cook until browned.

Lyonnaise Baked Potates. 1. Select baking potatoes of medium size. Cut each in 4 crosswise slices; place a slice of onion, salt, pepper, and butter between slices and wrap each in aluminum foil. Bake at 400° F. until potatoes are almost done. Open foil and return to oven to brown tops.

Oven-browned Potatoes. 1. Pare and cut potatoes in uniform pieces. Place in baking pan containing a small amount of fat. Turn potatoes so that all sides are coated with fat. Sprinkle with salt. Bake in hot oven until browned and tender. Turn as necessary for even browning. 2. Parboil potatoes approximately 15 min. before placing in baking pan, to shorten baking time. 3. Brown raw potatoes in deep fat before placing in oiled baking pan.

Oven-fried Potatoes. Prepare potatoes as for French fried potatoes. Place in oiled shallow pan to make a thin layer and brush with oil or melted fat, turning to cover all sides. Bake 20–30 min. at 450° F., or until browned, turning occasionally. Drain on absorbent paper and sprinkle with salt.

Persillade New Potatoes. Pare and cook uniform small potatoes. Pour over them a mixture of lemon juice and butter, then roll in minced parsley.

Potato Balls. Pare potatoes and cut into balls with a French vegetable cutter. Cook. Season with lemon juice and butter and roll in minced parsley.

Potatoes Continental. Peel and cook small potatoes in meat stock with bay leaves until tender. Drain and season with onion browned in butter. Garnish with minced parsley and paprika.

Potato Croquettes. Mash potatoes, add butter, salt, cayenne, and well-beaten egg yolks. Shape into croquettes. Egg and crumb. Chill. Fry in deep fat.

Potatoes in Jackets. Wash medium-sized potatoes and remove any blemishes. Steam until tender and serve without removing skins.

Potato Pancakes. Grate or grind 15 lb. raw potatoes and 4 oz. onions; drain. Add 6 beaten eggs, 8 oz. flour, 3 T. salt, 1 t. baking powder, ¾ c. cream or milk. Drop with No. 20 dipper onto a hot oiled griddle. Fry until golden brown on each side. Serve with applesauce.

Potato Rosettes. Force Duchess potatoes through a pastry tube, forming rosettes or fancy shapes. Bake at 350°–400° F. until browned. Use as a garnish for planked steak.

Riced Potatoes. Pare potatoes and boil or steam until tender; force through potato ricer or coarse strainer. Pile lightly in hot serving dish and sprinkle with salt and paprika.

Rissolé Potatoes. See Oven-browned Potatoes 3.

Stuffed Baked (Potatoes in the Half Shell or Double Baked Potato). Cut hot baked potatoes into halves lengthwise (if potatoes are small, cut a slice from one side). Scoop out contents. Mash, season with salt, pepper, butter, and hot milk. Pile lightly into shells, leaving tops rough. Bake until tops are browned. Grated cheese or pieces of pimiento may be placed over the top.

French Fried Potatoes

Amount	Ingredient	Method
15–18 lb. (E.P.)	Potatoes	Pare and cut into uniform strips from ⅜ to ¼ in. thick.
		Cover with cold water to keep potatoes from darkening. Just before frying, drain well or dry with paper towels. Place potatoes in frying baskets. Fry according to method 1 or 2.

Method 1. Half fill frying kettle with fat or oil. Preheat to 365° F. Fry for 6–8 min. Drain; sprinkle with salt if desired.

Method 2 (Two-stage method).

(a) Heat fat to 360° F. Place drained potato strips in hot fat, using an 8 to 1 ratio of fat to potatoes, by weight, as a guide for filling fryer basket. Fry 3–5 min., depending on thickness of strips. The potatoes should not brown.) Drain.

(b) Reheat fat to 375° F. Place about twice as many potato strips in kettle as for first-stage frying. Fry 2–3 min., or until golden brown. Drain; sprinkle with salt if desired.

Note: Select a mealy type potato for French frying. For best results, store potatoes at room temperature 2 weeks before frying.

Variations: 1. **Shoestring Potatoes.** Cut potatoes into ⅛-in. strips. Fry 3–10 min. at 325–335° F.
2. **Lattice Potatoes.** Cut potatoes with lattice slicer. Fry 3–10 min. at 350–375° F.
3. **Potato Chips.** Cut potatoes into very thin slices. Fry 3–6 min. at 325° F.
4. **Deep-fat Browned Potatoes.** Partially cook whole or half potatoes. Fry in deep fat 5–7 min. at 350–375° F.

Glazed or Candied Sweet Potatoes

AMOUNT	INGREDIENT	METHOD
25 lb. (A.P.)	Sweet potatoes	Steam or boil until tender. Peel. Cut into halves lengthwise. Arrange in shallow pans.
	Pour over potatoes	
1 lb. 12 oz.	Sugar, brown	
1 pt.	Water	Mixed and heated to boiling point.
8 oz.	Butter or margarine	
½ t.	Salt	

Bake approximately 20–30 min. at 400° F.   Serving: Approximately 4 oz.

NOTE: Baste frequently with sirup.
VARIATIONS: 1. **Candied with Almonds.** Proceed as for Glazed Sweet Potatoes; increase butter
or margarine to 12 oz.; reduce brown sugar to 1½ lb. and water to 1 c. Add
1 c. dark sirup and 2 t. mace. When partially glazed, sprinkle top with
chopped almonds and continue cooking until almonds are toasted.
2. **Orange Slices.** Add 4 T. grated orange rind to sirup. Cut 5 oranges in half and
slice thinly; add to sweet potatoes when sirup is added.

Sweet Potato and Apple Casserole

AMOUNT	INGREDIENT	METHOD
15 lb.	Sweet potatoes	Cook potatoes in skins. Peel and slice.
5 lb.	Apples, pared and sliced	
	Place alternate layers of sweet potatoes and apples in baking pan.	
	Add	
1 lb.	Sugar, brown	
8 oz.	Sugar, white	
2 T.	Salt	Made into a sirup.
8 oz.	Butter or margarine	
1 qt.	Water	

Bake 45 min. at 350° F.   Serving: Approximately 4 oz.

NOTE: During last 5 min. of baking 1 lb. marshmallows may be placed on top.
VARIATION: **Cranberry-Sweet Potato Casserole.** Substitute 3 lb. cooked cranberries for apples, omit
brown sugar, and add 3 lb. granulated sugar.

Sweet Potato and Almond Croquettes

Amount		Ingredient	Method
12 lb.		Sweet potatoes	} Pare, cook, and mash.
		Add	
16		Egg yolks, beaten	} Mix well.
	1 c.	Cream	
		Add	
	2 t.	Nutmeg	
	5 T.	Sugar	} Mix well.
	1 T.	Salt	
1 lb.		Almonds, chopped	

Measure with No. 12 dipper. Chill in refrigerator 2 hr., or longer. Remove ½ hr. before frying. Dip in egg mixture (p. 32).

Amount	Ingredient	Method
	Roll in	
1 lb.	Cornflakes, crushed	

Shape as croquettes or patties.

Fry in deep fat 3–4 min. at 375° F.   Serving: 1 3-oz. croquette.

NOTE: May be baked. Place on oiled baking pan. Spread with 8 oz. butter or margarine. Bake 30–45 min. at 350° F.

Baked Tomatoes

Amount		Ingredient	Method
50		Tomatoes (4–5 oz. each)	} Wash. Cut cone-shaped piece from center.
		Add	
	2 T.	Salt	} Sprinkle ⅛–¼ t. in center of each tomato.
		Allow to stand 1 hr.	
		Add	
	6 oz.	Butter or margarine, melted	
	2 oz.	Bread crumbs, coarse	{ Combine. Place 2 t. crumbs in each tomato.
	6 oz.	Onions, chopped fine	

Bake 12–15 min. at 400° F.   Serving: 1 tomato.

NOTE: Tomatoes may be cut in half and spread with crumb mixture. Bake 10–12 min.
VARIATIONS: 1. **Mushroom-stuffed Tomatoes.** Add 2 lb. sautéed, sliced, or chopped mushrooms to crumb mixture.
2. **Broiled Tomato Slices.** Cut tomatoes in ½-in. slices. Salt, dot with butter, and broil.

French Fried Onions

Amount	Ingredient	Method
8 lb. (E.P.)	Onions	Cut into ¼-in. slices; separate into rings. Soak in milk 1 hr. if desired.
	Dip in	
12 oz.	Flour	
2 t.	Baking powder	
1½ t.	Salt	Made into a batter.
2 c.	Milk	
6	Eggs, beaten	
	Fry in deep fat 3–4 min. at 350–375° F. Drain.	

VARIATIONS: 1. **French Fried Cauliflower.** Dip 10 lb. cold cooked cauliflowerets into batter and fry 3–5 min. at 370° F.
2. **French Fried Eggplant.** Pare, cut into crosswise ¼-in.-thick slices. Soak in salt water (2 T. salt per qt.) 1 hr. Dip in batter and fry 5–7 min. at 370° F.

Baked Onions

Amount	Ingredient	Method
50	Onions (4 oz. each)	Peel. Make small cavity in center. Steam until tender.
	Sprinkle with	
1 lb.	Bread crumbs, buttered	
2 T.	Salt	
	Pour over onions	
1 qt.	Water, broth, or milk	

Bake 20–30 min. at 400° F., or until browned.

VARIATIONS: 1. **Stuffed Baked Onions.** Scoop out center of onions. Fill with mixture of 1½ qt. Thin White Sauce (p. 295), 1 lb. butter or margarine, 6 beaten egg yolks, and onion centers cooked and chopped. 12 oz. chopped toasted almonds may be added. Cover tops of onions with buttered crumbs.
2. **Spanish Baked Onions.** Place steamed onions in baking pan. Pour Spanish Sauce (p. 293) over onions and bake 20–30 min. at 400° F.

Buttered Cabbage

AMOUNT	INGREDIENT	METHOD
15 lb. (E.P.) 4 gal. 2 T.	Cabbage Water, boiling Salt	Remove outer leaves. Cut into quarters and remove stalk. Cut quarters in several pieces or shred. Cook in boiling salt water or steam until tender (approximately 20 min.).
8 oz.	Drain and add Butter or margarine, melted	Serving: 3 oz.

NOTE: Cabbage will cook in a shorter time if shredded and will yield a more desirable product.

VARIATIONS: 1. **Creamed Cabbage.** Omit butter or margarine. Pour 2 qt. Medium White Sauce (p. 295) over the cooked, drained cabbage.

2. **Scalloped Cabbage.** Omit butter or margarine. Pour 2 qt. Medium White Sauce over cabbage wedges. Cover with buttered crumbs. Bake 15–20 min. at 400° F. Grated cheese may be added.

Hot Slaw

AMOUNT		INGREDIENT	METHOD
1 lb.	5 oz. 1½ T. 4 oz. 2 t.	Sugar Salt Flour Mustard, dry	Mix.
1 qt. 1¼ qt.		Add Milk, hot Water, hot	Stir and cook until thick.
	8	Add Eggs, beaten	Stirring constantly.
	2⅔ c.	Add Vinegar, hot	
12 lb.	4 t.	Pour sauce over Cabbage, raw, shredded Celery seed	Yield: 4 qt. Serving: Approximately 3 oz.

NOTE: Do not pour hot sauce over cabbage until ready to serve. This sauce may also be used as a cooked salad dressing.

Buttered Spinach

Amount	Ingredient	Method
15 lb.	Spinach	
	Remove roots, wilted leaves, and coarse stems. Wash 2–5 times, lifting leaves out of water each time. Enough water will cling to leaves so it is not necessary to add water to cook. Cook in uncovered kettle, approximately 20 min., stirring frequently with a fork until leaves are wilted. Do not overcook. Drain if necessary.	
	Add	
1½ T.	Salt	
8 oz.	Butter or margarine, melted	
		Serving: 3 oz.

Notes: 1. May be cooked in steamer (p. 316).
2. May be served with sliced new beets.
3. Garnish with 12 sliced or chopped hard-cooked eggs or 1 lb. bacon cooked until crisp, then crumbled.

Spanish Green Beans

Amount	Ingredient	Method
8 oz.	Bacon, diced	
6 oz.	Onion, chopped	Fry until onions are browned.
4 oz.	Green pepper, chopped	
	Add	
4 oz.	Flour	Stir until smooth.
	Add	
2 qt.	Tomatoes, hot	Stir well.
1 T.	Salt	
	Add	
2 No. 10 cans (or 10 lb.)	Green beans, drained	
	Simmer approximately 30 min.	
		Serving: 3 oz.

Variations: 1. **Southern-style Green Beans.** Cut 1½ lb. bacon or salt pork into small pieces. Add 6 oz. chopped onion and fry until onion is lightly browned. Add to hot, drained green beans. Serve with boiled ham and corn bread.
2. **Creole Green Beans.** Omit bacon. Sauté onion, green pepper, and 8 oz. celery in 2 oz. butter or margarine. Add 2 oz. sugar to tomatoes.

Harvard Beets

Amount	Ingredient	Method
1 t.	Cloves, whole	
2 qt.	Beet juice	Heat to boiling point.
1	Bay leaf	
	Add, stirring constantly,	
12 oz.	Sugar	
1½ T.	Salt	Mixed.
6 oz.	Cornstarch	
	Cook until thick, add	
4 oz.	Butter or margarine	
1½ c.	Vinegar	
	Add, and reheat	
2 No. 10 cans	Beets, sliced, drained	
		Serving: Approximately 3 oz.

NOTE: 12 lb. fresh beets may be substituted for canned beets.
VARIATIONS: 1. **Beets with Orange Sauce.** Omit bay leaf and vinegar; add 1½ c. orange juice.
2. **Hot Spiced Beets.** Drain juice from two No. 10 cans sliced beets and add 1 T. cloves, 1½ T. salt, ½ t. cinnamon, 1 lb. brown sugar, 8 oz. granulated sugar, and 1 qt. vinegar. Cook 10 min. Pour sauce over beets and reheat.

● SUGGESTIONS FOR SERVING VEGETABLES[1]

Artichokes. Serve whole with melted butter, margarine, or Mayonnaise Dressing.

Asparagus with Cheese Sauce. Serve 5 or 6 stalks of cooked asparagus with 1 T. Cheese Sauce.

Fresh Asparagus with Hollandaise Sauce. Serve 1 T. Hollandaise Sauce over cooked asparagus.

Creamed Asparagus on Toast. Add 1 gal. Medium White Sauce to 10 lb. (E.P.) asparagus, cooked. Serve on toast.

Green Beans Almandine. Add 8 oz. slivered almonds lightly browned in 8 oz. butter or margarine to freshly cooked and drained beans.

French Green Beans. Cook frozen French cut beans. Drain and season with 1 c. Mayonnaise, ¾ c. cultured sour cream, 2 T. vinegar, salt, pepper, and 2 oz. onion sautéed in 2 oz. butter or margarine.

Green Beans and Mushrooms. Add 2 lb. sautéed chopped mushrooms to cooked, drained beans arranged in a serving pan. Cover with 6 10½-oz. cans of cream of mushroom soup. Top with toasted almonds. Bake uncovered about 25 min. at 350° F.

Julienne Beets. Shred cooked beets into thin strips. Season with mixture of 8 oz. butter or margarine, ½ c. sugar, 4 t. salt, 1 c. lemon juice.

[1] For preparation and detailed cookery methods, see pp. 313–316.

Beets in Sour Cream. Grate fresh cooked beets and season with a mixture of 1½ c. lemon juice, 1½ T. onion juice, 2 t. salt, and 1¼ c. sugar. Toss lightly. Serve with a spoonful of cultured sour cream on each portion.

Broccoli with Hollandaise Sauce or Lemon Butter. Serve cooked spears of chopped broccoli with 1 T. Hollandaise Sauce or 1 t. lemon butter.

Almond-Buttered Broccoli. Brown slivered almonds in butter and pour over cooked and drained broccoli.

Brussels Sprouts. Serve with melted butter.

Julienne Carrots and New Peas. Cut carrots into long narrow strips, cook, and add butter. Place 4 or 5 strips on each plate and place 1 T. buttered peas in the center.

Buttered Latticed Carrots. Cut the carrots with a lattice slicer and cook until tender; serve with melted butter.

Mint-glazed Carrots. Peel and cut into quarters lengthwise; cook until almost tender. Drain. Melt 8 oz. butter or margarine, 8 oz. sugar, 1½ T. salt, and 1 c. mint jelly. Blend. Add carrots and simmer a few minutes.

Cranberry Carrots. Cut raw carrots diagonally into 1-in. pieces. Cook. Add 2 T. salt, 8 oz. butter or margarine, and 3 c. cranberry sauce. Reheat.

Candied Carrots. Cut into 1-in. pieces. Cook until tender but not soft. Melt 12 oz. butter or margarine, add 9 oz. sugar, 1½ T. salt. Add to carrots. Bake 15–20 min. at 400° F. Turn frequently.

Carrots and Celery. Combine 7 lb. carrots and 3 lb. celery sliced about the same thickness. Cook until tender and season with butter or margarine, salt, and pepper.

Savory Carrots. Cook sliced carrots in a small amount of beef or chicken broth. Remove from broth and season with butter or margarine, salt, pepper, and lemon juice. Sprinkle with chopped parsley.

Lyonnaise Carrots. Arrange cooked carrot strips in baking pan. Add onion that has been cooked until soft in butter or margarine. Place in a 375° F. oven until reheated and lightly browned.

Creole Cabbage. Sauté chopped onion until soft in butter or margarine. Add 3 qt. canned tomatoes, 2 c. chopped green peppers, 12 whole cloves, 1 bay leaf, ¾ c. brown sugar, and 2 t. salt. Simmer about 15 min. Remove cloves and bay leaf. Add this sauce to 10 lb. shredded cabbage cooked 7 min. Mix, reheat, and serve.

Fried Cabbage. Place 1 lb. fat in small steam-jacketed kettle or heavy aluminum pan. Add 13 lb. (E.P.) shredded cabbage and 2 T. salt. Cook about 25 min., stirring frequently.

Cabbage Polonnaise. Arrange cooked cabbage wedges in baking pans and cover with 3 qt. Medium White Sauce. Sprinkle with buttered bread crumbs. Bake about 25 min. at 350° F.

Cabbage au Gratin. Alternate layers of 7-min. cooked coarsely shredded cabbage, Medium White Sauce, and grated sharp cheese in an oiled baking pan. Sprinkle with buttered crumbs. (Use 10 lb. cabbage, 3 qt. White Sauce, 12 oz. cheese, 8 oz. crumbs, and 4 oz. butter.) Bake about 25 min. at 350° F.

Cauliflower with Almond Butter. Season 12 lb. freshly cooked cauliflower with 2 c. slivered almonds that have been browned in 8 oz. butter or margarine.

Cauliflower Casserole. Place 12 lb. (E.P.) cooked, drained cauliflowerets in baking pan. Cover with a mixture of 18 eggs, 2 qt. milk, 12 oz. grated cheese, and 1 T. salt. Set in a pan of hot water and bake about 45 min. at 325° F. Serve with Tomato Sauce (p. 292). With crisp bacon, this casserole may be served as a luncheon dish.

Cauliflower with New Peas. Combine 7 lb. freshly cooked cauliflower with 5 lb. cooked frozen peas. Season with melted butter or margarine.

Cauliflower with Cheese Sauce. Pour 2–3 qt. Cheese Sauce over 12 lb. (E.P.) cooked fresh cauliflower.

Corn with Green Pepper Ring. Place a ring of green pepper on each serving of buttered whole-grain corn.

Corn Pudding. Three 46-oz. packages uncooked frozen corn or 1 No. 10 can, 3 qt. milk, 6 oz. melted butter or margarine, 2 T. salt, and 24 egg yolks, beaten. Mix and fold in 24 beaten egg whites. Pour into baking pan and place in pan of hot water. Bake approximately 45 min. at 325° F.

Corn in Cream. Add 1¼ qt. light cream, 6 oz. butter or margarine, 2 T. salt, and 1 T. white pepper to 10 lb. frozen whole-grain corn, cooked. Bring just to boiling point and serve immediately.

Baked Corn on the Cob. Remove husks and silks, and wrap each ear with bacon or season with butter. Wrap in a square of aluminum foil, seal with a "drug-store" foil wrapping. Bake approximately 1 hr. at 350° F. Serve in the foil wrapping.

Corn with Bacon. Place two No. 10 cans cream-style corn in well-oiled baking pans. Cover top with cheese cracker crumbs and arrange slices of raw bacon on top. Allow 1 slice bacon and ½ c. corn for each serving. Bake about 25 min. at 400° F., or until corn is hot and bacon is crisp.

Scalloped Corn. Add 1 qt. cracker crumbs, salt and pepper to 8 oz. melted butter or bacon fat. Mix 1 qt. whole milk with 4½ qt. cream-style corn. Place alternate layers of buttered crumbs and corn mixture in oiled baking pan. Bake approximately 45 min. at 325° F.

Corn and Tomato Casserole. Add to 1 No. 10 can of whole-kernel corn 1 gal. chopped fresh tomato, 1½ c. chopped green pepper, 2 T. salt, and ½ t. pepper. Place in oiled baking pan, cover with 4 c. crushed crisp cereal, 3 c. grated sharp cheese, and 8 oz. butter or margarine.

Corn O'Brien. Drain 2 No. 10 cans whole grain corn. Add 1 lb. chopped bacon, ¾ lb. chopped green pepper, and ¾ lb. chopped onion that have been sautéed until lightly browned. Just before serving, add 3 oz. chopped pimiento, salt, and pepper.

Scalloped Cucumbers. Pare 15 lb. cucumbers. Slice lengthwise and remove hard seeds. Steam 3 min. and drain. Arrange in oiled baking pan. Sprinkle with 1½ T. salt and 1 t. pepper. Pour over the cucumbers 2½ qt. Medium White Sauce (p. 295) and 6 oz. chopped pimiento. Cover with 8 oz. buttered crumbs. Bake 30 min. at 350° F.

Creole Eggplant. Melt 1 lb. fat, add 1 lb. chopped onion, 8 oz. coarsely chopped green pepper, and 1 lb. coarsely chopped celery. Cook until tender. Add 2 qt. tomatoes, 5 lb. diced eggplant, 3 T. salt, 1 t. pepper, and 1 T. sugar. Pour into baking pan. Cover with buttered crumbs. Bake until eggplant is tender.

Fresh Mushrooms. Clean thoroughly. Peel all but tender young caps. Sautéed: add sliced or whole small mushrooms to butter or margarine. Cover and cook over low heat until tender, approximately 10 min. Broiled: remove and chop stems, season and use to fill hollows of caps. Place in shallow pan. Dot with butter or margarine. Broil.

Creamed Pearl Onions. Cook tiny unpeeled white onions in boiling salted water until tender, drain, then peel. Add 2 qt. Thin White Sauce, to which 4 oz. additional butter or margarine has been added. Garnish with paprika.

Onion Casserole. Combine 10 lb. cooked tiny onions, 10 oz. chopped walnuts, 1 c. pimiento strips, and 8 10½-oz. cans cream of mushroom soup. Cover with 1½ c. grated cheese. Bake approximately 30 min. at 400° F.

Browned Parsnips. Place 10 lb. cooked parsnips, cut lengthwise into uniform pieces, in counter pan. Sprinkle with 1½ T. salt and 4 oz. sugar. Pour 8 oz. melted butter or margarine over top. Bake 425° F. until browned.

New Peas with Mushrooms. Add 2–3 lb. fresh mushrooms, sliced, sautéed in 8 oz. butter or margarine, to 10 lb. cooked frozen peas.

Creamed New Potatoes and Peas. Combine 7 lb. freshly cooked new potatoes and 5 lb. cooked frozen peas with 3 qt. Thin White Sauce.

Green Peas and Sliced New Turnips. Combine 2 40-oz. packages frozen peas, cooked, with 3 lb. new turnips, sliced and cooked. Add 8 oz. melted butter or margarine and salt to taste.

Green Peas with Pearl Onions. Combine 3 40-oz. packages frozen peas, cooked, with 3 lb. pearl onions, cooked. Add 8 oz. butter or margarine or 2–3 qt. Thin White Sauce, to which 4 oz. extra butter or margarine has been added.

Wilted Lettuce or Spinach. To 10 lb. chopped lettuce or spinach, or a combination of the two, add 2–2½ qt. Vegetable Sauce (p. 292) just before serving.

Zucchini Italian. Cook 1½ lb. sliced onions in 1 c. hot salad oil until tender but not brown. Add 5 lb. raw tomatoes that have been peeled, sliced, and cooked about 3 min. Add 12 lb. sliced zucchini, 2½ T. salt, 4 t. pepper. Cook slowly about 20 min., adding small amount of water if necessary. Add 1 bay leaf if desired.

Baked Acorn Squash. Cut 25 squash into halves, remove seeds, bake upside down in shallow pan with a little water, 20–25 min., or until just tender. Place hollow side up, add 8 oz. butter or margarine, 1½ T. salt, 12 oz. brown sugar, and reheat until sugar is melted. For a luncheon dish, place a 4-oz. sausage pattie or 2 link sausages, partially cooked, in each squash half, and continue baking. Cavity may also be filled with No. 12 dipper of a mixture of 5 qt. steamed rice, 4 lb. chopped cooked meat, 4 oz. sautéed minced onion, moistened with meat stock.

Mashed Butternut Squash. Cook 15 lb. peeled butternut squash until tender. Mash and add 1½ qt. hot milk, 8 oz. butter or margarine, 2 T. salt, and 8 oz. brown sugar. Whip until light. May be garnished with toasted slivered almonds.

Broiled Zucchini Squash. Remove ends of squash and cut in halves lengthwise. Simmer in boiling salted water, or steam until almost tender. Drain and arrange in a baking pan. Cover with melted butter or salad oil. Sprinkle with garlic salt, white pepper, grated Parmesan cheese, and a little oregano. Broil or bake in hot oven until lightly browned.

Baked Sweet Potatoes. Select small even-sized sweet potatoes. Scrub and bake 40–45 min., or until done, at 425° F.

Mashed White Turnips. Cook turnips, drain, and mash as potatoes. Season with 8 oz. butter or margarine, 1 T. salt, ½ t. pepper, and 1 c. hot milk or cream.

Breaded Tomatoes. Add 1 lb. cubed bread, 8 oz. butter or margarine, and ¾ c. sugar to 2 No. 10 cans tomatoes. Bake approximately 30 min. at 350° F.

Creole Tomatoes. Drain 2 No. 10 cans tomatoes. To the juice add 1 lb. celery, 4 oz. onion, and 8 oz. green pepper, coarsely chopped. Cook about 15 min. Add the tomatoes, 2 T. salt, and ¾ t. pepper and place in oiled baking pan. Cover with 2 qt. toasted bread cubes and bake about 30 min. at 350° F.

part three • **menu planning**

menu planning

● PRINCIPLES OF MENU PLANNING

A carefully planned menu is the initial step toward a successful meal. It should provide food for adequate nutrition, tempt the appetite, and result in satisfaction for the guest. For the food service, the menu will predetermine the work to be done and largely control the resulting profit or loss. So important is the menu that, without it, there will be no successful food service.

Factors basic to menu planning may therefore be divided into two areas: those relating to the guest, and those to the food service management. The first includes age, sex, and occupation of the group, their nutritional needs and food preferences. The second deals with the type of food service, number to be served, equipment available, number and experience of employees, distribution of work, availability and seasonability of foods, and the food budget.

Meals outside of the home are eaten in such widely diversified places as the school lunchroom, university cafeterias and residence halls, hospitals, homes for children and adults, summer camps, industrial cafeterias, and many types of restaurants. Each of these services is planned to meet the needs of a particular group of customers. To insure that a menu will meet the demands of the customer, careful consideration must be given to each of the following factors:

1. *Age, sex, and occupation of group to be served.* The menu planner must consider the age, sex, occupation, nutritional needs, food habits, and preferences of the individual members of the group. For example, the type of food suitable for a men's civic club would in most cases, not be enjoyed by a group of high school girls, nor would a luncheon considered "perfectly delicious" by high school girls be fully appreciated by the men's club.

In a situation in which no choice of food is offered, as in homes for children and adults, meals must be planned to meet the complete nutritional needs of members of the group and also offer enough variety to minimize monotony and meet, in so far as possible, their food preferences.

Wherever a multiple choice of foods is offered, redundant care must be taken to provide foods from which the individual patron may choose a well-balanced meal. The choice also must include enough variety to make it possible for him to select a meal that he will enjoy at a price he wishes to pay.

2. *Climate and season.* The factor of climate and season is important in the choice of foods. Cool, crisp, fresh foods are often more appealing in hot weather, but at least one hot food should be included in each summer menu. In cold weather, the heavier foods high in caloric value may be used. A festive touch may be added on holidays and other special occasions by including foods not served regularly, and by adding unusual garnishes and special decorations.

3. *Flavor and appearance of the food.* Flavor combinations should receive special consideration. A balance should be maintained between tart and sweet, mild and highly flavored, light and heavy foods. Certain flavors seem to belong together, and if carefully selected will complement each other. Foods of the same or similar flavor, such as tomato soup and tomato salad, should not be repeated in one menu. A definite contrast in flavor between the foods of different courses is desirable.

Acid foods, such as grapefruit, stimulate the appetite and digestion. They are used effectively as a first course or with a bland entrée. Sweet foods are satiating and should be used sparingly. They are served to best advantage as dessert.

Foods selected for a menu should be of harmonious colors that present an inviting appearance on the plate, the hospital tray, or cafeteria counter. Just as uninteresting, colorless meals are to be avoided, so should those offering foods that clash in color, such as beets and carrots. When planning menus for a cafeteria or a buffet meal, foods that are to be displayed together, such as vegetables, salads, or desserts, should offer a pleasing color contrast.

Contrast in shape and form of different foods appearing on a plate likewise lends interest to the meal. Variety in preparation makes it possible to present food shaped in varied forms and sizes. Care should be taken to avoid too many mixed foods of similar shape at the same meal, such as beef stew, mixed vegetables, tossed green salad, and fruit cup. Indiscriminate use of the dippers when serving may cause all the food to assume the shape of tennis balls. A suitable sauce or garnish may be used effectively to give an appearance of unity to the plate.

There should be balance between soft and solid foods. A soft entrée calls for a crisp vegetable or salad. A mashed or creamed vegetable may be served more successfully with a solid meat than with a casserole dish.

Two foods prepared in the same manner, such as creamed, buttered, fried, or mashed, should not be served together.

4. *Variety.* Variety is introduced not only in the kind of food, but also in the method of preparation, combinations, textures, and garnishes. With the exception of staples, the same food should not be served too often or repeated on the same day of the week. If the same food must be served often, a change in the method of preparation and the accompanying foods will give desired variety.

The menu planner, in considering the needs and wishes of the guest, must be aware also of the problems of management that affect the food offerings. These factors include:

1. *Type of food service.* The menu pattern will be influenced by the type of food service. The simple cafeteria meal planned for the child eating in a school lunchroom will be quite different from the meal served family style in a university residence hall or from the menu offered in a restaurant catering to business executives.

2. *Number to be served.* Besides affecting the variety of food that can be included in the menu, the number to be served also influences the method of preparing the food. For example, it would be difficult, under usual institutional conditions, to prepare grilled tomatoes or stuffed baked potatoes for a large group.

3. *The food budget.* The amount of income allotted for raw food cost and labor is a determining factor in the type of menu that can be planned and served. The menu planner should not only know how much money is available for food and labor, but should check this amount against the actual cost of the menu as served.

4. *Available equipment.* To prepare suitable meals with the available equipment in a given length of time presents one of the major problems of those responsible for planning menus. Special attention needs to be given to oven capacity, refrigeration facilities, number and size of steam-jacketed kettles and steamers, and availability and capacity of mixers. Certain combinations of menu items often must be avoided because of lack of pans or dishes.

5. *Number and experience of employees.* The man hours of labor available and the efficiency and skill of employees are important to the successful preparation of any meal. When there is a lack of experienced workers, the menu items must be limited to simple foods, easily prepared.

6. *Distribution of work.* The distribution of work among the various areas of preparation is of prime importance in meeting a time schedule and in maintaining the morale of the workers. In determining a day's work load, the menu planner needs to consider not only one day's menu

but any prepreparation necessary for meals for the following day or for several days. Foods prepared by the salad and bakery departments are often of the type that require long-time preparation and need to be carefully scheduled to equalize the load. On days when the work load is light, foods may be prepared and stored in the freezer for future use.

The wise planner will make it possible to spread the employee's work load so that a limited number of foods requiring time-consuming preparation may be included. To add interest to the menu, foods such as stuffed baked potato, individual salads, fresh grapefruit sections, fresh fruit plates, homemade noodles, and tarts may be included in a menu if combined with other food items that require minimum preparation. The wide variety of ready-to-cook frozen foods, preprepared vegetables, and other convenience foods now makes possible a less restricted menu than can be offered when all food preparation is done in the kitchen. Discrimination in the selection and use of many of the prepared foods is needed to maintain high food standards and to preserve the individuality of the food service.

Some foods, including fresh and frozen vegetables, mashed potatoes, hot breads, and certain meats and fish, require last-minute cooking to assure products of high quality. To avoid confusion and delayed meal service, the menu should be so planned that there is a balance between items that may be prepared early and those that must be cooked just prior to serving.

7. *Availability and seasonability of foods.* Availability of foods in the local markets will exert a limited influence on the menu items. Although most foods are now available in fresh or frozen form in all sections of the country, fresh foods produced locally are often of better quality and less expensive during the growing season than are those shipped from distant markets.

8. *Cooked foods on hand.* Unused cooked foods are more often used to effect changes in a menu than as the basis of the original menu. However, the successful use of foods on hand requires careful thought and imagination to incorporate them in such a way that they will be acceptable.

Some foods may be offered in their original form as a choice on a selective menu. Others may be incorporated into combinations such as hash, meat roll, barbecued sandwiches, and croquettes. These dishes are often better made from cooked foods than from raw. Cooked vegetables, which should be reused sparingly, may be included in salads and casserole dishes. If suitable, they may be used in soup, or ground and combined with meat loaf or other luncheon entrées. Fresh fruits may be used in fruit cup, gelatins, or mixed salads, and stewed fruits may be combined in an appetizing compote. Cake and bread crumbs often are utilized in puddings, cakes and cookies, and for breading. However used, the food product must be prepared in such a way that it is as acceptable in the combined form as in its original state.

9. *Recipes.* Many a well-planned menu has been a failure because sufficient thought was not given to the selection of recipes. Cooks should be provided with standardized recipes, so that there will be no question as to the yield or quality of the finished product. If deviations from the original recipes are necessary, great care should be exercised in making substitutions that may affect both quality and yield.

● MENU-PLANNING PROCEDURES

The Menu Planner

The importance of menu planning to the success of any food service cannot be overemphasized. The effectiveness of the planning is largely influenced by the attitudes and ability of the planner, who should recognize that his task is an important one requiring imagination, creative ability, and a deep interest in food. It is important that the menu maker be free of prejudices and food dislikes. Menu planning should not be regarded as a routine duty, but as an opportunity to work through the medium of food to present a 3-dimensional picture of food beautiful to look at, nutritionally sound, and delightful to taste.

The Menu-planning Center

If at all possible, the menu should be planned during uninterrupted time in a place away from noise and confusion, and at a desk or table large enough to accommodate menu-planning materials. These include:
1. Menu forms as dictated by type and needs of food service
2. Standardized recipe file.
3. Cook books, for large and small quantity cookery.
4. Periodicals, institutional and household.
5. Idea file of pictures and other material clipped from magazines.
6. Menu suggestion lists, as shown on pp. 359–366.
7. File of previous menus.

Cycle Menus

The trend in institutional meal planning is toward the construction and use of cycle or rotating menus. Such a set of menus is planned well in advance of the time it is to be used. Although many factors influence the length of the cycle, many institutions find a cycle of 3 to 5 weeks satisfactory. To ensure serving of foods that are appropriate to the season, many food services have a slightly different cycle for each of the 4 seasons.

Thoughtfully planned menus may be rotated successfully and have many advantages over short-time planning. Such a procedure results in keeping repetition of foods at a minimum and tends to aid in the control of food and labor costs. It further facilitates food purchasing, reduces waste, and provides for the effective use of employees' time. Most important, rotating menus are time-saving for the food service manager, as their use greatly reduces the time spent in menu planning and food ordering. Carefully planned menus offer variety and interest in meals and bring greater satisfaction to patrons or guests. Interest may be added to cycle menus by varying the cookery methods of frequently recurring foods.

Steps in Menu Planning

Successful menus are planned systematically and should follow a definite pattern, about in the following order:

1. *Meat or other entrée.* First, determine the entrées for the entire time for which the menus are being planned, whether for a 5- or a 1-week cycle. Many managers who plan menus weekly like to schedule the entrées for a longer period, 4 or more weeks. When this has been completed, plan the remainder of each meal around the meat or main dish. In a multiple-choice menu, the entrées may consist of a roast or other "solid" meat, meat extender, poultry, fish, and a meatless entrée. Where no choice is offered, the meat or main dish needs to be varied from day to day. Variety may be obtained through the use of different kinds of meat, as well as different cuts and forms, such as roasts, cutlets, chops, ground and cubed meat. Beef, veal, pork, lamb, poultry, fish, and variety meats may be prepared and served in many interesting ways to offer a wide variety in appearance and flavor.

2. *Vegetables.* Vegetables appropriate to serve with the planned entrées should be considered next. Although there are a few widely accepted staple vegetables that necessarily must be repeated often,

variety may be obtained through varied methods of preparation. Maximum use should be made of fresh vegetables when in season.

3. *Salads.* The choice of salads is of great importance in adding color, texture, flavor, and interest to the menu. There should be a well-balanced distribution of fruit, vegetable, and gelatin salads. Combinations are almost unlimited, and care should be taken to serve a dressing and a garnish that will complement the salad ingredients. On a cafeteria menu, certain basic salads are usually offered daily. These might include head lettuce, combination vegetable salad, relishes, and cottage cheese.

4. *Bread.* A standard assortment of breads is usually offered, and one or more hot breads. Available oven space may be a limiting factor in offering a choice of hot breads.

5. *Desserts.* Dessert is the last item of the dinner and luncheon menu to be planned. The type of dessert offered depends on the rest of the meal. Where no choice is offered, a light dessert should be served with a heavy main course and a rich dessert with a light main course. When a choice is to be offered, it is customary to plan a two-crust pie, soft pie, cake, pudding, and gelatin dessert. In addition, ice creams and fruits are usually offered daily.

The menu is then completed by adding beverages, first course, if one is to be served, and breakfast items. Variety in the breakfast menu may be introduced through a choice of entrées, hot breads, fruits, and fruit juices.

Recording the Menu

The recording of menus on a planning sheet is essential. The menu form to be used by office and kitchen personnel should include the listing of sauces, gravies, and accompaniments, as well as specific directions for preparation and service. The menu as presented to the customer will be in a different form from that designed for the preparation and service areas. In preparing the customer's menu, follow these two widely accepted rules: (1) list food items in the order of service; (2) capitalize all words except prepositions and conjunctions.

In many cases, the menu card is the customer's or patient's preview of the food and service he can expect. This emphasizes the importance of the appearance and wording of the menu. Suggestions for writing a menu card are:

1. Write the main dish of each course across the center of the sheet.

Write one accompaniment on the line below, on the right hand or in the center. If there are two accompaniments, write one at the right and one at the left on the line below.

Cream of Mushroom Soup
Melba Toast

Cream of Mushroom Soup
Celery Sticks   Melba Toast

2. If more accompaniments are served, balance on sheet.

Breaded Veal Cutlet
Parsley Creamed Potatoes   Buttered Asparagus
Tossed Vegetable Salad
Butterhorn Rolls   Raspberry Jelly
Mocha Almond Frozen Pie
Coffee

3. Write beverage at the bottom of the menu or with the course with which it is to be served.

4. Do not include on the written menu such accompaniments as cream and sugar, salt and pepper, and condiments, such as mustard, catsup, and vinegar.

5. Use wording that is as descriptive as possible. Describe ham as Roast Sugar Cured Ham, Hawaiian style; or use terms to indicate the method of preparation, such as candied or honey-glazed. The method of preparation or some descriptive term should always be used for each item on the written menu.

Points to Remember in Menu Planning

1. Leave nothing to chance. Be specific when recording menus. For example, pork chops should be shown as barbecued, stuffed, breaded, or whatever method of preparation is desired.

2. Avoid too many foods with accompaniments, sauces, and garnishes. This will increase the work load and may complicate the service.

3. Watch for "hidden" methods of preparation for different food items, as the name may not always be descriptive of the method. For example, breaded pork chops, ham croquettes, cheese balls, browned potatoes, French fried onion rings are all fried foods, but only one is so indicated by name.

4. Avoid food clichés. Food combinations such as ham and pineapple, pork and apples, are highly acceptable, but should not always be served together. New combinations add interest to the menu.

5. Watch for repetition as menus are being developed. Strive for variety through the use of good basic standardized recipes and different methods of presentation, garnishes, and sauces. The menu maker should be aware of ingredients used in all recipes to avoid repetition of any one food. Sunshine salad, vegetable soup, braised liver, vegetable cheese pie, buttered carrot strips, frozen mixed vegetables all contain carrots, although "carrots" appear in the name of only one menu item.

6. Check completed menu carefully for all factors basic to successful menu planning.

The responsibility of the menu planner does not end with the writing of the menu. The task is completed only when the food has been prepared and served, the reaction of the consumer noted, and the relationship of raw food and labor costs to the selling price recorded.

• MENUS FOR SCHOOL LUNCHES

The school lunch program has expanded rapidly since the National School Lunch Act was passed by Congress in 1946, and is now an integral part of the total educational program of elementary and secondary schools. The objective of a school lunch is to offer a nutritionally adequate meal that provides at least ⅓ to ½ of the child's nutritional requirements for the entire day. Schools participating in the School Lunch Program under the National School Lunch Act must meet minimum nutritional requirements for type A lunch as follows:

1. ½ pint whole pasteurized milk, to be used as a beverage.
2. 2 oz. processed meat (cooked weight), poultry meat, cooked or canned fish, or cheese, or ½ c. cooked dry beans, or 4 T. of peanut butter, or 1 egg. The protein requirements may be furnished by the main dish, or by the main dish and one other menu item to meet sufficient protein as listed above.
3. ¾ c. fruit and vegetable combination, preferably one raw. ¼ c. full-strength juice may be used to meet part of this requirement.
4. A food high in vitamin C must be served each day, and a food high in Vitamin A 2–3 times a week.
5. A portion of bread or hot bread made of whole-grain cereal or enriched flour (crackers do not substitute for bread).
6. 2 t. butter or fortified margarine, which may be used in cooking or baking as well as a spread for bread (1 lb. is sufficient for 50).

In addition to meeting the nutritive requirements, the school lunch should provide satisfaction and pleasure to the pupil and help in the development of good eating habits. Planning menus that meet the nutritive requirements and are attractive, appetizing, and palatable at a price that pupils can afford to pay presents a challenge to the ability of those responsible for this function of the program.

The major factors to be considered by those planning school lunch menus include: variety in texture, color, flavor, and methods of preparation; use of foods in season; use of commodities distributed to lunchrooms operating under the National School Lunch Program; number, ability, and experience of personnel; amount and adequacy of equipment and space; time available for food preparation; and food habits of the group to be served.

When all of these factors are taken into consideration, the foods suitable for a school lunch group themselves into the following classifications: soups, hot dishes, vegetables, salads, beverages, sandwiches, breads, and desserts.

If separate items are offered, one or more choices for the day may be made from each of the following categories:

Soups. Cream of tomato, cream of spinach, cream of potato, corn chowder, split pea, vegetable beef, beef noodle.

Hot Dishes. Meat balls or patties; meat loaf; hot meat sandwich; hamburgers in buns; frankfurters in buns; sauerkraut and wieners; scalloped potatoes and sausage; baked beans with bacon; stuffed wieners; meat pie; shepherd's pie; beef stew; liver; veal stew with vegetables; pork and noodle casserole; Creole spaghetti; Spanish rice with meat; creamed chipped beef; cream hamburger; tamale pie; chili con carne; chop suey; scalloped potatoes and ham; Lima beans with bacon or ham; ham and potato omelet; scrambled eggs and bacon; baked beans; creamed salmon; salmon loaf; baked fish; fish fillets; tuna and noodles; macaroni and cheese; toasted cheese sandwiches; corn and cheese rarebit; cheese fondue.

Vegetables. Peas; carrots; green and wax beans; beets; spinach; tomatoes; cabbage; broccoli; asparagus; corn; squash; potatoes; sweet potatoes. Most vegetables may be creamed, buttered, or scalloped to offer variety.

Salads:

1. *Fruit salads.* Peach, pear, pineapple, orange, and apple; apple, pineapple, and marshmallow; Waldorf; stuffed prune, apple, and banana; banana and nut; apple, grape, and banana; raisin and carrot; cranberry relish; combination; grapefruit.

2. *Vegetable salads or relishes.* Sliced tomato; head or leaf lettuce; celery stuffed with cheese or peanut butter; vegetable combination; carrot and celery; cole slaw; cabbage and pineapple; asparagus; apple, cabbage, and raisin; chopped lettuce and hard-cooked eggs; pickled beet; spiced pear or peach; carrot, celery, cauliflower, and turnip strips.

3. *Hearty salads.* Kidney bean; potato; cottage cheese; deviled eggs; salmon; tuna.

4. *Gelatin salads.* Perfection; jellied Waldorf; pineapple and carrot; jellied fruit; jellied vegetable.

Sandwiches. Cold meat; ground meat moistened with salad dressing and mixed sweet pickle relish; egg salad; cottage cheese and nut; cheese; lettuce and tomato; nut bread; chicken salad; peanut butter and raisin; peanut butter and honey; peanut butter and cheese; raisin and date; date and nut; egg and bacon; egg and celery; rye bread and jelly; prune and cottage cheese; bacon and tomato.

Desserts:

1. *Puddings.* Tapioca; rice; custard; bread; divinity; blanc mange; brown Betty; Norwegian prune; chocolate cream; lemon snow; lemon cake; Bavarian cream; vanilla cream; vanilla cream with fruit; chocolate fudge; date; butterscotch.

2. *Fruit.* Fresh, canned, or dried fruit; fruit cup; orange-banana-coconut combination; jellied fruit cup; fruit whips; baked apple; stuffed dates.

3. *Gelatin.* Fruit gelatin; fruit whip; Bavarian cream.

4. *Cakes.* Plain with fruit sauce; cherry, applesauce prune, or banana; fudge; chocolate cup; coffee; upside-down fruit; cottage pudding; Washington pie; jelly roll; gingerbread.

5. *Cookies.* Oatmeal; ginger; sugar; butterscotch drop; filled; icebox; peanut butter; chocolate chip; brownies; prune; fruit bars; Russian rocks.

6. *Pastry.* Fresh, frozen, canned or dried fruit cobbler or pie; cream puffs; fruit turnovers or dumplings.

7. *Ice cream.*

Beverages. Chocolate and plain milk; malted milk; cocoa; vegetable juices; fruit juices.

Suggested School Lunch Menus (Plate Lunches)

1	2	3	4	5	6	7	8
Beef Stew with Vegetables	Pizza	Orange Juice	Pork and Noodle Casserole	Tomato Soup	Steamed Frankfurter	Macaroni and Cheese	Chili-Crackers
Raw Spinach and Lettuce Salad	Buttered Green Beans	Hot Meat Sandwich	Buttered Spinach	Grilled Cheese Sandwich	Scalloped Potatoes	Buttered Broccoli	Celery Sticks
Hot Biscuit, Butter	Cole Slaw	Mashed Potatoes	Cabbage Pineapple Salad	Crisp Carrot Strips	Head Lettuce Wedges	Deviled Egg	Corn Bread, Butter
Cinnamon Applesauce	Hot Rolls, Butter	Lettuce-Egg Salad	Bread, Butter	Banana Cake	Bread, Butter	Cinnamon Roll, Butter	Canned Pear
Milk	Canned Peach	Jellied Fruit	Peanut Butter Cookie	Milk	Orange (cut)	Cherry Cobbler	Milk
	Milk	Milk	Milk		Milk	Milk	

1	2	3	4	5	6	7	8
Meat Loaf	Spanish Rice with Meat	Hamburger in Bun	Chop Suey with Chow Mein Noodles	Baked Fish Fillet	Meat Balls and Spaghetti	Creamed Chipped Beef	Vegetable-Beef Soup
Creamed Potatoes	Buttered Green Beans	Scalloped Corn	Sliced Tomatoes	Buttered Peas	Combination Green Vegetable Salad	Baked Potato	Peanut Butter-Honey or Peanut and Cheese Sandwich
Raw Vegetable Relishes	Apple, Celery, Nut Salad	Lettuce Wedge	Kolaches, Butter	Molded Carrot-Pineapple Salad	Rolls, Butter	Peach with Cottage Cheese Salad	Raw Vegetable Relishes
Rolls, Butter	Rolls, Butter	Ice Cream	Fruit Cup	Corn Meal Rolls, Butter	Apple Crisp	Lettuce Sandwiches	Chocolate Pie
Cake with Pineapple Topping	Coconut Cream Pudding	Milk	Milk	Icebox Cookie	Milk	Gingerbread with Lemon Sauce	Milk
Milk	Milk			Milk		Milk	

● MENUS FOR THE UNIVERSITY CAFETERIA

The trend in menu planning for a university cafeteria is toward simplicity in offerings, with emphasis on pleasing combinations and well-prepared food. Menus that meet nutritional needs, offer variety, and can be sold at a moderate cost must be planned for students, faculty, and off-campus guests. The uncertainty of numbers and often unexpectedly small volume of business creates a problem of excess prepared food and of food cost control.

The use of a cycle menu is of value in some situations. However, the need for using leftovers and the desirability of including seasonable foods available on the market lead some directors to plan for periods as brief as one week, and others prefer a five-week cycle.

The menu patterns for lunch and dinner in a university cafeteria are so similar that the suggested menus planned for this type of operation pp. 346–347) may be used for either lunch or for dinner for a two-week period.

The breakfast menu should offer some choice in food items each day, although there is less need for variety from day to day than is desirable for lunch and dinner. Breakfast should include one or more citrus juices and one other juice; fresh fruits in season; cooked or ready-to-eat prepared cereals; breakfast hot breads and toast; eggs and bacon, ham, or sausage; jam and jelly; and a choice of beverages.

In addition to the items listed on Suggested Luncheon and Dinner Menus for a University Cafeteria (pp. 346–347), certain other items are available daily.

These include:

Entrées: Four entrées including one meat and three others. These may be a meat extender, a meatless entrée, poultry, or fish. This variety may be increased or decreased to fit the demands of the food service.

Vegetables: Mashed potatoes.

Salads. Cottage cheese, head lettuce, tossed fresh vegetable salad with assorted dressings, carrot and celery sticks.

Breads: Whole wheat bread, white bread, and a hot bread.

Desserts: Baked custard, fresh fruit in season, fruit juices, and a variety of ice creams.

Beverages: Coffee, tea, hot and iced, cocoa, milk, whole, nonfat and cultured buttermilk.

Suggested Luncheon and Dinner Menus for a University Cafeteria

Pattern	Monday	Tuesday	Wednesday	Thursday	Friday	Saturday	Sunday
Soup	Vegetable	Barley	Pepper Pot	Mushroom	Bean	Tomato Bouillon	French Onion
Entrées	Swiss Steak Creamed Chipped Beef on Corn Bread Baked Haddock Mushroom Puff	Roast Pork Turkey Loaf Codfish Balls Macaroni and Cheese	Pot Roast Beef Chicken a la Maryland Salmon Loaf Egg Cutlet	Deviled Pork Chop Meat Loaf Chicken Turnover—Mushroom Sauce Russian Salad Bowl	Roast Leg of Lamb Creamed Ham & Celery on Hot Biscuit Fried Whiting Corn Fritters	Country Fried Steak Sweetbread Cutlets Pizza Cheese Soufflé—Shrimp Sauce	Baked Ham with Honey Glaze Fried Chicken Baked Fillet of Sole Beef Stew with Dumplings
Vegetables Mashed potatoes available daily	Baked Potatoes Chilled Tomatoes Broccoli au Gratin Corn on the Cob	Scalloped Sweet Potatoes—Apples Buttered Wax Beans Buttered Asparagus Tips Julienne Carrots	French Baked New Potatoes Cauliflower—Cheese Sauce Buttered Mixed Vegetables Scalloped Tomatoes and Celery	Sautéed Green Tomatoes New Corn in Cream Buttered Spinach with Lemon Mashed Summer Squash	Parsley Buttered Potatoes Baked Tomatoes Braised Celery Buttered Green Peas	French Fried Potatoes Wilted Greens Buttered Zucchini Squash Creole Corn	Baked Sweet Potato Buttered New Beets and Greens Creamed Onions Buttered Baby Limas
Salads	Spicy Apricot Mold Grapefruit—Orange—Red Apple Section Cabbage—Cucumber—Tomato—Green Pepper Beet Relish	Perfection Stuffed Tomato Waldorf Deviled Egg	Lime Gelatin—Spiced Grape—Celery Cucumber and Onion Sour Cream Shredded Carrot—Pineapple Mixed Fruit	Molded Pineapple—Cottage Cheese Tomato—Avocado Sections Banana Slice—Cubed Pineapple—Orange Sections Cabbage—Green Pepper—Pimiento	Jellied Beet Cantaloupe—Honeydew Wedge—Grape Vegetable Nut Stuffed Celery—Cheese	Cabbage Parfait Salad Banana—Nut—Mint Garnish Sliced Tomatoes Carrifruit	Raspberry Ring Mold Fresh Fruit Bowl Sliced Orange—Onion Ring Green Bean—Pimiento
Hot Bread	Blueberry Muffins	Dinner Rolls	Kolaches	Bishop's Bread	Corn Bread	All Bran Muffins	Vienna Bread
Desserts	Green Apple Pie Lemon Pie Applesauce Cake Prune Whip	Blueberry Pie Coconut Cream Pie Lemon Sponge Cake Cherry Crisp	Apricot Pie Strawberry Glazed Cream Pie Angel Food Cake Apple Brown Betty	Cherry Pie Chocolate Chiffon Pie Fruit Upside-Down Cake Caramel Custard	Raspberry Pie Frozen Lemon Pie Burnt Sugar Cake Blue Plum Cobbler	Apple Pie—Cheese Crust Date Cream Pie German Chocolate Cake Peach Crisp	Fresh Rhubarb Pie Pecan Pie Lady Baltimore Cake Strawberry Shortcake

Pattern	Monday	Tuesday	Wednesday	Thursday	Friday	Saturday	Sunday
Soup	Cream of Potato	Creole	Tomato	Clam Chowder	Split Pea	Vegetable Beef	Cream of Tomato
Entrées	Breaded Pork Cutlet / Corned Beef—Horseradish Sauce / Meat Roll / Grilled Cheese Sandwich	Roast Veal / Ham Soufflé / Baked Halibut	Chicken Tahitian / Braised Liver	Grilled Ham Slices / Spaghetti Creole / Scalloped Chicken / Fruit Plate with Cottage Cheese	Veal Chops in Sour Cream / Beef Pot Pie / Fried Shrimp / Cheese Balls with Pineapple	Barbecued Spareribs / Baked Meat Croquettes / Chicken Fricassée / Tuna Salad	Roast Turkey / Mock Drumsticks / Hungarian Goulash / Steamed Salmon / Lemon Butter
Vegetables / Mashed potatoes available daily	Fried Hominy / New Peas in Cream / Buttered New Cabbage / Spanish Green Beans	Baked Beans / Green Rice / Scalloped Tomatoes / Buttered Brussels Sprouts / Sautéed New Carrots	Stuffed Peppers / Scalloped Corn with Bacon / New Potatoes with Peas / Buttered Broccoli / French Fried Eggplant / Succotash with Green Beans	Creamed Potatoes / Fresh Spinach with Bacon / Corn on the Cob / Harvard Beets	New Potatoes in Jackets / Grilled Tomatoes / Green Peas with Mushrooms / Hot Slaw with Poppy Seed	Lattice Potatoes / Buttered Green Beans with Celery / Baked Onions with Cheese / Buttered Summer Squash	Browned New Potatoes / Buttered Fresh Asparagus / Diced Turnips with Hollandaise / Buttered Apples
Salads	Molded Grapefruit / Cranberry Relish / Prune—Apricot / Tomato—Cucumber	Frosted Cherry Mold / Cabbage Relish / Asparagus—Pimiento / Green Applesauce	Frozen Fruit / Avocado—Orange Sections / Cabbage—Pepper Slaw / Stuffed Peach	Autumn Mold / Pineapple—Cream Cheese—Date / Melon Slice—Bing Cherry / Tomato—Shrimp	Apple—Grapefruit Mold / Green Pepper—Cottage Cheese / Orange—Endive / Fresh Pineapple—Strawberry	Molded Pineapple—Cucumber / Fruit Salad Bowl / Raw Spinach—Egg / Spiced Apple	Under the Sea Salad / Avocado—Grapefruit / Stuffed Prune / Peaches—Banana—Grape
Hot Bread	Whole Wheat Rolls	Boston Brown Bread	Cinnamon Rolls	Raised Muffins	Butterhorn	Honey Cornflake Muffins	Butter slices
Desserts	Fresh Peach Pie / Custard Pie / Chocolate Angel Food / Tapioca Cream	Boysenberry Pie / Butterscotch Pie / Jelly Roll / Orange Cream Puff	Dutch Apple Pie / Eggnog Pie / Pineapple—Cashew Cake / Apricot Whip	Gooseberry Pie / Banana Cream Pie / Fudge Cake / Fruit-Cup—Cookies	Plum Pie / Chocolate Cream Pie / Lazy Daisy Cake / Date Pudding	Cherry Pie—Lattice Crust / Lemon Chiffon Pie / Chocolate Cup Cake / English Toffee	Loganberry Pie / Mocha Almond Frozen Pie / Marble Cake / Apple Dumplings

● MENUS FOR THE RESIDENCE HALL

The daily menu in the residence hall must be adequate to meet the nutritional needs of the residents. The number to be served is fairly constant, so amounts may be carefully planned, resulting in little or no waste. Although there are many halls that still serve a "fixed" or complete meal three times a day, others are finding the use of selective menus for breakfast or lunch or both popular and advantageous. In this case, the selective menus are simplified cafeteria menus, and cafeteria style of service is used for breakfast and lunch, with a more formal type of service for dinner.

There is little difference in menus planned for men and women except in the size of the servings. Usually the men require larger portions than the women. However, this varies with the groups to be served. In many women's halls, fruit is replacing a cooked dessert on the menu for one meal a day.

Suggested Menu Outline for a Residence Hall Serving 3 Meals a Day

BREAKFAST	LUNCH		DINNER
	I or II		
Fruit	Main dish	Soup	Main meat dish
Cereal, hot and/or cold	Vegetable	Salad	Potato or other starchy
Protein dish	Salad or	and/or	vegetable
Toast or hot bread	relish	sandwich	Vegetable
Accompaniment, i.e.,	Bread, butter	Dessert	Bread, butter
jam, jelly, or sirup	Fruit or	Milk	Salad, ice, or relishes
Coffee, cocoa, or milk	other light		Dessert
	dessert		Beverages
	Milk		

Daily Recommended Food Allowances for College Women

1 citrus fruit
2 vegetables in addition to potatoes, 1 of which should be green or yellow and 1 raw
1 pint or more milk per person, in addition to that used in cooking
Fresh fruit
3 whole grain or enriched cereals, including bread
2 protein foods:
   1 meat dish
   1 dish including eggs, cheese, beans, or meat extender
1 T. or more butter or fortified margarine
1 egg, or 4 weekly in addition to those used in cooking.
Frequently 1 glandular organ, such as liver, heart, tongue, or sweetbreads.

Menus for a Women's Residence Hall

BREAKFAST

Monday	Tuesday	Wednesday	Thursday	Friday	Saturday	Sunday
Assorted Fruits	Assorted Fruits	Assorted Fruits	Assorted Fruits	Assorted Fruits	Assorted Fruits	Orange Juice
Hot and/or Cold Cereal	Hot and/or Cold Cereal	Hot and/or Cold Cereal	Hot and/or Cold Cereal	Hot and/or Cold Cereal	Hot and/or Cold Cereal	Prepared Cereal
Bacon Slices	Fried Scrapple—Sirup	Link Sausage	Poached Eggs	Scrambled Eggs	Bacon	Sweet Rolls
Toast—Jelly	Coffee, Cocoa, Milk	Biscuits—Honey	Toast—Orange Marmalade	Toast—Jelly	Bishop's Bread	Coffee, Cocoa, Milk
Coffee, Cocoa, Milk		Coffee, Cocoa, Milk	Coffee, Cocoa, Milk	Coffee, Cocoa, Milk	Coffee, Cocoa, Milk	

LUNCH

Monday	Tuesday	Wednesday	Thursday	Friday	Saturday
Creole Spaghetti	Vegetable-Beef Soup	Pizza	Chef's Salad Bowl	Cheese Soufflé	Barbecued Hamburger
Buttered Limas	Egg Salad Sandwiches	Buttered Green Beans	Hot Muffins	Baked Tomato	Potato Salad
Relish Plate	Head Lettuce Salad	Carrifruit Salad	Chocolate Cream Pudding	Cinnamon Rolls	Relish Plate
Bran Muffins	Thousand Island Dressing	Oatmeal Cookies	Milk—Hot Tea	Small Fruit Plate	Peach Half
Pears	Fruit Gelatin	Milk		Milk	Ginger Cookies
Milk	Milk				Milk

DINNER

Monday	Tuesday	Wednesday	Thursday	Friday	Saturday	Sunday
Roast Beef	Braised Liver	Ham Patties on Pineapple Slice	Chilled Fruit Juice	French Fried Shrimp	Swiss Steak	Tomato Juice—Cheese Crackers
Browned Potatoes	Parsley Buttered Potatoes	Buttered Broccoli	Chicken à la Maryland	Creamed Potatoes	Baked Potato	Roast Pork Loin
Cauliflower with Cheese Sauce	Breaded Tomatoes	Buttered Whole Kernel Corn	Fried Rice with Almonds	Buttered Peas	Julienne Carrots	Mashed Potatoes-Gravy
Tossed Green Salad	Stuffed Celery	Vienna Bread	Buttered Asparagus	Salad Greens with Grapefruit	Creamy Cole Slaw	French Green Beans with Mushrooms
Dinner Rolls	FanTan Rolls	Apple Dumpling	Lemon Ice	Hard Rolls	Whole Wheat Rolls	Molded Cranberry Salad
Chocolate Chiffon Pie	Strawberry Sundae	Beverage	Cloverleaf Rolls	Pineapple-Cashew Cake	Fruit Cup	Finger Rolls
Beverage	Beverage		Blueberry Glazed Tarts	Beverage	Beverage	Frozen Filled Angel Food
			Beverage			Coffee

EVENING MEAL (Buffet Service)

(Sunday)

Tuna Salad
Shoestring Potatoes
Bread and Butter Sandwiches
Fresh Fruit Bowl
Brownies

Beverage

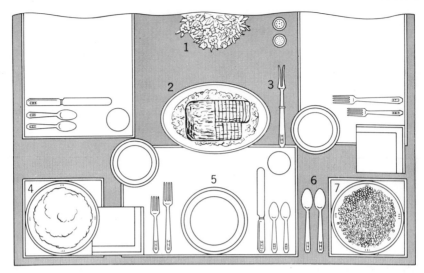

Fig. 16. Section of a table set for family service in a residence hall. (1) Decoration; (2) meats; (3) serving fork; (4) potatoes; (5) stack of plates; (6) serving spoons; (7) vegetable.

● MENUS FOR HOSPITALS

The basis for the successful operation of any hospital dietary department is the production and service of high-quality foods that not only meet the nutritional requirements of patients and personnel but are provided at a cost within budgetary allowance. Although often more complex, the principles of meal planning in a hospital are the same as in other types of institutions. For one service period, foods must be provided for many kinds of diets. These may range from liquid, ground, soft, or regular to bland, low-sodium, fat-restricted, with a wide range in caloric requirements. Often foods must be available 24 hours a day. For those responsible for hospital food service, such demands present multiple problems not found in other types of institutions. These must be solved in an acceptable manner if a high degree of efficiency in the production of nutritious, attractive, and palatable food is maintained.

When developing a hospital meal pattern, the first step is to plan a regular or normal diet that will supply all food essentials necessary for good nutrition. This pattern then becomes the foundation for most diets required for therapeutic purposes, and is the core of all meal planning in a hospital of any type or size. Patients requiring other than a normal diet will receive various modifications of the regular diet to fit their particular needs.

Usually food for hospital personnel is served in one dining room, cafeteria style. Here the menu also may be a modification of the patient menu, with a few additions to offer a wider selection than is desirable for the patients.

In planning a normal or regular diet, meals should be planned for each day as a unit; that is, for breakfast, dinner, and supper. Each day's menu then may be checked to be sure that all essential foods have been included. A suggested menu pattern for a normal diet follows:

Breakfast	Dinner	Supper or Lunch
Fruit or juice	Soup (optional)	Cream Soup or
Cereal with milk	Meat, poultry or fish	Main dish (made with
Egg	Potato or alternate	meat, fish, poultry,
Bread or toast	starchy vegetable	egg, or cheese)
Butter or	Green or yellow vegetable	Vegetable or salad
margarine	Salad: fruit or	Bread with butter or
Beverage	vegetable	margarine
	Bread with butter or	Fruit or other simple
	margarine	dessert
	Dessert	Beverage
	Beverage	

Many hospital dietary departments use diet manuals written by members of their staff or other authorities in this area of nutrition as a guide for planning modified diets. However, most small hospitals and nursing homes must operate without the services of a dietitian. For those persons responsible for menu planning in such situations, A Guide for Planning Diets is shown on preceding page.

● MENUS FOR HOMES FOR CHILDREN AND ADULTS

Characteristic factors involved in menu planning for institutional homes caring for children or adults are somewhat similar. With few exceptions, all 3 meals are eaten in the same place every day throughout the year. Under such conditions, the nutritional needs of the individuals being served must be met in the daily food provided for them, usually at a per capita cost at or below that termed the irreducible minimum. Careful thought must be given to menu planning to incorporate variety and interest into the menu in order to prevent the low-cost foods commonly used from falling into a monotonous pattern. However, menus planned specifically for children should use unfamiliar foods sparingly. Such foods should be introduced carefully to avoid rejection. The type of foods suitable for children will be similar to those suggested for the school lunch, p. 344.

Those responsible for planning menus for older people should be aware of the food problems peculiar to this group. Their fixed habits and food preferences may influence, but should not determine, the foods planned for them. Adults also need a well-balanced diet and in planning the day's food, it is well to follow the basic pattern for the normal diet, with emphasis on the inclusion of protein foods, including milk, meat, eggs, and whole-grain cereals. Individual problems of the group members, such as difficulty in chewing solid foods and special diet requirements, must be of major concern to those planning menus for the older adults.

Suggestions that might be met by the budget and that would add interest and variety to menus in homes for children and adults may be found on pp. 359–366.

● MENUS FOR SUMMER CAMPS

The rapid increase in the numbers of children and adults in attendance in organized summer camps has been paralleled, in most situations, by an equally rapid expansion in the educational plans of camp directors and leaders. An important phase of this expanding program is the provision of adequate dietary departments. Few staffs of well-organized camps are considered complete without the inclusion of an experienced dietitian. The problems met by a camp dietitian are often accentuated by the lack of adequate mechanical equipment, the limited market facilities for fresh foods, and the inexperienced helpers usually employed. These inconveniences are compensated for in part by satisfactions which come from feeding hungry, happy children.

The menus planned for a camp should be simple and based on the nutritional needs of the growing children, the climate, the children's acceptance of foods, and any religious restrictions of certain foods. Consideration should also be given the equipment available for food preparation, type and skill of kitchen employees, and the time required for preparation. The amount of food to be prepared is usually larger in proportion to the number served than is usual for most other types of services. Portions are larger, and there is usually a demand for "seconds."

Meal patterns suggested for a camp are as follows:

BREAKFAST	LUNCH [1]	DINNER
Fruit juice or fresh fruit when available	High-protein dish (or soup and sandwiches)	Meat or meat extender Potatoes
Cereal, hot or cold	Hot vegetable, creamed or buttered	Hot vegetable
Bread (type depending on the equipment)	Salad or relish	Salad or relishes Dessert
Milk or hot cocoa	Simple dessert, such as pudding	Milk
	Milk	

Before making an order list of foods, determine fresh food supplies available at local markets; then plan all menus to be served each group. Amounts of foods to be ordered may be determined by consulting the proper tables (pp. 3–8). Since the group membership may change very week or 10 days, menus found suitable for one group may be repeated with necessary variations.

● MENUS FOR INDUSTRIAL RESTAURANTS

Those engaged in operating the many types of industrial feeding units are responsible for reflecting the standards, goals, and desires of management while supplying plant employees with food that is nourishing, sanitary, well-prepared, attractive, and reasonably priced. These objectives are achieved if the food provided helps to build employee morale, if it contributes to individual health and vitality, increases plant production, and if it lessens absenteeism.

Menu planning for an industrial cafeteria or restaurant has much in common with menu planning for other cafeterias. Consideration must be given to the basic rules of successful meal planning and food combination as well as the specific requirements of the industrial establishment being served. As in any other food service, labor is one of the largest items of expense and one of the most difficult to control. The use of preportioned foods such as catsup, jelly, and butter, of portion-ready entrées such as chicken legs and prefabricated meat cuts, of ready-to-cook foods such as French fried potatoes, and of other built-in labor-saving devices is of major importance in effecting economies of time and cost.

The use of rotating menus has proved valuable in reducing the time spent in planning and as an aid in the equitable distribution of labor

[1] See suggested menus for school lunchrooms and residence halls, pp. 341–344, 349.

and food. Four (1-week) menus comprise a cycle suitable for the 5-day week of industry. This cycle is repeated 3 or 4 times, and then a new cycle is begun. Cycles should correspond with the seasons of the year, with appropriate adjustments being made for holidays, vacation shutdown periods, and the Lenten season. Breads, sandwiches, salads, desserts and beverages are planned on a separate menu. A 4-week winter menu cycle (pp. 355–358) which has been successfully used in one large industrial cafeteria follows.

Industrial Cafeteria Weekly Winter Menu Cycle: Menu 1

ITEM	MONDAY	TUESDAY	WEDNESDAY	THURSDAY	FRIDAY
Soup	Chicken Gumbo	Scotch Broth with Barley	Yellow Split Pea	Turkey Noodle	Clam Chowder
Entrée 1	Special Chipped Beef on Toast	Boston Baked Beans with Brown Bread	Baked Eggs and Noodles	French Fried Cauliflower with Rarebit Sauce	Macaroni and Cheese Loaf with Tomato Sauce
Entrée 2	Salisbury Steak with Brown Sauce	American Chop Suey with Steamed Rice	Barbecued Beef on Bun Plate Potato Chips Pickle	Baked Ham Loaf Glazed Pineapple Ring	Deep-sea Scallops Cole Slaw Tartar Sauce
Entrée 3	Roast Leg of Lamb Mint Jelly Brown Sauce	Country Smoked Loin of Pork with Sauerkraut	Roast Turkey Mashed Potatoes Cranberry Sauce Dressing Gravy	Potted Swiss Steak with Vegetable Sauce	Baked Pork Chops with Dressing and Gravy
Hot sandwich	Roast Pork with Gravy	Roast Veal	Baked Ham	Roast Beef	Corned Beef
Potatoes	Mashed Potatoes	Scalloped Potatoes	Mashed Potatoes	Mashed Potatoes	Parsley Potatoes
Vegetables	Cauliflower Polonaise Garden Green Beans	Sliced Beets Baked Squash	Garden Frozen Peas with Mushrooms Cream-style corn	Stewed Tomatoes Baby Lima Beans and Garden Carrots	Fresh Carrots Frozen Brussels Sprouts

Industrial Cafeteria Weekly Winter Menu Cycle: Menu 2

ITEM	MONDAY	TUESDAY	WEDNESDAY	THURSDAY	FRIDAY
Soup	Potato and Leek	Navy Bean	Vegetable	Beef Broth with Barley	Mushroom
Entrée 1	Asparagus au Gratin	Smoked Link Sausage	Baked Lima Beans with Salt Pork	Banana Fritters with Maple Sirup	Scrambled Eggs on Toast
Entrée 2	Braised Beef Stew with Dumpling	Potato Pancakes with Applesauce	Turkey Pot Pie	Spaghetti with Meat Sauce, Grated Cheese French Bread	Breaded Haddock with Tartar Sauce
Entrée 3	Baked Ham with Raisin Sauce	Yankee Pot Roast of Beef with Noodles Vegetable Gravy	Baked Liver with Bacon	Breaded and Fried Quarter Chicken with Baked Rice	Country-fried Veal Steak Cream Gravy
Hot sandwich	Hot Turkey	Roast Lamb	Corned Beef	Roast Pork with Gravy	Roast Beef
Potatoes	Lyonnaise Potatoes	Paprika Potatoes	Au Gratin Potatoes	Mashed Potatoes	Mashed Potatoes
Vegetables	Baked Acorn Squash Frozen Garden Spinach	Whole Kernel Corn O'Brien Hot Slaw	French Fried Eggplant Harvard Beets	Garden Broccoli Cuts Mixed Vegetables	Garden Peas Julienne Carrots in Sauce

Industrial Cafeteria Weekly Winter Menu Cycle: Menu 3

ITEM	MONDAY	TUESDAY	WEDNESDAY	THURSDAY	FRIDAY
Soup	Homemade Chicken	Minestrone	Philadelphia Pepper Pot with Spatzels	Green Split Pea	Tomato with Barley
Entrée 1	Oven Baked French Toast with Maple Sirup Link Sausage	Baked Corn Pudding	Mostaccioli with Marinara Meat Sauce French Bread Grated Cheese	Vegetable Chop Suey Steamed Rice	Scalloped Macaroni
Entrée 2	Veal Ragout with Spaghetti	Stuffed Bacon Wrapped Frankfurter on Bun Potato Chips Sliced Tomato	Pork Patties Baked Acorn Squash Applesauce	Baked Meat Loaf with Mushroom Sauce	Salmon Patties with Egg Sauce
Entrée 3	Vienna Cubed Steak	Brisket of Corned Beef with Cabbage	Braised Short Ribs of Beef with Vegetable Sauce	Roast Loin of Pork with Stewed Apples Gravy	Roast Round of Beef with Natural Gravy
Hot sandwich	Roast Pork with Gravy	Roast Veal	Roast Lamb	Hot Turkey	Baked Ham
Potatoes	O'Brien Potatoes	Parsley Potatoes	Mashed Potatoes	Browned Potatoes	Oven-roasted Potatoes
Vegetables	Frozen Baby Lima Beans Whole Kernel Corn	Fresh Cabbage Glazed Carrots	Acorn Squash Garden Peas	Mashed Rutabagas Hot Spiced Beets	Cauliflower Polonaise Garden Green Beans

Industrial Cafeteria Weekly Winter Menu Cycle: Menu 4

Item	Monday	Tuesday	Wednesday	Thursday	Friday
Soup	Lima Bean	Vegetable	Chicken Broth with Rice	Beef Broth with Barley	Clam Chowder
Entrée 1	Ravioli with Meat Sauce and Italian Cheese	Baked Corned Beef Hash	Chili Con Carne on Plain Spaghetti	Eggs à la King on Crisp Chinese Noodles	Scalloped Tuna and Peas
Entrée 2	Hamburger and Cheese on a Bun Plate Potato Chips Cole Slaw or Pickle	Turkey and Vegetable Fricassée with Corn Bread	Stuffed Cabbage Rolls, Creole Style	Braised Lamb Stew with Vegetables	Halibut Steak with Lemon Butter
Entrée 3	Roast Leg of Veal with Baked Peach and Gravy	Fried Pork Chops with Applesauce	Boiled Beef with Horseradish Sauce	Roast Round of Beef with Natural Gravy	Baked Ham Loaf with Mustard Sauce
Hot sandwich	Corned Beef	Roast Beef	Baked Ham	Smoked Pork Butt	Hot Turkey
Potatoes	Cottage Potatoes	Mashed Potatoes	Parsley Potatoes	Hash-browned Potatoes	French Fried Potatoes
Vegetables	French Fried Eggplant Frozen Mixed Vegetables	Garden Peas Braised Red Cabbage	Garden Carrots and String Beans Onions in Cream Sauce	Frozen Garden Spinach Cream-style Corn	Stewed Tomatoes Mashed Squash

Menu-planning Suggestions: Entrées

MEAT	MEAT EXTENDERS	POULTRY	FISH	MEATLESS DISHES
BEEF:	Baked Hash	TURKEY:	FRESH AND FROZEN FISH:	Cheese Rarebit
Corned Beef	Corned Beef Hash	Roast Turkey	Fried Salmon Steaks	Cheese Balls on
Roast Beef	Stuffed Peppers	Baked Turkey Roll	Poached Salmon	Pineapple Slice
Pot Roast	Beef Roll		Baked Halibut Steak	Cheese Croquettes
Broiled Steak	Beef Upside-down Pie	CHICKEN:	Poached Halibut Steak	Cheese Soufflé
T-Bone	Spaghetti with	Baked Chicken	Fried Halibut Steak	Cheese Fondue
Sirloin	Meat Sauce	Broiled Chicken	Fried or Baked Fillets	Macaroni and Cheese
Fillet Mignon	Creole Spaghetti	Fried Chicken	Haddock, Perch,	Scalloped Macaroni
Club	Beef and Pork	Barbecued Chicken	Sole, Whitefish,	Baked Rice and Cheese
Cubed Steak	Casserole	Chicken Tahitian	Catfish	Rice Croquettes with
Country Fried Steak	Spanish Rice	Breast of Chicken	Fried Whole Fish	Cheese Sauce
Spanish Steak	Creamed Beef	with Ham Slice	Whiting	Chinese Omelet
Swiss Steak	Creamed Chipped Beef	Chicken à la Maryland	Smelts	Rice with Mushroom
Steak with Vegetables	Creamed Chipped Beef	Fricassée of Chicken	French Fried Shrimp	and Almond Sauce
Steak Straganoff	and Peas	Chicken with Dumplings	Creole Shrimp with Rice	Fried Mush
Mock Drumsticks	Chipped Beef and	Chicken with Noodles	French Fried Scallops	Baked Eggs with
Barbecued Kabobs	Noodles	Chicken Pie	Fried Clams	Cheese
Barbecued Shortribs	Veal Croquettes	Chicken or Turkey Loaf	Fried Oysters	Curried Eggs
Braised Shortribs	Meat Turnovers	Chicken Soufflé	Scalloped Oysters	Creamed Eggs
Beef Pot Pie	Veal Soufflé	Chicken Turnovers	Deviled Crab	Egg Cutlets
Beef Stew with	Curried Veal with Rice	Chicken and Rice	Crab Casserole	Egg and Noodle
Vegetables	Creamed Ham and	Casserole	Broiled Lobster	Casserole
Beef Stew with	Celery	Chicken à la King		Noodle Casserole
Dumplings	Ham à la King	Singapore Curry	CANNED FISH:	Hot Stuffed Eggs
Beef Ragout	Ham Croquettes	Creamed Chicken:	Salmon Loaf	Eggs à la King
Hungarian Goulash	Ham Soufflé	on Biscuit	Salmon Croquettes	Scalloped Eggs and
Chop Suey	Ham Timbales	in Patty Shell	Creamed Salmon	Cheese
Meat Loaf	Ham and Egg Scallop	in Toast Cups	on Biscuit	Scrambled Eggs
Swedish Meat Balls	Creamed Ham on	on Chow Mein Noodles	Salmon Biscuit Roll	Omelet
Spanish Meat Balls	Spoon Bread	on Spoon Bread	with Creamed Peas	Spanish Omelet

Menu-planning Suggestions: Entrées (continued)

MEAT	MEAT EXTENDERS	POULTRY	FISH	MEATLESS DISHES
Meat Balls with Spaghetti	Ham Biscuit Roll	Chicken Croquettes	Scalloped Salmon	Vegetable Casserole, with Pinwheel Biscuits
	Ham Turnover with Cheese Sauce	Chicken Cutlets	Salmon and Potato Chip Casserole	
VEAL:	Ham Shortcake	Scalloped Chicken	Casserole of Rice and Tuna	Cauliflower Casserole
Roast Leg of Veal	Ham and Sweetbread Casserole	Chicken Timbales		Vegetable Timbales
Roast Veal Shoulder		Chicken Chow Mein	Tuna Croquettes	Spinach Timbales with Poached Egg
Baked Veal Chops	Sausage and Dressing	Chicken Biscuit Roll-	Creamed Tuna on Toast	
Veal Chops in Sour Cream	Sausage and Apple Dressing	Mushroom Sauce	on Biscuit	Mushroom Puff
Breaded Veal Cutlets	Sausage Rolls	Chicken Salad	Tuna Soufflé	Cheese Puff
Veal Birds	Sausage Cakes	Chicken Salad in Cranberry or	Scalloped Tuna	Spoon Bread
Veal Fricassée with Poppyseed Noodles	Fried Scrapple	Raspberry Mold	Tuna Biscuit Roll with Cheese Sauce	Corn Rarebit
Veal Stew with Vegetables	Bacon and Potato Omelet	Hot Turkey Sandwich	Tuna-Cashew Casserole	Corn Pudding
Veal à la King	Pork and Noodle Casserole	Chicken Salad Sandwich	Codfish Balls	Scalloped Corn
Veal Patties with Bacon	Baked Lima Beans	Sliced Turkey Sandwich	Tuna and Noodles	Hot Potato Salad
Veal Paprika with Rice	Boiled Lima Beans with Ham		Crab Salad	Creamed Asparagus on Toast
Curried Veal with Rice	Baked Lima Beans with Sausage	VARIETY MEATS:	Lobster Salad	French Toast
	Baked Navy Beans	Braised Tongue	Shrimp Salad	Plain Fritters
LAMB:	Chili Con Carne	Braised Liver	Tuna Salad	Corn Fritters
Roast Leg of Lamb	Chili-Spaghetti	Liver and Bacon	Salmon Salad	Fruit Fritters
Roast Lamb Shoulder	Ranch Style Beans	Liver and Onions	Cold Salmon with Potato Salad	Grilled Cheese Sandwich
Broiled Lamb Chops	Baked Eggs and Bacon Rings	Baked Heart	Hot Tuna Bun	Egg Salad Sandwich
Lamb Stew	Pizza	Braised Heart	Tuna Sandwich, Plain or Grilled	Fruit Plates
Braised Lamb Riblets	Cold Luncheon Meat with Macaroni Salad	Sweetbread Cutlets		Cottage Cheese Salad
Barbecued Lamb		Creamed Sweetbreads		Deviled Eggs
				Brown Bean Salad
		MISCELLANEOUS:		Stuffed Tomato Salad
		Frankfurters with Kraut		
		Cheese-stuffed Wieners		

Lamb Patties with
  Bacon
Curried Lamb with
  Rice
Lamb Fricassée with
  Noodles

PORK (FRESH):
Baked Fresh Ham
Roast Pork Loin
Roast Pork Shoulder
Roast Pork with
  Dressing
Baked Pork Chops
Breaded Pork Chops
Deviled Pork Chops
Barbecued Pork Chops
Stuffed Pork Chops
Breaded Pork Cutlets
Barbecued Spareribs
Spareribs with Kraut
Spareribs with
  Dressing
Pork Birds

PORK (CURED):
Baked Ham
Baked Ham Slices
Grilled Ham Slices
Baked Canadian Bacon
Ham Loaf
Ham Patties
Glazed Ham Balls

Cold Baked Ham with
  Potato Salad
Chef's Salad Bowl
Russian Salad Bowl
Baked Ham Sandwiches
Ham and Cheese
  Sandwiches
Ham Salad Sandwiches
Bacon and Tomato
  Sandwiches
Bacon and Tomato on
  Bun with Cheese Sauce
Hamburgers on Buns
Barbecued Hamburgers
Wieners with Meat
  Sauce on Bun
Hot Luncheon Sandwich
Hot Roast Beef
  Sandwich
Hot Roast Pork
  Sandwich
Barbecued Ham,
  Pork, or Beef
  Sandwiches
Western Sandwich
Toasted Chipped Beef
  and Cheese Sandwich

Menu-planning Suggestions: Vegetables*

POTATOES OR SUBSTITUTE

POTATOES, IRISH:
Au Gratin
Baked
Browned
Buttered New
Chips
Creamed
Croquettes
Duchess
Fried
French Fried
Lyonnaise
Mashed
O'Brien
Potato Cakes
Potato Pancakes
Potato Salad, hot or cold
Rissolé
Scalloped
Stuffed Baked
POTATOES, SWEET:
Baked
Candied or Glazed
Croquettes
Mashed
Scalloped
MACARONI AND SPAGHETTI:
Macaroni and Cheese
Macaroni Salad
Scalloped Macaroni
NOODLES:
Buttered
Poppyseed
RICE:
Buttered
Curried
Fried Rice with Almonds
Green Rice
Croquettes

OTHER STARCHY VEGETABLES

CORN:
Buttered
In Cream
On Cob
Corn and Tomato
Corn Pudding
O'Brien
Scalloped
With Celery and Bacon
With Green Pepper Rings
Succotash
LIMA BEANS:
Buttered
In Cream
With Bacon
With Mushrooms
With Almonds
PARSNIPS:
Buttered
Browned
Glazed
SQUASH:
Baked Acorn
Baked Hubbard
Mashed Butternut
Mashed Hubbard

GREEN VEGETABLES

ARTICHOKES:
With Butter or Mayonnaise
ASPARAGUS:
Buttered or Creamed
With Cheese Sauce or Hollandaise
BEANS, GREEN:
Buttered or Creamed
Creole
With Almonds or Mushrooms
Southern Style
BROCCOLI:
Almond Buttered
Buttered
With Cheese Sauce, Lemon Butter, or Hollandaise
Brussels Sprouts, Buttered
CABBAGE:
Au Gratin
Buttered or Creamed
Creole
Hot Slaw
CELERY:
Buttered or Creamed
CELERY CABBAGE:
Buttered
PEAS:
Buttered or in Cream
With Carrots, Cauliflower, Celery, or Onions
With Mushrooms or Almonds
SPINACH:
Buttered
Wilted
With Egg or Bacon
With New Beets

OTHER VEGETABLES

BEETS:
Buttered
Harvard
Julienne
In Sour Cream
With Orange Sauce
Hot Spiced
Pickled
CARROTS:
Buttered or Creamed
Candied
Glazed
Lyonnaise
Mint Glazed
Savory
With Celery
With Peas
Parsley Buttered
Sweet Sour
CAULIFLOWER:
Buttered
Creamed
French Fried
With Almond Butter
With Cheese Sauce
With Peas
CUCUMBERS:
Scalloped
EGGPLANT:
Creole
Fried or French Fried
Scalloped
MUSHROOMS:
Broiled
Sautéed

ONIONS:
Au Gratin
Baked
Buttered
Casserole
Creamed
French Fried
Stuffed
With Spanish Sauce
RUTABAGAS:
Buttered
Mashed
SQUASH, SUMMER:
Buttered
Mashed
TOMATOES:
Baked
Breaded
Broiled Tomato Slices
Creole
Scalloped
Stewed
Stuffed
TURNIPS:
Buttered
In Cream
Mashed
With New Peas
FRUITS SERVED AS VEGETABLES:
Apples
Buttered
Fried
Hot Baked
Bananas
Baked
French Fried
Grapefruit
Broiled
Peaches
Broiled
Pineapple Ring
Broiled
Sautéed

* For additional vegetable suggestions, see pp. 327–330.

Menu-planning Suggestions: Salads and Relishes

Fruit Salads*	Vegetable Salads†	Gelatin Salads	Salad Ices	Relishes
Apple and Celery	Beet Pickles	Applesauce Mold	Apricot	Relishes
Apple and Carrot	Beet Relish	Autumn	Cherry	Burr Gherkins
Apple and Cabbage	Brown Bean	Beet	Cranberry	Carrot Curls
Carrifruit	Cabbage Relish	Bing Cherry	Grapefruit	Carrot Sticks
Cranberry Relish	Cabbage	Cabbage Parfait	Lemon	Cauliflowerets
Cranberry Sauce	Cabbage-Carrot	Cranberry Ring Mold	Lime	Celery Curls
Frozen Fruit	Cabbage-Marshmallow	Frosted Cherry	Mint	Celery Fans
Mixed Fruit	Cabbage-Pineapple	Frosted Lime	Orange	Celery Hearts
Waldorf	Carrot-Raisin	Grapefruit	Pineapple	Celery Rings
	Celery Cabbage	Jellied Citrus	Raspberry	Cherry Tomatoes
	Cole Slaw	Jellied Vegetable	Rhubarb	Cucumber Slices
	Creamy Cole Slaw	Jellied Waldorf	Strawberry	Cucumber Wedges
	Cucumber-Onion	Molded Pear	Tomato	Green Pepper Rings
	in Sour Cream	Perfection	Watermelon	Olives
	Hawaiian Tossed	Molded Pineapple-		Green
	Head Lettuce	Cheese		Ripe
	Potato	Molded Pineapple-		Stuffed
	Red Cabbage	Cucumber		Onion Rings
	Salad Greens with	Molded Pineapple-		Radish Accordions
	Grapefruit	Relish		Radish Roses
	Stuffed Tomato	Molded Pineapple-		Spiced Crabapples
	Tossed Green	Rhubarb		Spiced Peaches
	Tomato	Raspberry Ring Mold		Spiced Pears
	Tomato-Cucumber	Ribbon Mold		Stuffed Celery
	Vegetable-Nut	Spicy Apricot		Tomato Slices
		Sunshine		Tomato Wedges
		Swedish Green Top		Watermelon Pickles
		Tomato Aspic		
		Under-the-Sea		

* For additional fruit salad combinations, see pp. 242–244.
† For additional vegetable salad combinations, see pp. 248–249.

Menu-planning Suggestions: Desserts

Cakes and Cookies	Pies and Pastries	Puddings	Frozen Desserts	Miscellaneous Desserts
CAKE:	**ONE-CRUST PIES:**	Apple Crisp	**ICE CREAMS:**	**CHEESE, assorted:**
Angel Food, Plain, Chocolate, and Filled	Apricot Cream	Apple Dumplings	Apricot	With Crackers and Fruit
Applesauce	Banana Cream	Apple Brown Betty	Banana	**FRUIT:**
Banana	Butterscotch	Baked Custards	Butter Brickle	*Baked or Stewed:*
Boston Cream	Chiffon	Banana Cream	Caramel	Apples
Burnt Sugar	Coconut Cream	Bavarian Cream	Chip Chocolate	Fruit Compote
Chiffon	Coconut Custard	Bread Pudding	Chocolate	Pears
Chocolate and Jelly Rolls	Custard	Butterscotch Pudding	Coffee	Rhubarb
Coconut	Date Cream	Caramel Tapioca	Lemon Custard	*Canned or Frozen:*
Cup Cakes	Dutch Apple	Cherry Crisp	Macaroon	Apricots
Fruit Upside Down	Frozen Pies	Chocolate Cream	Peach	Berries
Fudge	Fruit Glazed Cream	Coconut Cream	Peanut Brittle	Cherries
German Sweet Chocolate	Pecan Cream	Cottage Pudding	Pecan	Figs
Gingerbread	Pineapple Cream	Cream Puffs	Peppermint Stick	Fruit Cup
Lazy Daisy	Pumpkin	Date Cream	Pineapple	Peaches
Marble	Rhubarb Custard	Date Pudding	Pistachio	Pears
Pineapple Cashew	**TWO-CRUST PIES:**	Date Roll	Raspberry	Pineapple
Poppy Seed	Apple	English Toffee Dessert	Strawberry	Plums or Prunes
Spice	Apricot	Floating Island	Toffee	Rhubarb
White	Blackberry	Fruit Gelatin	Tutti Frutti	*Raw:*
COOKIES:	Blueberry	Fruit Whips	**PARFAITS**	Apples
Brownies	Boysenberry	Fudge Pudding	**SHERBETS:**	Apricots
Butter Tea	Cherry	Icebox Dessert	Apricot	Bananas
Butterscotch	Gooseberry	Lemon Snow	Cherry	Berries
Chocolate Chip	Mincemeat	Meringue Shells	Cranberry	Cherries
Coconut Macaroon	Peach	Peach Crisp	Green Gage Plum	Figs
Date Bars	Pineapple	Peach Melba	Lemon	Grapefruit
Oatmeal	Plum or Prune	Pineapple Cream	Lime	Grapes
Fudge Balls	Raisin	Royal Rice Pudding	Orange	Melons
Ginger, Crisp	Rhubarb	Shortcake	Mint	Oranges
Marshmallow Squares	Strawberry	Steamed Pudding	Pineapple	Peaches
Peanut Butter	**COBBLERS, FRUIT:**	Tapioca Cream	Plum	Pears
Sandies	(same fruits as for Pies)	Vanilla Cream	Raspberry	Pineapple
Sugar Cookies			Rhubarb	Plums or Prunes
			Watermelon	

Menu-planning Suggestions: Garnishes

YELLOW-ORANGE	RED	GREEN	WHITE	BROWN-TAN
CHEESE AND EGGS: Balls, Grated, Strips Rosettes Egg, Hard-cooked or Sections Deviled Egg Halves Riced Egg Yolk FRUIT: Apricot Halves, Sections Cantaloupe Balls Lemon Sections, Slices Orange Sections, Slices Peach Slices Peach Halves with Jelly Spiced Peaches Persimmons Tangerines SWEETS: Apricot Preserves Orange Marmalade Peach Conserve Peanut Brittle, Crushed Sugar, Yellow or Orange VEGETABLES: Carrots, Rings, Shredded, Strips MISCELLANEOUS: Butter Balls Coconut, Tinted Gelatin Cubes Mayonnaise	FRUIT: Cherries Cinnamon Apples Cranberries Plums Pomegranate Seeds Red Raspberries Maraschino Cherries Strawberries Watermelon Cubes, Balls SWEETS: Red Jelly, Apple, Cherry, Currant, Loganberry, Raspberry Cranberry Glace, Jelly Gelatin Cubes Red Sugar VEGETABLES: Beets, Pickled, Julienne Beet Relish Red Cabbage Peppers, Red; Rings, Strips, Shredded Pimiento: Chopped, Strips Radishes, Red; Sliced, Roses Stuffed Olives, Sliced Tomato, Aspic, Catsup, Chili Sauce, Cups, Sections, Sliced, Slices, Broiled MISCELLANEOUS: Paprika Tinted Coconut Cinnamon Drops "Red Hots"	FRUIT: Avocado Cherries Frosted Grapes Green Plums Honeydew Melon Lime Wedges SWEETS: Citron Green Sugar Gelatin Cubes Mint Jelly Mint Pineapple Mints VEGETABLES: Endive Green Pepper: Strips, Chopped Green Onions Lettuce Cups Lettuce, Shredded Mint Leaves Olives Parsley, Sprig Chopped Pickles Burr Gherkins Strips, Fans, Rings Spinach Leaves MISCELLANEOUS: Coconut, Tinted Mayonnaise, Tinted Pistachios	FRUIT: Apple Rings Apple Balls Grapefruit Sections Gingered Apple White Raisins Pear Balls Pear Sections VEGETABLES: Cauliflowerets Celery Cabbage Celery Curls, Hearts, Strips Cucumber Rings, Strips, Wedges, Cups Mashed Potato Rosettes Onion Rings Onions, Pickled Radishes, White MISCELLANEOUS: Cream Cheese Frosting Sliced-Hard-cooked Egg White Shredded Coconut Marshmallows Almonds Mints Whipped Cream Powdered Sugar	BREADS: Crustades Croutons Cheese Straws Fritters, Tiny Noodle Rings Toast Cubes, Points Strips, Rings MISCELLANEOUS: Cinnamon Dates French Fried Cauliflower French Fried Onions Mushrooms Nutmeats Nut-covered Cheese Balls Potato Chips Rosettes Toasted Coconut BLACK Caviar Chocolate-covered Mints Chocolate Sprill Chocolate, Shredded Chocolate Sauce Olives, Ripe Prunes Prunes, Spiced Pickled Walnuts Raisins, Currants Truffles

Menu-planning Suggestions: Utilization of Excess Prepared Foods

BREAD AND CRACKERS:
Bread Crumbs—for crumbing Cutlets, Croquettes, and other fried food; thickening steamed and other puddings
Canapés
Cinnamon Toast
Croutons—as soup accompaniment
Desserts — Bread Pudding, Brown Betty
French Toast
Hot Dishes—Cheese Fondue, Scalloped Macaroni, Soufflé, Stuffing for Meat, Poultry, or Fish
Melba Toast
Toast Points—as garnish

CEREALS:
Chinese Omelet
Fried or French Fried Corn Meal Mush or Hominy Grits
Meat Balls with cooked cereal as an extender
Rice and Tuna
Rice Croquettes
Rice Custard
Soup with Rice, Spaghetti, or Noodles

CAKES AND COOKIES:
Baked Fruit Pudding
Cottage Pudding
Crumbs to coat balls of ice cream
Crumb Cookies
Icebox Cake
Spice Crumb Cake

EGGS:
Boiled or Poached—add to Cream Sauce, Mayonnaise, or French Dressing, as a garnish for Vegetables, Egg Cutlets, in Salad
Scrambled — Potato Salad, Sandwich Spread
Egg Whites, raw—Angel Food Cake, Bavarians, Fluffy or Boiled Dressing, Macaroons, Meringue, Prune Whip, White Sheet or Layer Cake
Egg Yolks, raw—Cooked Salad Dressing, Custard Sauce, Filling, or Pudding, Duchess Potatoes, Hollandaise Sauce, Hot Cake Batter, Scrambled Eggs, Strawberry Bavarian Cream Pie, Yellow Angel Food Cake

FISH:
Creamed, à la King or Scalloped
Fish Cakes or Croquettes
Salad
Sandwich Spread

FRUIT:
Applesauce Cake
Apricot or Berry Muffins
Frozen Fruit Salad
Fruit Slaw
Fruit Tarts
Jellied Fruit Cup or Salad
Jelly or Jam
Mixed Fruit Salad or Fruit Cup
Prune or Apricot Filling for Rolls or Cookies
Sauce for Cottage Pudding

MEAT:
Apple stuffed with sausage
Bacon in sauce for vegetable
Baked Beef Hash
Boiled Lima Beans with Ham
Chili con Carne
Chop Suey
Creamed Ham or Meat on Toast
Creamed Ham in Timbale Cases
Creole Spaghetti
Ham or Bacon Omelet
Hot Tamale Pie
Meat Croquettes
Meat Roll or Meat Pie
Meat Turnovers
Salad
Sandwiches
Scalloped Potatoes with Ham
Scrapple
Stuffed Peppers

MILK AND CREAM, SOUR:
Biscuit Brown Bread
Butterscotch Cookies
Fudge Cake
Griddle Cakes
Salad Dressing
Sour Cream Pie
Spice Coffee Cake
Veal Chops in Sour Cream

POULTRY:
Chicken and Rice Casserole
Chicken Timbales
Creamed Chicken in Patty Cases
Chicken à la King
Croquettes
Cutlets
Jellied Chicken Loaf
Pot Pie
Salad
Sandwiches
Soufflé
Soup
Turnovers

VEGETABLES:
Combination — Carrots and Peas, Corn and Beans, Corn and Tomatoes, Peas and Celery
Fritters
Potatoes—Duchess, Hashed-brown, Lyonnaise, Cakes, Omelet, Salad (hot and cold)
Salad, in combination (when suitable)
Soup
Vegetable Pie
Vegetable Timbales

Menu Terms

à la (ah lah), *Fr.* To the, with, in the mode or fashion of, or in, as in *à la Crême*, with cream; *à la Newburg*, Newburg fashion; *à la Moutarde*, in mustard.

à la carte, *Fr.* On the menu, but not part of a complete meal, usually prepared as ordered.

à la king, *Fr.* Served in cream sauce containing green pepper, pimiento, and mushrooms.

à la mode, *Fr.* in style. When applied to desserts, means with ice cream. *Beef à la mode*, a well-larded piece of beef cooked slowly, in water with vegetables, similar to braised beef.

à la Newburg. Creamed dish with egg yolks added, originally flavored with lime or sherry. Most often applied to lobster, but may be used with other foods.

allemande (al-mângd), *Fr.* German; a smooth yellow sauce consisting of white sauce with the addition of butter, egg yolk, catsup, etc.

amandine. Served with almonds.

anglaise (ng-glayz), *Fr.* English; *À la anglaise*, in English style.

antipasti (än-tēē-päs tēē), *It.* Appetizer; a course consisting of relishes.

au gratin (o grat-ang), *Fr.*, made with crumbs, scalloped. Often refers to dishes made with a cheese sauce.

au jus (o zhüs), *Fr.*, meat served in its natural juices or gravy.

Bardé (bar-day), *Fr.* Larded. Covered with salt pork or with slices of bacon. *Un poulet Bardé de Lard*, a pullet larded with bacon.

bar-le-Duc (bar-luh-dük), *Fr.* A preserve originally made of selected whole white currants seeded by hand with the aid of knitting needles. Now gooseberries, strawberries, etc., may be used. It frequently forms a part of the cheese course.

Bavarian Cream. A gelatin dish into which whipped cream is folded as it begins to stiffen.

Bavarois (bav-ar-wâz), *Fr.* Bavarian.

Béchamel (bay-sham-ayl), *Fr.* Refers to a sauce supposed to have originated with the Marquis de Béchamel, maître d'hôtel of Louis XIV. A cream sauce made of chicken stock, cream, or milk, and usually seasoned with onion. Sometimes applied to all sauces having a white sauce foundation.

beef à la mode (bēf ah lah mōd), *Fr.* A well-larded piece of beef cooked slowly in water with vegetables, similar to braised beef.

bellevue (bel-vü), *Fr.* A pleasing sight; in aspic. *À la bellevue*, a food enclosed in aspic through which it can be plainly seen.

Bénédictine (bay-nay-dik-tang), *Fr.* A liqueur made principally at the Abbey of Fécamp in Europe. *Eggs à la Bénédictine*, poached eggs served on broiled ham placed on split toasted muffins and garnished with Hollandaise sauce.

beurre (buhr), *Fr.* Butter. *Au beurre noir*, with butter sauce browned in a pan; *Beurre Fondue*, melted butter.

beurré (buhr-ay), *Fr.* Buttered.

biscotte (bis-kot), *Fr.* Rusk, biscuit.

bisque (bisk), *Fr.* A thick soup usually made from fish or shellfish. Also a frozen dessert. Sometimes defined as ice cream to which finely chopped nuts are added.

blanquette (blâng-ket), *Fr.* A white stew usually made with veal. A cheese similar to Roquefort.

bleu (bluh), *Fr.* Blue. *Au bleu*, plain boiled; Used with reference to fresh-water fish.

boeuf (buhf), *Fr.* Beef. *Boeuf à la lardinière*, "braised beef with vegetables; boeuf kôti, roast beef.

bombe (bongh), *Fr.* Also called *bombe glacée*. A frozen dessert made of a combination of two or more frozen mixtures packed in a round or melon-shaped mold.

bonne femme (bong fam), *Fr.* Good wife; in simple home style. Applied to soups, stews, etc.

bordelaise (bord-lĕz), *Fr.* Of Bordeaux. *Sauce bordelaise*, a sauce with Bordeaux wine as its foundation, with various seasonings added.

borsch or **bortsch** (bōrsh), *Rus.* A Russian or Polish soup made with beets. Often sour cream or citric acid is added to give an acid taste.

bouillabaisse (bool-yab-ays), *Fr.* A national soup of France. The word comes from the verbs *bouiller*, to boil, and *abaisser*, to go down. A highly seasoned fish soup made especially at Marseilles. Served in plates with dry toast.

bourgeoise (boor-zhwâz), *Fr.* Middle-class, family-style. *À la bourgeoise* usually means served with vegetables.

brioche (bre-yosh), *Fr.* A slightly sweetened rich bread of French origin.

broche (brosh), *Fr.* Skewer, spit for roasting. *À la broche,* cooked on a skewer.

café (kaf-ay), *Fr.* Coffee; coffee house; restaurant. *Café au lait,* coffee with hot milk; *Café noir,* black coffee, after-dinner coffee.

canapé (kan-ap-ay), *Fr.* Originally couch, sofa, or divan; now an appetizer served either hot or cold. Usually fried or toasted bread spread with or supporting a wide variety of highly seasoned foods. Generally used as the first course of a meal as an hors d'oeuvre and eaten with the fingers, unless accompanied by a sauce or otherwise made impossible to eat this way. Often served on a doily.

carte (kart), *Fr.* Card; bill of fare. *À la carte,* according to the bill of fare; *carte au Jour,* bill of fare or menu for the day.

Chantilly (shâng-tē-yē), *Fr.* Name originally given to savoy cakes, which were scooped out, filled with preserved fruit, and garnished with whipped cream; now applies to anything served with sweetened and flavored whipped cream. *Chantilly cream,* sweetened and flavored whipped cream.

Chartreuse (shar-truhz), *Fr.* Having a hidden filling or stuffing, as meat molded in rice or molded aspic filled with vegetables, meat, or fruit filling in the center; also famous liqueur.

chaud (shô), *Fr.* Hot.

chemise (sh-mēz), *Fr.* Shirt. *En chemise,* with their skins on; generally applied to potatoes.

chiffonade (shēf-fōn-äd), *Fr.* Rags; minced or shredded vegetables or meat sprinkled over soups or salads.

cloche (klosh), *Fr.* Bell, dish cover. *Sous cloche,* under cover.

confit or **confiture** (kong-fee), *Fr.* Preserves or jam made from fruit.

Consommé (kon-so-may), *Fr.* A clear soup usually made from 2 or 3 kinds of meat.

creole (krē'ōl), *Fr.* Relating or peculiar to the Creoles, made with tomatoes, peppers, onions, and other seasonings. Applies to soups, garnishes, sauces, etc. so prepared.

crépe suzette (krayp), *Fr.* The product is small, very thin and crisp pancake served for tea or as dessert.

croissant (krwâ-sâng), *Fr.* Crescent. Applied to rolls and confectionery of crescent shape.

curry (kŭr'ĭ). Highly spiced condiment from India, a stew seasoned with curry.

déjeuner (day-zhuh-nay), *Fr.* Breakfast, lunch.

de jour, *Fr.* Ready to serve.

de la maison, (de-lah-mā-zōn'), *Fr.* Specialty of the house.

demi-tasse (dŭh-mee-tâss), *Fr.* Half-cup; after-dinner coffee served in small cups.

dîner (de-nay), *Fr.* Dinner; to dine.

duglère (doog-lâr), *Fr.* After French restaurateur who popularized tomatoes. Signifies the use of tomatoes.

écarlate (ay-kar-lat), *Fr.* Scarlet; a red sauce containing lobster roe, red tongue, etc.

entrecote (ângtr'kôt), *Fr.* Between ribs; a steak cut from between the ribs. Supposed to be second in quality only to the fillet or tenderloin.

entrée (âng-tray), *Fr.* Dish served between the main courses of a dinner. Usually a "made" dish of unusual food or of food prepared in an unusual manner. It is garnished and may be accompanied by a sauce. It should be easy to eat and pleasing to the appetite but not satisfying. More often refers to the main course.

espagnole (ays-pah-nyol), *Fr.* Spanish; brown sauce.

fanchonette (fâng-sho-net), *Fr.* Small pie or tart covered with a meringue.

farci (far-see), *Fr.* Stuffed.

fermière (fayr-myayr), *Fr.* Farmer's wife; in plain country style.

foie gras (fwâ gra), *Fr.* Fat liver. Applied especially to the liver of fat geese. *Foie gras au naturel,* plain cooked, whole foie gras; *Pâté de foie gras,* cooked livers seasoned with truffles, wine, and aromatics; most popular form of foie gras.

fondu (fong-dü), *Fr.* Melted or blended.

Franconia. Ancient German duchy; in the culinary sense, browned. Franconia potatoes, whole potatoes browned with the roast.

frappé (frap-pay), *Fr.* Beaten and iced. Applied to a water ice frozen to a mush while stirring; usually drunk rather than eaten with a spoon or fork.

glacé (glah-say), *Fr.* Iced, frozen, glassy, glazed, frosted, candied, crystallized. *Glacé fruit,* fruit dipped in a hot sirup which has been cooked to a hard-crack stage.

gumbo. Okra; a rich, thick Creole soup containing okra.

haché (hah-shay), *Fr.* Minced, chopped.

hors d'oeuvre (or-duh-vr'), *Fr.* Side dish or relish served at the beginning of a meal. Used for luncheons, but not for dinners in France.

Italienne (e-tal-yang), *Fr.* Italian style.

Jardinière (zhar-de-nyayr), *Fr.* The gardener's wife; a dish of mixed vegetables.

julienne (zhü-lyayn), *Fr.* Vegetables cut into fine strips or shreds. Named from the famous chef, Jean Julienne, who invented clear vegetable soup with the vegetables cut into match-like strips.

jus (zhüs), *Fr.* Juice or gravy. *Au jus,* meat served in its natural juices or gravy.

kippered. Scotch term originally applied to salmon; now a method of preserving fish, especially herring and salmon. The fish are split, then lightly salted and smoked.

kosher (kō'shēr). Jewish term. *Kosher meat,* meat from a strictly healthy animal that has been slaughtered and prepared in accordance with the Jewish requirements.

Kuchen (kōō-ckhen), *Ger.* Cake, not necessarily sweet.

Laitue (lay-tü), *Fr.* Lettuce.

Lebkuchen (lāp'kōō-ckhen), *Ger.* Famous German cake, sweet cakes or honey cakes.

limpa. Swedish rye bread.

lox. Smoked salmon.

lyonnaise (lyo-nayz), *Fr.* From Lyons; seasoned with onions and parsley, as *Lyonnaise potatoes.*

macédoine (mah-say-dooan), *Fr.* Mixture or medley; usually applied to cut vegetables, but also to fruit.

maître d'hôtel (maytr' dotayl), *Fr.* Steward. In the culinary sense, implies the use of minced parsley. *Maître d'hôtel sauce* (parsley butter), a well-seasoned mixture of creamed butter, chopped parsley, and lemon juice. Served on broiled meats, broiled or boiled fish, and on some vegetables, as potatoes.

marinade (mar-e-nad), *Fr.* French dressing in which foods, as cooked vegetables and meats, are allowed to stand to render them more palatable. Also used with uncooked meat to soften tough fibers and to keep meat fresh, in which case it may be no more than a brine or pickle solution.

marinate. To treat with a marinade.

milanaise (me-lan-ayz), *Fr.* From Milan. Implies the use of macaroni and Parmesan cheese with a suitable sauce, often Béchamel.

Minestrone (mēē-nāys-trō'nĕ), *It.* Famous Italian thick vegetable soup.

Mulligatawny. Derived from two East Indian words signifying pepper water. A highly seasoned, thick soup characterized chiefly by curry powder. Meats, vegetables, mango chutney, coconut flesh, rice, cayenne, etc., may be added to taste.

Napoleans. Puff pastry kept together in layers with a custard filling, cut into portion size rectangles, and iced.

Neapolitan. (Also **Harlequin** and **Panachée**). Molded dessert of 2 to 4 kinds of ice cream or water ice arranged lengthwise in layers. The mixture is sliced across for serving. Also applied to a gelatin dish arranged in layers of different colors.

Nesselrode pudding. Frozen dessert with a custard foundation to which chestnut purée, fruit, and cream have been added. Has been termed the most perfect of frozen puddings.

Newburg. Creamed dish with egg yolks added, originally flavored with lime or sherry. Most often applied to lobster, but may be used with other foods.

noisette (nooâ-zet), *Fr.* Literally hazelnut; nut-brown color. May imply nut-shaped. A small piece of lean meat. Generally a chop minus the bone (fillet). Potatoes Noisette, "potatoes cut into the shape and size of hazel-nuts and browned in fat."

normande (nor-mând), *Fr.* From Normandy. *À la Normande,* a delicate, smooth mixture often containing whipped cream.

O'Brien. Cubed potatoes cooked in a small amount of fat with chopped onion and pimiento.

pané (pan-ay), *Fr.* Covered with bread crumbs or breaded.

parfait (par-fay), *Fr.* Perfect; a mixture containing egg and sirup which is frozen without stirring. May be molded, but is more commonly served in parfait glasses.

parmentière (par-mang-tyayr), *Fr.* Potato. Named after Baron Augustine Parmentier, who introduced potatoes to France and originated many methods of preparing them. À la parmentière, with or of potatoes.

pastrami (pa-strä'mi), *Hung.* Boneless beef cured with spices and smoked.

pâte (pât), *Fr.* Paste, dough.

pâté (pâ-tay), *Fr.* Pie, patty, pastry. Also a meat preparation packed in earthenware jars and small tins, prepared largely in Germany and France, so called because it was sold in pies of *pâté* form. *Pâté de foie gras,* paste of fat livers.

persillade (payr-se-yad), *Fr.* Served with or containing parsley.

petit pois (puh-tee pooâ), *Fr.* A fine grade of very small peas with a delicate flavor but of low food value.

petits fours (puh-tee foōr), *Fr.* Small fancy cakes.

piquant (pe-kâng), *Fr.* Sharp, highly seasoned. Applied to sauces, etc. *Sauce piquante,* "a highly seasoned brown sauce containing lemon juice or vinegar, capers, pickles, etc."

plank (plänk). Hardwood board used for cooking and serving broiled meat or fish. Thought to improve the flavor of foods so cooked. *Plánked steak,* a broiled steak served on a plank attractively garnished with a border of suitable vegetables or fruits.

plat (plah), *Fr.* Dish. *Plat au jour,* food of the day, as featured on the menu.

Polenta (po-lĕn'ta), *It.* Popular Italian dish originally of chestnut meal, but now often made with farina or corn meal. Cheese is usually added before serving.

polonaise (po-lo-nay), *Fr.* Polish. Dishes prepared with bread crumbs, chopped eggs, brown butter, and chopped parsley.

pomme de terre (pom de tare), *Fr.* Apple of the earth potato. *Pommes de terre à la Lyonnaise,* Lyonnaise potatoes.

purée (pü-ray), *Fr.* Foods rubbed through a sieve; also a nutritious vegetable soup in which milk or cream is seldom used.

ragout (rag-oo), *Fr.* Stew; originally something to restore the taste and tempt the appetite. Generally a thick, well-seasoned stew containing meat.

ramekin (răm'e-kĭn). Small, individual baking dish or a pastry shell; also a cheese cake.

ravigote (rav-e-got), *Fr.* Sauce seasoned with tarragon vinegar, chives, shallots, etc.

ravioli (rä'vē-ō'lē), *It.* Little shapes of Italian or noodle paste rolled thin, one half spread with a filling of minced meat or vegetables and moistened with a sauce if necessary, then folded over and poached in stock.

rémoulade (ray-moo-lad), *Fr.* Pungent sauce made of hard-cooked eggs, mustard, oil, vinegar, and seasonings. Served with cold dishes.

rissoler (re-so-lay), *Fr.* To roast until golden brown; to brown. *Rissolé,* browned.

rouelle (roo-ayl), *Fr.* Round slice or fillet.

roulade (roo-lad), *Fr.* Roll; rolled meat.

roux (roo), *Fr.* Browned flour and fat used for thickening sauces, stews, etc.

Sabayon *Fr.* Custard sauce with wine added.

scallion. Any onion which has not developed a bulb.

Schaumtorte (schoum tor′te), *Ger.* Foam cake; layers of meringue and crushed fruit.

shallot. Onion having a stronger but more mellow flavor than the common variety.

sorbet (sor-bay), *Fr.* Sherbet made of several kinds of fruits.

soubise (soo-bēz), *Fr.* White sauce containing onion and sometimes parsley.

Springerle (spring′er-le), *Ger.* A popular Christmas cake or cookie. The dough is rolled into a sheet and pressed with a springerle mold before baking.

table d'hôte (tabl' dôt), *Fr.* Table of the host or innkeeper. *Service table d'hôte,* a meal planned by the establishment at a set price, permitting a wide choice of foods.

terrine (tay-reen), *Fr.* Tureen, an earthenware pot resembling a casserole. *Chicken en terrine,* chicken cooked and served in a tureen.

torte (tôr′te), *Ger.* Rich cake made from crumbs, eggs, nuts, etc.

tortilla (tô-tē′ya), *Sp.* A round thin "bread" made of corn meal.

tortoni (tôr-tōn′ēē), *It.* Originally *tortonois,* meaning from the Italian city Tortona. *Biscuit tortoni,* a frozen mixture containing dried, ground macaroons and chopped, blanched almonds.

tournedos (tōōr-nāy-dōz), *Sp.* Small round fillets of beef.

truffles (trŭf′ls). A species of fungi similar to mushrooms, found chiefly in France. They are black and grow in clusters under oak trees, several inches below the surface of the ground. They are rooted out by pigs trained for the purpose. Used chiefly for garnishing and flavor.

velouté (vu-loo-tay), *Fr.* Velvety; a rich white sauce usually made of chicken or veal broth. Considered the principal white sauce just as *Espagnole* is the chief brown sauce, although some confusion exists in the use of the terms.

volaille (vo-lah-yuh), *Fr.* Poultry.

vol-au-vent (vol-o-vang), *Fr.* Flying at the mercy of the wind; large patties of puff paste made without a mold and filled with meat, preserves, etc.

Wienerschnitzel (vē′nēr shnit′s′l), *Ger.* An entrée made of thin veal steak (cutlets) breaded and fried slowly in butter.

Yorkshire pudding. English dish, usually served with roast beef, consisting of a popover-like mixture which may be baked with the meat or separately with some of the drippings.

Zwieback or **Zwiebach** (tsvē′bäk), *Ger.* Twice-baked bread, crisp and slightly sweet. Now used largely as a food for very young children.

part four • special meal service

special meals

Meals for special occasions may call for the organization of a special temporary service staff. Procedures will differ in many ways from those established for the usual routine of daily food service. To many the organization and administration of these unusual meals is a task to be dreaded and, if possible, to be avoided. This attitude is often common among persons without institutional training, although it is not infrequently found among trained directors who are completely preoccupied with their daily tasks.

When a meal is to be served outside of the routine daily schedule, a temporary organization is often set up for the unusual task. The cooks who will prepare the meal may be experienced in large-quantity food preparation, but waiters and waitresses may be untrained.

The major responsibilities of the manager or food service director in charge of a special meal are as follows:

1. Confer with representatives of the organization to be served to determine such details as the type of group and number to be served, the service desired, price to be paid, and time and place of service.

2. Plan menu with the organization representative.

3. Determine quantity, quality, and estimated cost of food to be served.

4. Place food order.

5. Check dishes and equipment on hand. Make arrangements for obtaining additional items needed.

6. Set up temporary organization.

   (a) Assign cooks, regular or special, to prepare food.
   (b) Assign cooks and other personnel to the serving counter from which the plates will be filled.
   (c) Assign and instruct waiters or waitresses for dining room service.

7. Make detailed work schedule for each group of workers, if inexperienced.

8. Supervise the preparation and service of food.

375

9. Supervise the dishwashing and cleanup of preparation and service areas.

10. Write a detailed report including information concerning numbers served, income and expenses, and useful comments for service of similar meals in the future.

Suggestions for the organization and administration of a typical simple meal for 150 people, such as might be prepared and served in various types of food services, are offered here as an aid for those inexperienced in the service of meals for special occasions. Most schools have kitchens in their student centers, residence halls, or lunchroom in which special meals may be prepared by the regular cooks. Many communities and church centers also have well-planned and adequately equipped facilities for preparing and serving special meals. The plan presented here can be adjusted to other situations to meet changes in the menu, the number served, and equipment and labor available.

PLANNING THE MEAL

It is desirable that the person acting as manager for the special meal confer with an authorized representative of the group to be served. Such a conference provides information as to the menu to be planned, the estimated or guaranteed number to be served, the price to be charged for the meal, the type of service, the date, time, and place the meal is to be served. It is well also to discuss program arrangements and responsibility for table decorations.

Duplicate copies of the menu plans should be signed and kept by the group's representative and the food director. This confirms the agreement and may prevent a misunderstanding of details and avoid last minute changes. Menu plans may be recorded on a blank, such as that shown on p. 377.

After the menu has been planned, the next step is to determine the kind and amount of food to be purchased. A list of foods and amounts needed for the suggested menu is given on p. 378.

A carefully planned work schedule is important to the success of any special meal. The number of workers and time required for preparation will depend largely on equipment available and the experience of the workers. The work schedule on pp. 380–381 is offered only as a guide. In this plan for a Father and Son Dinner, to be served in a school lunchroom, the detailed schedule assumes that the kitchen used for the preparation of the meal is equipped with an electric mixer with attachments, adequate oven and refrigerator space, and a mechanical dishwasher. The cooks are experienced in quantity food preparation; the waiters and waitresses are students. If there is less equipment and the cooks are inexperienced, an adjustment in work schedules will need to be made.

A list including the amount and kind of linen, dishes, silver, glassware, and serving utensils required should be made by the manager and arrangements made for assembling these, at least one day before they are to be used. Such a list is shown on p. 379.

Central High School

		Menu
Date to be served	*Nov. 10*	
Dining room	*North*	*Hot Spiced Tomato Juice*
Time	*6:15 P.M.*	*Cheese Crackers*
Organization	*Father and Son*	*Honey-glazed Baked Ham*
Plates estimated	*150*	*Potatoes au Gratin*
Plates guaranteed	*145*	*French Style Green Beans with Almonds*
Price per plate	*$1.50*	*Ginger Ale Fruit Salad—Chantilly Dressing*
Number served		*Dinner Rolls—Butter*
Amount paid		*Pumpkin Pie—Whipped Cream*
Cash		*Coffee, Milk*
Charge		
Comments		

Representative of Organization _____ *George Johnson* _____

Food Director _____ *Helen Smith* _____

Food to Be Purchased[1]

MENU ITEM	FOOD	QUANTITY
Spiced Tomato Juice—Cheese Crackers	Tomato juice	10 46-oz. cans
	Onions	1½ lb.
	Consomme	5 46-oz. cans
	Cheese crackers	6 pkgs.
Honey-glazed Baked Ham	Ham, cured, ready-to-eat boned, sliced and tied	50–55 lb.
	Honey	1 qt.
	Orange juice, frozen	2 6-oz. cans
Potatoes au Gratin	Potatoes	45–50 lb.
	Cheese, Cheddar	6 lb.
Green Beans with Almonds	Frozen green beans, French cut	12 2½-lb. pkg.
	Almonds, slivered	1 lb.
Ginger Ale Fruit Salad	Gelatin, lemon-flavored	3 24-oz. pkg.
	Ginger ale	6 qt.
	Grapes	3 lb.
	Apples	4 lb.
	Celery	3 bunches
	Pineapple chunks	3 No. 10 cans
	Lemon juice, frozen	1 6-oz. can
	Lettuce, head	1 doz.
	Mayonnaise	2 qt.
Rolls, Dinner	Yeast, compressed	9 oz.
Pumpkin Pie	Pumpkin	9 No. 2½ cans
	Eggs	5 doz. (for pie and rolls)
	Milk	12–15 gal. (for cooking and serving)
	Shortening	6 lb. (rolls and pastry)
Cream	Cream, whipping	3 qt. (for pie and salad dressing)
	Cream, half-and-half	2 qt.
Coffee	Coffee, regular grind	2–3 lb.
Butter	Butter or margarine	7 lb. cooking and serving
Sugar	Sugar, granulated	10 lb. cooking and serving
	Sugar, brown	3 lb.
	Sugar, powdered	1 lb.

[1] Flour, condiments, and spices in stock. Based on menu to serve 150 (p. 377).

Dish List for Father and Son Dinner

ITEM	NUMBER
CHINA:	
Service plates (6-in.)	150
Dinner plates (9-in.)	160
Salad plates (6-in.)	150
Dessert plates	150
Cups	100
Saucers	100
GLASSWARE:	
Glasses for water and milk	250
Sugar bowls	20
Creamers	20
Salts and peppers	20
Water pitchers	12
Punch cups	150
LINEN:	
Place mats	150
Napkins	175
SILVERWARE:	
Knives	150
Forks	300
Teaspoons	175
Extra silver or trays	10 each
MISCELLANEOUS:	
Turner for meat service	3
Solid serving spoons	3
Slotted serving spoons	3
Hot pan holders	6
Dish towels	1 doz.
Roll baskets or plates	15
Coffee servers	6

The plans for organization that have been presented have presupposed some one person to be in charge, with others working under her direction, either as students or employees. Such is not the case with many special meals that are prepared and served by community and church organizations. These meals are a responsibility which many women, active in church and community life, are asked to assume. Often these women, who are efficient organizers in their own homes, are at a loss to know how best to proceed in the preparation and planning of food for a large group. Detailed plans previously presented as necessary for the efficient management of a special meal (p. 375) may be modified to fit the needs of a group of adult women. This group may be familiar with time requirements for food preparation but who have

Suggested Work Schedule for Cooks and Waitresses

Time	Cook I	Cook II	Waitresses 1-2-3	Waitresses 4-5-6	Waitresses 7-8-9	Waitresses 10-11-12
10:00	Make and roll out pastry for pies	Make salad and prepare lettuce for salads				
11:00		Refrigerate				
11:45	Make pie filling Bake pies	Prepare pans for rolls				
12:30		Make roll dough				
1:00	Eat lunch	Eat lunch				
1:30	Pare and cook potatoes	Assist Cook I with potatoes				
2:30		Count dishes and silver and instruct waitresses				
3:00	Cube potatoes Make cheese sauce					
3:45	Place hams in pans. Place in oven Combine tomato juice ingredients Assist Cook II shape rolls	Shape rolls			Set tables	Set tables
4:30	Heat water for coffee and beans	Heat water for coffee and beans				

Time	Cook	Head cook	Waitresses 1-2-3	Waitresses 1-2-3	Waitresses 4-5-6		
4:45	Remove hams from oven; Glaze and return to oven	Instruct and assist waitresses in cutting butter and salads	Cut butter	Cut butter	Cut salads	Cut salads	Cut salads
5:15	Combine potatoes and cheese sauce	Make salad dressing	Place salad and butter on salad plates	Place salad and butter on salad plates	Arrange lettuce cups and place on salad plates		
5:30	Remove hams from oven	Cook beans					
5:40	Bake rolls; Bake potatoes au Gratin	Make coffee; Assist waitresses in setting up serving counter	Set up serving counter; Place salads on table	Place crackers on serving plate; Place salads on table	Fill water glasses with ice and water; Place salads on table		
6:00	Prepare hams for service on counter	Heat tomato juice					
6:10	Remove rolls from oven; Remove potatoes from oven	Season beans, add almonds	Place rolls on plate and on table	Place rolls on plate and on table	Duties same as for waitresses 4-5-6		
6:15	Remain in kitchen during serving period; Assist in placing pie on plates	Pour tomato juice; Serve plates from counter; Remove food from counter; Place pie on plates	Pour tomato juice; Serve plates from counter; Fill pitchers with coffee; Stack dishes; Place whipped cream on pie	Place tomato juice after guests are seated; Remove first course; Place plates on table; Serve coffee and milk; Clear plates from table; Serve dessert			
7:00	Put away food	Clean counter and stack dishes	Stack dishes	Clear tables of all food and dishes			
7:15	Eat	Eat	Eat	Eat			

A helper for the cooks will report at 4 P.M. to assist cooks, wash pots and pans, and remain to wash dishes.

had little experience in the managerial aspects of institutional meal preparation, including the division of labor and the delegation of various responsibilities. A necessary initial step in such planning is the assignment of definite tasks to committees. A suggested plan for such a group follows:

Duties and Procedure of Committees

PLANNING COMMITTEE:
  1. Plan menu.
  2. List foods to be purchased.
  3. Plan amounts of food to be purchased.
  4. Select and assemble recipes.
  5. Appoint the following committees: Preparation, Serving, Clean-up.
  6. Furnish copies of menu and amount to be prepared and served to above-named committee.

PREPARATION COMMITTEE (number determined by menu and amounts to be prepared):
  1. Study menu and recipes.
  2. Make a preparation work schedule.
  3. Prepare food according to the work plan.

SERVING COMMITTEE:
  1. Make lists of, and have available when needed, necessary dishes, silver, linen and other table appointments.
  2. Arrange tables.
  3. Lay covers and decorate tables.
  4. Serve food on plates.
  5. Serve food to guests in dining room.

CLEAN-UP COMMITTEE:
  1. Provide space for soiled dishes.
  2. Scrape and stack soiled dishes and cooking utensils. Wash.

● SERVING THE MEAL

Preparation of the Dining Room

All personnel assisting with the food service should be given definite instructions. A mimeographed sheet of detailed procedures and instructions should be given to everyone new on a job.

The first step toward the service of a meal is the preparation of the room. It should be thoroughly cleaned, lighted, and ventilated; and the temperature should be regulated, if possible. The tables and chairs must be placed so there will be adequate space for serving after the guests are seated. Serving stands, conveniently placed, make service faster. Such provision is especially important when the distance to the kitchen is great.

Arrangement of the Table[1]

In order that the food may be properly served, great care must be taken to follow certain accepted rules for table setting. The physical setup, help available, or other conditions may demand some deviation from the rules given. However, there is often more than one right way.

1. *Silence Cloth.* When a damask tablecloth is chosen, first lay the silence cloth, which is usually of felt or of quilted or double-faced cotton material made for this purpose. It should have a drop of about 3 in. Fit it over the table tightly. The corners may be folded, if the table is square, and pinned or tied tightly beneath the table. The silence cloth serves three purposes: it prevents noise, protects the table, and improves the appearance of the tablecloth.

2. *Tablecloth.* Lay the tablecloth, unfolding it carefully on the table to avoid creases. Place the cloth upon the table so that the center lengthwise fold comes exactly in the middle of the table and the four corners are an equal distance from the floor. The cloth should extend over the table top at least a quarter of a yard at each end. The tablecloth should be ironed with one lengthwise fold down the center, the cloth opened up, and each side folded to the center crease, to make 3 lengthwise creases. Because of its length, institutional linen is usually folded crosswise to facilitate handling and storage.

3. *Place Mats.* Place mats make an attractive table setting when the finish of the table top permits. They are often used in institutions where no linen is available. Rectangular place mats may be sufficiently large that a single one will provide protection for the entire cover. If the mats are small, however, it is necessary to have enough paper doilies, of assorted sizes, to put under glasses, cups and saucers, bread and butter plates, and dishes containing food. In many institutions polished wood, lacquered, glass, or attractive composition table tops are used so the cover may be laid without cloth.

4. *The Cover.* The plate, silver, glasses, and napkin to be used by each person are called a "cover." Consider 20 in. of table space as the smallest permissible allowance for each cover; 25 or 30 in. is better. Arrange covers as symmetrically as possible. Place all silver and dishes required for one cover as close together as possible without crowding.

[1] Adapted from Department of Foods and Nutrition, Kansas State College, *Practical Cookery and the Etiquette and Service of the Table,* New York, John Wiley & Sons, 1956.

5. *Silver*. Place the silver about 1 in. from, and at right angles to, the edge of the table. If the table is round, only the outside pieces can be thus arranged. Place knives, forks, and spoons in the order of their use, those first used on the outside with the possible exception of the dinner knife and fork which may be placed immediately to the right and left of the plate, thus marking its position. Some prefer to place the salad or dessert fork next to the plate as the menu dictates.

Place the knives at the right of the plate, with the cutting edge turned inward. If the menu requires no knife, omit it from the cover. Place the spoons, bowls up, at the right of the knives. Place the forks, tines up, at the left of the plate. Oyster and cocktail forks are exceptions to this rule; place these at the extreme right of the cover beyond the spoons.

The fork may be substituted for the knife at a luncheon where no knife is needed. Place it on the right side of the plate with the spoon beside it, if one is used. If more than one spoon is needed, the balance is better if the fork is placed to the left of the plate. With two forks and a spoon it also is probably better to place the forks in the usual position.

Lay the butter spreader across the upper right hand side of the bread and butter plate, with the cutting edge turned toward the center of the plate. It may be placed straight across the top of the plate or with the handle at a convenient angle. The butter spreader is sometimes placed

Fig. 17. Cover for a simple meal. (1) Bread and butter; (2) water glass; (3) napkin; (4) salad fork; (5) fork; (6) knife; (7) spoon.

with the other knives at the right of the plate beyond the spoons. This practice is followed chiefly in public places.

Do not place the dessert silver on the table when the cover is laid, except when the amount of silver required for the entire meal is small. Never lay covers with more than 3 forks or a total of 6 pieces of silver. If a dinner is sufficiently elaborate to require too much silver to be put on at one time, place that needed for the later courses quietly at the covers just before the course is served.

If it is necessary to wash silver for use in the later courses, see that it is chilled before returning it to the table. Bring in the extra silver needed during the meal on a serving tray unless it is brought in with the course.

7. *Napkin.* Place the napkin at the left of the forks. It may be placed between the knife and fork if space is limited.

8. *Glass.* Place the glass at the tip of the knife or slightly to the right. Goblets and footed tumblers are often preferred for luncheon or dinner and should be used at a formal dinner.

9. *Bread and Butter Plate.* Place the bread and butter plate at the tip of the fork or slightly to the left.

10. *Salt and Pepper.* Salt and pepper shakers should be provided for each 6 covers. They should be placed parallel with the edge of the table and in line with sugar bowls and creamers. Salt shakers are placed to the right.

11. *Nut or Candy Dishes.* Place individual nut or candy dishes directly in front of the cover. Larger dishes for nuts or bonbons are placed symmetrically upon the table, usually allowing 1 dish for each six or eight guests.

12. *Chairs.* Place the chairs so that the front edge of each touches or is just below the edge of the tablecloth. The chair should be so placed with relation to the table that it need not be moved when the guest is seated.

13. *Decorations.* The decorations of the table should be in charge of someone not connected with the food service, although it is sometimes necessary for the food director to assume this as an added responsibility. Some attractive decoration should be provided for the center of the table. It should be low so the view across the table will not be obstructed. The decoration usually varies in elaborateness with the formality of the meal. Cut flowers should harmonize in color with the menu, the appointments of the table, and the room.

The use of candles in the daytime is permissible only when the lighting is inadequate or the day is dark. When used they should be the sole source of light. Do not mix candlelight and daylight or candlelight and electric light. Candles often form part of the decorations. Tall ones in low holders should be high enough so that the flame is not on a level with the eyes of the guests.

Seating Arrangement

Place cards should ordinarily be placed on the napkin or above the cover. Menu cards, or booklets containing the menu and program, are commonly used at banquets. Infrequently the placing of cards is left to the food director. It is extremely difficult to lay down arbitrary rules for the seating of guests, since the matter is governed largely by the number and by the degree of formality of the meal. The guest of honor, if a woman, is usually seated at the right of the host; if a man, at the right of the hostess. The woman next in rank is seated at the left of the host. At a women's luncheon, the guest of honor sits at the right of her hostess. At banquets and public dinners, a woman is seated at the right of her partner.

Table Service

1. Waitresses should report to the supervisor to receive final instructions at least 15 min. before the time set for serving the banquet.

2. If the salad is to be on the table when the guests arrive, it should be placed there by the waitresses not more than 15 min. before serving time. It should be placed at the left of the fork. If space does not permit this arrangement, place salad plate at tip of fork and the bread and butter plate if used, directly above the dinner plate between the water glass and the salad plate.

3. Place creamers at right of sugar bowls.

4. Place relishes on the table, if desired.

5. For small dinners, the first course may be placed on the table before dinner is announced. For large banquets, however, it is best to wait until the guests are seated. Soups or hot canapés are always served after the guests are seated. To simplify service and to create an atmosphere of cordial hospitality, a first course of fruit or vegetable juices and accompaniments may be served as the guests arrive in the reception area.

6. Place butter on the right side of the bread and butter plate. If no bread and butter plate is used and the salad is to be on the table when the guests arrive, place the butter on the side of the salad plate. This is often necessary where dishes and table space are limited.

7. Place glasses filled with ice and water just before guests are seated.

8. When the guests are seated, waiters or waitresses line up in the kitchen for trays containing the first course. Two persons work together, one carrying the tray and the other placing the food. Place the cocktail glasses, soup dishes, or canapé plates on the service plates, which are already on the table.

9. Place and remove all the dishes from the left with the left hand, except those containing beverages, which are placed and removed from the right with the right hand.

10. Serve the head table first, progressing from there to the right. It is preferable to have the head table the one farthest from the kitchen entrance.

11. When the guests have finished the first course, waitresses line up for removing the dishes. Follow the same order in removing dishes as in serving.

12. Waitresses line up in front of the serving table for the dinner plates, each waitress taking 1 plate in each hand. The line then advances as a unit to the dining room, each waitress stopping back of every second guest. There at a signal from the waitress at the head of the line, each waitress simultaneously places first, the dinner plate in her left hand in front of the guest and then, transferring the other plate from the right hand to the left, places it in front of the next guest. Every precaution should be taken to prevent the seemingly haphazard service that results from allowing the waitresses to serve without a line organization.

An alternate type of service requires tray stands on which are placed plate carriers or large trays holding several plates. Each waitress serves the plates to a specified group of guests.

A third method is often used in serving large groups. A tray of filled plates is brought from the kitchen to a particular station in the dining room, where waitresses serve the plates. The waitresses remain at their stations during the serving period.

Fig. 18. The salad is placed at the left of the fork when salad and beverage are both served with the main course. If space does not permit, place salad plate at tip of fork and bread and butter plate above the dinner plate. (1) Bread and butter plate; (2) sherbet dish; (3) water glass; (4) salad plate; (5) dinner plate; (6) cup and saucer.

13. Place the plate 1 in. from the edge of the table with the meat next to the guest.

14. As soon as a table has been served with dinner plates and salad, specially appointed waitresses should follow immediately with the ice, rolls, and coffee.

15. At a large banquet, when serving a sherbet with the dinner course, carry it in on trays and place directly above the plate. Two waitresses work together as for first course.

16. Serve rolls at least twice. Offer them at the left at a convenient height and distance. Plates or baskets of rolls may be placed on the table to be passed by the guests.

17. Place the coffee at the right of the spoons with the handles of the cups toward the right.

18. Refill water glasses as necessary. If the tables are crowded, it may be necessary to remove the glasses from the table to fill them. Handle the glass near the base.

19. At the end of the course, remove all dishes and food belonging to that course. Remove dishes from left of the guest.

20. The silver for the dessert may or may not be placed on the table when the table is set. If passed later, take in on a tray and place at the right of the cover.

21. Serve desserts 2 at a time and in the same order that the plates were served.

22. Coffee is served by waitreses who served it with the dinner course.

23. If possible, the table should be cleared except for decorations before the program begins.

24. The handling of dishes should cease before the program begins. The rattling of dishes has ruined many banquets and is an unnecessary offense to the guest.

Servers

Waitresses may wear black or dark dresses with dainty white aprons or light wash dresses; however, uniforms are usually preferable. Shoes with low, or medium-low, rubber heels should be worn. Waiters should wear dark trousers, white shirts, dark ties, and white coats. Waiters or waitresses should observe the following points:

1. Be immaculately clean in person and dress.

2. Report promptly on duty at scheduled time.

3. Be quick to see errors in table setting or service and to give help in case of accidents.

4. Appear pleasant and courteous at all times.
5. Step lightly, move quickly, but do not show a flurried manner.
6. Close doors without noise. Handle dishes and silver quietly.
7. Do not converse unless it is absolutely necessary.
8. Be as inconspicuous as possible.

Kitchen Organization

Food should be served from hot counters if these are available. If there are no hot counters, the utensils containing food should be placed in hot water in order that food may be served hot. Some provision must also be made for keeping plates and cups hot. For serving 50 plates or less, the plan should provide that 1 person serve meat, vegetables, 1 potatoes, and so on. Such an arrangement for serving may be termed a "setup." For 60 to 100 persons, 2 setups should be provided in order to hasten service. For more than 100 persons it is well to provide additional setups.

It is usually convenient to have the food placed on the hot counter in the following order: meat, potatoes, vegetables, and sauces. Butter, garnish, and relishes are placed on an adjoining table.

The supervisor should demonstrate the size of portions to be given and their arrangement on the plate by serving the first plate and calling attention to the points to be considered.

There should be a checker at the end of the line whose responsibility it is to remove with a damp cloth any food spots from the plate, to check the plate for completeness, arrangement, and uniformity of servings.

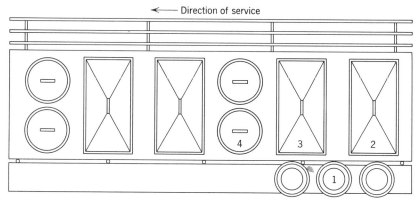

Fig. 19. Food arranged on a steam table in the order it is to be placed on the plate facilitates service. (1) Plates; (2) meat; (3) potatoes; (4) vegetable.

Portions

The importance of standardized serving can hardly be overestimated, for on this may depend the enjoyment of the guests and the financial success or failure of a meal.

There are various ways in which standard portions may be obtained. Perhaps the first way is by specifying the size or weight of units comprising the purchase if these are to serve as individual portions. Meats such as veal cutlets, chops, or steaks may be ordered 3, 4, or 5 to the pound, as desired, thus providing for standardized service.

Many foods cannot be brought under this plan because they are mixtures or combinations of various foods, or are served in a form quite different from that in which they are purchased. Meat balls, croquettes, mashed potatoes, pudding, cakes, and pies all illustrate this point. Several different methods are followed to obtain standardized individual portions in foods belonging to this group:

1. Portions may be determined by weight during the process of preparation, as is sometimes done in the making of chicken pie.

2. Portions may be determined by the use of dippers of standardized size (p. 25). This method is commonly used in the preparation of such foods as meat balls and sandwich ingredients. Dippers are also used for serving puddings and salads.

3. Foods that take the form of the container in which they are prepared, such as gelatin salads, desserts, cakes, pies, and meat loaf, are prepared in pans of uniform size, and the prepared product is cut into uniform portions.

To obtain standardized portions by any of these methods, it is essential that the recipe used be standardized.

● MENUS FOR SPECIAL MEALS

Special Dinner Menus

The Selective Menu Planner (pp. 391–397) is designed as a guide for those responsible for planning dinners for special occasions. Food combinations suggested here may be suitable for community meals, special occasions in residence halls, school banquets or holiday meals, or wherever a special meal for a group is being planned.

To use the guide, first decide on the entrée, then select 1 or 2 vegetables, salad, bread and dessert within the group. Any combination of items within a group, with minor adjustments, is designed to make a well-balanced dinner menu. If a first course is desired, see pp. 44–48 for suggestions for appetizers.

Selective Menu Planner

Roast Entrée Group I	Vegetable	Salad	Bread	Dessert
1. Roast Top Round of Beef O'Brien Potatoes Brown Gravy	Mint-glazed Whole Carrots	Celery Hearts Radishes, Olives	Raised Muffins	Chocolate Mint Parfait Butter Cookie
2. Roast Leg of Veal Dressing Mushroom Sauce	Butternut Squash	Mixed Salad Greens with Parisian Dressing	Sesame Twists	Apple Pie with Streussel Topping
3. Standing Rib Roast Parsley Buttered New Potatoes	Blue Lake Snap Beans	Bing Cherry Mold—Chantilly Dressing	Cornflake Muffins	Walnut Chiffon Cake—Praline Topping
4. Roast Sirloin of Beef au Jus Yorkshire Pudding	Asparagus Polonaise	Melon Boats Fresh Fruits Thick French Dressing	Orange Rolls	Cream Puffs
5. Rump Roast Small Corn Fritters	Zucchini Italian	Hearts of Romaine with Anchovy French Dressing	Whole Wheat Twin Rolls	Ice Cream Balls Hot Chocolate Sauce
6. German Pot Roast Egg Noodles in Casserole Gravy	French Fried Onion Rings	Pink Grapefruit Sections—Avocado Poppyseed Dressing	Ice Box Cloverleaf Rolls	Lemon-Orange Sherbet with Fresh Strawberries Sandies

Selective Menu Planner (Continued)

BROILED STEAK ENTRÉE GROUP II	VEGETABLE	SALAD	BREAD	DESSERT
1. Broiled Center Cut Lamb Chop Creamed New Potato Chutney	Buttered Frozen Peas with Mushrooms	Pineapple, Melon and Orange. Celery Seed Fruit Dressing	Glazed Pecan Rolls	Chocolate Chiffon Pie
2. Broiled T-Bone Steak Baked Rice Parsley	Baked Stuffed Tomato	Under-the-Sea	Hard Rolls	Pineapple-Cashew Cake
3. Broiled Sirloin Strip Steak French Fried Potatoes	Green Beans Amandine	Avocado and Orange Sections Fresh Fruit Salad	Butterhorn Rolls	English Toffee Dessert
4. Fillet Mignon Baked Potato with Sour Cream and Chives	Cauliflower—Whipped Lemon Butter and Paprika	Crisp Green Salad Bowl Roquefort Dressing	Cranberry Nut Muffins	Peach Melba
5. Porterhouse Steak Stuffed Baked Potato Green Corn Relish	Fresh Julienne Beets	Head Lettuce with Avocado and Grapefruit Sections—Piquante Dressing	Hot Biscuits Jelly	Mocha Almond Frozen Pie

Fresh Pork Entrée Group III	Vegetable	Salad	Bread	Dessert
1. Stuffed Pork Chops Glazed Apple Ring	Cauliflower Cheese Sauce Pimiento Strip	Grapefruit and Orange Sections on Curly Endive French Dressing	Cornbread	Chocolate Sundae Pie
2. Roast Loin of Pork Sage Dressing	Broccoli Drawn Butter	Cranberry Jewel Mold	Butterhorn Rolls	Meringue Shells Ice Cream and Fresh Strawberries
3. Barbecued Pork Chops Baked Rice	Buttered Green Peas	Guacamole and Tomato	All Bran Muffins	Lemon Cake Pudding
4. Breaded Pork Tenderloin Scalloped Potato	Frozen Asparagus Tips	Bibb Lettuce Chiffonade Dressing	Crown Rolls	Fruit Sherbet— Fudge Balls
5. Pork Chops in Sour Cream Baked Sweet Potato	French Green Beans	Stuffed Prune and Peach	Cinnamon Knots	Frozen Filled Angel Food Cake

Selective Menu Planner (Continued)

CURED HAM ENTRÉE GROUP IV	VEGETABLE	SALAD	BREAD	DESSERT
1. Baked Ham Slices Mustard Sauce	Mashed Potato or Sweet Potato	Waldorf and Pineapple Slice	Oatmeal Muffin	Rainbow Ice Cream Balls
2. Broiled Ham Slice Cranberry Relish	Creamed Pearl Onions	Ginger Ale Fruit	Poppyseed Twin Rolls	German Sweet Chocolate Cake
3. Glazed Baked Ham Currant Jelly	Buttered Whole Kernel Corn— Green Pepper Ring	Combination Fresh Julienne Vegetables	Parkerhouse Rolls	Strawberry Shortcake
4. Grilled Ham Golden Sauce Asparagus Spear Garnish	Green Lima Beans in Cream	Melon—Fresh Pineapple— Cherry	Pecan Rolls	Chilled Fresh Fruit Cup with Lime Sherbet Tea Cookie
5. Ham Loaf Horseradish Sauce	Southern Style Green Beans	Head Lettuce Roquefort Dressing	Pan Rolls	Fresh Peach Pie

POULTRY ENTRÉE GROUP V	VEGETABLE	SALAD	BREAD	DESSERT
1. Brown Fricassée of Chicken Hawaiian Sweet Potato	Fresh Green Beans with Dill Sauce	Head Lettuce with Florida Fruits— Mint Leaf	Hot Biscuits Honey	Pink-Frosted Ribbon Layer Cake
2. Roast Tom Turkey Dressing Giblet Gravy Orange-Cranberry Relish	Glazed Carrots	Crisp Cole Slaw Green Pepper Ring	Parkerhouse Rolls	Baked Meringue Pears— Chocolate Spritz Cookies
3. Barbecued Chicken Wild Rice Casserole Parsley	Fresh Frozen Peas with Sautéed Mushrooms	Peach Apple Salad Pecan Garnish	Small Hard Rolls	Strawberry Pie
4. Country Fried Chicken Cream Gravy Mashed Potatoes Spiced Apricot	Buttered Fresh Corn	Sliced Cucumbers in Sour Cream	Bran Rolls	Sherbet— Melba Sauce
5. Chicken Tahitian Fried Rice with Almonds	Chive Baked Tomato	Mixed Salad Greens Chiffonade Dressing	Dinner Rolls	Pumpkin Pie

Selective Menu Planner (Continued)

Fish Entrées Group VI	Vegetable	Salad	Bread	Dessert
1. Baked Salmon Steak Bernaise Sauce Parsley New Potatoes	Buttered Julienne Beets	Stuffed Apricot Sliced Orange and Glazed Prune	Cornmeal Muffin	Date Torte Whipped Cream
2. Broiled Fillet of White Fish and Mushrooms Lemon Butter Corn on Cob	Sliced Buttered Zucchini Grated Italian Cheese	Jellied Raspberry with Cream Cheese Balls	Butterscotch Pinwheels	Apple Dumpling Nutmeg Sauce
3. Poached Halibut Amandine Sauce Green Rice	Broiled Fresh Tomato	Assorted Relishes	Tea Biscuits	Lemon Chiffon Pie
4. Stuffed Fillet of Sole Cucumber Sauce— Pimiento Baked Idaho Potato in Foil	Fresh Green Peas—Drawn Butter	Head Lettuce Thousand Island Dressing	Braids	Chilled Melon Lime Wedge
5. Fried Deep-sea Perch Tartar Sauce Scalloped Potatoes	Broccoli Polonaise	Pear on Orange Slice with Lime Gelatin and Cherry Garnish	All Bran Rolls	Vanilla Ice Cream Hot Mincemeat Sauce

Braised Steak Entrée Group VII	Vegetable	Salad	Bread	Dessert
1. Cubed Steak Swiss Style Oven Browned Potato Radish Rose	Brussels Sprouts Brown Butter Sauce	Melon and Grape-fruit Salad Honey Lime Dressing	Blueberry Muffin	Cheese Apple Crisp
2. Country Fried Steak Mushroom Gravy Stuffed Baked Potato	Fresh Garden Spinach	Green Salad with Avocado Mexican French Dressing	Sesame Seed Bread	Peppermint Mousse Cookie
3. Baked Veal Cutlets in Sour Cream Glazed Sweet Potato	Jumbo Asparagus Spears Hollandaise	Stuffed Peach and Strawberry French Dressing	Orange Rolls	Ice Box Dessert
4. Veal Birds Broiled Tomato	Buttered New Beets and Greens	Cheese-Stuffed Celery	Parkerhouse Rolls	Red Cherry Tarts
5. Mock Drumsticks Lyonnaise Potato Cranberry Jelly	Baby Lima Beans and Carrots Julienne	Molded Spiced Fruit	Cheese Biscuits	Washington Cream Pie
6. Breaded Veal Steak Parsleyed New Potato Spiced Crabapple	Whole Kernel Corn O'Brien	Tossed Fresh Vegetable Salad Bowl Roquefort Dressing	Cinnamon Twists	Hot Chocolate Sundae

Special Luncheon Menus

(1)

French Onion Soup   Melba Toast
Chicken Salad in Raspberry Ring Mold
Buttered Lima Beans   Stuffed Celery
Hot Butterhorn Rolls
German Sweet Chocolate Cake
Coffee

(2)

Chilled Fruit Juice   Canapés
Cheese Soufflé with Shrimp Sauce
Buttered Broccoli   Broiled Fresh Pineapple Slice
Green Salad Bowl
Bran Muffins   Jelly
Fresh Strawberry Sundae   Macaroons
Coffee

(3)

Lime Ice Cocktail
Breast of Turkey with Wild Rice and Mushrooms
Buttered Asparagus Tips
Spiced Peach
Molded Cranberry Salad
Fan Tan Rolls
Orange Cream Puffs with Chocolate Cream Filling
Coffee

(4)

Hot Spiced Tomato Juice
Ham Loaf   Horseradish Sauce
Green Beans with Almonds
Buttered Whole Kernel Corn
Hawaiian Salad Bowl
Crown Rolls
Apricot Chiffon Pie
Coffee

(5)

Cheese Soup
Fresh Fruit Plate
Small Chicken Sandwiches
Filled Angel Food Cake
Coffee

(6)
Deviled Pork Chops
Stuffed Baked Potatoes
Buttered Cauliflower with Green Peas
Tossed Green Salad
Twin Rolls   Jelly
Fresh Peach Pie
Coffee

● BUFFET SERVICE

Buffet suppers and luncheons are increasing in popularity as a means of serving relatively large groups of people. They are characterized by an atmosphere of informality and friendliness, which extends their appeal to people in every age and occupation group. Some commercial food directors regard buffet service as ideal for the food service to which the family may bring the children. Others stress its suitability for festive occasions in residence halls and clubs. The menu may be simple or elaborate. In general the buffet meal is limited to two courses, but an assortment of hors d'oeuvres and a refreshing drink may be served to the guests before they are brought to the buffet.

A large part of the success of the buffet service depends upon the attractiveness of the buffet table. Gay colors may be introduced in the cloth, the serving dishes, the food, or the decorations. Not infrequently a bowl of fruit, gourds, and nuts replaces the more usual floral decorations in the buffet service. Consideration must be given contrasts in colors, shapes, and sizes in the food and to the selection of harmonizing floral or other decorations. Another important factor in the satisfaction afforded by the meal is the delicious flavor of the food and the combining of food flavors. It is much better to limit the kinds of hot foods served to those that can be prepared and served nicely rather than risk an overcrowded table and the overcooked food sometimes resulting from attempting too much.

Arrangement and Service

Food in a buffet service is arranged in the order in which it is usually served: Meats or other entrées, potatoes, vegetables or salads, and relishes. If more than one kind of cold meat or cheese is included in the menu, a pleasing grouping of the various kinds of food of this type is usually made on one platter. Fig. 20.

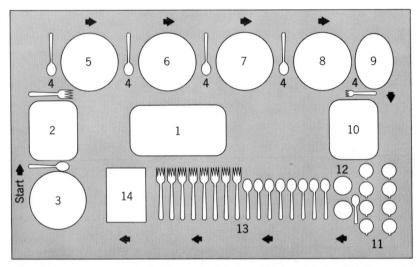

Fig. 20. Table arrangement for buffet service. (1) Centerpiece; (2) main dish; (3) stack of plates; (4) serving silver; (5–6) vegetable dishes; (7–8) salads, relishes; (9) rolls; (10) coffee service; (11) cups; (12) cream and sugar; (13) silver; (14) napkins.

Desserts may be placed on a table other than the one containing the main course, from which the guest will later serve himself. Usually if the guests are seated, the dishes from the first course will be removed and the dessert served.

The type of service depends largely upon the equipment available. If ample table space is provided places may be set with covers, rolls, and water, and provision may be made for the beverage to be served by a waiter. In this case, the guests need only to pass before a buffet table and select the foods desired. Hot foods at the buffet may be served by a hostess, by a waiter or waitress, or the guest may serve himself. When his plate is filled he takes his place at one of the covers prepared. If table room for all is not available, each guest may be given an individual tray on which to place silver, napkin, water, glass, and the plate containing the assembled food. Hot beverages and rolls are then commonly served by a waitress.

Food for Buffets

In planning a menu for a buffet, certain precautions must be observed:

1. Care must be taken to keep the service as simple as possible, i.e., to avoid foods difficult to serve; or those which are soft or "soupy" on the plate; or foods that require extra utensils as bread-and-butter spreaders, or salad or cocktail forks.

2. Hot dishes should include only food easily kept hot. Essential equipment for this may be large or individual casseroles, chafing dishes or perhaps shells for deviled fish and similar food.

3. Attractive garnishing is important. The menu should include a few attractively decorated foods, assorted salads, and an assortment of relishes.

4. A larger variety of food should be included than can be offered at table d'hôte meals.

5. The menu may be planned for men, women, or a mixed group, depending on the group to be served.

6. A salad bowl may be used for interest.

7. Jelly or jam facilitates the introduction of a color note and makes a pleasing accompaniment.

8. Dessert for a buffet service has no limitation except that it fit into the meal as planned.

Suggested Foods for Buffet Menus

MAIN DISHES

Shrimp Creole
Scalloped Chicken
Creamed Ham and Mushrooms
Deviled Crab
Creamed Sweetbreads and Mushrooms
Sweetbread Cutlets
Chicken à la King, Rosettes
Chicken Pie
Chicken Tahitian
Ham Patties with Pineapple Ring

Sliced Ham and Turkey
Scalloped Oysters
Curried Veal with Rice
Veal Birds en Casserole
Tuna Cashew Casserole
Chicken Salad in Raspberry Ring Mold
Tomato Stuffed with Crab or
  Shrimp Salad
Chicken-Rice-Almond Casserole
Singapore Curry

VEGETABLES

Latticed Potatoes
Shoestring Potatoes
Sweet Potato Croquettes
Buttered Peas, Mushrooms
Broiled or Baked Tomatoes

Cut Green Beans, Almond Butter
Baby Limas in Butter
Shredded New Harvard Beets
French Fried Onions
Green Rice

SALADS

Stuffed Tomato
Frozen Fruit
Spiced Pear and Orange
Orange and Grapefruit Sections
Stuffed Cinnamon Apple
Assorted Relishes

Potato
Pineapple-Tomato
Fruit Combinations
Molded Fruit Gelatins
Lettuce Hearts, Blue Cheese

SALAD BOWLS

Julienne Vegetables   Tossed Green Salad
Cabbage Slaw   Hawaiian Tossed Salad
Salad Greens with Grapefruit   Celery Curls and Carrots

DESSERTS

Filled Angel Food Cake   Orange Cream Puffs with Chocolate
Meringue Shells with Strawberries   Filling
   or other Fruit Filling   Pecan Pie
Lemon or other Chiffon Pie   German Sweet Chocolate Cake
Peach Melba   Assorted Cheese and Crackers
                                        Assorted Fresh Fruits

Buffet Menus

(1)

Chicken Pie in Casseroles
Buttered Lima Beans
Grapefruit-Orange Salad   Caraway Cole Slaw Salad Bowl
Spiced Peach   Apple Jelly
Relishes
Cloverleaf Rolls
Frozen Filled Angel Food
Coffee

(2)

Pork Cutlets with Mushroom Sauce en Casserole
Buttered Cauliflower with Peas   French Baked Potatoes
Stuffed Tomato Salad   Frozen Fruit Salad
Celery Curls, Olives
Garlic Bread
Blueberry-glazed Cream Pie
Coffee

(3)

Sliced Baked Ham and Turkey
Buttered Brussels Sprouts   Potatoes au Gratin
Grapefruit, Orange, and Avocado Salad
Crown Rolls
English Toffee Dessert
Coffee

(4)

Veal Paprika with Poppyseed Noodles
Glazed Carrots
Molded Cranberry Salad   Julienne Vegetable Salad Bowl
Whole Wheat Rolls   Apple Jelly
Pumpkin Pie
Coffee

(5)

Ham and Sweetbread Casserole
Buttered Broccoli
Pear Salad with Stuffed Prune Garnish
Carrot Strips, Radishes, Olives, and Pickles
Assorted Hot Breads
Strawberry Tarts
Coffee

(6)

Chicken Tahitian
Broiled Tomatoes   Green Rice
Spicy Apricot Mold
Peppermint Ice Cream   Hot Chocolate Sauce
Iced Tea or Coffee

(7)

Singapore Curry[1]
Half Cantaloupe with Lime Sherbet
Tea

Singapore Curry (50 servings)

Singapore Curry, an unusual combination of foods, is popular not only in the Far East where it originated but has been well accepted by those persons interested in "something different." Basically, this is a curried meat served over rice with a variety of accompaniments.

For the curried meat, a good combination is chicken and fresh pork. However, other meat, such as lamb or veal, may be used. For a generous serving, allow about ½ lb. meat per person. Brown the meat and simmer in meat or chicken broth. When done, dice meat and add to a sauce made from 5 quarts broth, 1 lb. 4 oz. flour, and 1 lb. fat. When thick, season with salt, pepper, and curry powder to taste. Add diced meat and

[1] Recipe follows.

stir gently. Let set to blend flavors. Taste and add more seasoning as the meat takes up the curry flavor. It should be quite yellow in color and have a distinct curry flavor. Serve with accompaniments:

5 lb. rice cooked (p. 227)	2 No. 10 cans pineapple chunks
50 servings French fried onion rings	2 lb. coconut
10 lb. tomatoes, sliced	1 lb. salted peanuts
15 lb. bananas, sliced or diced	2 1-lb. jars chutney

Arrange on buffet table in the following order: rice, curried meat, French fried onions, sliced tomatoes, sliced bananas, pineapple chunks; shredded coconut, salted peanuts and chutney. Each guest serves rice in the center of his plate, dips curried meat over the rice, then adds accompaniments. A well-served plate will be nicely rounded and self-garnished. Only a dessert need be added to make a complete meal. Fruit, melons, sherbet, or sundaes are especially good for dessert. Hot tea should be served.

● TEAS AND COFFEES

A table set for tea or coffee service depends upon its attractive appointments for its charm. The table covering, centerpiece, the tea service, silver, and serving dishes should be the best available and the foods colorful, dainty, and interestingly arranged. The selection of appointments and their arrangement on the table is influenced by the type of event, the number to be served, and the menu. To prevent a crowded appearance, there should be a limited amount of silver, china, napkins and food on the table when service begins, to be replaced as needed. A double table setup facilitates service to a large group. Figure 21 (p. 405) shows a tea table arrangement for two-way service.

Informal Tea

If tea is to be served to a large number of guests, the tea table usually contains a complete service of food, china, and silver. In this informal service, the guests file around the tea table and help themselves. Tea and coffee may both be served. They are placed on either end of the table and served by friends of the hostess, the guest helping herself to the accompaniments. In warm weather an iced beverage may be served to replace one or both of the hot drinks. The types of food usually served at a large informal tea include:

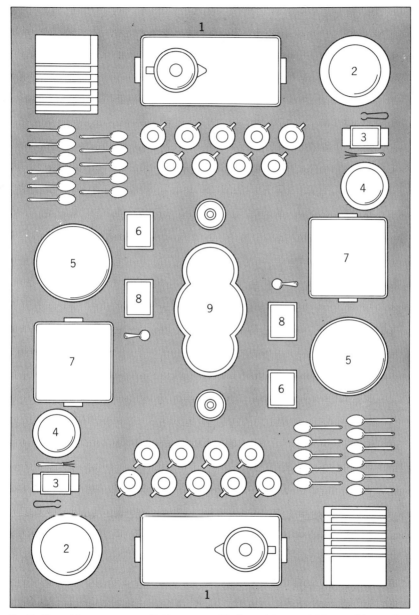

Fig. 21. Tea-table arrangement. (1) Tea service; (2) plates; (3) sugar; (4) lemon; (5) tea cakes; (6) candy; (7) sandwiches; (8) nuts; (9) decoration.

BEVERAGES

Hot: Coffee, Russian tea, chocolate, French chocolate, spiced grape juice, spiced cider, or spiced tea.
Iced: Tea, fruit punch (plain or with sherbet).

BREAD AND MISCELLANEOUS

Sandwiches, open: Assorted fancy shapes spread with desired filling and decorated.
Sandwiches, closed: Assorted breads as nut, orange, banana, date, cheese, or plain with suitable filling. Rolled, ribbon, checkerboard, pinwheel, or 2-tone sandwiches.
Miscellaneous: Cheese wafers, cheese straws, or miniature cream puffs filled with cream cheese or chicken salad.

CAKES AND COOKIES

Petits fours, small cup cakes, macaroons, kisses, shortbread, chocolate or date bars, tiny cookies—rolled or dropped.

ICE CREAMS, SHERBETS, OR ICES

Any desired flavor—served in individual cups in which frozen or in sherbet glasses.

NUTS AND CANDIES

Nuts: Salted, toasted, spiced, or crystallized. Preserved ginger, candied orange or grapefruit peel, mints in various pastel colors, and flavors; chocolate mint patties, small hard candies, opera sticks, crystallized mint leaves. Turkish paste in various flavors, colors, and shapes, and stuffed or candied fruits.

MISCELLANEOUS ACCOMPANIMENTS

Cube or loaf sugar—plain or decorated.
Orange—cut into thin slices or sections.
Lemon—cut into fancy shapes, sections, or slices; often garnished with whole cloves.

Informal Tea Menus

(1)

Butter Tea Cookies   Sandies
Small Frosted Brownies
Mints
Tea   Coffee

(2)

Nut Bread Sandwiches   Cheese Pinwheel Sandwiches
Assorted Tea Cookies
Spiced Pecans
Tea

(3)

Assorted Sandwiches: Ribbon, Rolled, and Banana Bread
Frosted Tea Cakes   Coconut Pecan Bars
Candied Orange Peel   Salted Nuts
Spiced Tea

(4)

Small Toasted English Muffins   Red Raspberry Jam
Cranberry Bread Finger Sandwiches
Plate of Bite Size Frosted Fruits   Cheese Plate
Coffee   French Chocolate

Formal Tea

Formal tea service is similar to the informal type, except that in the formal service the guests are seated and the food is brought to them by waitresses or assistants to the hostess. At a formal sorority house tea, members of the organization serve their guests. The foods served at a formal tea or reception are of the same type as those served at an informal tea, except that they are often more elaborately prepared and of greater variety.

Formal teas are usually used for entertaining large groups. The occasion may be a wedding anniversary, to introduce someone to a group, or to honor one or more individuals. The degree of formality will vary with the occasion and the desires of the hostess.

A formal tea served in the place of supper is sometimes called a high tea. It is more elaborate than afternoon tea and is similar to a buffet supper.

Formal Tea Menus

(1)

Assorted Open-Face Sandwiches   Two-Tone Sandwiches
Tiny Cream Puffs   Chicken Salad Filling
Raspberry Sherbet
Fudge Balls   Scotch Short Bread
Decorated Mints   Spiced Walnuts
Tea   Coffee

(2)

Christmas Tea
Christmas Bread Finger Sandwiches
Thin-sliced Turkey Sandwiches   Open-face Shrimp Canapé
Assorted Christmas Cookies from Foreign Lands
Thin Slices of Fruit Cake
Candy Stripe Mints   Salted Nuts
Sparkling Cranberry Punch
Coffee

(3)

Wedding Reception
Strawberry Ice Cream Balls in Fluted Pastel Cups
Bride's Cake   Groom's Cake
Wedding Punch   Coffee

(4)

Wedding Breakfast
Hot Creamed Chicken and Cashews on Rosettes
Spiced Peaches   Ripe Olives
Assorted Tea Sandwiches
Mint Sherbet
Wedding Cake
Punch   Coffee

Commercial Teas

Hotels, department stores and other food services sometimes offer pay-
ing guests an afternoon tea menu. The menu usually includes a wider
choice of foods than is provided at the usual afternoon tea. Food for this
type of service may include: hot tea biscuits and rolls; toasted English
muffins; various types of waffles, plain or pecan with sirup; toasted
breads, marmalades, jellies or jams; assorted sandwiches; small cookies,
cakes, French pastries; ice cream and sundaes. Simple salads, usually of

fruit, sea food or chicken, may be added. Beverages include hot tea with various accompaniments, hot chocolate, coffee and iced drinks.

A typical commercial tea menu follows:

AFTERNOON TEA À LA CARTE

Beverages

Tea—Orange Pekoe, English Breakfast, Oolong
Chocolate with Whipped Cream
Coffee

Breads

Dry or Buttered Toast   Toasted English Muffins
Strawberry Jam   Orange Marmalade

Sandwiches

White Meat of Chicken Salad
Olive-Nut

Salads

Bartlett Pear with Cream Cheese   Shrimp Stuffed Tomato

Desserts

Filled Angel Cake   French Pastries
Butter Pecan Ice Cream   Pineapple Sherbet
Swedish Mints

Informal Coffee Hour

Inviting friends and neighbors for a Morning Coffee or Kaffeeklatsch is a pleasant way to entertain informally and is growing in popularity. The food served is usually more substantial and the variety more limited than is the tea menu. There is always an ample supply of hot fresh coffee served with one or more hot breads. These may include: pecan rolls, glazed marmalade rolls, doughnut holes, Bishop's bread, quick coffee cake, Kolaches, Danish pastry and toasted English muffins. Fresh fruit or juice may also be included on the menu. A fruit tray, with bite size pieces of fresh fruit arranged on a silver or wooden tray, serves as an attractive centerpiece as well as an interesting addition to a coffee hour.

A 6-layer Ribbon Butter Cake is the only coffee accompaniment necessary for a simple and elegant afternoon Coffee Hour. Napoleans, Cheese Cake, Bismarcks, Danish pastry, and Crown Rolls are also popular Kaffeeklatsch items.

● FOREIGN BUFFETS

Increased interest shown by the average American in foreign foods is indicated by the many books dealing with food habits and choice recipes of various countries and by frequent magazine articles treating various aspects of the subject. One has only to observe the frequent appearance of chow mein, pizza, or chili con carne on menu cards to realize that the American taste is becoming cosmopolitan. This interest may be effectively capitalized by the presentation of dishes of a given foreign land at a buffet luncheon or supper. The foreign buffet affords a ready means of introducing variety and interest into meals that might tend to become routine.

In the following pages there are given some typical foreign buffet menus typical of certain countries, together with the recipes necessary for the successful preparation of the meal. Recipes are not given for foods often used on American menus, for foods ordinarily purchased ready to serve, or for recipes included in other sections of this book.

Chinese Buffet Suppers

Americans find Chinese dishes enjoyable and unlike those of any other nation except possibly Japan. Food items desired by a Chinese cook might include: Litchi nuts, mushrooms, dry lotus seeds, bamboo shoots, lotus roots, bean sprouts, shark fins, very fine noodles, rice, millet, rice flour, ginger root, bean meal, shell fish and other fish, chicken, pork, chestnuts, almonds, and walnuts. Preserved eggs, condiments and preserved fruits and ginger are frequently used. Chinese sauce or soya sometimes takes the place of salt in Chinese cookery. Peanut oil is used for frying.

Tea is the popular beverage and is served without cream or sugar in small covered cups without handles. A party menu usually contains several meat dishes—including chicken, fish, goose, pork, lobster, crab, or shrimp. Each dish is said to be 1 course. Tea may be served with each course. Almond meal cookies and fruits are common desserts.

Suggested Chinese Menu and Recipes

Menu is suggested for

CHINESE CHOW

Boo Loo Gai (Pineapple Chicken) Celery Hearts
Hop Too Guy Ding (Almond Chicken) Kumquat and Ginger Preserves
Egg Foo Yung (Omelet) Plain Boiled Rice
Chow Lon Fon (Fried Rice) Soya Sauce
Fried Shrimp Litchi Nuts
Almond Cakes (Gum Loo) Fortune Cookies

Fruit: Fresh and Candied
Jasmine Tea

The Dishes:

PINEAPPLE CHICKEN (Boo Loo Gai)

Cut a young chicken as for fried chicken, season with soya sauce, salt, and sugar and let stand 1 hr. Drain, dredge with flour and brown in hot fat. Add a little hot water and simmer until tender. Add 1 small can of diced pineapple and 1 t. soya sauce. Thicken liquid with flour and serve as soon as flour is cooked. Garnish with parsley.

ALMOND CHICKEN (Hop Too Guy Ding)

Fry 2 c. shredded onions, 2 c. shredded water chestnuts, and 2 c. shredded celery until slightly browned, then add chicken broth or white stock to cover, and cook until vegetables are tender. Add 1 young chicken that has been cut into cubes and cooked in peanut oil (or vegetable oil). Thicken liquid with a little cornstarch and water mixed. Add 1 T. soya sauce and place in a hot casserole. Add 1 c. toasted almonds just before serving.

OMELET (Egg Foo Yung)

Beat 12 eggs and add 1 c. bamboo shoots, ½ c. shredded water chestnuts, 2 T. chopped green onions, 1 c. cooked pork or chicken cut into fine strips, and 1 T. soya sauce. Mix all together lightly and fry as an omelet in hot peanut oil or ham fat. When omelets are cooked pour off fat. Add ½ c. broth, 1 T. cornstarch, and 1 T. soya sauce mixed and cooked 2 minutes. Serve as soon as the omelets have absorbed a little of the gravy.

CHOW LON FON (Fried Rice)

2 c. cooked rice 1 onion, shredded
12 oz. ham, finely cubed ½ c. cooked mushrooms
3 eggs 1 c. chicken stock
½ green pepper, shredded

Fry the rice in peanut oil until it is evenly browned. Fry the ham, onion, mushrooms, and green pepper for a few minutes. Add a little cold water and cook slowly 15 min. Season with salt and soya sauce. Add rice which has been mixed with beaten eggs. Add hot chicken stock and cook a few minutes. Garnish with chopped parsley.

Fried Shrimp

Fry shrimp in hot peanut oil until brown. Place shrimp and shredded green pepper in a flat pan; add hot chicken broth and cook a few minutes. Season with soya sauce and serve.

Almond Cakes (Gum Loo)

1 c. flour	1 egg, beaten
¾ c. powdered sugar	3 T. vegetable oil
¼ c. almonds, chopped	

Mix dry ingredients. Add oil and then the beaten egg. Mold into small balls, brush with egg, garnish with a whole almond, and bake in a moderate oven.

Litchi nuts have a characteristic flavor and may be purchased dried or canned.

Hungarian Buffet Suppers

Knowledge of Hungarian cookery is for many people restricted to the more or less enthusiastic acceptance of Hungarian goulash, a dish said to be "the savory ancestor of all stews." Historically, goulash has an honorable record in that for more than a thousand years it has brought gastronomic delight to the peoples now called Hungarian. It exemplifies a common practice in Hungarian cookery, that of cooking meats such as pork and beef with vegetables.

The vegetables in common use are similar to those in the American dietary and include beets, red and white cabbage, sauerkraut, carrots, cauliflower, kale, kohlrabi, peppers, and lettuce. The popular fruits include apples, apricots, cherries, melons, peaches, pears, and bananas. The large rôle of cereals in the diet is shown by the appearance of noodles and bread dumplings in many menus along with rye breads and fancy rolls.

Cheese is used freely in cooked dishes and in its natural state, and on the other hand butter is used sparingly and then unsalted. Sour cream is widely used both as a garnish and as an ingredient in cooking. Its use with paprika is regarded by many as the characterizing feature of a Hungarian dish, so popular are both with these people. Paprika, although popular, is only one of the numerous condiments used, as the Hungarians are fond of spicy foods.

Suggested Hungarian Menu and Recipes

HUNGARIAN BUFFET

Paprika Chicken with Spatzels
Stuffed Squash   Green Beans with Dill Sauce
Cucumber Salad—Sour Cream Dressing
Poppyseed Crescent Rolls   Sweet Butter
Cheese Cake   Fresh Fruit Compote
Coffee

PAPRIKA CHICKEN

Cut chicken as for frying, salt, and let stand 2 hours. Slice 2 large onions and fry in hot fat until light brown. Dredge each piece of chicken in flour and brown in the fat. When brown add the yolks of 2 eggs mixed with 1 c. of sour cream, sprinkle with 1 T. of paprika, a little salt and pepper, and let simmer until the chicken is tender.

STUFFED SQUASH

Select 12 uniform acorn squashes and cut each into halves and remove seeds. Steam until almost tender, then place in a flat pan. Place a No. 12 dipper of the following mixture in each half: 2½ qt. steamed rice, 2 lb. chopped cooked veal, 1 small onion minced and fried in ¼ c. of butter. Pour around the squash the following liquid: 1½ qt. stock, 2 oz. flour and 4 oz. butter made into a sauce. Sprinkle with chopped parsley. Baste and bake for half an hour. Add sour cream before serving if desired.

Swedish Buffet Suppers

Sweden is famous for its Smörgåsbord, or hors d'oeuvres, which is an ancient tradition and an important accompaniment to all Swedish dinners. The hors d'oeuvres for a family of moderate means are grouped in the center of a long table laid with a spotless white linen tablecloth, plates, and silver. The guests are seated at the table and the hors d'oeuvres are passed and eaten just before a regular meal of two or more courses is served. A maid removes the dishes from the first course. Typical food for the family hors d'oeuvres might include: Meats—cold spiced tongue, smoked venison, smoked salmon (sliced), fish in aspic jelly, anchovies, herring served in two ways, large shrimps with Thousand Island dressing, parsley, and dried beef; vegetables—radishes, sliced tomatoes, salads (two or more kinds), and a scalloped dish; bread —rye bread, white bread baked in ornamental shapes; cheese—served in a big piece on a cheese plate with a cheese knife.

Hors d'oeuvres for a family, or for a hotel, might be arranged on a separate table as for a buffet supper. Each guest would help himself and then take his place at the dining table.

The service by waitresses or waiters would be much the same as for the less elaborate meal described above. The food would be of greater variety, including 20 to 125 articles—Rye Krisp, butter curls, 6 or 7 kinds of cheese, very small Swedish meat balls fried in deep fat, a hot scalloped dish of fish or vegetable, pickled onions, pickled beets or cucumbers; vegetable salads—similar to our own, a bowl of mayonnaise; jellies and marmalades. A regular 3- or 4-course dinner is served after the hors d'oeuvres are eaten.

The use of colorful foods or decorations is an outstanding feature of the Swedish table. Candles are not used for decorations except for banquets. Flowers are always used and often two or more bouquets are placed on the table, if long.

A Swedish buffet supper suitable for service in this country is planned to include only the Smörgåsbord and the dessert, omitting what the Swedish diner would regard as the main part of the meal.

Suggested Swedish Menus and Recipes

SMÖRGÅSBORD

Pickled Herring   Canapés
Pickled Beets   Celery Curls   Radish Roses
Deviled Eggs with Parsley Garnish   Sliced Tomatoes
Cucumbers in Sour Cream
Seasoned Cottage Cheese   Assorted Cheese
Swedish Meat Balls   Potato Sausage
Cold Sliced Baked Ham or Spiced Tongue
Parsley Buttered Potatoes or Potato Salad
Swedish Brown Beans or Green Beans with Mushrooms
Fruit Salad Mold   Swedish Green Top Salad
Cabbage Slaw
Swedish Salad Bowl
Rye Bread   Swedish Tea Ring
Cheese Pudding with Thickened Grape Juice
Lingenberry Tarts
Swedish Apple Cake   Assorted Cookies
Swedish Mints
Coffee

Bordstabbel Bakels (Lumberpile Cookies)

½ c. butter	1¼ c. flour
1 c. light brown sugar	½ t. soda
1 egg	¼ t. salt
½ t. vanilla	½ c. chopped nutmeats

Cream butter and sugar. Add well-beaten egg and vanilla. Add flour sifted with soda and salt, then nutmeats dredged in portion of flour. Mold dough. Let stand in refrigerator overnight. Cut into strips, 3 inches by 1 inch. Bake in a moderate oven. When done, cover with White Mountain Frosting and sprinkle with chopped almonds, caraway seed, or candies. Pile like lumber on serving plates.

Sandbakelser (Sand Tarts)

1 lb. butter	1 c. white sugar
pinch of salt	1 T. cream or milk
⅓ t. baking powder	2 eggs
5 c. flour (about)	3 T. almond extract

Cream butter and sugar. Add eggs. Blend well, add extract, then flour. Press into small "picture" tins or put through cookie press. Chopped almonds may be added to dough if "picture" tins are used. Turn out of tins at once after baking or they will stick.

Smörbakelser (Butter Cookies)

1 c. butter (sweet)
1 c. powdered sugar
2 c. flour

Mix and pat out in 2 10-inch baking tins. Bake in a moderate oven approximately 20–30 min. Cut as soon as removed from oven. This is the same as Scotch Shortbreads.

Svenska Kringlor (Swedish Kringle)

1 c. butter	3½ c. flour or enough to make soft
1¼ c. brown sugar	dough
½ c. milk	2 T. baking powder
2 eggs	1 T. cinnamon

Sift dry ingredients. Cream butter and sugar. Add egg yolks and flour and milk alternately. Fold in beaten whites. Bake as drop cookies.

Svenska Peppar Nötter (Swedish Peppernuts)

The oldest of all the cakes we know today are the peppernuts. They were in popular use long before the 11th century.

4 eggs	1 t. cardamon (ground)
2 c. sugar	½ c. nuts
1 c. butter	½ c. raisins
1 t. cinnamon	4 c. flour (bread)
1 t. cloves	1 t. soda
1 t. pepper	2 T. hot water

Drop on cookie sheet and bake at 450° F.

Fattigman Bakels (Poorman's Crullers)

2 eggs	f.g. cardamon
2 T. sugar	3 T. heavy sweet cream
⅛ t. salt	1¾ c. flour (or less)

Beat eggs until light, add sugar, salt, spice, and continue beating. Add cream and enough flour to make a soft dough. Turn out on floured board, roll very thin. Cut into diamond shapes. Slash opposite ends. Pull end through slit, or cut in star shapes. Fry in deep fat. Drain on heavy paper. Dust with sugar.

Swedish Salad Bowl

1 can of pineapple (size 2½)	1 stalk celery
1 tart apple	5 tomatoes
lettuce	½ cucumber

Cut the pineapple and tomato into wedges, dice the apple and celery, cut the cucumber en julienne. Mix with pineapple dressing just before serving and add shredded lettuce leaves.

Pineapple Dressing

Mix 2 raw egg yolks with the juice drained from the can of pineapple, stir constantly, and cook over a low heat until thick. Cool, then add 1 mashed cold hard-cooked egg yolk that has been mixed with ¼ t. mustard and 3 T. of vinegar. Fold in 2 c. whipped cream.

Serve salad in a salad bowl. Yield approximately 10 servings.

Ost Kaka (Cheese Pudding)

2 gal. milk	6 eggs
2 c. flour	1½ qt. cream, coffee
½ cake of cheese rennet	½ c. sugar
(purchased from drug store)	

Heat the milk until lukewarm and stir into it the flour that has been smoothed to a paste. Add the cheese rennet that has been dissolved in 2 T. water. Stir well and let stand. As soon as the milk has set, stir gently to separate the curds and whey. Let stand a few minutes then pour off whey or use a strainer to remove curds. (The curds should be quite moist.) Place curds in 2 medium-sized casseroles and pour over them a custard mixture made from the eggs, cream, and sugar. Sprinkle nutmeg over the top. Bake and test as a plain custard. Serve warm with strawberry jam or grape juice thickened to the consistency of thick cream.

KÖTTBULLAR (Meat Balls)

1 lb. beef loin	3–4 egg yolks
8 oz. veal	3 T. onion, chopped
8 oz. pork	2 T. salt
½ c. bread crumbs, dry, ground	½ t. pepper
1 c. cream	⅛ t. allspice
½ c. soda water, dilute	1 c. butter

Pass the meat through a meat grinder three times or more if a coarse grinder is used. Add the bread crumbs, which have been soaked in the cream. Add soda water and egg yolks, mix well, and shape into small balls. Fry the onion in butter but do not brown; add the meat balls and fry, using a low heat. Fry in deep fat. Shake the pan occasionally to keep the balls in shape. Place balls in casserole and pour over them the fat in which they were cooked. Garnish with a border of fried onions.

KROKONER

¼ c. sugar	1 c. milk
1 c. butter	f.g. salt
4 t. baking powder	1 t. vanilla (or ½ t. vanilla and
flour to make a roll dough	½ t. almond)
1 egg	

Roll dough and cut into strips 5 inches long and 1½ inches wide. Bake over semicircular tins 12 inches long, so that cookies form a semicircle when baked. Ice with orange icing and decorate with tiny colored candies.

German Buffet Supper

German people show a decided preference for heavy food, that is, food containing much fat and starch. They also use many sauces and gravies. Many foods are seasoned with vinegar and often sugar is added. With the exception of some typical dishes, German food is very similar to our own. Many kinds of sausages, sauerkraut with dumplings and spareribs, beef with sour sauce, noodles, and rye bread with caraway seed are typical German foods. The following menu is characteristic of the "feast food" popular with the German people for New Year's parties and similar festive occasions.

Suggested German Menu and Recipes

German New Year's Eve Buffet

Hasenpfeffer or Veal in Sour Cream
Poppyseed Noodles
Potato Pancakes   Applesauce
Kraut with Apples
Tomato Salad   Green Bean Salad Bowl
Cold Platter: Pickled Herring, Cold Tongue
Ham, Goose Liver, Smoked Salmon and Cervelat
Caraway Rye Bread   Vienna Rolls
Crullers   Cookies   Zwieback Cheese Cake
Coffee

Hasenpfeffer (Sour Rabbit)

Cut rabbit into pieces and cover with water to which has been added 1 c. vinegar, bay leaf, sliced onion, a few cloves, peppercorns, and salt. Let stand overnight. Remove rabbit from liquid, dredge in flour, and brown in fat. Add a little sugar and few slices of lemon and some of liquid in which rabbit was soaked. Let simmer until tender. Mix flour with about 4 T. heavy cream and thicken liquid. Serve with noodles or mashed potatoes.

Blitzkuchen

8 oz. butter	8 oz. flour, cake
8 oz. sugar	4 eggs
4 oz. (E.P.) almonds	Rind of 1 lemon

Cream butter and sugar until very creamy. Add eggs 1 at a time, then the grated rind of 1 lemon and the flour. Spread very thin in oiled pan. Cut blanched almonds very thin. Mix with sugar and cinnamon and sprinkle over the batter. Bake in a quick oven. Cut into squares and remove from pan as soon as taken from oven.

Sour Cream Dressing (for Green Bean Salad)

Mix 1 c. thick sour cream, 2 T. vinegar and chopped chives or onions. Add sugar, salt, and pepper to taste.

Lebkuchen

8 c. sifted flour	2 c. brown sugar
½ t. soda	2 eggs slightly beaten
1½ t. cinnamon	1½ c. çandied orange peel,
¼ t. cloves	shredded (6 oz.)
¼ t. nutmeg	1½ c. candied citron
1⅓ c. strained honey (1 lb.)	
2 c. almonds (blanched and	
shredded)	

Sift flour once, measure. Add soda and spices and sift together 3 times. Boil honey, sugar, and water 5 minutes. Cool, add flour mixture, eggs, fruits, and nuts. Work into loaf and place in refrigerator. Let ripen 2 or 3 days. Roll on slightly floured board to ¼-in. thickness. Cut in strips 1 in. x 3 in. Bake on greased baking sheet in moderate oven (350° F.) 15 minutes. When cool, cover with Transparent Icing. Lebkuchen should ripen in a covered cake box at least 5 days before using. Place raw apple in box for moisture. Yield 10 doz. Lebkuchen.

Transparent Icing (for Lebkuchen)

2 c. confectioner's sugar
3 T. boiling water
1 t. vanilla

Combine sugar and water. Add vanilla. Beat thoroughly. Drop from teaspoon on Lebkuchen. Makes enough to cover 10 doz. cookies.

Springerle

4 eggs	Grated rind of 1 lemon
1 lb. powdered sugar, sifted	1 t. baking powder (scant)
1 lb. flour	¼ t. salt
6 t. anise seed, pounded	Hartshorn, about 1 t.

Beat the yolks of the eggs until light colored and thick, beat whites until dry, then beat together; add very gradually grated lemon rind and sugar. Beat all the time. Last add the flour with the baking powder and salt. All the flour may not be required. Knead and cover closely; let chill two or three hours; then roll, a small piece at a time, into a sheet ⅛ in. thick. With a very close sieve dust the sheet of dough lightly with flour, then press the wooden springerle mold very hard upon the dough, so as to leave a perfect impress of the pictures upon the dough. Cut out the little squares with a knife and set aside, on a board lightly floured, over-night. In the morning transfer to baking tins, buttered and sprinkled with anise seed, and bake in a slow oven until a light straw color. These little cakes are quite universally made in Germany a few weeks before Christmas and Easter.

Pfeffernüsse

1 lb. sugar	½ T. cloves
1 lb. flour	½ T. mace
Grated rind of one lemon	½ T. nutmeg
½ c. fine chopped citron	2 t. baking powder
1 T. cinnamon	5 eggs

Sift together flour, sugar, spices, and baking powder. Add the citron and lemon rind and mix to a dough with the beaten whole eggs. Shape into small balls, the size of a hickory nut. Drop on waxed or buttered paper, 1 in. apart. Bake approximately 15 min. at 350° F. These resemble macaroons.

ZWIEBACK KÄSEKUCHEN (Zwieback Cheese Cake)

1½ pkg. zwieback   1 t. cinnamon
1 c. sugar   4 oz. butter

Grind zwieback, add sugar and cinnamon. Take out 1 c. of the mixture to sprinkle on top of the cake. To the remainder, add the melted butter. Line a cake pan with the mixture, both sides and bottom. Pour cooled filling into this, smooth with spoon, and sprinkle remaining cup of crumbs over top. Dust with cinnamon and bake 1 hr. in a slow oven at 325° F.

FILLING:

5 eggs   1 pt. cream
1 c. sugar   1½ T. flour
1 pt. dry cottage cheese   1 t. lemon extract

Beat eggs well; add sugar, cottage cheese, cream, and flour. Cook in a double boiler until thick like custard. Cool thoroughly. Add lemon extract.

STERNLEIN (Almond Cakes)

1 lb. sugar, sifted   ⎫
8 egg whites, beaten stiff   ⎬ Stir with large
1 T. cinnamon   ⎭ motion for 1 hr.

Put aside 6 T. of above for frosting and add to remainder 1 lb. almond meats, blanched and grated. Mix well and roll ⅛–¼ in. thick on board dusted with half flour and half sugar. Cut into star and moon shapes, frost with egg mixture, bake on buttered tins in moderate oven. Store in tightly sealed tins. Bake several days or a week before using.

index